ONLINE JOURNALISM

STEVE HILL # PAUL LASHMAR

ONLINE JOURNALISM
THE ESSENTIAL GUIDE

Los Angeles | London | New Delhi
Singapore | Washington DC

Los Angeles | London | New Delhi
Singapore | Washington DC

SAGE Publications Ltd
1 Oliver's Yard
55 City Road
London EC1Y 1SP

SAGE Publications Inc.
2455 Teller Road
Thousand Oaks, California 91320

SAGE Publications India Pvt Ltd
B 1/I 1 Mohan Cooperative Industrial Area
Mathura Road
New Delhi 110 044

SAGE Publications Asia-Pacific Pte Ltd
3 Church Street
#10-04 Samsung Hub
Singapore 049483

Editor: Mila Steele
Editorial assistant: James Piper
Production editor: Imogen Roome
Copyeditor: Neil Dowden
Proofreader: Kate Harrison
Marketing manager: Michael Ainsley
Cover design: Francis Kenney
Typeset by: C&M Digitals (P) Ltd, Chennai, India
Printed and bound by
CPI Group (UK) Ltd, Croydon, CR0 4YY

MIX
Paper from
responsible sources
FSC® C013604

© Steve Hill and Paul Lashmar 2014

First published 2014

Library of Congress Control Number: 2013940297

British Library Cataloguing in Publication data

A catalogue record for this book is available from
the British Library

ISBN 978-1-4462-0734-5
ISBN 978-1-4462-0735-2 (pbk)

Contents

About the Authors   xii
Acknowledgements   xiii
So what are these weird QR codes?   xiv

Introduction   1

Section 1   Foundations of Online Journalism   5

1   What are the Essential Skills?   7
    Introduction   7
    Objectives   8
    The Multimedia Mindset   8
    Traditional Journalism versus the Multimedia Mindset: a Conflict of Interests?   9
    Multimedia Working Practices   10
    Mobile Reporting Tools   13
    Going Mobile   14
    Mobile Operating Systems   15
    Smart Smartphone Features   15
    Apps for Journalists   15
    Understanding the Media Business   16
    Interview: Kim Gilmour, Freelance Journalist and Author   17
    Journalism as a Conversation   18
    Data Journalism: More than Pretty Pictures   19
    Case Studies   21
    Tools of the Data Journalist's Trade   22
    Summary   24
    Exercises   24
    Further Reading   24

2   Understanding Your Users   25
    Introduction   25
    Objectives   26
    Why Online Users Are Different to Newspaper and Magazine Readers   26
    How We Seek Out News Based on Niche Interests   28
    Personalized News   28

Sites that Provide Personalization 29
Challenges Posed by Personalization 33
Social Bookmarking Sites 33
How Users Multi-Task 33
Analysing User Behaviour 34
Problems with Analytics Data 37
Writing an Audience Profile 39
Interpreting the Data 40
The Digital Divide 41
Summary 42
Exercises 43
Further Reading 43

Section 2 Skills for the Multimedia Journalist 45

3 Writing for the Web 47
Introduction 47
Objectives 48
Interacting with Text 48
Snacking on Content 49
Making Copy Scannable 49
Preparing to Cover Breaking News 50
The Importance of a Great Intro 52
Giving Your Copy Pace 54
Examples: Keeping It Short 54
Giving Your Copy Impact 54
Interviewing: the Art of Listening 55
The Seven Enemies of Good Writing 56
Writing Headlines and the Rise of SEO 57
Example: Headlines from BBC Surrey (Local News Site) 58
Keep Your Opinions to Yourself 58
Types of Online Writing 59
Interview: Paul Douglas, Editor, TechRadar.com, Future Publishing 63
Summary 63
Exercises 64
Further Reading 64

4 Telling the Story with Images 65
Introduction 65
Objectives 67
How Images Work with Text 67
Composition 70
Things to Avoid 71
The Art of Good Caption Writing 72
Q&A: Sue Steward, Former *Daily Telegraph* and *Observer* Picture Editor 73
Editing Photographs 75

Displaying Your Images Online: Creating a Slideshow 76
How Images Can Be Used to Deceive 78
Using the Images of Others 79
Infographics 80
Using Maps 80
Cartoons 81
Summary 81
Exercises 82
Further Reading 82

5 Using Audio and Podcasts 83
Introduction 83
Objectives 84
Audio Journalism 84
Audio in a Converged World 84
A Short History of Audio 85
Podcasting 88
Making an Audio Package 89
Tips for Writing for Audio 90
Interviewing for Audio Packages 91
Recording Digital Audio 93
Digital Audio Recorders (DARs) 94
Editing Your Audio Using Audacity 95
Tips for Editing 97
Interview: Sutish Sharma, Experienced Radio Reporter 97
Interview: Chris Ledgard, BBC Producer 98
Uploading Audio to the Web 99
Summary 100
Exercises 100
Further Reading 101

6 Working with Video 102
Introduction 102
Objectives 103
Video Journalism for Online 103
How Newspapers Use Video 105
Finding the Story 106
Write to Pictures 106
Creating Packages with Different Lengths 108
Interview: Kurt Barling, BBC London Reporter 108
Learn to Really See 110
Signposting 111
Choosing a Video Camera 111
Capturing Good Video 112
Editing 114
Sound 115

Contents

Graphics		116
Uploading Video to the Web		116
Summary		118
Exercises		118
Further Reading		118
7	Doing Investigative Reporting	120
	Introduction	120
	Objectives	122
	Investigative Skills	122
	A Short History of Investigative Journalism	123
	Phone Hacking	124
	WikiLeaks	125
	The Death of Investigative Journalism?	126
	Key Concepts	128
	Methods	129
	The Importance of Research	129
	Undercover Reporting	130
	Freedom of Information	131
	Sources and Whistleblowers	132
	Computer-assisted Reporting	134
	Crowdsourcing: The Insight of Crowds	134
	New Investigative Journalism Models	136
	Summary	137
	Exercises	137
	Further Reading	137
Section 3	Building Communities, Interaction and Entrepreneurship	139
8	Social Media and Building Online Communities	141
	Introduction	141
	Objectives	142
	So What *Exactly* is Social Media?	142
	How Does Social Media Relate to Journalism?	144
	How Journalists Use Social Media	147
	Interview: Zoe Kleinman, Technology Reporter, BBC	149
	Finding Stories on Social Media	150
	Handling Hoaxes	151
	Facebook Pages	153
	Encouraging Users to Share News Content	153
	Levels of Engagement with Social Media	154
	Academic Concerns about Social Media	155
	Summary	158
	Exercises	158
	Further Reading	159
9	Blogging and Participatory Journalism	160
	Introduction	160

Objectives		161
What is a Blog?		161
Blogs as Citizen Journalism		162
Do Blogs Expand the Public Debate?		164
Setting Up a Blog		165
Setting Up a Blog on WordPress		167
Writing Your First Blog Post		168
Linking		169
Categories and Tags		170
Plugins and Widgets		170
How to Cope with Comments		171
Taking Your Blog to the Next Level		172
Key Academic Issues in Blogging		173
Summary		176
Exercises		176
Further Reading		177
10	Freelancing and Entrepreneurial Journalism	178
	Introduction	178
	Objectives	179
	What is an Entrepreneur?	180
	How to be an Entrepreneur	181
	Learning to Fail Well	183
	Interview: Mike Butcher, European Editor, TechCrunch	184
	Going Niche and Hyperlocal	185
	Online Local News	185
	How Sites Generate Revenue	186
	Google's Role in Online Advertizing	187
	Writing a Business Plan	188
	The Freelance Journalist	189
	Interview: Fiona Webster, Freelance Journalist	190
	Commissioning Editors	191
	Freelance Finances	191
	Why all Journalists Need to Learn about Business	193
	Summary	194
	Exercises	194
	Further Reading	194
11	Outputting for Web, Smartphone, and Tablet	196
	Introduction	196
	Objectives	197
	The Digital Newsroom	197
	Headlines and Deadlines	198
	Interview: James Fyrne, Co-Founder, Independent News Website SoGlos	199
	Setting Up a News Site	200
	Open Source Content Management Systems	200
	Setting Up a News Site Using Joomla!	202

Programming Languages 206
Editorial Issues in Website Production 207
Search Engine Optimization (SEO) 208
Creating Apps for Mobile Smartphones 210
Intergrated Development Environments 211
How to Design an App 212
iPad and Other Tablet Computers 212
Creating Magazine Content for the iPad 213
Key Academic Issues in the Digital Newsroom 214
Summary 216
Exercises 216
Further Reading 216

Section 4 Becoming a Thinking Journalist 217

12 Ethics and Good Practice 219
Introduction 219
Objectives 220
Journalism Concepts and Ideas 220
Gatekeeping Theory 225
Commercial Pressures 225
How Do Proprietors Influence News? 226
Regulation 227
Ethics Online and Offline 227
'Rocking the Boat' 228
How Corrections and Clarifications Should Be Handled 228
Online Ethics 228
NUJ Code of Conduct 229
A Blogger's Code of Conduct? 230
How You Portray People is an Ethical Issue 230
Basic Ethical Questions 230
The Cautionary Tale of Johann Hari 232
Final Ethical Questions 232
Summary 234
Further Reading 235

13 Law and Regulation 236
Introduction 236
Objectives 237
An Uncertain Universe 237
Defamation 239
Copyright (Intellectual Property) 243
Contempt 246
Privacy 249
Summary 254
Exercises 255
Further Reading 255

14 How the Internet Transformed Journalism   256
    Introduction   256
    Objectives   257
    Milestones in Technology   257
    The Web Is Not the Internet   260
    How Do Mobile Apps Use the Internet?   260
    The Web Gets Political   261
    Open Source Movement   261
    The Launch of Newspaper Websites   262
    Generating Revenue   262
    News as a Commodity   263
    Impact of the Net on Working Practices   263
    Online News Today   264
    The Network and Devices   265
    The Rise of Tablet Devices   267
    Predicting the Future (Based on the Past)   267
    Summary   270
    Exercises   270
    Further Reading   271

    References   272
    Index   284

About the Authors

Steve Hill is a senior lecturer in journalism at Southampton Solent University. He has worked in technology and business journalism for over 15 years and has written for the *Independent, Sunday Express, New Statesman, New Media Age* and *Web Designer* magazine among many other print and online publications. He has also appeared as a pundit on the BBC News Channel, Sky News, ITN and numerous radio outlets. During the late 1990s and early 2000, he reported extensively on the dotcom boom and bust as senior editor at *Internet Magazine* at EMAP in London. He holds postgraduate qualifications in journalism, is a fellow of the Higher Education Academy and is currently studying for a PhD. He blogs at www.new-journalismreview.com.

Paul Lashmar is a journalism course convenor at Brunel University. He is currently undertaking a PhD on the links between the media and intelligence services. He is also an investigative journalist and has worked in television, radio and print for 30 years. He has been on the staff of Granada Television's *World in Action* current affairs series and the *Observer* and *Independent* newspapers. He was awarded 'Reporter of the Year' in the 1986 UK Press Awards and has worked on all media platforms. For full details of his career please go to his website at www.paullashmar.com.

Andy Chatfield, the author of the chapter on law, is a journalism lecturer at Southampton Solent University. He is a highly experienced journalist in the regional press and former deputy editor of the *Oxford Mail*. His continuing professional practice includes working as a design consultant on recent re-launches of a number of newspapers, including the *Oxford Times,* the *Wiltshire Gazette & Herald* and the *Wiltshire Times*.

Acknowledgements

We would like to give special thanks to photographers Andy Blackmore and Gretel Ensigna for allowing us to use their exceptional news and sports images.

STEVE HILL

A book of this size is impossible to write without the help and support of a large number of people. Thanks go to Mila Steele, James Piper, Imogen Roome and everyone at Sage for their belief in the project. Thanks to my students and colleagues at Solent, particularly my office mates Mary Hogarth and Rick Taylor for their inspiring chats.

I am grateful to the journalists who were very generous with their time in answering my questions: Mike Butcher (www.techcrunch.co.uk), Zoe Kleiman of the BBC, Paul Douglas (www.techradar.com) and James Fyrne (www. soglos.com) as well as my good friend and former colleague Kim Gilmour (www.kimgilmour.com).

This book is for my wife Tina, who also works in journalism and is a fantastic editor. It is also for my mother and father who remain dedicated subscribers to the paper editions of the *Guardian*, *Observer* and *Surrey Advertiser*.

PAUL LASHMAR

I'd like to thank the journalism team at Brunel University, Professor Sarah Niblock, Murray Dick, Jacquie Hughes and Rachel Sharp, who are a delight to work with and who are both creative academics and journalism practitioners. My gratitude goes to Professor Julian Petley at Brunel for his academic mentoring. I'd also like to mention Dr Denis Gartside who thought I might make it as an academic.

Furthermore I would like to thank Jacquie Hughes for her excellent subbing skills, Paul Moody for advice on two chapters and picture editor Andy Blackmore for his advice. I owe Steve Bell a drink for letting us use his cartoons.

In recent years journalism has been under the microscope like never before over the phone-hacking scandal and it would be easy to forget some of the brave, clever, moral and often very funny people who make journalism a profession to be proud of. I've worked and known some of the best and I dedicate this book to them. These include David Leigh, James Oliver, Adrian Gatton, Andrew Jennings, Sarah Spiller, Sue Bishop, Kim Sengupta, Jon Lee Anderson, Scott Armstrong, Nick Davies and Jack Crossley, to name just a few.

ANDY CHATFIELD

Apart from those quoted in my chapter, I would like to thank my colleagues at Solent University for advice and feedback, particularly media law lecturers Kris Low and David Mascord, and my family for tolerating the additional absences the project entailed.

SO WHAT ARE THESE WEIRD QR CODES?

Tablet computers and smartphones are essential tools for the modern journalist. To reflect this, throughout the pages of this book you'll see QR codes dotted around. Scan one of the codes with your mobile device's camera to be instantly transported to relevant pages on our companion website.

Our website will:

- Provide practical examples of good journalism.
- Be multimedia. You will be able to listen to audio and watch examples of good video work.
- Include plenty of useful links to sites that provide more depth and additional information.
- Allow 'readers' to become 'users' and interact with the text.
- Be updated with the latest information.
- Allow you to find out more about the authors.

All you need to get started is a mobile device (tablet computer or smartphone) with a camera and QR reading software. You can download the software from your device's app store. Popular free choices include: QR Reader, ScanLife or Scan (they all do a similar job).

Want to give it a test drive? Point your mobile device at this page and scan the code to go to the homepage of our website at: **www.OnlineJournalismGuide.com**

INTRODUCTION

TO THE JOURNALIST

As a journalist you have chosen to join one of the most exciting of all professions. At its best, journalism gives you access to the most interesting people and places, travel opportunities and to be part of history. You will have seen journalists reporting from outside No. 10 Downing Street in London and the White House in Washington; you will have seen journalists reporting in war zones wearing flak jackets and helmets; and you will have seen journalists interviewing musicians, writers, actors and business leaders.

You have to be gutsy, but also really good to get a job, and this book is designed to help you to become exactly that – really good. To be a great journalist you need to have curiosity, be tenacious, a facility for storytelling and personable – it helps a lot if people like you.

You have joined at a time when the future of news is unclear. Legacy media companies, who once made huge profits by distributing journalism on paper, are switching to becoming multimedia digital operations that output their journalism over a whole new range of devices – smartphones, tablets and smart TVs. To some in the news industry the speed of this change has been terrifying. Given the opportunity, we are sure that some editors would like to switch off the internet and return to the 'good old days' of high circulation figures for print media and large advertising revenues which dominated the 1980s and early 1990s.

Rather than regarding this as frightening, we believe that the media is going through some of the most exciting periods in its history and this is an amazing time to study journalism. While it's impossible to predict precisely how journalism will change in the future, throughout this book you will see the key themes emerge:

- mobile;
- on demand;
- interactive;
- multimedia;
- participatory;
- social;
- entrepreneurial.

We will return to these themes regularly. They open up exciting and new opportunities for journalists to reach new users and markets.

The new world of journalism is dominated by new software and devices, but talk to any journalist and it is clear that editors and news professionals believe that learning how to write stories well is still at the heart of good journalism. Reassuringly it's still the facts, the story and the interviews which are the foundation on which all the technology skills you will learn rest on. Above all, it's about people and their stories.

Whether you are an undergraduate or postgraduate trainee journalist, this book will provide a basic primer in multimedia and online journalism. We encourage you to specialize and develop contacts in particular subject areas – for example current affairs, sport or business. You will also need to have in-depth specialist knowledge of at least one area. A journalist needs a hinterland, a place where they have their passions and interests, and that feeds into their journalism. This is the soil that their journalism will grow in. This is where they will get the stories that will make their reputation. In short, develop knowledge of a specific area and learn all the important names and companies within that area, but be platform-neutral. You need to be able to create text, images, audio and video content for a whole range of old and new devices.

Of course, to understand the new role of a journalist in these changing times requires more than a straightforward practical guide that simply lists the classic rules of journalism. In this book, we combine practical instruction within a framework of journalism theory, interviews with industry experts and modern examples. We practise what we preach. Along with the printed book, you have a regularly updated website. This will provide practical examples and up-to-date links. A textbook can't hope to cover all the skills needed to be a multimedia or online journalist, so, like any good news website, where appropriate we have linked to our source material that provide extra in-depth material.

You'll notice we don't call you a student – to us you are an early career journalist. There should be no boundary where you cease being a student and become a journalist; the student should dissolve as you become a confident professional. Start producing journalism as soon as you can. Learn to find your own stories. Employers are looking for people who are self-starters, who have published high-quality journalism online and have built up a loyal audience on YouTube, Twitter and the other social media sites. Equally none of us should stop learning when we get a job. We are all still learning about journalism but much, much more besides. Journalism is a university of the world.

Everything is up in the air. Will newspapers survive? Who will pay for good journalism? Is investigative journalism dying? How will news work online? We don't know the answers to these questions yet but we can see what we need to do to prepare you. The one thing that is certain is that the news industry will survive in some modified form and the current upheavals will benefit you if you are imaginative and creative. More and more journalists are freelance and we talk about surviving and blossoming as a freelance. While the mainstream media contract, the possibilities to develop online websites providing news grow. So we devote a chapter to encouraging you to think entrepreneurially – including how to set up your own business rather than rely on others.

You are also coming into journalism in the UK in the wake of the phone-hacking scandal. This has raised all sorts of questions about the ethics and practices of journalism in parts of the news media. As we will point out in depth in this book, proactive professional journalism is vital in a democracy; without it to bring the rich and powerful to account democracy would be undermined by corruption. As journalism lecturers we make it clear that when people apply to join our courses we like applicants who clearly have a pre-existing and demonstrated interest in journalism but above all we are looking for people who are engaged with the world and fascinated by what happens, whether in your locality or across the globe in a profound way. All journalists, and we mean all journalists, should be on top of the daily news agenda. We hope you find the book assists you getting your qualification, your training council award if you are taking one, and most importantly that you get the journalism job of your dreams.

The book is divided into four sections:

- Section 1: Foundations of Online Journalism
- Section 2: Skills for the Multimedia Journalist
- Section 3: Building Communities, Interaction and Entrepreneurship
- Section 4: Becoming a Thinking Journalist

Each section has a number of chapters, and each chapter stands alone so you can dip in and out depending on your emphasis at any time in your course. Each chapter features:

- examples of good practice;
- interviews with leading industry experts;
- an introduction that sets out what the chapter covers;
- objectives – a set of five learning objectives in the chapter;
- exercises – so that you can develop the ideas and practices;
- a summary – reminding you of the key points in the chapter;
- further reading – five websites, books or documents that are important to read to develop what you have just learnt;
- and a range of tips, examples and questions for you to answer.

A QUICK WORD TO TUTORS

This textbook has the ambition to support and provide direction to tutors looking to embed multimedia and online journalism throughout their courses, an essential process that can prove fiendishly complex in practice. In these times of limited teaching resources and large numbers of trainees, pressure is on to get the teaching right first time. Yet as tutors it can feel like the ground is constantly moving as we cope with an unprecedented rate of industry change. Those who feel that things will eventually 'settle down' will have a long wait. Of course it's important that tutors, as well as students, adopt a mindset that is open and adaptable to change.

The book also has the ambition to help in some way to bridge the gap between theory and practice. We have strong vocational values and believe the important thing this book can do is help trainees get the job they want, whether this is in journalism or the wider field of media communications. But we also encourage trainees to act as 'thinking journalists' and we also discuss the theory and context of journalism throughout the book. It's these types of thinking skills we hope will help trainees anticipate and cope with the constant and radical nature of change to working practices.

It is not just a question of learning a series of skills but having a wider picture. A journalist needs an insightful understanding of their profession. While it is good for the trainee journalist to learn skills from a lecturer or a more senior journalist about how they succeeded, this leaves out an important factor – rule breaking. If everybody just did exactly what had been done before then journalism would remain

exactly the same decade on decade. Clearly it does not. What is important about having new blood entering journalism each year is that the new journalist should bring new ideas and challenge how things are done. The trainee journalist should know the rules but be prepared to innovate. They need to develop the confidence to challenge the old order, while remaining respectful of the traditions of the profession. One of the most effective ways to develop this ability to critically analyse one's own work and the work of those around you is through reflexive (or reflective) practice.

The industry training councils are rapidly moving towards a platform-neutral approach to media skills. It is well worth noting that the National Council for the Training of Journalists (NCTJ) – the body which sets the training standards for reporters based on industry requirements – now has a range of different modules and is developing more. The NCTJ used to be primarily focused on training print journalists, as the Broadcast Journalism Training Council sets the criteria for broadcast journalists and the Periodicals Training Council (PTC) sets the criteria for magazine journalists. Now the boundaries have broken down. For example, the NCTJ has embraced convergence and has made a number of major changes for their new revised diploma. This, for instance, includes a 'video for online' module that requires aspirant reporters to be able to shoot, script and edit a news package that achieve a standard very similar to one that you would expect on a regional TV news bulletin. The NCTJ is also very keen that journalists are able to think entrepreneurially and they are working on modules to encourage business. This book's chapters are designed to match the key elements of the Training Council's courses.

Figure I.1   *The Economist* homepage has links to stories delivered in text, video and audio formats. *The Economist* also uses all the main social media sites to interact with its users. (© The Economist Newspaper Limited, London, 2013)

SECTION 1

Foundations of Online Journalism

What are the Essential Skills?   7

Understanding Your Users   25

CHAPTER 1

What are the Essential Skills?

INTRODUCTION

In the aftermath of the summer 2011 riots in cities across England, the *Guardian* newspaper embarked on one of its most ambitious interactive projects to date. To try to understand how rumours and speculation to do with the riots spread using social media, the newspaper, in collaboration with a team of academics, examined 2.6 million tweets. The *Guardian* found it was full of outlandish misinformation. There were false rumours that tanks were being deployed by the government and that rioters had broken into London Zoo and were releasing the animals. The *Guardian* produced an interactive visualization on its website that charts how misinformation spreads widely on social media and, more interestingly, how users quickly self-correct false rumours.

The *Guardian*'s Riots Interactive Project is just one example of how journalism is undergoing a radical transformation brought about by the internet and associated digital technology. It is traditional, public interest, verification (fact-checking) journalism for the modern age. It explains a complex topic to a non-specialist audience in a visually appealing and easy to understand way. As Bill Kovach and Tom Rosenstiel (2003) write in their classic text on media ethics *The Elements of Journalism*, the role of journalism is to provide citizens with the information they need to be 'free and self-governing' and it must be 'independent, reliable, accurate, and comprehensive'.

However, data journalism is just one way that technology is being used to better inform our audience. In this chapter, we examine a series of new practical and theoretical issues you will need to understand to survive and thrive in the new digital environment. Journalism just became infinitely more interesting.

>>OBJECTIVES<<

In this chapter, you will learn:

- mindset skills for coping with constant change;
- the core principles of journalism;
- how convergence affects our professional lives;
- new forms of journalism including mobile, social and data journalism;
- why it is important that journalists are numerate.

THE MULTIMEDIA MINDSET

Many experienced journalists love newsprint. Newspapers have a smell to them and a tactility that gives the format an emotional appeal. We experience a buzz when we see our work appear on the newsstand, which is very different to seeing work appear on a website.

But newspapers and magazines in print format are expensive to produce when compared with a digital output and their audience is falling. A few exceptional magazines in the UK retain readers while providing very little online content. Satirical magazine *Private Eye* retains a circulation of over 200,000 an issue with a modest internet presence. Some papers have made a unique selling point of being non-digital. The French satirical magazine *Le Canard* (The Duck) states defiantly on its single page website (www.lecanardenchaine.fr), 'Le Canard ne vient pas barboter sur le net'; or to crudely translate, 'The duck does not splash on the internet'. The editor writes that *Le Canard* sees its role to 'inform and entertain our readers with newsprint and ink' and politely points out that readers should pay a visit to their local newsagent to find their favourite magazines.

We love newsprint, but users are increasingly consuming and interacting with content on a range of internet-enabled mobile devices such as smartphones and tablet computers – the evidence is all around us to see whenever we take a bus or train. Ken Doctor, a US-based media analyst, in a 2011 blog post entitled 'The Newsonomics of Oblivion', warned the newspaper industry that only by adopting a digital-first strategy, where digital media takes priority over paper, and re-organizing themselves to 'scrap old structures, budgets, job descriptions—and, massively, costs', will they have any hope of survival in the new, mainly digital, age.

Simon Waldman (2010), the former head of digital at the *Guardian* newspaper, studied how legacy businesses (companies who have been successful in the pre-web days) have adapted to what he terms the 'creative disruption' caused by the internet. Some companies have successfully re-invented themselves as digital companies. Many, such as high-street retailers like HMV and Blockbuster, have not.

Forward-thinking newspapers and magazines have re-branded themselves as multimedia businesses. Regional newspapers that once came out daily in print are now coming out weekly. The print versions focus on longer opinion and feature articles, which is what print media do best. Meanwhile, online outputs, such as websites and mobile apps (smartphone or tablet computer software applications), are being used to keep users up-to-date with breaking news; this is sometimes known as a digital-first strategy.

A new range of independent news websites have launched with smaller editorial teams and lower production and distribution costs, such as politics site the *Huffington Post* (www.huffingtonpost.com). These online-only news outlets are usually run on shoestring budgets compared to those of national newspapers, but they are forcing the mainstream media brands to re-invent themselves. As professional journalists, we also need to adopt digital working practices and this will involve learning many new skills throughout our careers and adopting a multimedia mindset.

So what is a multimedia mindset?

1 It understands that in our careers as journalists we will face yet more constant, rapid change in our working practices caused by new technologies. We must not succumb to common human emotional responses to change, which include fear, resistance and denial. Instead, we should actively seek out new opportunities that technology affords us to keep our users informed and deliver on our core journalistic principles.

2 We understand that we can learn a lot from those with expertise in computing. We become more employable if we understand just a little bit about computer programming.

3 We understand that we need to be flexible in how we work. There will be periods of time that we will work as a full-time employee for one media publisher and other times when we work on a freel-ance basis for a number of websites, broadcasters, charities and other employers simultaneously. Our skills as journalists are remarkably transferable. We need to become jugglers and cope with competing demands for our time.

4 We must learn about the media business and how content can be monetized (how it generates revenue). François Nel (2010) from the University of Central Lancashire writes: 'I've argued before that being in-dependent from commercial pressures is not the same as being ignorant of commercial imperatives, and that for journalists to understand the various aspects of the business they're in is crucial.' We couldn't agree more. Our role is simple – we serve our users. Our role is not to serve politicians, members of the public relations industry and certainly not advertisers. However, we don't feel we are tarnishing our journalistic ethics by understanding how journalism generates revenue. It makes us more responsible.

5 We must be numerate and understand statistics. What is it about journalists not being skilled in maths? The joke is that while a journalist can spell 'innumerate', they won't be able to tell you how many letters are in it. Yet numbers are the heart of some of the biggest news stories such as the global financial crash.

6 We must understand the traditions and importance of journalism. We need to understand how the technology works, but it is a means to an end. It is the story that matters most.

What would Google do?

One massively successful digital company is the search engine Google. Although not a media content pro-ducer as such, it is a huge distributor of content produced by others and also runs a massively successful online advertising network. Jeff Jarvis in his 2009 book *What Would Google Do?* urges readers to ask them-selves the question in the book's title when looking at the challenges we face as journalists. Jarvis refers to a post-information scarcity, open source and gift economy. That's to say we live in an era where journalistic content is easily available to our audience and often for free at the point of consumption.

TRADITIONAL JOURNALISM VERSUS THE MULTIMEDIA MINDSET: A CONFLICT OF INTERESTS?

In the section above, we have highlighted how journalists are adapting to digital working practices. By far the biggest challenge is how we learn the new skills required while retaining traditional journalistic values.

Bill Kovach and Tom Rosenstiel (2003) list nine key principles which are worth remembering as we contend with difficulties caused by the growth of digital technology:

1 Journalism's first obligation is to the truth.
2 Its first loyalty is to citizens.
3 Its essence is a discipline of verification (fact checking and accuracy).
4 Its practitioners must maintain an independence from those they cover.
5 It must serve an independent monitor of power.
6 It must provide a forum for public criticism and compromise.
7 It must strive to make significant events interesting and relevant.
8 It must keep the news comprehensive and proportional.
9 Its practitioners must be allowed to exercise their personal conscience.

We need to think how the internet and new digital technologies can make us more efficient at delivering on these nine points and improving our skills at verifying and reporting the facts in explaining complex issues in the most appropriate formats for our audience. Nick Davies, an investigative journalist for the *Guardian* and author of *Flat Earth News* (2008), highlights both the strengths and weaknesses of digital technology. He writes:

 By delivering news electronically, the Internet has the potential to slash the cost of production, reducing or completely removing the heavy costs of printing and distributing conventional newspapers. If those savings were recycled back into the newsrooms, to employ more journalists, we could start to reverse the process which has made the media so vulnerable to Flat Earth News.

The book's title refers to how journalists re-print news that is just as false as saying the world is flat. He outlines how journalists increasingly fail to perform the simple functions of the profession, like the checking of basic information and verifying facts. This is often caused by cuts to newsroom editorial budgets, which means that journalists are having to work faster than ever before. He warns: 'So far, media owners have shown every sign of grasping electronic delivery as yet another chance to cut costs and increase revenue without putting anything back into journalism.'

It's certainly easy to be blinded by techno-optimism. New technology is sold to media companies by computer firms as having almost revolutionary powers. They highlight supposed labour-saving efficiencies, while ignoring potential negative consequences. Media companies have often believed the hype and invested in expensive technology only to find it doesn't do the job. Trade unions representing media workers, such as the National Union of Journalists (NUJ), say that its members are often placed under immense pressure by their employers to learn new skills and produce stories at an increasingly fast rate.

MULTIMEDIA WORKING PRACTICES

Convergence is one of the most widely used of the numerous multimedia buzzwords currently in circulation and it is likely to affect the way you work. Put simply, convergence describes a coming together of two or more things. So what are these 'things'?

We can view the World Wide Web as being an arena for convergence as it allows us to produce multimedia content news packages that include: text, audio, video, interactive graphics and still images together. Just try getting all of this onto a printed page!

Academic Janet Kolodzy (2006) describes how convergence can improve journalists' storytelling abilities. She writes: 'Convergence refocuses journalism to its core mission – to inform the public about its world in the best way possible. But nowadays, the best way is not just one way: newspaper or television or the internet. The best way is a multiple media way.'

Robert Peston (2009), the BBC's business editor, told the Edinburgh International Television Festival how distinctions between television, radio and print journalists are 'quite close to being obsolete'. He says:

> When I started in journalism, I wrote one or two stories a week on a clunky mechanical typewriter – it was the last century but it really wasn't that long ago. Now I write up to five or six blogs in a single day, I broadcast on the [BBC radio] *Today* programme, the [BBC television] *Ten O'Clock News*, as the broadcasting pillars of my output – and up to 20 or so other channels and programmes in a single day.

Peston is saying that his day-to-day working practices simply reflect what viewers, listeners and web users are doing. Audiences increasingly act in a platform-neutral way. That is to say they really don't care where they obtain their news from – whether it's on a laptop, smartphone, tablet, TV, radio or in print. They move from each platform with ease throughout the day, choosing the most convenient device to engage with news at any given moment. While the PC dominates online news consumption, both mobiles and tablet computers, such as the Apple iPad, are rapidly growing in usage.

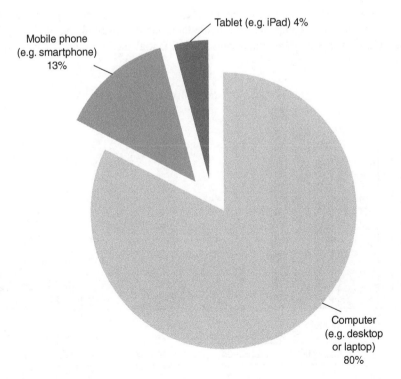

Figure 1.1　In 2012 those who accessed online news mainly did so through desktop or laptop computers, although usage of tablets and smartphones is likely to increase. (Source: Reuters Report, 2012)

Peston concludes: 'What matters is what has always mattered – the facts, the story. The skill for a journalist is unearthing information that matters to people and then communicating it as clearly, accurately – and if possible as entertainingly – as possible.'

Stephen Quinn of Deakin University, Australia, has written extensively on the subject of convergence and lists five types (2005):

- Ownership convergence (sharing of multimedia content within a media organization, such as the BBC)
- Tactical convergence (content sharing arrangements and partnerships that have arisen among media companies with separate ownership)
- Structural convergence (changes in newsgathering and distribution) – as you will see in Chapter 11, newspapers such as the *Guardian* and *Daily Telegraph* have set up convergent newsrooms which allow journalists working on a range of media to work side-by-side
- Information gathering convergence (requires reporters to have multiple skills in using technology)
- Storytelling or presentation convergence (journalists must appreciate the potential of each media platform for content output and interaction)

There are yet more types of convergence. As Janet Kolodzy identifies:

- Technological convergence: Anyone who has used a mobile phone to browse the web, snap a picture, or send a short message service (SMS) knows that mobile feature phones and more advanced smartphones seem to do just about everything. They represent technological convergence as they bring many functions together.
- Economic convergence: Larger media companies seek to buy up or merge with weaker rivals and it's now common to find companies that made their name in print media buying up TV, radio and websites. German media giant Bauer runs 80 influential media brands in the UK. Many of its

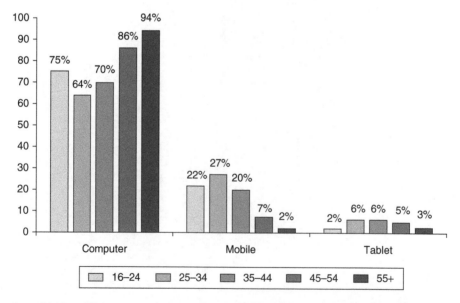

Figure 1.2   Accessing via mobile is most popular among 25–34 year olds – these tend to be young professionals. (Source: Reuters Report, 2012)

magazine titles, including men's lifestyle magazine *FHM*, celebrity magazine *Heat*, and women's titles *Grazia* and *Closer*, were bought from ailing media publisher EMAP in 2008. A large number of these 'magazine' titles have been turned into multimedia brands. For example, *Heat*, which started life as a magazine in 1999, is available today as a digital TV channel, music radio station, website and on mobile.

So convergence is often considered to be healthy for journalists. It makes us more efficient and better reflects the demands of audiences consuming content through multimedia technology. However, there are concerns. When it comes to news journalism, the UK traditionally has had strict controls to prevent one commercial operator from dominating the media landscape. Rupert Murdoch's News Corporation bid in 2011 to take over BSkyB was opposed by politicians and commercial rivals due to concerns over a reduction in media plurality and reduced choice for customers. The take over was eventually abandoned. Local World, an alliance of 180 local newspaper titles and 60 websites from former rivals Northcliffe Media and Iliffe News and Media, received approval from the regulators the Office of Fair Trading (OFT) in June 2013. The OFT concluded that the merger would not reduce plurality in the local news market or result in price increases.

Plurality ensures that media power is not held by too few companies. Others argue that to survive in the digital age media companies must be allowed to merge or form alliances. They say that concerns regarding plurality are less important than they once were due to the vast range of diverse opinions represented on news sites and blogs.

MOBILE REPORTING TOOLS

Technology has become cheaper, more portable and easy to use than ever before. Mobile technology such as smartphones and tablets are becoming one of the main ways that users, particularly educated young men, consume journalistic content. It is also used by journalists as a reporting tool to edit and produce content.

A study by the Pew Research Center's Project for Excellence in Journalism (2012) discovered that more than 40 per cent of men get news daily on either their smartphone and/or tablet, compared with roughly 30 per cent of women. On tablet computers specifically, men visit news apps and watch news videos online more than women. Women, on the other hand, are more likely than men to use social networks as a way to get news.

The rise of handheld, internet-enabled devices has also led to a new breed of reporter – the mobile journalist. These all-in-one, jack-of-all-trades journalists aim to write content for different media, and can often shoot digital stills and record video and audio.

A basic reporting kit will include:

1 Smartphone: This can be used to shoot basic digital images, audio and high definition video. A range of apps (mobile phone software applications) can be used to carry out basic editing of multimedia material on the phone. At a push, copy (the text of a story) can be written on a smartphone using the tiny onscreen keyboard and emailed to a newsroom or uploaded directly to a news site. If you install the main social media apps, such as Twitter and Facebook, you can post short, breaking news-style headlines online. Oh yes, and we nearly forgot, you can actually use a smartphone to make calls. Indeed, talking to real people remains important as ever!

2 Batteries: Using the smartphone's camera, Wi-Fi or GPS function will kill the battery. Using them all at once and we would not be surprised if your phone dies within 30 minutes. So the golden rule is to pack plenty of spare batteries and a mains charger.

3 SIM Cards: High-speed third generation and fourth generation mobile broadband coverage is patchy at best. If you are sending larger files such as audio and video from a mobile device you may be better off using a free public Wi-Fi hotspot in the area. Most of the large coffee shop chains or fast food outlets offer this to customers.

Case study: Covering the riots of 2011

BBC Radio 5 Live's correspondent Nick Garnett, speaking to Journalism.co.uk (Marshall, 2012), described how he used his smartphone to cover the riots of 2011 in the UK. Covering such events is always dangerous for reporters and in Manchester a radio car was burnt out. Garnett says: 'Using one device I was able to take stills, video, file copy, monitor TV, radio.' He also broadcast live using a voice over internet app called Luci Live (www.luci.eu/) which works a bit like Skype. But it all requires a good mobile broadband signal. 'The most important thing is that you have a good signal. If you don't have a good signal it will go wrong,' Garnett warns.

Figure 1.3   The Flip Video Ultra HD is the video camcorder of choice for mobile journalists; however, a high-quality smartphone can be just as good for video. (Source: Steve Hill)

Mobile journalists have to be multi-skilled and are at least competent in doing many of the jobs that were once carried out by dedicated professionals such as camera workers, sound recordists and photographers (known as snappers, in the trade). They may also have to tweet or live blog from the scene of event and file their copy from the field. It is a fact of human nature that few of us have the skills to be equally proficient in text, images, audio and video. You may feel concerned that by doing all these forms of journalism may mean that none are done very well.

Whatever your personal views on mobile journalism, you should understand and experiment with the functions of your mobile phone. There may be times when this is the only bit of kit you have available on which to file a story.

GOING MOBILE

Mobile smartphone and tablet devices are predicted to become the primary platform for the consumption of entertainment content, leap-frogging both television and the computer screen. In many areas of the developing world where computers are expensive and fixed line broadband not universally accessible, mobile phones are the primary way of accessing online services.

Academics Andreas Kaplan and Michael Haenlein (2010) write:

> In India, for example, mobile phones outnumber PCs by 10 to 1. In Thailand, only 13 per cent of the population owns a computer, versus 82 per cent who have access to a mobile phone. It is therefore not surprising that the Pew Research Center Washington-based think tank estimates that by 2020, a mobile device will be the primary internet connection tool for most people in the world.

MOBILE OPERATING SYSTEMS

Smartphones run on an operating system (OS). The two most common OSs are Google's Android and Apple's iOS:

Google's Android: This is a Linux-based mobile operating system for tablets and smartphones. As of June 2012 there were more than 600,000 apps to download in the Google Play store. Samsung and HTC are just a few of the manufacturers whose mobile devices run Android. The first commercially available phone to run it was the HTC Dream in 2008. There are a variety of versions of Android being used 'in the wild' – all with tasty names such as Gingerbread, Ice Cream Sandwich and the current edition at the time of writing, Jellybean. All these different versions cause a headache for Android app developers.

Apple iOS: This runs exclusively on mobile devices made by Apple – that's the iPod Touch, iPhone and the tablet iPad at the time of writing. It is more costly to develop apps for iOS and Apple places strict quality thresholds on developers who submit their progams to the App store.

SMART SMARTPHONE FEATURES

Phones include features that journalists can use for content generation:

- The camera: Mobiles provide a way for both journalists and users to contribute to the news – through tweeting comments and posting photos and video from the scene of live news events. Apps such as CNN's iReport encourage users to post news stories to the CNN website.
- The Global Positioning System (GPS): This allows users to read content, view maps, and access profiles of friends based on their location at any given time. Content can be geo-tagged – which allows information about a users location to appear in tweets and photos, etc.
- The accelerometer: This tool senses movement and gravity and is most commonly used in mobile gaming and in app design.
- Speech recognition: While touch commands remain the primary way of interacting with a phone, tools such as Apple's Siri and Android's Voice Actions allow users to speak common tasks.

APPS FOR JOURNALISTS

Smartphones can act as multimedia production studios for journalists on location. You can shoot, edit and upload video directly into a newsroom production system in just a few easy clicks. In most cases these apps are available in the Google Play and Apple app stores:

Note-taking

Evernote (www.evernote.com) allows you to save notes and images to the cloud from your mobile device and each element of content is made searchable. Cloud computing is an important term that you will see used throughout this book. This is where data is saved on a remote server and users have access to it on any internet-connected device.

Website development

Apps are available for all the main content management systems (CMS) including WordPress, Tumblr, Blogger and Joomla! which we look at in Chapters 9 and 11. These apps allow you to upload content to your website on the go.

Social media

Hootsuite (http://hootsuite.com) provides the ability to post content to the main social media sites and allows for the searching of the posts of others.

Recording interviews

Most phones are able to act as a digital dictaphone to record interviews. SoundCloud (https://soundcloud.com/) and AudioBoo (http://audioboo.fm/) are two options for editing and publishing audio online, and they are discussed in Chapter 5.

Video: recording and editing

iMovie (www.apple.com), a simplified version of the popular video editing software is available only for Apple devices and is discussed in Chapter 6. ReelDirector (http://www.nexvio.com/product/ReelDirector.aspx) and Voddio (http://vericorder.com/solutions/mobile-reporting) are also worth a look.

Broadcasting live using your phone

A smartphone is much cheaper than hiring a satellite truck for a day. Increasingly news organizations use Skype (www.skype.com) for live interviews. But have a play around with dedicated broadcasting tools such as Ustream (www.ustream.tv), Luci Live (http://www.luci.eu/) and Bambuser (http://bambuser.com) for live video streaming from your smartphone.

Photo editing

Most smartphones have basic image editing packages as standard. Adobe's (www.adobe.com) Photoshop and Axiem Systems' (www.axiemsystems.com) Photo Editor apps provide extra functionality.

UNDERSTANDING THE MEDIA BUSINESS

Business skills are particularly important when working as a freelance journalist. To survive as a freelance you'll need to keep track of income, expenses and profit (or lack of!), and pay your taxes. Compared to the fun of writing stories, doing the business paperwork is a drag. Yet we can't over-estimate how important is to keep on top of this as we discuss in Chapter 10 on entrepreneurial journalism.

A freelance journalist is self-employed and works for a range of different employers. It's likely that you will spend periods of your career working freelance and other times working full-time for just one employer, e.g. as a reporter or editor on a magazine.

One of the fun parts of being freelance is that you can carry out a varied range of work. The types of work that freelance journalists do can include:

1 Creating content: Most large newspapers, magazines and websites will employ journalists on a freelance basis to create content. Most work from home and those with subject-specific specialist skills tend to do well.
2 Shift work: You may be invited do one or two days per week working in a newspaper, magazine or website's office. The type of work is often sub-editing, production or reporting work.

3 Public relations and other corporate work: Public relations agencies recruit journalists to write press releases or create content for corporate in-house magazines and websites. For those looking to build a reputation for independent and honest journalism, this type of work is dangerous territory as it blurs the lines between journalism, PR, marketing and advertising. However, it can be very lucrative work for established journalists.

Your name as a freelance journalist is also your brand name. You can use the internet to build up a loyal following of people who enjoy what you produce. How do you do this?

1 Register your own name as a domain – as a .com or .co.uk. If your real name is quite common it is highly likely that it will have been registered by someone else. In this case, you may wish to adopt a pen name.
2 You will want to create a professional website that advertises your skills, a blog and profiles on all the main social media sites. The aim is to ensure your work can be found on Google and other search engines.
3 Take part in the online debate and contribute comments to blogs in the area you specialize in. Get your name out there and associated with high-quality journalism content online. This is essential for obtaining freelance jobs and improving your prospects of getting full-time work.

INTERVIEW: KIM GILMOUR, FREELANCE JOURNALIST AND AUTHOR

1 Which type of work is most personally enjoyable? Or is that purely who pays the most!

A job that pays well is great, but being able to chat to people about a topic I'm interested in such as social networking, digital photography, online music or web design, learning something new that I can share with others, is very rewarding.

2 How do you go about getting jobs?

I was a full-time staffer [in magazines] in both Australia and the UK for about nine years before I entered the world of freelance, so in that time I was lucky enough to have gathered a range of industry contacts. Work comes to me from previous workplaces, or I'd pitch ideas to former colleagues.
It is really a case of who you know sometimes!

3 How has working freelance changed over the years?

Freelancers work from anywhere. All you need is a Wi-Fi connection, a laptop and, most importantly, constant access to strong coffee. But because anyone can set up a blog or tweet their opinions, it's becoming harder to stand out from a global crowd. They have to forge an online personality and engage with people a lot more than before, in order for potential editors (and readers) to trust them.

4 You have worked as a commissioning editor for magazines and a freelancer. What makes for a good story idea?

I often encountered pitches [a writer's description of a potential story to an editor] that were clearly cut-and-pasted and sent to a range of similar publications. Feature editors want exclusive ideas that you haven't pitched to anyone else; ideas that are clearly targeted to their readership.

Figure 1.4 Freelance journalist Kim Gilmour. (Photo credit: John Trenholm)

5 There is a new breed of e-lance sites which some freelancers use to pick up work. Would you recommend them?

The problem with the e-lance sites is that when it comes to writing, you'll probably be working for peanuts, as you'll be competing with people in different parts of the world where £5 for a feature article might be a meaningful day's wage. Either that, or there'll be literally dozens of people competing for the same meagre job as you, in the hope for extra cash.

6 What are your top tips for surviving as a freelance journalist?

Move away from the mainstream. Find a niche interest to write about, follow that and become an expert on that topic.

Use social networking to market yourself and build up a following. Editors will eventually take note of your abilities.

If you're applying for a job or pitching one, the first thing an editor will do is Google you – and it's always a good idea to have something professional come up in the search results.

Get involved with emerging trends in social media like online pinboard Pinterest or social media storymaker Storify. These might end up being fads, but it's always a good idea to register and reserve a decent web address at these places, as they could serve to tie into your overall social networking presence and reputation in the future.

JOURNALISM AS A CONVERSATION

Journalists need to be aware of the changing producer–consumer relationship. This is discussed in the next chapter, but for the time being it is enough to say that audiences increasingly produce as well as passively consume content. You may be able to think of many sites that mix journalistic content produced by professionals with user-generated content (UGC). As the name suggests, UGC is a general term for when non-professionals produce online content. It reflects how technology such as video cameras and blogging tools have become cheaper and easier to use over the years. Sites such as YouTube, Twitter and Flickr are full of user material.

Formally known as the audience

There is a new model of journalism – the social journalist or the social news gatherer that engages with users online on news sites, blogs and social media to generate news tips, research stories and gain feedback. The social journalist's role is to collect, authenticate and reproduce content produced by audiences, particularly content with news value that has been uploaded to social media sites.

Key theorists including academics Jay Rosen and Clay Shirky and technology writer Dan Gillmor have highlighted how journalists need to appreciate that our users often know more than we do about the topics that we write about. Of course, this makes a lot of sense. As journalists, one day we may be writing about homelessness in London and the next poor exam results in local schools. Those in our audience that have direct experience in these areas may clearly have useful information to offer us and the internet allows us access to a wide range of expert opinion. This aspect of social journalism is closely aligned with the concept of collective intelligence and the wisdom of the crowd. If you post a question in an online social forum you may be staggered by how quickly people respond. Social journalism is also related to the concept of collaborative journalism where journalists work with members of the public to research stories.

Skills of a social journalist

So how does this translate to practical skills? Vadim Lavrusik of the website Mashable (2010) writes:

> **"** To be a social journalist and one that engages in online communities, journalists will have to practice blogging regularly and serve as curators of other content on the web ... Journalists of tomorrow will be participating in the link economy by gathering, synthesising and making sense of other content across the web. **"**

Content curation is an important term that is used throughout this book. It involves the journalist sorting, categorizing and presenting information from a wide range of sources in a format that is easy for the user to digest. Social journalism contrasts with the traditional producer–consumer, journalist–audience relationship, where journalists were viewed as authoritative figures on the topic they wrote about. For their part, journalists appeared aloof and distant from the audiences that they served. The social journalist is involved in an ongoing conversation with audiences using social media tools.

The rise of social journalism is one of the most significant trends in recent times and best of all it helps us to deliver on those traditional journalism values listed above. The internet makes it so easy to connect with a wide variety of people in the local community who may have expertise that can help improve our reporting.

A positive view of social journalism is that it can help on delivering one of the most important roles of giving a voice to people who traditionally lacked access to the media. A critical view is that often it merely provides pseudo-empowerment to audiences. That's to say journalists give the impression that users can make a difference, yet audiences often remain sceptical.

Academic Clare Wardle (2007) carried out audience engagement studies at the BBC. She found that user participation in news is a minority activity. Contributors were overwhelmingly white, educated, middle-class, and already heavy news users. Typically, they were already activists in the local community, i.e. they had previously written letters to MPs or were members of local political, church or charity organizations.

So a key role for journalists is to encourage involvement in journalism not just from target readers, but also the wider community. It's well worth thinking about how you can involve the readers at every stage of the news reporting and production process as social journalism is likely to become even more important in the future.

DATA JOURNALISM: MORE THAN PRETTY PICTURES

Reporters are swimming in a sea of data as government and other official bodies publish their research online. If you want to know the number of adoptions in the UK, the number of adults with psychotic disorders living in private households or rates of crime down your street you can find it online. In fact, we've moved from information scarcity to information overload. One of the biggest challenges journalists face is how we go about interpreting these statistics so they make sense to our users and this is what data journalism is all about.

Data journalism is closely aligned with computer-assisted reporting (CAR) which has a long history dating back to the 1950s. Often CAR involved a trip to the public library to search government databases, reference books and CD-ROMs. Today, most government data is placed online. Data journalism began receiving attention with the release of data concerning the war in Afghanistan by WikiLeaks in spring 2010. One spreadsheet had over 92,000 rows of data, each one containing a detailed breakdown of a military event in Afghanistan. The *Guardian* and the *New York Times* newspapers brought in large teams to interpret it and seek out stories.

Key data journalism sites

 Data.gov.uk (www.data.gov.uk) – publishes massive amounts of facts and figures from various government departments as well as the Office of National Statistics (ONS) at www.statistics.gov.uk.

 The *Guardian* newspaper has a massive searchable data of statistics from agencies throughout the world at www.guardian.co.uk/world-government-data.

 Data journalism is closely aligned with the work of important organizations such as the Open Knowledge Foundation (http://okfn.org/) and the UK's My Society (www.mysociety.org/) which build applications around government data to make it more easily accessible to the public.

Jonathan Gray et al.'s *The Database Journalism Handbook* (2012) (http://datajournalism handbook.org/1.0/en/index.html) is an invaluable resource. Cynthia O'Murchu (cited in Gray et al., 2012) of the *Financial Times* says:

> Data journalism is another way to scrutinize the world and hold the powers that be to account. With an increasing amount of data available, now more than ever it is important that journalists are of aware of data journalism techniques. This should be a tool in the toolkit of any journalist: whether learning how to work with data directly, or collaborating with someone who can.

So where do you start when planning a data journalism project? It's frequently based on a hunch that there may be a story in some data that has just been released. Data journalism, like investigative journalism, is rarely an 'easy win'. It takes time to analyse pages of data and may involve a team of journalists working together. So it's well worth thinking about the likely impact of any resulting stories. Will it allow users to better understand a complex story? Will it reveal details of an existing story that was previously unknown? Most data comes in the format of large tables and spreadsheets which are intimidating to our users, so can you present the data, or visualize data, in a format that is searchable to users and easier to interpret? Most importantly, does your data journalism project have a public interest value? That's to say is it important information that should be available to the public to help them make an informed decision in a democratic society.

It's certainly worth heeding O'Murchu's warning:

> **"** The exercise should not be about just analysing data or visualizing data for the sake of it, but to use it as a tool to get closer to the truth of what is going on in the world. While numbers can be interesting, just writing about the data is not enough. You still need to do the reporting to explain what it means. **"**

Journalism is about people and not numbers. Often the best way to explain the importance of a story is to interview someone who has some personal experience.

A data journalist requires an eye for detail and numeracy skills. Data can be inaccurate or missing details, which can in itself be a story. Be suspicious about why certain categories of information in a table are grouped together in the way they are. A simple example from the area of crime statistics is that certain types of crime, such as rape and vandalism, can go under-reported to the police. In some cases the police will target specific offences and the rates of crime can appear to artificially go up for a short while.

Data journalism cases studies

Data journalism can be an intimidating area of study. One of the best ways to start is by analysing successful data journalism projects. The *Guardian*'s datablog (www.guardian.co.uk/news/datablog) provides all the full datasets behind its news stories, so users can have a play around with the raw data themselves.

CASE STUDIES

The Detail: How quickly did help arrive?

www.thedetail.tv/issues/72/ambulance-response-times/how-quickly-did-help-arrive-where-you-live

Purpose: Investigate the disparity in ambulance response times to Category A (life threatening) calls made to the Northern Ireland Ambulance Service during 2010 and 2011. Obtain data and create a visualization, in this case an interactive Google map that allows users to enter their postcode to determine likely ambulance response times.
Hunch: Ambulance response times have increased, particularly in rural areas of Northern Ireland, following the closure of accident and emergency units in the area.
Data source: An analysis of response time to 215,349 emergency calls made to the Northern Ireland Ambulance Service (NIAS) during 2010 and 2011.

BBC: Student finance calculator

www.bbc.co.uk/news/education-14785676

Purpose: Investigate the costs of going to university based on the new tuition fees implemented from September 2012 in England and Wales. The result was an online calculator that allowed prospective students to discover approximately the total costs of the repayment of tuition fees on their likely career earnings.
Hunch: How much students will pay off in loans and interest may vary depending on chosen career and future earnings.

Data source: Uses government-supplied data on the various interest rates charged and repayment periods for tuition fee loans; data from the ONS about average earnings, broken down by sex, age group and career group.

The BBC's student finance calculator presents potentially complex data in a simple to understand format that produces a result that is personalized to the needs of the user. So how does it work? Briefly, at the heart is an assumption that earnings at any age may be estimated by looking at how much the average person at that age, based on particular career groups, would have earned today. The figure is then adjusted for predicted growth in the economy over the user's career lifetime. So clearly the creators are making a few assumptions – most significantly that the economy will grow in size! History tells us that this is likely, but even the best economists can only hazard a guess by how much or when.

The user selects a 'career path' that they would like to take. However, one career category such as 'health' may include a wide range of job roles and frustratingly, data from the ONS includes non-graduate jobs mixed in with graduate positions. Ideally, the data journalist would attempt to 'clean' the data by filtering out non-graduate results to improve accuracy.

Data journalists face these issues all the time and we are not being critical. A key question is always what exactly is being counted in the data set? The second question is always – what data could be missing and has anything (like the fact the economy will improve!) been assumed?

One of the leading users of data journalism is Paul Bradshaw, journalist and academic at Birmingham City University, who lists four important stages of data journalism:

- finding data;
- interrogating data;
- visualizing data;
- mashing data.

It is important to be thorough and sceptical in your approach.

 See the companion website for an example of data journalism from the *Guardian*.

TOOLS OF THE DATA JOURNALIST'S TRADE

Spreadsheets

Spreadsheet software, such as MS Excel and Google Spreadsheets, are often at the heart of data journalism and most data will have to be processed using it. Bradshaw recommends that when requesting data, you ask for it to be in a comma-separated values (.CSV) file format. This type of data is stored in tabular plain text format and is easy to import into a spreadsheet for processing. The worst-case scenario is when data comes in a PDF file or in hard-copy format. In both cases, you may need to spend hours inputting figures and this is a recipe for errors to creep in.

Spreadsheets are incredibly powerful tools and it is worth spending a few hours getting to grips with what they can do. Even having a basic understanding how data is imported, sorted, key formulas and how data is outputted visually is a good start and you will find plenty of 'how-to books' for the main packages in your local library. There are added benefits as many freelancers use spreadsheets to monitors their income and outgoings for tax purposes.

Google Maps, Bing Maps and Google Earth

Maps are wonderful tools for visualizing data. What better way to do this than to make a searchable map? The BBC's massive Every Death on Every Road in Great Britain 1999–2010 (www.bbc.co.uk/news/uk-15975720) is a great example. Paul Bradshaw recommends OpenHeat (www.openheatmap.com) as a mapping tool, 'As long as your data is categorized by country, local authority, constituency, region or county'. Advanced data journalists use Google Fusion Tables to host, manage, collaborate on, visualize and publish data tables.

Yahoo! Pipes

Yahoo! Pipes (http://pipes.yahoo.com/pipes) allows you to aggregate (bring together) feeds and mash-up information from around the web. When it comes to web development (as opposed to music!), a mash-up is where data or functionality is combined to create a new service that makes data more useful to the user. They often use application programming interfaces (APIs). Many social media sites, such as Facebook and Twitter, publish their APIs to allow web developers to create new applications that integrate with user data on social media sites.

The Pipe beneath allows a search to be done on Yahoo! News and Google News for a celebrity's name. It is possible to create a live feed of news about a particular celebrity and this could be added to your website or blog.

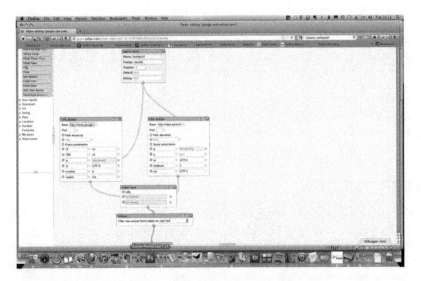

Figure 1.5   An example of a Yahoo! Pipe allowing a search to be done on a celebrity's name. (Source: Yahoo!)

 See the companion website for more tips for understanding figures.

>>Summary<<

1 Faced with declining circulations and what Simon Waldman refers to as 'creative disruption' brought about by the internet, many newspaper companies have undergone a process of re-invention. Most have streamlined their operations to make digital output the core of their business.

2 Technological change is constant. We must understand that in our careers we will have to re-main flexible and invest in life-long learning.

3 Despite technological change, the core journalist skills of unearthing information that matters to people and then communicating it as clearly, accurately and, if possible, entertainingly re-main as important as ever.

4 There is a new model of journalism – the social journalist or the social news-gatherer. These journalists engage with users on news sites, blogs and on social media to generate news tips, research stories and gain feedback.

5 With an increasing amount of data available, now more than ever it is important that journal-ists are aware of data journalism techniques.

EXERCISES

1 Invite an editor or journalist from a local newspaper to discuss how the use of the internet and digital technologies has affected professional working practices in news production.

2 Data journalism can be an intimidating area for the novice, so start by choosing any data set to do with crime or health statistics from Data.gov.uk (www.data.gov.uk) and consider how you will make the information relevant or searchable by your users.

3 Use only your smartphone to file your next story. Using the free Wi-Fi in a local coffee shop or bar, see if you can file copy, images, video and audio to your website. How easy was it to work using just your smartphone? Make notes of any problems or challenges you faced in the process. (We strongly suggest you take a spare battery or charger for your phone when out on this assignment!)

FURTHER READING

Briggs, Mark. 2012. *Journalism Next*, Washington: CQ Press.
  A practical guide, including step-by-step instructions, to digital reporting and publishing.
Gray, Jonathan et al. 2012. *The Data Journalism Handbook*. Open Knowledge Foundation.
  Comprehensive guide to data journalism. Available for free under creative commons licence.
Jarvis, Jeff, 2009. *What Would Google Do?* London: Collins.
  The *Guardian* newspaper media contributor asks the simple question, 'What would Google do?', when examining the challenges brought about by the internet.
Kovach, Bill and Rosenstiel, Tom. 2003. *The Elements of Journalism*. London: Atlantic Books.
  An essential book for all journalists on media ethics. It lists nine key principles of good journalism.
Peston, Robert. 2009. Peston's Picks: What Future for Media and Journalism? Available: www.bbc.co.uk/blogs/thereporters/robertpeston/2009/08/what_future_for_media_and_jour.html [8/31/2011]
  Raises numerous points for class discussion about the changing role of journalism.

CHAPTER 2

Understanding Your Users

INTRODUCTION

The first thing that hits you when enter the Telegraph Media Group's convergent newsroom in London is its sheer size. It's nearly the size of a football pitch, covering 67,000 ft. To one side there is a 100 ft multimedia display projected onto a wall where, alongside the front page of the *Daily Telegraph*'s website (www.telegraph.co.uk), it has what is known as the eyeball chart. This live top ten list keeps the journalists working in the newsroom updated with the most popular news stories on the site based on the number of unique user hits.

Most news sites compile similar lists; indeed many also publish them on their homepage. They provide a fascinating insight into the content that visitors to websites find newsworthy. Depressingly for us as journalists, the public tend to have some peculiar tastes. Suppose you have just filed an exclusive interview with the British Prime Minister. You go back to the newsroom, write it up, it's uploaded to your website and you sit back and wait for hits to come rolling in. You wait and wait, but far from setting the world alight, your story doesn't even make it into the top ten chart of most viewed stories. The top story is some rubbish video of a dog that has learned to surf the waves at the local beach.

This example highlights a central purpose of this chapter, to understand how website users consume, interact and produce content online. We must understand that our users are not necessarily like us and this has always been the case in media publishing. David Randall of the *Independent* writes in *The Universal Journalist* (2000) that journalists 'often inhabit circles and have lifestyles, habits and tastes that are far removed from those of their readers'. They may be older, wealthier, have different political affiliations and live in another part of the country to you.

For example, it is relatively common for women to edit magazines and websites that are aimed at men and vice versa. This is not a problem as long as the editor has that fundamental journalistic skill – to have empathy and understanding of the audience. Luckily we can learn a lot about our online visitors by deploying analysis tools (known as analytics software). These allow us to access detailed information about what visitors do when they are on our sites. We can monitor precisely what they are clicking on at any given moment and the popularity of individual stories and sections. This provides the online journalist with far deeper understanding and near immediate access to data on the likes and dislikes of their users. The depth of data is far greater than is available for those journalists who work in traditional print or broadcast.

However, some worry that online news is becoming market driven. That is to say, news websites may become solely reactive to the whims of their users to generate hits and that much-needed online advertising revenue. This normally entails increased coverage of content that is cheap to produce and is popular with users. As a result, websites may focus on crime news and celebrity scandal that has perceived shock value, at the expense of other types of journalism, such as investigations and international news coverage. As journalists we need to understand the crucial difference between journalism that is of interest to members of the public and the concept of public interest journalism. We discuss the meaning of public interest journalism in Chapter 7.

>>OBJECTIVES<<

In this chapter, you will learn:

- how online users are different to newspaper and magazine readers;
- about the rise of populist, market-driven news that focuses on crime, celebrity and sport;
- about the key traffic statistics and audience jargon;
- how you can monitor audiences on your own news website or blog;
- how the digital divide – the gap between the information rich and the information poor – in the UK and around the world affects how journalists output content.

WHY ONLINE USERS ARE DIFFERENT TO NEWSPAPER AND MAGAZINE READERS

How should we refer to the people who read our content on websites?
Do we refer to them as:

- the audience;
- readers;
- consumers;
- viewers;
- visitors;
- users;
- interactors;
- the community?

Or perhaps you can think of another term to describe them.

In this chapter we refer to website users, rather than the audience. The term audience is problematic as we tend to imagine a bunch of people passively watching television in a living room or watching a movie in the cinema.

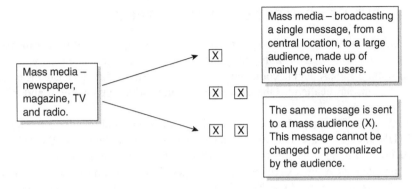

Figure 2.1   We can visualize traditional mass media as working in a broadcast pattern

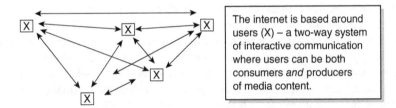

Figure 2.2   We can visualize the web as a community of users. It lacks the 'centrality' of traditional media where content is published from a single point

Media theorist Clay Shirky (2008) says that broadcast media are shaped, conceptually, like a megaphone, amplifying a one-way message from one sender to many receivers.

The internet allows for many different modes of communication. It lacks the centrality of traditional media where the producer of a media message is usually easy to identify. On the internet users can be both consumers of content *and* producers of journalistic content. The global nature of the internet, the huge number of mainstream and independent news sites, and lack of centrality makes online communication far harder to understand and study compared with traditional media.

Websites often allow users to contribute user-generated content (UGC) and participate in the creation of news content alongside professional journalists. Jay Rosen (2006) of New York University coined the phrase 'the people formerly known as the audience' to describe the full range of online activities that website users can choose to take part in when they switch on their computers. The phrase sounds somewhat clumsy and broad, but it provides a good explanation of the changing producer–consumer relationship between journalist and audience. He describes how TV, radio, newspapers and magazines broadcast a single message to an audience made of passive receivers. However, thanks to digital technology, things have changed. He writes:

> The people formerly known as the audience are those who were on the receiving end of a media system that ran one way, in a broadcasting pattern, with high entry fees and a few firms competing to speak very loudly while the rest of the population listened in isolation from one another—and who today are not in a situation like that at all.

Media theorist Henry Jenkins (2008) regards user participation as an integral part of a 'new economy' online where 'the ideal consumer is active, emotionally engaged, and socially networked'.

HOW WE SEEK OUT NEWS BASED ON NICHE INTERESTS

In the previous chapter, we spoke about convergence – a coming together of different media, e.g. onto single multi-function devices such as smartphones. But when it comes to audiences, website users are fragmented – consuming and producing content through a wide variety of media channels based on often very niche interests. This has challenged the traditional notion of what mass media is and individualizes the communication process.

This is not just a result of the web; there is more choice in media channels available through digital TV and radio. In the UK there are more than 500 TV channels available via digital satellite. The long established large audience, mainstream channels, such as BBC and ITV, have been joined by hundreds more that appeal to niche interests. A few examples are the Gospel Channel, Gem Collector, Wedding TV and Horse & Country. These receive small numbers of viewers and are usually run on shoestring budgets, but they make money by providing focused advertising opportunities to companies seeking to target niche audiences.

Of course, user fragmentation is most obvious on the web where there are many more than 500 channels to consume. On the web we have an almost unlimited choice of destination. The number of media voices available online has expanded and this has led to an explosion in choice. No matter what sports team, political party or celebrity you support – you can find news that caters for your individual interest. However, choice can be bewildering to some and most website users regularly visit a relatively small number of very popular websites. Data from Nielsen Online (Netimperative, 2009) found a sample of internet users spent half of their time online on just ten media brands: Facebook, MSN, Google, eBay, Yahoo!, AOL, BBC, YouTube, Microsoft and Apple.

A small number of well-known and very popular sites get the lion's share of users' attention. For example, the most popular site in the Nielsen survey was Facebook. Users spent 13 per cent of their total internet time using this site alone. Sites like Facebook are the equivalent of U2 and Coldplay, the types of globally popular bands that play arenas throughout the world. There are also an almost unlimited number of less well-known websites that cater for niche or specialist interests. These are the bands that play at your local pub or club. Each of these sites has small, sometimes tiny, numbers of users. This supports the long tail theory of economics developed by American journalist Chris Anderson (2006) which is discussed in Chapter 9.

PERSONALIZED NEWS

Social media consultant J.D. Lasica (2002) described the great shortcoming of mass media as that which exists 'to serve people's general interests while serving no individual's specific needs'.

Just think about the last time you bought a Sunday broadsheet newspaper, like the *Observer* or the *Sunday Times*. Now, think how much of the newspaper you actually read. Perhaps you read most of the sports and news section and perhaps you glanced at the TV guide. What about the glossy lifestyle supplement, the personal finance or the business pages? Were these thrown straight into the recycling bin? Why are our Sunday newspapers not more like the internet? Why can't we choose which sections we want to buy and leave the rest with the newsagent?

So why do 'the Sundays' pack in so much content? Most newspaper editors realize that publishing in print format is highly inefficient. Few people have the time to read it all, even if they had the inclination. The problem is that when it comes to mass media, general interest, newspaper publishing, the package *is* the product. The newspapers take a scattergun approach where the aim is to pack in as much content as possible to appeal to a wide variety of interests and audience demographics. Those glossy lifestyle magazine supplements, full of articles about celebrities and health products, attract advertising. In fact, they do much to supplement cross-subsidizes the expensive international news and investigative journalism that is so crucial for public interest journalism and wins the newspaper prizes.

Newspapers have always mixed the serious with the surprising or funny. Indeed, evidence suggests that readers like to be surprised by stories they didn't know they would be interested in. But Sue Cross (Wayne, 2009) of Associated Press writes: 'Boots on the ground news reporting has always been a "loss leader". It reinforces the brand and establishes a news organization's credibility for the seriousness and intelligence. Rarely have people been willing to pay for it directly.'

On the web, the traditional newspaper package is broken up and this is a concern to many traditional publishers. On the web we can understand what individual news articles are popular and which are not at any given moment. Users can also personalize their news experience to their own individual tastes and niche interests. Loyalty to any individual newspaper brand is in short supply when you have so much freedom to choose and select the stories you wish to read.

The daily me

Nicholas Negroponte in his best-seller *Being Digital* (1995) predicted a future of highly personalized newspapers dedicated to the user's individual tastes – he called it the 'Daily Me'. Despite the web being only in its infancy, Negroponte writes: 'Mass media will be redefined by systems for receiving personalized information and entertainment.'

The role of personalization in news can be overstated. There will always be space for what J.D. Lasica refers to as 'broad-brushstroke news', so mass media is hardly dead. Users will still watch TV news to find out what is going on in the world. However, he says audiences also want 'narrowcast' news to find out that is personalized to their individual needs, e.g. the latest news in their specific field, local film listings and reviews and breaking news about the football team they support.

SITES THAT PROVIDE PERSONALIZATION

'My sites'

As early as 1995 cable news channel CNN and the portal Yahoo! were offering personalized 'my' versions, e.g. MyCNN and MyYahoo! Users of these sites could choose news headlines and other modules of content from a limited selection of content to create a personalized homepage. But 'my sites' have had only limited success. For example, the BBC launched MyBBC in 2000, only to close it three years later. Martin Belam (2007), a former website producer at the BBC, blogs:

> MyBBC didn't have a massive user base, although those who did use it were fiercely loyal to it and had grown accustomed to it as their homepage. It seemed that in some ways that level of personalization was a challenge for the BBC's very mainstream online audience.

This highlights the fact that personalization demands a degree of effort from the user. Many users, perhaps even the majority, may like to receive news based on an editorial selection process of others. My sites have also been overshadowed by apps which are a popular way of delivering personalized news content.

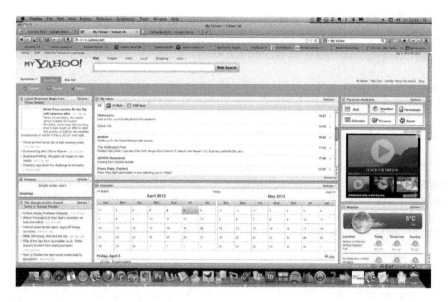

Figure 2.3   MyYahoo!: It allows users to select modules of content to create their own personalized homepage (Source: Yahoo!)

News aggregation sites

News aggregation or 'scraper' sites use a computer program that pulls together (aggregates) headlines from news sources around the world. Google News (http://news.google.com) is dominant in this sector, although there are older sites, including London-based NewsNow (www.newsnow.co.uk), which was set up by two technology journalists in 1998, and TechMeMe (www.techmeme.com). Google News lists 4,500 English-language news sources worldwide, while NewsNow has over 10,000. These sites are a very valuable resource, not least for journalists looking to keep up-to-date with subject specific news. However, some newspaper publishers have been less keen. The *Independent* newspaper wrote in a leader in October 2009:

> Google and other websites make big money from the audiences they attract for their content, which is Hoovered up from countless news sources all around the world. The creators of that content, meanwhile, earn not a bean from such aggregators – they often do not even give their permission for it to be taken – and are unable to sell it for themselves online because it has already been made freely available. To add insult to injury, having seen their content filched by the search engines, newspapers then find themselves beholden to them. In order to attract visitors to their own sites – and thus generate advertising revenue – newspapers must strive to ensure their content appears as prominently as possible with the aggregators.

Some news providers see news aggregators as competitors, all be it rivals that use software rather than human journalists to determine what the public should see. In other words, where once journalists would hold a morning editorial meeting to determine the prominence of each story within a newspaper, Google News uses a powerful computer to do this job. Instead of relying on traditional editorial news values,

Google uses complex algorithms to rank the importance of stories. This is a new form of journalism gatekeeping. Traditionally journalists were viewed as the main filters and selectors of information for their audiences, thus having a powerful control over information flow to the public. Individuals can act as information gatekeepers by deciding what to publish on their blogs and on social media.

Some media publishers are concerned about the control that search engines have over the news distribution network, something that newspapers are used to owning themselves.

The distribution of newsprint is an expensive business. It involves bundles of newspapers being slung onto trucks and distributed to newsstands throughout the country in the middle of the night. In the online world, the news aggregators have control of the virtual trucks.

So who do you support in the battle between aggregators and newspaper websites? On one hand, aggregators need content from news sites to sell targeted advertising around. However, they do not pay for the content which is written by journalists. Aggregators argue that all they are doing is giving content providers a huge amount of free online exposure and the way these sites are set up is that users who are interested in reading the full story always have to click through to the news site. So maybe news websites should actually pay the aggregators to have their content listed? This debate is likely to run for a long time.

Aggregation is certainly a controversial practice. As we will see in Chapter 9, some bloggers have been accused of being mere aggregators of original news content produced by others (usually mainstream media).

Really Simple Syndication

RSS (Really Simple Syndication) feeds are a text file of a headline and a summary of a news story that can be 'read' by RSS news reading software. RSS feeds allow users to aggregate content themselves and provide a deeper level of personalization than the aggregation sites.

RSS readers for journalists:

- NewsBlur (www.newsblur.com)
- Feedly (www.feedly.com)
- The Old Reader (http://theoldreader.com)

We also must appreciate the downside as RSS allows the pooling of reporting from a vast range of sources, thus weakening user loyalty to individual websites. However, most journalists will subscribe to RSS feeds from a range of news websites, companies and blogs in their area of specialism, and the best thing is that it's always free.

Social news

Have you seen that YouTube video of the baby panda sneezing? Man, it's so cute! Social news, the sharing of news content between friends, both funny and serious, is an important trend in news distribution and consumption.

When a friend posts a 'you simply must see this …' message followed by a link to a news story, they are harnessing the power of personal recommendation. We trust our friends who know us to recommend news content that we are likely to find significant. In this respect, our friends are acting as the information gatekeepers. We know of some people who claim their daily news diet is based exclusively on news shared with them by friends on social media, a fact that we find a little worrying! As journalists we need to understand the social web and seek to make our content easier to share – we discuss practical ways to do this in Chapter 7. The aim is normally to get our content to 'go viral' on social media which means that it will be seen by hundreds, maybe even thousands, of users.

Facebook and Twitter are two of the most important sites for the distribution of social news. How do we discover what people are interested in on social media?

Twitter.com – if you hold a Twitter account you probably know that you view a top ten list of the most popular words being used on Twitter (this is known as 'trending') in the UK, worldwide or by country. Some journalists use the list to inspire news story and feature ideas.

Flipboard (http://flipboard.com/) – an app for tablet and smartphones, demonstrates the potential of personalization. It presents personalized news based on a user's existing interest. It automatically aggregates content from a user's Facebook, Twitter, and RSS feeds in a highly readable and attractive magazine-style format. Flipboard also suggests news articles that a user may like based on their previous reading habits.

Figure 2.4   Flipboard (www.flipboard.com) for the iPad presents personalized content in a 'magazine' style. (Source: © Flipboard)

In doing so, personalization shifts the balance of power away from editors and towards the news consumer. Lasica (2002) says: 'Personalization does not mean that journalists should abandon their role of sorting, filtering, prioritising and making sense of the news. It does mean that users need to be brought into the process in a direct and meaningful way.'

CHALLENGES POSED BY PERSONALIZATION

Editors now accept that loyalty to individual news brands online is weak when users can now select content from a huge range of sources based on their personalized and individual tastes. *Daily Telegraph* journalist Shane Richmond writes:

 Now, audiences can form at article level, driven by new aggregators such as Techmeme, social bookmarking sites such as Delicious, and news sites such as Digg, that are 'edited' by their users. There are still audiences, and large ones, but they are not loyal to a single title. (Richmond, 2008).

SOCIAL BOOKMARKING SITES

Social bookmarking sites harness the knowledge of users (sometimes known as collective intelligence or the wisdom of the crowd) to sort or edit content:

 Delicious (www.delicious.com) – perhaps the best-known social bookmarking site. It works as a search engine in a similar way to Google, except the popularity of a site is based on how many Delicious users have bookmarked it. In contrast to Google which uses a computer algorithm to compile its search results, Delicious uses the 'collective intelligence' of its users.

 Digg (www.digg.com) – a people-powered news site, where thousands of users are invited to 'Digg', i.e. recommend stories on the internet for others to see. Reddit (www.reddit.com) works in a similar way, where users 'vote up' stories that users find interesting. It is fascinating to look at the types of stories that prove popular on these sites and compare with what appears in the newspapers.

HOW USERS MULTI-TASK

News and entertainment content, rather than being in short supply, is all around us and freely available. One way we cope with information overload is by multi-tasking. We can be searching on a website while texting on our phone or tuning in to a YouTube video while exchanging emails on a laptop.

Clifford Nass (2010) of Stanford University writes:

 When people multitask with media they are consuming two or more streams of unrelated media content … It doesn't matter exactly what information they are taking in or what devices they are using; just the act of using two or more media streams simultaneously means that consumers are engaging in what is an increasingly frequent pursuit in our digital age.

We must understand that our users consume and interact with our content in challenging environments where they are easily distracted, such as on the bus or train. We look at how to adapt journalistic writing styles to cope with multi-taskers in the next chapter about writing content for web and mobile devices.

ANALYSING USER BEHAVIOUR

The first and most important stage of creating content is to understand the user who we are creating it for. We aim to target our users with appropriate content, on appropriate devices and at the best time for our users.

The study of website user behaviour, sometimes known as internet analytics, is full of jargon and buzz-words that can bemuse and amuse you in equal measure. Website editors study user analytics closely in an attempt to discover trends. The number of clicks (known as the click-stream) is monitored to assess the popularity of individual news stories, columnists and website sections. The vast amount of data produced by analytics software will often challenge traditional news values and will often lead to lively discussions in newsrooms about what stories are worth covering. Some newspapers, such as the *Daily Mail* in the UK, have become skilled at targeting different audiences for their print and online outputs.

Essential jargon

Here a few bits of jargon that you'll need to understand when assessing the popularity of websites:

- *CPM*: cost per thousand impressions. This is the amount companies pay to show adverts on a site. It is based on the number of times a banner advert is shown to site visitors.
- *Traffic*: A general term to describe the number of visitors to a specific website or a page.
- *Unique visitors*: One of the most widely used metrics, it represents the number of visitors to a website. Each visitor is counted just once in a given period no matter how many times they visit a website from the same computer.
- *Loyalty*: Number of repeat visits to a site by a user.

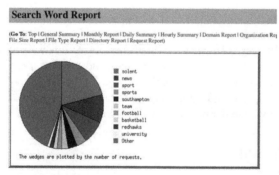

Figure 2.5   Most web hosts supply basic statistics about traffic to your site, including the words that people type into search engines to find you. (Source: Steve Hill)

- *Engagement*: What is the visit duration, i.e how long are they on your site for? Users may browse your site for minutes or even seconds before moving to a different site.

Analytics software

Free tools, that are becoming increasingly sophisticated, help us monitor user trends and understand what content users are clicking on when they visit our sites.

Your website's hosting company will normally provide some audience traffic statistics based on their own server logs, although usually the statistics collected are quite limited.

Google provides one of the best free tools for the generation of quantitative data. Google Analytics (www. google.com/analytics/) is particularly strong at monitoring how people find your site; this is known in the jargon as referrals. Referrals are the links that users click to find news content. Search engines and social media sites are important ways that our users find our content. Google dominates searches in the UK, but this is not the same everywhere. For example, in China the massive internet market search site Baidu (www. baidu.com) dominates and at the time of writing there are plans to launch an English-language version.

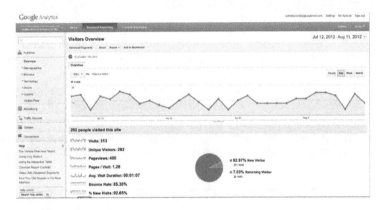

Figure 2.6   Google Analytics is one of the best tools for user analysis. (Source: Google)

How to use Google Analytics on your site

1   Go to Google and get an account.
2   Create an account at www.google.com/analytics/. You may have a Google account already, particularly if you use Gmail email or have a blog on Blogger.com which are both sites owned by Google.
3   Install the tracking code: When you sign up you will be invited to install a tracking code that is used by Google to monitor visitors to your site. The code is unique to you and you need to copy and paste it into the bottom of your content pages. It needs to be pasted very accurately and immediately before the </body> tag of each page you are planning to track. If you use a content management system (CMS) for your news site, you only need to include the tracking code once in your website's template (see Chapters 9 and 11 for more on CMS) to get it to monitor all the pages of your site.

It normally takes up to 24 hours after you have installed the tracking code for user data to start to appear.

Google Analytics outputs data in a range of attractive bar charts and pie charts covering five key sections – audience, advertising, traffic sources, content and conversion. The amount of data you will get access to is truly staggering and may well be overkill for smaller news sites.

The type of data you'll be able to see includes:

- location of visitors (by country);
- whether users are new or returning visitors;
- frequency of visit (how often they visit your site);
- how long visitors stay on your site (measured in minutes and seconds);
- web browser (e.g. Firefox or Google Chrome);
- whether visitors access your site on a smartphone or tablet computer;
- if visitors found your site using a search engine, it lists the words typed into the search engine box.
- top ten lists of the most popular pages on your site.

Case study: Analysing users of a sports site

A class of journalism students at Southampton Solent University discovered that the main sources of referrals to their university sports website were Google and Facebook links. In particular, people seeking out news about the university's American football team, the Solent Redhawks. As a result, the class made a few decisions. First, they decided to cover the Redhawks matches in far greater depth than before. Second, they decided to re-design the menus system to make it easier to find news about American football on the website. Other less popular pages were grouped together under the navigation button of 'Other Sports'. Finally, a mobile version of the site was created that was fast to load to appeal to users who access the site on their phones. Google Analytics software was used to monitor any boost in traffic as a result of these changes.

Advanced jargon

The world of user analytics is full of jargon and here are some key phrases to understand:

- *ABC1*: This is a British demographic classification used to describe users' different social grade, income and earnings levels. It is based on a scale from A, B, C1, C2, D and E. Most websites will attempt to target the potentially lucrative ABC1 user – people in the middle class and above. These people tend to work in the professions and have a disposable income that will appeal to online advertisers. You will need to carry out an online survey of your users to discover this type of demographic information.
- *Average page depth*: The average number of pages on the site that the visitor views during a single session.
- *Bounce rate*: The percentage of single page visits or visits to which the person left your site after viewing just one page. A high bounce rate is normally a bad sign indicating poor user loyalty.
- *Conversion rate*: Describes when a casual visitor to the site takes part in a desired activity. Examples may include clicking on a video link, banner advert or making an online purchase.
- *Hits*: Many sites quote high numbers of 'hits' to their sites. However, this is not a serious *measure of success* as a hit is simply a request to the web server for a file. A single web page can be made

up of dozens of files (e.g. images, video or audio files). A more reliable measurement is unique visitors.

- *Landing page or entrance page*: The first webpage that a user views. Exit page is the final page that users view during a session on your site.
- *Location*: If your site is written in English it's likely that a large numbers of users come from the USA such is the size of the market. Local newspaper websites may generate a lot of traffic from ex-pats living abroad.
- *Page view or page impression*: A page view is an instance of a page being loaded by a browser.
- *Returning visitor*: Record of a visitor returning to a webpage.
- *Sticky content or sticky eyeballs*: Any content that holds a visitor's attention and encourages loyalty, i.e. people returning time and time again to the site.
- *Visit/session*: A period of interaction between a visitor's browser and a particular website, ending when the browser is closed or shutdown or when the user has been inactive for a specified period of time.

PROBLEMS WITH ANALYTICS DATA

There are problems with relying too much on data from analytics software. Here are a few questions you may wish to ask.

Who are these people behind the numbers?

Analytics software provides a bewildering amount of data. You'll be able to discover the country and city where users are located and even what mobile devices they access your site on, but they won't tell you important information about the humans behind the numbers. Demographic data such as the gender, age, profession, etc. are likely to remain a mystery unless you carry out a survey of your users.

Does the analytics software take into account how people browse the web?

As we have already said, online usage is fragmented. A single visitor may access your site in the same month using a range of devices in a single day – a tablet at home, a computer at work or using a smartphone. The unique visitor metric counts visitors only once over a given period. Clearly, a visitor accessing the site over multiple devices in different locations could be measured many times in a single month making data meaningless.

How does the analytics software use cookies?

Most analytics tools rely on cookies – text files being placed on a user's computer to anonymously record their activities while on a site and record when a user returns to a site. Despite the tasty name, cookies are controversial as they raise privacy concerns. Some sites have used them to track users as they move around the web, obtaining valuable marketing data in the process. In 2012 Information Commissioner's Office (www.ico.org.uk) forced British websites to obtain 'implied consent' from their users if they wish to use cookies. Users must be told how data obtained through cookies will be used by a site. It is now common to see messages on websites such as: 'We use cookies on this website. By using this site, you agree that we may store and access cookies on your device.'

Carrying out online surveys

You may wish to conduct an online survey of your users to fill in some of the gaps left by analytics data – such as the users' age, gender, race, education, family income, profession (or are they students, retired people, unemployed), why they visit your site and how satisfied they are with the experience. Free Online Surveys (http://freeonlinesurveys.com) or Survey Monkey (www.surveymonkey.com/) are two of the best online survey websites.

While free survey tools are easy to set up, you'll need to think carefully about how you determine a sample, what questions you ask and how user data is processed. Universities often have internal ethics policies that must be adhered to when conducting research for student projects and the UK has data protection laws to prevent the release of personal data.

Comparing websites and understanding trends

Finding out the popularity of rival sites can be difficult. Alexa (www.alexa.com) monitors visitors to a range of popular sites and provides plenty of free demographic information. Its methodology relies on a sample of web users, mostly based in the USA, who have installed a special toolbar that monitors the sites that they visit. Google Trends (www.google.com/trends) offers a fascinating insight into what is popular online at any given moment based on what people are currently searching for.

Many news sites publish their eyeball chart (list of their most popular stories of the day) online. The *Guardian* (www.guardian.co.uk/zeitgeist) and BBC News (http://news.bbc.co.uk/1/shared/bsp/hi/live_stats/html/map.stm) are two of the most informative.

Why not compare the types of stories that are popular online with what appears in the following day's newspapers? Do you find evidence of newspapers following the online news agenda or are the newspapers covering very different topics. The types of news stories to dominate the online popularity lists tend to focus on crime, celebrity and sports stories over more serious investigative and international news content. However, your research may challenge this argument.

How large news sites audit their users

Companies looking to advertise on news websites demand reliable data about who visits each site, so most large new sites commission independent traffic measurement companies to supply the data. These include:

 ABC (Audit Bureau of Circulations) – www.abc.org.uk

 ComScore – www.comscore.com

Experian Hitwise – www.hitwise.com/uk

 Nielsen Netratings – www.nielsen-online.com

These firms use a number of techniques to monitor website traffic, which reflects the complexities of obtaining the most accurate data. They may install software at the servers of internet service providers (ISPs) to monitor visits to their clients' websites. One firm uses an opt-in panel of web users with a sample of 25 million people worldwide, including eight million in the UK. The aim is to provide the most comprehensive measurement across all devices and locations, including mobile devices, tablets, secondary PCs and access points outside of home and work locations.

WRITING AN AUDIENCE PROFILE

It is worth writing an audience profile for your website. It allows all the journalists and contributors to understand, as accurately as is possible, who a typical reader is and what interests them.

Case study: The NME (www.nme.com) user profile

Here is the user profile of the news site the NME:

NME.com is Europe's biggest and most viewed music website. It has earned worldwide respect for its rock music news and features, which are updated around the clock. With 1.3 million unique users generating over 13 million page impressions, nme.com is the UK's premier music content website. It offers unparalleled access to an affluent young audience and a unique opportunity to communicate with them in an environment that they relate to and return to frequently – 63% visit the site weekly or more frequently. The nme.com audience is made up of key demographic groups that can be difficult to target through other media:

65% male

50% aged 16–24

(Continued)

INTERPRETING THE DATA

It is important that we understand as much as possible about our users. As journalists, we need to know who is looking at our site as this will impact many things, including the design of the site, the news that is covered and its treatment (the angle on stories). It is also the way that a site will correctly value its advertising spots so it can generate as much revenue as possible.

It can be depressing to discover that your opinion piece about the state of a local care home or an interview with a leading local politician performs poorly online, often being overshadowed by something more dramatic such as CCTV video footage of a local bank robbery which was supplied by the police, or maybe just the football results!

The rise of market-driven news

A Reuters Institute Digital Report (2012) discovered that people in the UK are more interested in celebrity news and sport and less interested in domestic politics than those in other countries. Celebrity news is particularly popular with young British women. The report states:

> Almost 50 per cent of 16–24 women say they are interested in celebrity and entertainment news –
> that's twice as many as express interest in news about the economy. It is also striking that the biggest
> single driver of celebrity and entertainment news has been online newspaper websites such as the
> *Daily Mail* and the *Sun*. Almost a third (29%) of Mail Online readers say that they are interested in
> celebrity news, compared with 19% of those who read the printed newspaper. The *Daily Mail* edito-
> rial agenda online has been heavily focused on celebrity and these figures show how successful this
> strategy has been – helping it become the world's largest online newspaper according to Comscore.

Academics have related to the popularity of celebrity news with a decline in political participation. The Reuters Report (2012) says: 'The low level of interest in UK political news amongst women is especially striking – and reinforces other studies, which suggest that Westminster politics in particular is not helped by gender inequalities in political representation.'

This supports research from Markus Prior of Princeton University (2005) which has found that the internet has caused increased segmentation between users who consume news and those who prefer a diet largely made up of entertainment on TV and on the internet. Prior found that it was even possible to predict how likely people were to vote in an election based on the type of media content that they consumed online. He writes:

> "The optimists claim that the greater availability of political information [on the internet] will lead more people to learn more about politics and increase their involvement in the political process. The pessimists fear that new media will make people apolitical and provide mind-numbing entertainment that keeps citizens from fulfilling their democratic responsibilities."

In fact both are true. For those interested in politics the internet increases their knowledge and involvement, but Prior warns conversely: 'People who prefer entertainment abandon the news and become less likely to learn about politics and go to the polls.'

News-U-Like

It is important to consider whether as journalists we simply, based on our user analytics data, give people what they want. Some websites have gone in this direction and pursue a populist news agenda – perhaps focusing on a diet of celebrity, crime, or sport.

Technology columnist John Naughton (2011), referencing a 1996 study by American journalist James Fallows, describes the rise of market-driven news which he describes as:

> "news agendas that are driven not by some professional assessment of what's important and relevant, but by research into what viewers like and respond to. Put crudely, such an approach leads to news programming that plays down politics and economics in favour of coverage of crime, celebrity and sport. News-U-Like, as it were."

The pressures facing online journalists are illustrated in a slide from an AOL presentation which was leaked to *Business Insider* (Carlson, 2011). Under the heading 'Decide What Topics to Cover', the slide lists four factors to be considered:

- Traffic potential ('How many page views will this content generate?');
- Revenue/profit ('What CPM will this content earn?');
- Turnaround time ('How long will it take to produce?');
- Editorial integrity ('Will this content conform to AOL's editorial standards?').

This highlights how the sheer amount of user data we have access to can challenge traditional journalistic news values and our editorial judgements. While most journalists will like to know what stories do well and which perform poorly on their sites, we must never become slaves to the data. Rather than simply reacting to what users have liked in the past, we should lead the way by surprising our users with something they didn't know they would find interesting. We need to be risk takers and not pursue a narrow range of stories based on analytics data.

THE DIGITAL DIVIDE

A study of traffic data will tell you who is looking at your site, but what about those who can't access the net. Should journalists really care about them?

A digital divide exists between the information rich and the information poor – those who have access to digital technology and those who do not.

The global digital divide

There is a divide between the first world and developing countries in their access to the internet and associated digital technologies. In the UK over 80 per cent of the population have used the internet. In some central African countries internet usage can be as low as 2 per cent. However, the spread of cheaper internet-enabled mobile phones is slowly improving access in developing nations.

The UK's digital divide

The UK government is keen to get more people online and in 2009 the e-commerce entrepreneur Martha Lane-Fox was appointed its digital inclusion champion with the task of getting the estimated ten million UK adults (Race Online, 2011) who are offline onto the net. The north-east of England has the largest concentration of working-age people who are offline. Rural and coastal areas have the highest concentration of older people who don't use the internet. Research by Dr Ellen J. Helsper of the Oxford Internet Institute (2008) found that barriers to online engagement were: a poor education, being elderly, disabled, unemployed or retired.

Why does the digital divide matter to journalists?

It is said that 'knowledge is power' and the digital divide reinforces and deepens existing disadvantages between social groups. Those without internet access have limited access to information with which to improve their lives and often miss the cheapest deals on utilities and other products. Journalists use social media to locate contacts and generate story ideas and some assume that 'everyone uses Facebook', but this is not always the case. A key role of the journalist is to give a voice and representation to those who often feel marginalized in society and these groups are often not heavy users of the internet.

Inadequate broadband and mobile connectivity in rural areas may mean that streaming video content may be unwatchable. We need to present content over a range of media devices.

>>Summary<<

1 As journalists we often have lifestyles, habits and tastes that are very different to those of our users. We therefore need to have empathy for our users, understand who they are, why they visit our site and how they use our content.
2 Key trends in website user analysis include: fragmentation, participation, sharing, multi-tasking and personalization. Users enjoy 'broad brushstroke' general news which tells them about the world. But they also actively seek news based on their own narrow personal interests and tastes.
3 The internet gives us the opportunity to reach new international users who would be unable to access our content if it solely existed in print.
4 We should never become slaves to user data. Some news websites select stories to publish based on commercial factors such as traffic potential and potential advertising revenue. These market-driven journalism values promote a limited agenda of crime, sport and celebrity which often get large numbers of users. This is usually covered at the expense of investigative and international news.
5 A digital divide exists between the information 'have' and 'have nots'. In the UK those with limited access to the net tend to be poor, elderly, or live in rural areas. Africa is the continent with the lowest penetration of internet usage in the world.

EXERCISES

1   Carry out an online survey of your class or work colleagues to discover what sites, apps and devices they use to get their online news content.

2   If you run a news site or blog, sign up for a free analytics services and install the tracking code to monitor your site's visitors.

3   When running analytics software make a note of the following metrics:

   o   Location of visitors: What is the balance of visitors who live in the UK versus North America?

   o   What are the most visited pages on your website?

   o   Where does your referral traffic come from, i.e. what percentage of users come to your site via search engines, social media sites, blogs or news sites?

   o   How you can you use this information to make your content more appealing to your target users?

4   Sign into Twitter (www.twitter.com) and make a note of the top ten keywords that are 'trending' (getting the most mentions). Compare the list with what is appearing on the websites of mainstream media publishers. Are journalists covering the same issues that users of Twitter are finding significant?

FURTHER READING

Blackhurst, Rob. 2005. The Freeloading Generation, *British Journalism Review*, 16(3): 53.
   Blackhurst looks at why young and budget-conscious commuters seem unwilling to pay for news.
Negroponte, Nicholas. 1995. *Being Digital*. London: Coronet.
   This best-seller from the 1990s predicted the future of media, including personalization and the 'Daily Me'. You can play 'spot what came true'.
Richmond, Shane. 2008. How SEO Is Changing Journalism, *British Journalism Review*, 19(4): 51.
   The *Daily Telegraph* journalist explains the impact of search engine optimization (SEO) on journalism.

SECTION 2

Skills for the Multimedia Journalist

Writing for the Web   47

Telling the Story with Images   65

Using Audio and Podcasts   83

Working with Video   102

Doing Investigative Reporting   120

CHAPTER 3

Writing for the Web

INTRODUCTION

BBC journalist and political commentator Andrew Marr (2006) says:

> Words matter, although I am not sure how much print does. The smell of books, of bookshops, of newsprint; the sharp cut of black letters on creamy paper, bindings that reassure the fingers, the satisfying scrunch of a folded paper in a coffee shop as you smooth it down to read some fool's column – we all have sentimental reasons to love print. But if, in the end, we can download far more writing, a bigger selection of books and more news stories than we can get in a shop, and if we can do it quickly and search for references as efficiently, then these sentimental tugs are of secondary importance.

If you are reading these words printed in ink on paper (how retro!), you may like to consider the advantages and disadvantages that print has compared with digital media formats. Even if, as some have predicted, all newspapers eventually go electronic, there will always be a demand for well-crafted and reliable journalism. Despite the technological changes, words certainly still matter. The development of a clear and engaging style, and the ability to tell a story in an accurate and entertaining way remain at the heart of journalism. You are unlikely to be able to get a job in journalism without these essential skills.

Neil Thurman and Ben Lupton (2008) carried out interviews with senior staff at some of the UK's most influential online news providers. There was general agreement that many of the classic rules of writing for print media also apply to online journalism. These include:

1 being able to write quickly, clearly and accurately;
2 being able to spell;

3   having excellent grammar;
4   being able to write snappy headlines;
5   possessing the ability to spot a strong story.

We won't repeat all the basic rules of journalism here. Instead, we will contrast writing for the web and smartphones with other forms of output.

Journalistic writing is an idiomatic skill that may share similarities but is not the same as the 'fine writing' for literature and fiction. Journalism writing is also different to academic writing. Passive sentences and long paragraphs that are laden with technical language and other jargon are perfectly acceptable for academic dissertations and essays, but journalistic writing is very different and some students struggle to switch between these styles.

Words should never be seen as separate from other media outputs. Research suggests that our understanding of events and the way we perceive the world around us is put into context by strong and bold digital images and video. The image is an important communication tool in today's fast-paced world where many of us suffer from information overload. Yet reporters commonly regard 'words' as being their responsibility and multimedia is viewed as 'someone else's job'. Even worse, reporters may think about adding other multimedia content only as an afterthought, once the copy of an article is filed. We need to take an integrated approach to achieve our ultimate aim – to tell people's stories in the most compelling ways for our users.

>>OBJECTIVES<<

In the chapter, you will learn:

1   the essential skills of good reporting;
2   how to write content for the web that is easy to digest;
3   how smartphones and tablet computers are changing how users interact with content;
4   how to write compelling headlines, summaries, leads, sub-headings and body copy;
5   skills for online news, feature, review and opinion writing.

INTERACTING WITH TEXT

What are the key differences between writing for the web and print or broadcast? Before we even begin looking at writing techniques, we must take into account how users consume and interact with content online, whether they consume content on a desktop computer, smartphone, tablet or smart TV. The way users interact with our content impacts just about everything we produce – writing style, length of articles, and design and layout.

Research shows that online readers use vastly different sections of the brain than offline readers. Dave Copeland of ReadWrite.com (2012) says: 'The brain is conditioned to skip around when online reading, as clicking on a link, for example, will reward the brain with new images and content.'

He warns that many journalists write the same way online as they do for books, magazine articles and other long-form and traditional print mediums.

So when writing for websites, we must first face up to the shocking fact that it's highly *unlikely* that users will read to the end of a long news story, unless they are extremely interested in its content. The longer the story is the more likely they will give up part way through. The web is a challenging environment where users can easily be distracted by the almost infinite range of alternative news sources available to them at a click of the mouse. If they can't find the information they need they will quickly and ruthlessly abandon your site and move on.

Once described as the 'King of Usability', Jakob Nielsen is an expert at looking at how websites and computer programs can be made easier to use. Nielsen (2003) bluntly refers to website users as being 'selfish, lazy, and ruthless'. His research found that only 16 per cent of online users read web pages word-by-word. Most users just scan the

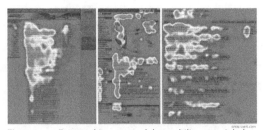

Figure 3.1   Eye-tracking research by usability guru Jakob Nielsen shows that users read news in an 'F' pattern. Headlines and intros must explain the story clearly, if the user is to read on. (Source: Useit.com)

text as they attempt to quench their thirst for a particular information hit, so we need to consider how this research affects the way we write our stories.

Studies vary, but some suggest that reading from a computer screen is 25 per cent slower than reading from the page. People simply don't read long articles on smartphones. However, in contrast, reading speed improves using tablets or e-readers. E-readers often use specially designed 'e-ink' made up of black text on a grey background. This reduces eyestrain and offers a huge improvement compared to reading from a bright computer screen. Quite simply the lesson here is we need to create content that appeals to our users and is easy to digest from a screen without having to print it.

Usability researchers use eye-tracking software to study the sections of websites that people look at the most. It does this by following where people look on a computer screen using a number of video cameras trained on a user's head. Cameras even track precise eye movements as they browse a web page. Jakob Nielsen (2010) found that users often browse a page in an 'F Pattern'. So we can conclude that the most important parts of a news story are the headline, sub-heads (headings beneath the main headline) and the lead paragraph (intro text to the story). These page elements should be used to explain clearly what the story is about and encourage users to read the main body text.

SNACKING ON CONTENT

Online users read in a different way to print readers. They tend to snack on content, often just reading the headline, the lead and first few paragraphs of the story and then moving on. A typical national newspaper news story may be 750 to 1000 words in length. While this word count would be acceptable for reading on a tablet, few would read it from a tiny screen on a smartphone. This highlights the need to check how our content is presented on all the main platforms and devices that it will be viewed on.

MAKING COPY SCANNABLE

Online readers tend to skip large blocks of text, so we must write our copy in a different way.

a   Include one idea per paragraph and put a line space between paragraphs.

b   Break up long articles into easily digestible chunks – a process appropriately called chunking. This includes using sub-headings to make text scannable and bullet points to attract people's attention.

c   Aim to create multiple-entry points into the story. This draws people into the page and encourages them to read the body copy.

Entry points to a page include:

- headlines;
- summary text or tasters;
- lead paragraphs;
- photos and captions;
- fact boxes;
- pull quotes;
- subheads and crossheads.

The first paragraph of the story (the lead) is vitally important. This is sometimes known as micro-content i.e. it must be content-rich, include search engine optimization (SEO) keywords, and usually be able to be understood without the users necessarily having access to the body of the story. SEO is an important new editorial skill. The aim is to make sure our stories appear high up in the listings on the major search engines such as Google. We discuss how to do this using SEO keywords in Chapter 11.

Depending on your website style, you may need to write homepage tasters that appear directly beneath the headline for each story. The aim is to summarize the story succinctly and entice the reader to 'click through' to read the full text. Space is limited on a homepage, so this text is specially written to a particular character count to fit with the site's template. Some sites have such strict word limits that the CMS will prevent the journalist from publishing a story if it contains headlines or summary text that goes over a pre-determined word count. Online journalists get used to writing headlines to limited word counts.

Once the user clicks through to the article page, they will normally see the headline and often a sub-head. This may be exactly the same text that is used for the homepage taster. Sub-heads are normally styled up in display text and in a font smaller than the headline, but larger than body text. Some CMS will automatically style headlines and sub-heads according to a pre-designed template and reporters won't need to worry about this.

Bulleted lists of content are very useful to those reading on small mobile phone screens. *The Yahoo! Style Guide* (2010) states: 'They [mobile users] tend to skim the left side of the screen looking for headings, bulleted lists, a word that jumps out at them.' Bulleted lists at the start of stories allow people to read the key points and then decide whether they would like to read on.

Statistics and facts can be hard to digest if they appear in body copy, so it is often best to include them as fact boxes. Once again, these act as useful visual entry points to the page.

Headings are used within body copy to break up longer text into chunks. These will entice a user who has begun reading the body copy to read on further. Those users, who are seeking particular information, can use headings within text to scan a story quickly and they should therefore be brief (one or two words) and descriptive about the content that appears beneath.

PREPARING TO COVER BREAKING NEWS

When covering a news story online, reporters need to carry out a range of important tasks.

Make contact with key sources

As soon as the story breaks, the first job is normally to establish the Ws of the story – who, what, where, when and why. Just as important is the H of the story – how it happened – but this information normally takes longer to establish. It is important to assess its impact for your users. This will give you some guide to how much coverage it is likely to require. You will need to make contact with news sources – these may be those people directly involved, local emergency services, eyewitnesses, etc. You'll need to make calls and arrange for them to be interviewed.

Search social media

Often eyewitnesses will tweet about what they have seen using their smartphones and may include images and video. Software such as TweetDeck (www.tweetdeck) allows you to search social media and receive real-time updates when specific words are mentioned. Hootsuite (http://hootsuite.com/) also provides tools to seek out potential contacts. Requests for information from eyewitnesses can also be tweeted.

Open up a Word file

Surprisingly many online journalists prefer to write their copy offline. That's to say, they write in MS Word rather than directly into the text editor of the CMS online. MS Word has a better spellchecker than those in most CMS and if your internet should go down, you won't lose your work. Don't style up the text in Word though; this will be done in the CMS.

Open CMS and create a new article or post

As soon as possible, get a brief summary story of what you know so far on your website. This may just be a headline and a paragraph or two, but it will alert the reader to the fact that important news is breaking. Alert your editor when you are ready to publish so your copy can be proofed. This story will be a work in progress; you will add extra information to this story as more facts emerge.

Promote the summary story on social media

As soon as the summary story is online, you should post the headline and link to friends and followers on social media. You can also put out another request for eyewitnesses if required.

Consider live blogging

For important or developing stories, you may wish to set up a live blogging system (see an example below). If you feel the story has become more significant, you will need to discuss with your editor whether coverage needs to be scaled up with extra resources being devoted to it.

Build the summary story

As you get more information, you will need to build on the summary story. You will need to add links, images and video at this stage. Once again, post a link to the updated story to social media.

Consider context articles

Over the hours and days following a major news story, there is often potential for context articles. These may include opinion and blog-style articles about the issues and controversies raised. When stories have run for a few days or even months users may not always remember what has gone on before. News sites like BBC News will often include separate background articles – often presented as a Q&A or interactive timeline of events – where they will explain the back-story, i.e. the story's history. We must never forget that while we may have an in-depth understanding of the issues and how situations emerged, users will need reminding of the background details.

 Click to access more about the importance of structure in news writing.

THE IMPORTANCE OF A GREAT INTRO

You need to think carefully about what type of information the user will want at the start of your summary story.

If you know your users, you'll have a sense of what interests them. In the case of the latest 'miracle' drug treatment, key questions may be:

- Will it work?
- Is it safe?
- When is it available?
- How does it affect me?

There are no prizes for burying important information low down in the body of the story.

During the reporting of breaking or developing stories, we should avoid allowing important information to become 'pushed' down the body copy. Summary stories can lose their 'shape' as the most important information may not necessarily be the latest information, causing confusion to users.

Research into the coverage of breaking news on UK websites by Kostas Saltzis (cited in SnurBlog, 2010) highlights how journalists update online stories as events are developing to form continuous news coverage. Saltzis found that web updates tended to lead to a steady increase in the stories word count. Typically, stories go from being very short when news breaks, perhaps a few sentences, to something much longer when a full picture of what is happening emerges. Interviews and reaction quotes also increase the length of the story. So we need to be aware of how the story structure is subtly changing and the potential for confusion that this may cause. The problem is that you are dealing with essentially two audiences – one looking for the overview summary of what happened and the other looking for breaking news updates. We should consider live blogging to cater for the latter audience.

 Find out how the traditional pyramid structure to write news works online.

What is live blogging?

When a major, rapidly developing story is occurring, we should offer users two types of content – a summary story that provides a definitive account of what the journalist knows and real-time live coverage. One of the easiest ways to blog about an event in real-time is to use free software such as CoverItLive (www.coveritlive.com). It allows the latest breaking news blog posts and tweets to be brought together and posted in a chronological format on a website. If you run a website using the WordPress CMS, which we discuss in Chapter 9, the live blogging extension (http://wordpress.org/extend/plugins/live-blogging) allows us to post content and photos in real-time as events develop.

With a real-time live blog the user is invited to make sense of the snippets of news posted by the journalist, which appeals to breaking news fans. However, there is still a role for a traditional summary-style news story that prioritizes the most important information first. Indeed, journalists will often be expected to work on both forms of output simultaneously.

Neil Thurman and Anna Walters from City University conducted research into live blogging:

> We believe live blogs are so popular because they meet readers' changing news consumption preferences. More and more news is being consumed at work, in the office. Live blogs provide this 'news-at-work' audience with what they're looking for: regular follow-up information on breaking news in 'bite-sized nuggets' which they can read – as several readers told us – while they are supposed to be working. (Thurman in Greenslade, 2012b)

An example of live blogging: panic buying of petrol (Guardian.co.uk, 30 March 2012)

The *Guardian* pioneered live blogging in sports coverage and in news events, including the London transport bombing in July 2005. Here is a short excerpt of how *The Guardian* covered a story to do with the panic buying of petrol in a live blog format:

> 6.02pm: Sky reports that ambulances in Yorkshire are running short of petrol, citing a doctor that contacted them. Sky also quote Chris Hunt, the director-general of the UK Petroleum Industry Association, who describes the situation as 'self-inflicted insanity'.
>
> 6.45pm: I [a *Guardian* journalist] have just spoken to the Department of Energy and Climate Change who assure me that there is no fuel shortage in the UK. 'Forecourts are being replenished and there is no break in the supply chain. If a forecourt is closed, it will probably open when it is re-supplied,' according to a spokesman. 'There is no need to queue. Queuing is causing additional disruption.'
>
> If things do get worse, the department is well prepared. On their website is the Downstream Oil Resilience and Emergency Planning page. On it you can access a document of Emergency Response Tools and a Memorandum of Understanding between the government, oil companies and trade unions.
>
> 7.11pm: Tanker drivers are normally only allowed to work nine hours per day but the government has waived the rule to allow them to work for 11 hours until next Thursday according to the BBC. The rules were introduced by the European Union to prevent drivers carrying dangerous loads from falling asleep at the wheel and causing accidents. So to add to the cocktail of panic-buying and 'self-inflicted insanity', we now have tanker drivers exceeding the 'safe' working limits.
>
> 7.38pm: I'll bring this blog to a close by referring you to the latest stories on the fuel crisis. Andrew Sparrow has filed this on political aspect of the crisis while Dan Milmo has been speaking to tanker drivers in Portishead.

GIVING YOUR COPY PACE

Newspaper journalists write tightly to fit a limited space on the page – this gives their reporting a sense of pace and urgency. Online journalists are wise to follow this style. Complex sentences are more difficult to comprehend when scanning online. Tabloids, like the *Daily Mirror*, rarely include sentences over 20 words in length. Even in a broadsheet newspaper, such as the *Guardian*, a typical sentence length may be no more than 35 words. Always consider whether you can cut the fat and sharpen things up by removing words without changing the sentence's meaning.

EXAMPLES: KEEPING IT SHORT

Here are some examples of news copy from the London *Evening Standard* and *Sunday Express*. We've included the word counts for each sentence; try and cut these sentences down even further without changing the meaning.

Cannibal on Trial for Murder

A self-proclaimed cannibal went on trial today accused of murdering and then eating a man. (15)
    Armin Meiwes, 42, killed computer expert Bernd Jurgen Brandes after he replied to an internet advertisement for someone willing to be eaten. (22)
    Mr Brandes was stabbed in the throat, carved up and eaten in front of a running video camera. (18)
    (Source: Allan Hall, *Evening Standard*, 3 December 2003)

Lastminute lines up 100 more sackings

More than 100 jobs at lastminute.com, the internet travel agency, are set to be axed next month. (17)
    The redundancies will come as a severe blow to staff, who have already seen their numbers slashed by 200, or 35 per cent, over the past two years. (28)
    (Source: Steve Hill, *Sunday Express*, 22 September 2002)

GIVING YOUR COPY IMPACT

Tabloids use a range of 'impact' adjectives to make their sentences exciting and generate emotion. However, we have to be careful, as some of these words have become tabloid clichés. You may be able to spot the impact words above. They include 'stabbed', 'carved' 'slashed', 'axed' and 'blow'.
    Try to sum up the story in a concise but dramatic way using the active rather than the passive form. Then build on that. Thus you might start, 'Police shot armed robber', which is more dramatic than, 'A man was shot by police'. That is the most important information and sums up the entire story.
    You can then develop out from that: 'Police shot an armed robber yesterday.' You can develop a bit further:'Police shot an armed robber during a bank raid in Uxbridge yesterday.'
    Then add a supporting sentence: 'The shotgun-brandishing gang was ambushed by Flying Squad detectives as they entered Lloyds in the High Street around midday.'
    Then a third sentence: 'Police shot an armed robber during a bank raid in Uxbridge yesterday. The shotgun-brandishing gang was ambushed by Flying Squad detectives as they entered Lloyds in the High Street around midday. The wounded man – said by eyewitnesses to be in his late 20s – was disarmed and taken away by ambulance.'

Then a fourth and fifth sentence. In many cases this will be a direct quote to liven up the copy and add colour: 'A Hillingdon hospital spokesman says the shot man is in a serious but stable condition. "A man suffering from gunshot wounds was admitted this morning. His injuries are not believed to life threatening."'

The NCTJ emphasizes a traditional approach to news writing which is based around a four par system (four sentences). It can be summarized as follows:

- Par 1 – Basic details of what happened/who did what, when and roughly where.
- Par 2 – Expansion on the points in par 1, a little more detail and elaboration.
- Par 3 – How/why it happened.
- Par 4 – What's happening now.
- Usually by par 5 it is good to bring in a voice, probably an interviewee. This brings authenticity to the story and another voice makes it easier to read.
- Remember that the most attention-grabbing stories are usually about other human beings. So get the human angle in early – deaths, injuries, saved/rescued – then tell people about damage to property and disruption to traffic.
- Get in all the key details – times, exact locations, names, ages, descriptions – this fulfils natural human concern curiosity.

Take this Maritime and Coastal Agency press release:

At 13.28 pm today a distress alert was received by the Coastguard from a 406 mhz EPIRB.

It was quickly identified as belonging to a fishing vessel registered in Buckie called Onward. The fishing vessel was in a position, 50 miles north west of Stromness.

Shetland Coastguard made a mayday relay broadcast to secure assistance from any other vessels in the area. A merchant vessel Nautica responded and diverted to the last known position.

A Maritime surveillance aircraft, Watch dog 65, was tasked to attend and report back. A rescue helicopter was requested from ARCC Kinloss and the Coastguard rescue helicopter R102 based at Sumburgh was sent.

Stromness RNLI lifeboat was also requested to launch, but has been stood down and the Nautica is continuing its passage.

Rescue 102 arrived on scene and found the fishing vessel had been on fire and that the crew had evacuated to liferafts. They were winched into the helicopter, and now all five crew have been evacuated to the hospital at Kirkwall suffering from hypothermia.

There are different ways to write the story. We could say, 'Emergency services assist fishing vessel on fire'. This is correct but not so dramatic. But the most interesting intro is, 'Five crew rescued by helicopter from burning fishing boat'. As is often the case with press releases the story is in the final paragraph.

INTERVIEWING: THE ART OF LISTENING

Journalism is all about finding new information and interviews play a crucial role. The more people you interview, the more you'll be amazed by the incredible stories people have to tell. Some interviewees will become trusted sources and may provide news tips that will be helpful for many stories to come. So make sure you add their details to your contacts book – whether you keep your contacts book stored in paper format (how old fashioned!) or in an electronic database. Try to get mobile-phone numbers of contacts as well as their email and social media details, as you often need to get hold of people quickly. Keep notes of any specialist knowledge or contacts they may have that could be useful in the future. There is no time like the present to start building your contacts database.

Don't limit yourself to carrying out research using internet archives or rely on pasting quotes into stories from press releases. The problem is that ordinary people don't issue press releases – it's normally companies or celebrities with something to promote. Information from the internet and press releases will rarely be exclusive and it's highly likely that other media outlets will use the same quotes as you. So it's always best to make time to interview someone, even when working to the tightest of deadlines.

A face-to-face interview is usually best as it allows a rapport to be built up between interviewee and journalist. Email, telephone and Skype interviews can work when time is short and the type of material that is required is mainly factual. Of course, you will need a way to record the interview.

Email interviews may be the only possibility when an interviewee lives in another time zone. But be aware the interviewee will get to see your questions in advance, which will reduce the spontaneity of a real-time conversation.

Quotes help to authenticate a story and this is particularly true for eyewitness accounts of news events where you will want a number of different sources confirming the basic details of what happened. Really simple questions such as: 'Will you tell me what happened?', 'What did you see?' and 'How did it make you feel?' work very well.

Quotes also add personality and colour to a piece. It is sometimes said that the web lacks personality, so we should always be on the lookout for quotes and pictures of people. One of the most exciting things about carrying out an interview is that we're never quite sure what people will say. An eyewitness may dispute the 'official' version of a news event given by some other 'respected' authority like the police. If so, you may well have a story.

THE SEVEN ENEMIES OF GOOD WRITING

- Passive verbs: Active verbs show people doing things (and people doing things make news). Passive sentences usually start with the receiver of the action. In active sentences, the thing doing the action is the subject of the sentence and the thing receiving the action is the object. Normally a good style for a sentence would be [Thing doing action] + [verb] + [thing receiving action]. There are cases where using the passive voice is appropriate if the object is what most people are interested in.
- Run-on sentences: Stick to one idea per sentence. A run-on sentence is really two sentences that should be separated by some kind of punctuation mark. If you find yourself with a run-on sentence, add some punctuation. A full stop or comma normally does the trick. Complex sentences with too many clauses are much harder to digest when scanning a page online. When in doubt keep it short.
- Mixed metaphors: When two or more metaphors are confused, you end up with a mixed metaphor. The following appeared in the London *Evening Standard* in a 2009 interview with a government minister: 'Her saucer-eyes narrow to a gimlet stare and she lets Mr Clarke have it with both barrels.' While the writer is trying to set a vivid scene, the reality is it simply sounds absurd.
- Mixed tenses: You need write in the past or present tense. Whatever you do don't mix your tenses within an article.

- Clichés: Whatever your specialist area, it is practically inevitable that you will start to repeat the same old phrases. In sports reporting you may find mentions of: 'A game of two halves', 'giving it 110 per cent,' 'match fit', 'acid test' and numerous others. These become tiresome to read.
- First person: Writing in the first person (I think, my view, etc) is best avoided. Often new journalists seem to feel they must get their own views into news stories. The best advice is to let the people you interview give their opinions on things – we are just reporters.
- Assuming too much knowledge of the user: When we write in technical language and jargon we risk confusing and alienating our users. However, a specialist business-to-business (B2B) website that is read by professionals working within a particular industry is likely to include a certain amount of jargon which will be understood by users. To have to explain every word would waste time, take up valuable space and could even be considered patronizing. Gossip blogs will often refer to celebrities by their first names. For example, 'Jen' = the actor Jennifer Aniston and 'Madge' = the singer Madonna. These sites seek to develop a shared language, which can encourage a sense of belonging and user loyalty. Determining how much specialist knowledge a user has is an art of a skilled editor rather than a science.

WRITING HEADLINES AND THE RISE OF SEO

Headlines in print must attract the reader's attention and give the gist of the story. On news websites, headlines are important for Search Engine Optimization (SEO) and act as clickable hyperlinks to the individual article page. Who writes the headlines? Traditionally, this was the sub-editor's job, but if you work on a small website with a limited staff it's likely the reporters will be required to at least suggest a headline for their stories, even if it is changed later by an editor.

British tabloid newspapers have sometimes used what we refer to as 'word play' such as alliteration (the repetition of an initial sound) and puns (two or more meanings of the same word or similar sounding words for humorous effect) and references to popular culture.

Here are some examples of tabloid headlines:

- 'Zip Me Up before You Go Go' (*Sun*): a story about when George Michael was arrested for lewd conduct in a public toilet.
- 'The Age of the Strain' (*Daily Mirror*): a story about the UK's crumbling railway system.

As fun as they are, puns and word play are not generally used for online headlines. The focus should be on keeping headlines simple for a global audience, making sure they contain SEO keywords and able to appear as standalone text in search engine listings. We can see that the example tabloid headlines are likely to perform badly online. Song titles are frequently used in tabloid headlines that appear in print, but only fans of 1980s pop tunes will understand the first headline (and if you are wondering who 'Wham!' are, you are proving our point!). The second headline is meaningless to anyone who can't remember the advert for the nationalized British Railways – 'this is the age of the train'.

Chris Moran (in Elliot, 2012), says: 'Even before we worry about [search engine] optimization of headlines, our subs need to consider the most profound difference between print and web – the almost endless number of places in which headlines will appear out of context. RSS feeds, Twitter and search results are just a few examples. Therefore we strive to tell the story of a piece clearly in every headline and aim to give readers all the help and information they need to make sure they are clicking on something of interest to them.'

Amelia Hodsdon of the *Guardian* (Elliot, 2012), says: 'In print, headlines often work only in conjunction with an image – "Phew!", the day after Team GB won its first gold medals, only made sense with the picture of a triumphant, relieved Bradley Wiggins.' A headline such as this, detached from its explanatory image, would be meaningless if it appeared in a search engine listing.

The Yahoo! Style Guide advises (2010):

1   Ask yourself which words you would use in a search to find your story.
2   Proper nouns – the names of people, places, and things – are good.
3   Avoid abbreviations, as people tend to spell out words in searches.
4   Subject–verb–object ('Hercules slays Hydra!') is often the best structure for a headline, because it puts the actor (subject) and the action (verb) first.

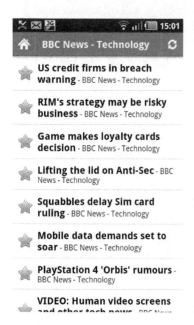

Figure 3.2   Keep headlines short and precise for reading on small mobile phone screens. (Source: Google Reader)

EXAMPLE: HEADLINES FROM BBC SURREY (LOCAL NEWS SITE)

Compared with the tabloids, online news headlines often seem very dull and boring. Here are some headlines from the BBC Surrey website:

- 'Body Found after Flat Explosion' (5 words, 32 characters)
- 'Good Samaritan Struck with Bottle' (5 words, 33 characters)
- 'Police Drop Ski Trips Fraud Probe' (6 words, 34 characters)

The headlines above are concise, informative and convey the gist of the stories, allowing the user to immediately decide whether they wish to click the headlines to read more. The BBC will vary its tone depending on the story. A story regarding a woman who is considering having her hand replaced with a bionic one after a motoring accident had a headline pitched as a dilemma – 'Should I Have My Hand Cut Off?' (7 words, 30 characters). This will immediately grab the user's attention and get them thinking about what they would do in such a situation. But a quick word of warning: in our attempts to summarize the story in as few words as possible, we must be wary of stating the obvious. Here are three examples from Stephen J. Dubner of Freakonomics (2012):

- 'Diana Was Still Alive Hours Before She Died'
- 'Frequent Sex Enhances Pregnancy Chances'
- 'Homicide Victims Rarely Talk to Police'

KEEP YOUR OPINIONS TO YOURSELF

In one of the best introductions to the basics of news reporting, journalist David Randall (2000) writes: 'If you take a room full of journalists and ask them who has got an opinion on an important topical news event, every hand will go up. Ask who has some fresh, unpublished information on this event and almost every hand will go down.'

The traditional view is that opinion should never appear in news copy. However, an article in *The Economist* magazine (2011) describes the Foxication of news – a reference to Fox News, the highly partisan, right-wing, cable news channel in the USA. The popularity of Fox suggests that there is a market for news tinged with opinion. Supporters of opinion-based news argue that with multiple news outlets audiences can make up their own minds which news outlets to trust. If you don't like the views of one provider there is always another one with a different take on the news, so the argument goes. *The Economist* article states: 'In a world where millions of new sources are emerging on the internet, consumers are overwhelmed with information and want to be told what it all means.' However, this has alarmed some journalists, academics and others who seek out trustworthy sources of news. We are wise to bear in mind the legendary words of C.P. Scott, former owner/editor of the *Guardian* newspaper: 'Comment is free, but facts are sacred.'

TYPES OF ONLINE WRITING

Now that we have looked at some tips for online news writing, let's look briefly at three key styles of writing – opinion, features and review writing.

Opinion blogging

A good opinion blog will:

1 include an original argument and focus on a controversial issue;
2 be backed up with detailed research and links to reliable sources of information;
3 be written in a lively, conversational, and entertaining style;
4 encourage users to respond – when a blogger deliberately goes out to stir up controversy it's known as providing link bait, as the aim is to provoke a debate among fellow bloggers.

Perhaps most importantly, a blog should be timely. The skill is to catch the moment when the reader is just beginning to think about a topic.

Getting the balance right between a conversational style and the precision of argument and thought is, arguably, the hardest element of opinion writing. You should avoid writing too much in the first person. The user will know it is you that is writing, so you can normally delete redundant phrases such as: 'I think ...', 'It is my view ...' and 'Most people would say ...'

Ideas for opinion articles could come from the following:

1 the news peg – what's currently happening in the news;
2 responding to a post written by another blogger – an argument between two bloggers tends to generate traffic for both parties;
3 something you are angry about – all opinion writers find it easier to write on topics where they have strong feelings, but take care, an opinion article should never simply become a rant;
4 an interesting personal experience that others can relate too;
5 what people are talking about on social media – look at the trending topics on Twitter.

Those who are serious about developing their skills in this area should subscribe to the RSS feeds of a few respected newspaper columnists and bloggers. It is useful to analyse the individual structures of their posts while you also work on developing your own voice.

EXAMPLES

News peg

Headline: 'Let's look after our victims more than our criminals'

Intro pars (paragraph):

> The last thing Betty Scoones said to son Darren was 'will you be in for tea, love?'

> Darren shouted back 'Aye, I will Mam' then drove off to work in his cab. A few hours later she saw him again, live on TV, a blood-splattered sheet over his body, which lay next to his taxi on the Whitehaven rank where Derrick Bird had murdered him ...

Last pars:

> A wise man once said that a test of a civilized country is how it treats its criminals. I'd say it's how it treats its victims of criminals.

> And we fail. Atrociously.

(Source: Brian Reade, *Daily Mirror*, 27 January 2011)

Personal experience

Headline: 'How Twitter changed the face of dissent'

Intro pars:

> If its founders hadn't invented such a silly name for Twitter, it would almost certainly have been closed down by now.

> The name suggests the cheery inanity of birdsong: it does not imply a considered and coherent back-channel of radical dissent. Without tweets, twibbons and hashtags, however, the public might not be aware that officers of the law recently assaulted a wheelchair user and dragged him behind riot lines.

> In the Parliament Square 'kettle' on 9 December, I happened to be standing next to Jody McIntyre when the police began to baton him and his brother, who was pushing his wheelchair. Within seconds, I had pulled out my phone to tweet about what I had seen; within minutes, the backlash had begun as outraged citizens all over the country found supporting evidence of the assault and let each other know what had happened. By the time I arrived home, bloody and bruised from further police violence, the assault on Jody had made the national press ...

Last pars:

> 'Thanks to the internet, the people are becoming the Panopticon – the all-seeing, ubiquitous power,' says Aaron Peters, who is working on a PhD on the political impact of social networking. 'With these tools, individuals can legitimately say, "we are everywhere".'

We are everywhere. That is what the young chanted in Parliament Square as the tuition fees vote came through. Behind the bonfires, you could see the scrawled words, 'This is just the beginning'. For this government and for any government that seeks to control citizens by monopolising information, the writing on the wall . . . is on the web.

(Source: Laurie Penny, *New Statesman*, 20 December 2010)

Features

Steen Steensen (2009) of Oslo University College describes the key characteristics of features:

1 Feature journalism is often narrative, and is thereby distinguished from the inverted pyramid structure of news journalism.
2 Feature journalism is usually not so deadline sensitive as news journalism.
3 Feature journalists are allowed to colour their text with subjective descriptions, reflections and assessments.
4 Feature journalism often portrays people and milieus and is therefore usually personal and emotional.
5 Feature journalism is usually visually attractive and presented in delicate layouts using multiple illustrations, mainly still photos.

The internet is suited to the breaking news, but relatively little academic research has been done into how long-form feature journalism works online. Steensen found that journalists did not consider feature journalism and online journalism (delivered to a desktop computer) as being compatible types as it is often believed that people simply don't read long articles online. However, e-readers and tablet computers may be changing user behaviour. They certainly make reading long-form journalism easier than from a computer monitor.

Reading a printed magazine is usually considered to be a passive and linear experience. The user starts at the top of the feature and simply reads to the end. The feature writer can take time to develop deeper arguments with longer blocks of text and narrative. This contrasts with a website experience, where users expect to be able to click links and comment on stories. While news story structures include the most important details of the story in the opening paragraphs, features traditionally take a more relaxed approach to their introductions.

Susan Pape (2006) says:

> In features, intros take on a different style and are able to 'breathe' a little more. Sometimes, this might be a harsh blast of hot or cold air that shocks the reader with a hard-hitting statement or fact; at other times it might be a gentle leisurely breath that seduces the reader by way of a description or anecdote that introduces a character or sets a scene; or, perhaps, a provocative question or an attention-grabbing or intriguing quote.

Figure 3.3 *The Economist* iPad app makes reading long-form journalism a pleasure. (© The Economist Newspaper Limited, London, 2012)

This leisurely approach to storytelling is the antithesis of web writing where users want hard facts delivered to them quickly.

So instead of simply pasting the text of a long feature on their websites, forward-thinking magazines and newspapers generate web-exclusive content based around the themes or ideas in a feature. These can exploit all the multimedia and interactive possibilities provided by the internet, such as image galleries, audio, video and social media content, to form a multimedia package. Publishers may also save their longer articles for delivery via tablet apps or on e-readers.

Reviews

Review sites have become very popular. Users will often read product reviews before making their purchases online, whether this is just a ticket to a film or play or the purchase of a big ticket item like a laptop or car. Journalists review just about anything that can be bought or sold.

Whether you are reviewing the latest smartphone or stage play, reviews share similar structures.

Before writing a review

- How much knowledge or experience do users have of what you are reviewing?
- What are their cultural references?
- Is the work or product being reviewed according to a set of criteria or are you comparing it with other work or products within its class or genre?

Structuring the review

Reviews are composed of a number of key elements:

- Identification: Users need to know the technical specifications for products; for example, if you are reviewing a car you would need to state the manufacturer, model, price, miles per gallon, cost, when and where it is available to purchase. These details will normally be provided by the PR company supplying the items being reviewed. In the case of creative works, other details will need to be accurately recorded. A film review will need to identify the title, certificate, length of film, director, main actors, and dates and times where the film is being shown.
- Summary: This is where good reporting comes in. In the case of films or a TV programme, you'll need to describe what happens (although you must do this in manner that doesn't give away a key twist in the story and never, ever, give away the ending to a film!). In the case of product reviews, you must try out the various functions to describe how it works. Whilst a summary is an essential element of the review it shouldn't be allowed to dominate the review.
- Informed opinion: Your criteria will allow you to judge the strengths and weaknesses of the reviewed product or creative work. If a film has an appalling script you may wish to quote a short snippet of dialogue to back-up your claim. *What Car?* magazine rates cars according to a criteria of: performance, ride and handling, safety and security, etc.
- Rating: It is common to give a star-rating, normally out of five. This allows users to discover an instant verdict on the products value or worth, without having to read the full review.

The independence of review sites

As with all areas of journalism, the golden rule is that you write for the user, not for the benefit of the artist or company whose work you are reviewing or advertisers. Most review websites generate revenue through showing online banner adverts, but this should not in any way impact the journalist's ability to write an honest and opinionated review. Any hint that a journalist is being unduly influenced by outside sources can instantly undermine trust.

It is worth having a clear mission statement. TechRadar has their 'reviews guarantee'. It states:

- We do not take payment for product reviews. Ever.
- We select products for review based on what we believe our readers would want to know.
- We'll tell you what we think, not what advertisers want you to hear.
- We say it as we see it. Our expert reviewers love technology and want you to love it too. If it's rubbish, we'll warn you off.
- If gear doesn't meet our high standards, we'll tell you why.
- If you think we're not living up to our promise, please email the editor in chief and we'll endeavour to put it right.

Figure 3.4 Paul Douglas, TechRadar.com, Future Publishing. (Source: Paul Douglas)

INTERVIEW: PAUL DOUGLAS, GLOBAL EDITOR-IN-CHIEF, TECHRADAR. COM, FUTURE PUBLISHING

TechRadar was launched in January 2008 and is the largest UK consumer technology and news and reviews site.

For us [product reviewing] is about depth and authority. Even if readers don't read every page of a long review, they trust our verdicts because they can see that we have tested every aspect of a product. Get one bit of your review wrong – a specification or a feature – and you've destroyed the credibility not just of that review but of all your reviews. So we make sure our reviewers are experts in their field. All TechRadar journalists are familiar with the principles of SEO, and so while the site has been set up to help with SEO – e.g. easily crawlable, automatic crosslinking to related content, etc – journalists are also expected to write search engine friendly headlines and article summaries. Online journalism changes so quickly that you can't learn a few rules and sit back and expect your working practice to remain unchanged.

>>Summary<<

1 The ability to write clearly, quickly and accurately, and possessing the ability to spot a strong story remains at the heart of good journalism practice.
2 When writing and editing content for online we must understand how our users will consume and interact with it. It is particularly important to make our text easier to digest and understand on mobile devices.

(Continued)

(Continued)

3　The aim of SEO is to make sure our stories appear high up in the listings on the major search engines. SEO is as important an editorial skill as learning about the traditional who, what, where, when, why and how of a story.

4　The once distinct writing skills of news, feature, review and opinion writing styles are slowly merging. That said, news stories should never be tainted by the writer's personal opinions.

EXERCISES

1　Try using the following approach for writing the first few paragraphs for your next news story. Begin by writing down what happened – it may be something straightforward like 'fire in block of flats in Southampton'. Then gradually build up the story by adding extra information (go through the five Ws if you get stuck). Keep your sentences to no more than 30 words.

2　Practise writing headlines that are short and concise. We prefer the method adopted by the BBC that limits its journalist to around five or six words per headline. Think about the keywords that users are likely to type into search engines to find your story. Try to get these words into the headline and story lead paragraph.

3　Experiment with live blogging a story. Insert CoverItLive or WordPress Live Blogging to your news website. Live blogging works particularly well when covering court cases (although you may not be able to post messages in the court itself!), conferences or music festivals that occur over a period of hours or days.

FURTHER READING

Carroll, Brian. 2010. *Writing for Digital Media*. London: Routledge.
　This provides an equal balance of theory and practice when looking at digital writing skills.
McKane, Anna. 2006. *News Writing*. London: Sage.
　A comprehensive guide to news writing for a range of publications.
Pape, Susan. 2006. *Feature Writing: A Practical Introduction*. London: Sage.
　Compared to news, there are far fewer guides to feature writing.
Wulfewmeyer, K. Tim. 2006. *Online Newswriting*. 1st edn. Ames, Iowa; Oxford: Blackwell.
　A practical guide to online writing which contains numerous examples of good online practice.
Yahoo! 2010. *The Yahoo! Style Guide: The Ultimate Sourcebook for Writing, Editing, and Creating Content for the Digital World*. London: Macmillan.
　The style guide from the online news portal and search engine.

CHAPTER 4

Telling the Story with Images

INTRODUCTION

Figure 4.1   London Fashion Week (© Photographer: Andy Blackmore)

You will have seen some news websites that are so unattractive that you don't want to even look at them. Then there are websites that are attractive and interesting and draw you in. How a page looks and how news stories are laid out is critical to winning an audience. A vital part of the journalist's job is to make the story compelling and to make it look as interesting as possible. We are always in the business of being concise and images can enhance the story in many ways, whatever the platform. Images provide information succinctly that should support the story and add to the audience's knowledge.

It is no longer enough for a journalist just to be able to compose text. It is now essential that they understand the interchange between text and images which give a website a visual identity. So journalists need to get into the habit of thinking in images.

The visual journalist uses digital images to help make news pages easy to read and informative. The visual journalist could be an editor, a website designer, a layout specialist, or it could be one person who does everything on a news website or it could be you. We deal with website design and layout in other chapters but here will deal with that vital ingredient – the digital image – including graphics, photographs and cartoons. Photographs have multiple uses and can show the scene and the subject and capture a moment in time.

Graphics supply complex information to the audience in a simple and clear way. Graphics like pie charts and bar charts have been used to support news stories for a long time. New technology is having an enormous impact on what we can do with digital images and in this chapter we will look at some of the great techniques that are available to us as visual journalists.

While we are going to discuss taking news photographs we are not going to try and turn you into a press photographer. To be a photojournalist in the modern world and make a living you need to be absolute master of photography. But we can guide you in the first steps. In the multimedia world a journalist is expected to be able to take photographs of reasonable quality. This chapter explains the basics of being able to take useful photographs.

The dominant and somewhat disturbing image we have now of press photographers is the paparazzi (the Italian word for 'buzzing insects') that snatch photographs of celebrities at every possible occasion. 'Paps' can fascinate or appal you but they are in a branch of photojournalism where there is still money to pay hefty fees for the right photo. The *Mail Online* website features dozens of 'pap'-style shots every day and it's one of the reasons why it gets more hits per day than any other UK news website. Most press photographers are not paparazzi but they are skilful, considerate journalists, working under time pressures to bring the pages of their news media alive. Most work for local or provincial newspapers where the photographer covers every possible subject from crime stories to business stories, hospital openings and village fetes. How you deal with the person you want a photograph of is vital. A good photographer can get the best out of their subjects and they learn to be able to make the people they are photographing comfortable. 'I have to be as much diplomat as a photographer,' said the great photographer Alfred Eisenstaedt.

Technology has quickly and effectively transformed photography. The camera using film to record images has made way for the digital camera which stores images electronically. Near enough every mobile phone has a camera capable of taking reasonable digital photographs. And what's more you can send them instantaneously to your editor using email or social media tools or just plain upload them yourself onto the website. There is no reason

Figure 4.2   Aftermath of 2005 London bombings: scene of the bus blown up by a terrorist bomb in Upper Woburn Place, London. (© Photographer: Andy Blackmore)

Figure 4.3   US landscape (© Photographer: Andy Blackmore)

for any reporter or journalist to leave the office without having at least a basic camera about their person. For multimedia journalists, different news organizations will expect varying levels of skill from you. If you are working for local or regional news outlet, besides reporting, you might be expected to produce photographs of events you are covering, and the people involved in them, on a daily basis.

>>OBJECTIVES<<

In this chapter, you will learn:

1 what a digital image is;
2 how to take good photographs;
3 how to create graphics;
4 how to use a cartoonist's work;
5 ethical and theoretical issues about digital images.

HOW IMAGES WORK WITH TEXT

Why use images?

There's a famous cliché that 'a picture is worth a thousand words' and like many clichés it does have a point. Sometimes there is no amount of words that could sum up what a photograph conveys. For example, if we give a text description of a criminal here, you are unlikely to have much of a reaction. If there is a picture of the person, then based on your personal experience, you will have an emotional reaction and make a decision about that person

Here we list some famous names:

- Andy Murray;
- Ken Livingstone;
- Ellie Simmonds;
- Salman Rushdie.

How do you respond? Now look at the pictures overleaf. Images are a much more powerful experience than just seeing the names in text.

We can feel instant sympathy for people we see in photographs when their plight is greater than our own. The most graphic example of this is the black and white image of a group of children, one of them naked after being severely burned, running down a road after their village was bombed during the Vietnam War in 1972. The image communicated the horrors of war in the most powerful way. The image can be found at http://en.wikipedia.org/wiki/Nick_Ut

Harry Evans (1997), one of the great British newspaper editors, says of the importance of photographs: '… most editors today would testify that for causing them anxiety and provoking readers there is still enormous power in a single still photograph'. Evans observed that while television has impinged on newspapers and magazines it has not killed still news photographs because it has a different function. Television, he says,

Figure 4.4   Sports photojournalism: Andy Murray poses with gold and silver medals after his win in the men's singles and mixed doubles matches at Wimbledon in the London 2012 Olympic Games. (© Photographer: Gretel Ensignia)

Figure 4.6   Ellie Simmonds wins gold in the women's 400m freestyle – S6 in the Aquatics Centre in the 2012 London Paralympics. (© Photographer: Gretel Ensignia)

Figure 4.5   Portrait: Ken Livingstone. (© Photographer: Andy Blackmore)

Figure 4.7   Sir Salman Rushdie. (© Photographer: Andy Blackmore)

 informs and excites but it cannot easily be recalled by the mind and it cannot be pondered. By contrast the still news picture, isolating a moment of time, has affinity with the way we remember. It is easier for us, most of the time, to recall an event or a person by summoning up a single image. In our mind's eye we can concentrate on a single image more easily than a sequence of images. And the single image can be rich in meaning because it is a trigger image of the all the emotion aroused by the subject. If you think of major news events, the likelihood is that you will visualise not a cine-sequence but a single scene from a single still news photograph which has been absorbed in the mind. 99

An effective image adds to the medium it is in. What does it do? It can:

1   tell us something unique that cannot be conveyed in words;
2   work with text to create a more interesting story;
3   support text by adding an element, like a portrait shot;
4   break up a text and make a page more interesting;
5   even tell a story using just pictures.

'I always thought good photos were like good jokes. If you have to explain it, it just isn't that good' (anonymous).

What camera to use

Today just about everybody uses digital cameras except a few photo-journalists who swear by the aesthetic quality of the old-style film camera. It's been a fast revolution. In 1981, Sony was the first company to introduce a film-less camera, the Mavica. Because the image quality was low, most photographers viewed the camera as a novelty. How wrong can you be?

Smartphone cameras are good basic tools as some have flash, zoom and the number of pixels is improving all the time. They have an advantage over most digital cameras, as they are internet-enabled, allowing users to upload images to websites instantly. However, they are no replacement for a high quality professional digital SLR with all its manual settings. The resolution for web work is normally 72ppi for web work, whereas print a typical minimum size is 300dpi. Online journalists spend a lot of time optimizing images to 72ppi for the web to make them fast to load using Photoshop or Photoshop Elements. The only time you would want image sizes larger is if users need to download them to print off.

Figure 4.8 News photo: nuns and make-up. Friends of *Father Ted* festival under way on the Irish island of Inis Mor. (© Photographer: Andy Blackmore)

The iPhone 5 has an 8 megapixel sensor which will create a 3264×2448 pixel photo. The camera has an aperture at f/2.4 (compared to f/2.8 of the iPhone 4), a hybrid infrared filter, and a five-element lens. The camera itself is 25 per cent smaller than the 4S, but the iPhone 5 can also take high definition (HD) quality images thanks to its smart filter, next-generation ISP, and faster photo capture photos are taken almost 40 per cent faster. The camera is also significantly better at low-light performance, and it's been enhanced with precision lens alignment and sapphire crystal.

That said, if you are going to take stills photography seriously you are probably going to need access to a quality camera. There are three main categories:

Figure 4.9 A Canon DSLR – a solid choice for professionals. (Source: Canon)

- the simple point to shoot;
- the camera that is simple but has some professional features (semi-pro);
- the professional camera e.g. digital SLR.

The price tends to go up with each stage. The point and shoot camera has few or no manual controls and the person can, well, point and shoot. If you have a mobile phone with a camera that is equivalent to an iPhone 5 it no longer makes sense to buy a separate point and shoot.

We recommend the Canon EOS D600 SLR professional level camera which is handy because it also records video and we recommend it in the next chapter as a good entry-level video camera. The 18Mp resolution, 3.7 frames per second (fps) shot rate, and 1080p video capture are all familiar features from this model's predecessor, the EOS 550D. But this model sports the rotatable LCD screen and creative shooting effects from some of the higher specification models in Canon's range. That is seriously high quality and should cost around £500. The number of photographs you can capture depends on your storage arrangements in the camera and the resolution you shoot at. The higher the resolution the more space the pictures will take up on your storage.

Figure 4.10　Portrait of comedian Lee Evans. The way the light falls on your subject is vital for the quality of the image. (© Photographer: Andy Blackmore)

The importance of light

Photography is light. No light, no photograph. So the way the light falls on your subject is vital for the quality of the image. You need to look at what you are about to photograph carefully and watch how the light and shadows fall. Don't just look at the central subject but what is in the background.

On a day that is likely to be bright, if you are able to pick the time of day to shoot your pictures, try to choose a time when the sun is low in the sky. Experienced photographers try to shoot in the early morning or late afternoon. Photographing people with the sun too high in the sky casts annoying shadows on the subject. The light in the early morning or late afternoon is that the colour of the light is 'warmer', reds and yellows are stronger. Strong light outside can result in some buildings being very bright and others will appear to be blacked out because the contrast is too much. Manoeuvre yourself so that you are dealing with a graduation of light rather than extreme contrasts.

Especially when photographing a particular person outdoors it is good to get the sun so it is behind either your right or left shoulder or even to the side of the subject.

Tips for shooting great images

a　Always take a tripod. A Gorillapod is a light camera tripod which allows you to secure your camera to just about any surface. They are available for just about any camera, including smartphones.

b　Keep a spare battery handy. Using the zoom a lot and using the flash will use up battery power quickly. The view screen also use a lot of power.

c　Always read your owner's manual. The owner's manual is the best way to learn how to care for you camera. It also describes the many features your camera has.

Types of images for different formats of images (JPEG, GIF, etc.) and explanation:

Figure 4.11　Canal barge photo – see how you eye is pulled to the horizon by the composition. (Source: Paul Lashmar)

COMPOSITION

If you are photographing an action event you may not have time to consider composition. Professional photographers have honed their compositional skills over hundreds of hours and it has become instinctive. As photographer Edward Weston once remarked: 'Now to consult the rules of composition before making a picture is a little like consulting the law of gravitation before going for a walk. Such rules and laws are deduced from the accomplished fact; they are the products of reflection ...' The rest of us do the best we can on the spot. Usually we have a little time to compose a shot and so try lots of different shots. The most important thing when composing a photograph is to consider where the viewer's eye is likely to be drawn. Ideally the composition pulls the viewer's eye to the most important thing in the picture, the thing we want the viewer to notice.

Figure 4.11 is a very simple example where the eye is pulled to the horizon, despite the large lifebuoy. It shows you the power of composition.

We can learn a lot about framing from the classic artists. Leonardo da Vinci used a very simple rule of composition for *Mona Lisa* known as the pyramid. The eye moves naturally to the face.

In modern photography we do not tend to place the person in the dead centre of the page especially if the photograph is landscape orientated.

Figure 4.12   The rule of thirds. (Source: Paul Lashmar)

What most amateurs do when taking a picture is to put the subject right in the centre of the frame. Instead, imagine a grid laid over your image divided into thirds both up and down. Place your subject's eyes at one of the 'thirds points' – the parts of the 3×3 grid where the lines intersect, i.e. usually top left or top right. It just looks better.

Avoid photographing lights or the sun as you will then get a hotspot. They are distracting as they draw the eye towards them instead of what you want the viewer to see.

Richard Avedon, a famous American photographer, said:

> A portrait is not a likeness. The moment an emotion or fact is transformed into a photograph it is no longer a fact but an opinion. There is no such thing as inaccuracy in a photograph. All photographs are accurate. None of them is the truth.

THINGS TO AVOID

a   Light flares.

Figure 4.13   What's the first thing your eyes are drawn to in the above image? It's not St Paul's Cathedral, it is the lights. (Source: Paul Lashmar)

b   White out: Even the best cameras can't cope with scenes that cause exposure problems. When the sun is too bright you often get areas of white. Where you have a choice, keep the sun behind your right or your left shoulder. This will give depth to your images as the sun will cast some shadow.

Figure 4.14   In this picture the sun reflects off the sea, whiting it out and ruining it as a professional photograph. Golden Cap, Dorset. (Source: Paul Lashmar)

c Backlighting: Another common problem that can happen in the field is
where the background is brighter than
the foreground.

d Strange objects: A classic is the pole
through the head. Watch out for anything
that is in the background and disrupts and
distracts the viewer's eye.

Figure 4.15 Shooting against the light causes numerous problems. (Source: Paul Lashmar)

Figure 4.16 Poor composition: subject has pole through head. (Source: Paul Lashmar)

THE ART OF GOOD CAPTION WRITING

The art of a good caption is important. Caption writing used to be the job of the picture editor or sub-editor, but as with many specialist areas of journalism, increasingly reporters will have to supply images and supply their own captions to run alongside. Captions act as an entry point to the page. Henri Cartier-Bresson, probably the greatest of all documentary photographers, said that if a photograph is really evocative it carries its own message, the only caption it needs is a label of when and where 'the who or what and the why are incorporated in the subject – or should – and the how is unimportant'. Well, we can take the point, but most of us will be photographing less earth-events than Cartier-Bresson and our photographs will need to be captioned.

Harry Evans (1997) said:

> The wordless picture story may have an aesthetic rigour but words can enhance both emotional and cognitive values. They are not competitive; they are complementary. They identify people and places, the first essential. They explain relationships. They fix the time. They may elaborate on what is happening. They can point to an elusive detail. They can attempt to counter our irritating perversity in drawing different, even contradictory, meanings from the same image. They can confirm mood. And with a single photograph only words can explain how the event occurred or what its effect might be.

Caption writing is rather like headline writing – it has to convey a lot of information in a few words. Don't state the obvious. If the picture is showing Prince Charles getting into a car, don't write, 'Prince Charles getting into a car'. Provide information that adds something useful, such as: 'The Prince had just opened a retirement home on his Poundbury development.' If the pictures doesn't show the who, what, when, why, where or how, then state it in the caption if it is important. Try to intrigue the reader. As Evans said: 'It is information that we want, not elaboration of the obvious. Often this means adding facts that cannot be drawn from the photo but which put the image in a context.'

Whatever you do, don't imply you know what someone is thinking or tell your audience what to think.

TIP

Andy Blackmore, picture editor of the *Metro*, says. 'If you send in a photograph to any new organization make sure the caption and credit (the photographer's name) is encapsulated into the image. We don't have time to match up images with emails for the caption. If you don't encapsulate it won't get used.'

To see how to encapsulate a caption in an image:

Q&A: SUE STEWARD, FORMER *DAILY TELEGRAPH* AND *OBSERVER* PICTURE EDITOR

Sue Steward is a former *Daily Telegraph* and *Observer* picture editor, and currently the photography critic at the *Evening Standard*, a writer for the *British Journal of Photography* and other magazines – in print and online – and a curator of photography exhibitions.

What do news organizations want from news photos?

'News pictures and text fit together really well. The text tells the facts of the story and the photograph fills in far more details and is often much more descriptive. Photos are obviously the selling point for a newspaper – and obviously also for the news screen. I think a lot of people look at the pictures and captions first, then go back to read the text.'

Figure 4.17 Sue Steward is a picture editor and writer on photography. (Source: Sue Steward)

How do news organizations choose what photos they want?

'The editor of the news organization will gather together all the other editors to discuss the contents for the day. The photo editor will be in on the conversation as the main stories are fleshed out. Then they will go through – on their computer screens – what stories have come in through the 'wires' – the photography agencies and the paper's staff photographers who are out and about – and will make sure they cover the photos for the main stories of the day. They might also look for some other images – maybe an amusing or gossipy story about, say, Madonna. That's done in the same way with the editor choosing something that could go with a brief article or a photo and caption. It will need a diversity of themes, a mix. The picture editor choosing the images will match the photos to the story but will choose them in terms of the look aesthetically and very importantly, the composition.'

How often would you use user-generated images?

'The photographs of the terrorists' attack on cricketers in Mumbai were all done on phones. On the first day of the crisis, the photos were all captured and sent around the world from mobiles phones. The photo editors don't mind sometimes poorer quality in these situations because these eyewitness pictures are so dramatic. Professional photographers are able to assess the situation and take photographs to give as much information as possible about what is happening. Digital cameras can obviously shoot huge numbers of pictures. So the professional clicks away then deletes like crazy. Composition is crucial. You must get the right person in the photograph or panoramic landscape to tell the reader/viewer as much as possible about what is happening.

Figure 4.18   Photojournalism in a war zone. Afghanistan: Camp Bastion Ranges. (© Photographer: Andy Blackmore)

Which photojournalists do you respect most?

'Tom [Stoddart] would photograph women in Sarajevo during the siege, running across the street called 'Snipers alley' to get food. He captured photographs of women putting on their lipstick who were saying, 'We will not be beaten down by this; even in a siege we can look good'. Powerful photographs. Tim Hetherington, who was killed in Libya in 2011, had a capacity for creating a relationship with his subjects, in the style of the old documentary photographers like the legendary Robert Capa, whose dramatic images of the Spanish Civil War are iconic. Lighting is crucial and Hetherington – like Stoddart – used it brilliantly. He took some moving and surprisingly beautiful photographs of a unit of American soldiers in Afghanistan – on and off duty, patrolling, playing basketball and golf, and sleeping. Simon Norfolk is another example – with him, much more in the tradition of the heroic, handsomely macho war photographer. In recent years, he began to document war and crises in a different way, confusingly

Figure 4.19   The power of the portrait: Sri Lanka – a fisherman from the Moratuwa shanty town devastated by Tsunami. (© photographer Andy Blackmore)

finding 'beauty in a war'. He called the style 'sublime photography' – and included scenes of ancient ruined buildings and a rather bleak, wrecked tank in a bleak landscape. That work developed into a whole new genre of war photography and it influences many young photographers behind him.

How should you think about tackling an assignment?

For instance, if you are sent out to cover a flood: normally water is a great element of photography, often beautiful especially with lights bouncing off it, and reflections in flowing water. In a flood situation you have to contrast that beauty with the reality of what's happening – unless you're not after a news photograph. You need to enter people's front rooms, people who have suffered from the flood and are showing you the awful damage. You have to get the faces of people who are devastated. You might want to get a picture of a couple holding a soggy photo album, covered in mud – their wedding pictures. This is where empathy comes in – you have to be thinking of the people you are photographing as people suffering. But you'll also need photos of cars or caravans floating on the current. We've all seen this kind of photograph – the man standing crying at the sight of devastation to his home.

Some pictures can lead the story – and the top-range photographers will be called in to get those kinds of iconic images – here's where the relationship between photographer and photo editor comes in; the photo editor has to know the best person for the story.

Photographs in newspapers can be distorted. Picture editors can choose a photo that is slanted to the angle of the story. For instance, if you are looking at a story that's slagging off a politician like Nick Clegg, the editorial team will ask for a picture that makes him look like a burk or frowning or happy with some achievement. You see this with Cameron all the time in the *Guardian*, for obvious political reasons, and you can see the slant of the picture to support the text.

What should you do to get better?

You must look through magazines and books to see the great photographs of the past, and look at websites that tell you about the best photographers of today. Whoever wants to be a good photographer really has to look at what other people are doing and how their photographs work. You will have to take it seriously; if you're just going out to snap, that's OK but if you're on a job, you need to think in advance, try to plan, consider situations, locations and expressions and postures of your subjects. The photo editor who commissioned you will explain what they want. And listen. And don't deviate to something *you* think would be better! Just obey! Because they've decided.

Don't forget, even if you are in Damascus or the scene of a massacre in Texas at the *Batman* film, try to get talking to the subject – you need connection – *unless* you are doing 'street photography' where you tend to want to be a bit secretive.

EDITING PHOTOGRAPHS

With the rise of user-generated content, a good percentage of the photographs that are available to any news site are not of professional quality. In most cases simple editing can improve them. They can be cropped, zoomed, rotated and have red eye removed and enhanced for improved colour and definition. Sometimes even professional photographs need to be improved especially if they are action pictures taken in the heat of the news moment. Or you might want to extract out of a picture of, say, a class group the portrait of one person.

There is a whole range of software that enables us to do this. Microsoft Picture Gallery comes with Microsoft programs and Mac has iPhoto. For professional use most people turn to the industry standard, Photoshop, as this provides a much more sophisticated array of tools.

The Adobe sales pitch on Photoshop is: 'You want powerful photo editing, but you also want it to be easy. With just a few clicks you can make any photo look amazing.'

A cheaper option

If you cannot afford Photoshop, then Pixlr is a cloud-based set of image tools and utilities, including a number of photo editor, as screen grabber browser extension, and a photo-sharing service. Founded in Sweden in 2008 by Ola Sevandersson, it was intended for non-professionals. It can be used on PCs, and on smartphones or tablets using an app. The suite of applications range from simple and playful to advanced photo editing.

Photoshop and manipulation

The ability of Photoshop and other editing programs not only to radically change a photograph to the point where it is virtually unrecognizable from the original raises serious ethical issues. Should a news photograph be an exact representation of reality? Or at least the reality as the photographer intended? We have already mentioned that the photographer influences what we see by their choice of the picture and composition. We rely on their professional skills as a journalist. But what happens when the photograph is manipulated by the photographer or editorial team to look different. 'They cannot be detected. They ought always to be admitted, the credibility of photojournalism must not be eroded by covert manipulation,' said Harry Evans (1997). In reputable news organizations there are strict rules about photo manipulation. If it is done then the user must be told.

But what is acceptable in nearly all newsrooms is choosing photographs that support the story. As Sue Steward points out 'The thing about photographs in newspapers is that they can be abused horribly and often are. Picture editors can choose a photo that is slanted to the angle of the story.'

To take the Nick Clegg example above, this may mean using a photograph of Nick Clegg that was taken some time ago but is the picture that most makes him seem either not very intelligent or somewhat sleazy. We all have seen photographs of ourselves that, just by the accident of light or angle, makes us look a bit stupid. But should an old photo be used to support the story of the day? Is this ethical? Photographs do have power and a bad photograph can be the one thing we are remembered for.

Harry Evans (1997) said of the picture editor:

> He can select, suppress, distort. He can blow up a single frame in a hundred and crop it to give a tiny detail the greatest significance: the yawn in a crowded political meeting rather than the candidate in the centre of a warming crowd. In his selection of prints from a take, or from the library, he can manufacture stereotypes, of heroes and villains – Saddam Hussein or Castro is, depending on the editor's whim a scowling belligerent or the idol of his people.

Evans points out there are four areas of sensitivity in choosing photographs to put on your news outlet: violence, intrusions into privacy, sex and public decency, and faking.

DISPLAYING YOUR IMAGES ONLINE: CREATING A SLIDESHOW

Creating a slideshow is a very effective way of delivering photographs when you are looking to tell the story through photographs. This is classically a set of say 12–15 photos. They can be about an occasion, e.g. highlights of a sporting event. They can be photographs by different photographers.

Depending how you set them up, photo galleries can play automatically or require the user to click a button. Then each photograph stays on screen for a pre-set time, say two or three seconds. You can caption photo galleries.

Audio Slideshows

An audio slideshow is an arrangement of photos which are automatically displayed one at a time and are sequenced to an audio report. They have proved popular with news sites as they are cheaper and quicker to produce than video reports, yet can also have real emotional impact.

Software

Journalists use a wide variety of packages. One of the best is paid-for software SoundSlides (www.soundslides). It was launched by photojournalist Joe Weiss in 2005 and is aimed at news websites. However, you could use Apple iMovie, or the combination of photo-editing software Google Picasa with audio editing tool Audacity, both free, can also do the trick.

Choosing images for a slideshow

Reuben Stern of the Missouri School of Journalism says that slideshows work best with stories where:

1 There is activity and/or people doing something observable (e.g. it is not a meeting story).
2 It is visually rich (e.g. lots of colour, decoration, contrast, rhythm, motion, scenery).
3 There are lots of different situations taking place and/or a variety of interesting moments (i.e. not a bunch of different people repeating the same thing).
4 The idea is emotional and/or humorous.
5 It features rich character or personality.

 Stern writes: 'The key is that both the sights and sounds involved should be interesting and important to the story.' We recommend you shoot a wide variety of shots – wide, medium and plenty of tight shots.

How many shots will you need? Timing is everything in producing a good audio slideshow. The rule of thumb is that you should plan for each photo to be on screen for about five seconds (or around 12 images per minute). Anything slower and your users will get bored. Don't forget you should also add captions to the images to help tell the story.

Adding commentary

You need to match up your words with the images. It's common for journalists to run an audio commentary or an interview over the images.

Slideshows used to almost always be Flash-based, but this doesn't work on Apple mobile devices. HTML5 is becoming increasingly common. As with video, you can host the slideshow on your own server or upload it to the video sharing site (then embed the code for your own site).

Figure 4.20   The sports photojournalist at work – David Weir wins gold in the men's 1500m T54 race at the Olympic Stadium in the London Paralympics 2012. (© Photographer: Gretel Ensigna)

Get inspired

Do a search on Google for audio slideshows and you will find plenty examples of news sites:

 Financial Times: www.ft.com/interactive/audio-slideshows

Guardian: www.guardian.co.uk/audioslideshows

What works really well is to use sound, and make it like video but using photographs instead of video footage. Photographs engage one of the five senses, and sound engages another and doubles the overall effect. You can use background sounds, music, archive recordings. Mostly you will record a commentary and or interviews with the people involved.

HOW IMAGES CAN BE USED TO DECEIVE

Photographs are as much an interpretation of the world as paintings and drawings are. (Susan Sontag, 1979)

Photographs are not value-free images capturing a moment of time. Every photograph involves decisions by the person taking the photo. Once you have a photograph you can manipulate it using computer programs. Software can allow you to radically change the image or even merge images. You can write a caption that gives the picture an entirely different meaning. The viewer, depending on many things including their culture and agenda, may see something different from what the photographer intended. This all raises some of the ethical and theoretical aspects of news photographs and we will discuss some of them later.

A photograph may appear to simply record what is 'real' before the photographer's eyes. But what is 'real' is an entirely subjective viewpoint. As the iconic art critic John Berger (1972) says, 'Every time we look at a photograph, we are aware, however slightly, of the photographer selecting that sight from infinity of other possible sights'. And, Berger observed, this is true even in the most casual family snapshot, for even with 'point-and-shoot' photography, the photographer is still pointing the camera at something. 'Yet, although every image embodies a way of seeing, our perception or appreciation of an image depend also upon our own way of seeing.' As we have discussed, when photographs are added to a news site they add new dimensions of meaning to a text. Our world-view is a construct of a range of socio-cultural influences including class, gender, race, religion, ethnicity, sexuality, age, family, health, nationality, education, political beliefs, occupation and ideology. These all influence how a photographer sees the world and how they photograph it. The audience's world-view will influence how they see the photograph. The famous photojournalist Ansel Adams once pointed out that even in landscapes there are personalities present: 'There are always two people in every picture: the photographer and the viewer.' One of the fundamental requirements for the functioning of the photographic system is that both the photographer and the audience have the same reference points.

Stuart Hall (1981) says:

News photos have a specific way of passing themselves off as aspects of 'nature'. They repress their ideological dimensions by offering themselves as literal visual-transcriptions of the 'real world'. News photos witness to the actuality of the event they represent. Photos of events carry a Meta (the overriding context) message: 'this event really happened and this photo is proof of it'. Photos of people – even the 'passport' type and size also support this function of grounding and witnessing: 'this is the man we are talking about, he really exists'. Photos, then, appear as records, in a literal sense, of 'the facts, and speak for themselves'. This is what Barthes calls the 'having been there' of all photographs.

One of the problems with some media theorists is that they rarely speak to practitioners. Therefore they would ascribe deep motives to the editorial team's use of a news photograph when the reality was rather more mundane.

Media academics Machin and Niblock (2006) observed this while talking about newsroom practice and practitioners. They say what became clear during their ethnographic study is the great difference in approach between the semioticians (academics who interpret text and images by identifying the signs within the images) and the approaches taken by practitioners.

> While the former strive to observe and describe systematic patterns in communication, the latter often describe design choices in terms of aesthetics, or simple practicalities of time, space and convention. Semioticians often fail to carry out a semiotic analysis in consultation with the text's producers in order to understand the economic motivations behind observed changes and to understand the motivations for choices of communicative tools. As a result, from the viewpoint of the practitioner, their analyses can seem absurd.

Figure 4.21   Photoshop. (Source: Paul Lashmar)

By talking to practitioners who specialize in visual journalism they discovered 'that a tremendous amount of research, reflection, and artistry takes place on behalf of journalistic staff.' They conclude: 'This tells a very different story from that of academic approaches which insist that journalists are in some way trying to impede information uptake or conceal and distort the real meaning of news events. From our observations, the case is quite the opposite.'

Figure 4.22   Here's a standard simple news page graphic. (Dreamstime)

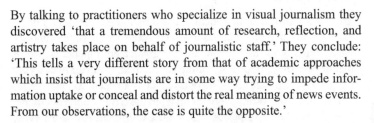

USING THE IMAGES OF OTHERS

Many blogs and personal websites use images stolen from other websites or simply downloaded from Google Images. Although this practice is widespread, it doesn't mean it is ethically or legally right. Just to be clear, unless you generated the image yourself (i.e. you took the picture) or have the permission of the copyright holder, you shouldn't use it. We must respect the fact that photojournalists need to make a living and you will need to negotiate a fee to use their images.

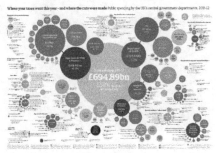

Figure 4.23   The *Guardian* has been at the forefront of infographics. This is an example from their guide to infographics, *Facts are Sacred* by Simon Rogers. (Source: Simon Rogers)

Figure 4.24   A Wordle cloud is an easy way to represent text of a story visually. This is a graphical representation of the Introduction chapter in this book which highlights the most frequently used words. (Wordle/Steve Hill)

Figure 4.25   Newsmap tracks trending topics. (Source: Newsmap)

Figure 4.26   Cartoonist Steve Bell makes a serious point about how British troops are treated once they return home (Copyright © Steve Bell 2011/2012 – all rights reserved)

Some photographers release their images under creative commons licences (see http://creativecommons.org/ and Chapter 13 for more information) as an alternative to full 'all rights reserved copyright'. A search on the image-sharing site Flickr (www.flickr.com) reveals many images that can be used for free as long as the name of the photographer is properly attributed.

If you are a photographer you may wish to license your work under creative commons as well. Many people who do this get a nice feeling of doing their bit to support the early founding principles of the web. However, in many cases it also makes business sense to give away work for free, particularly when you are building a name for yourself and it's more important that your work gets out there and you get the credit. Of course under creative commons licence, there are many settings – you may wish to eventually only offer your work for free to non-commercial use, but charge for commercial usage.

INFOGRAPHICS

Graphics are all about visualizing information. It can be very simple but graphics are really effective at taking complex information and making it very simple to understand.

A great source of royalty free graphics is Dreamstime and iStock, where you pay for the use of an image at quite low rates.

Word clouds

Wordle is a program for generating 'word clouds' from text. For instance, you can grab hundreds of tweets on a specific subject and see what words reoccur. The clouds give greater prominence to words that appear more frequently in the source text. You can tweak your clouds with different fonts, layouts and colour schemes.

Here's an interesting word cloud from the BBC. Police in Greater Manchester had completed a 24-hour experiment to record every incident they deal with on Twitter. They hoped it would give the public a better idea of the demands made upon them. The reporter turned the Twitter feeds into a word cloud.

USING MAPS

Mainstream media frequently make use of maps to illustrate stories.

Newsmap is an application that tracks trending topics. It employs a hierarchy of colour blocks to highlight the currently hottest stories on the websites of news outlets in 15 countries. It's a free service.

The Newsmap application 'scrapes' the Google News aggregator for what it needs to create an attractive, continuously changing one-screen picture of top Google News stories worldwide. It presents Google News headlines in a visually organized way across Newsmap's seven colour-coded categories: world and national affairs, business, technology, sports, entertainment and health.

Newsmap can compare the pages for several countries, say, the US, the UK and New Zealand, and show both the differences and similarities between what is considered the most important news in these places and how much play individual stories receive within particular news categories.

There are a range of programs that can help you create infographics, one of the best is Infogr.am (http://infogr.am). There are quite a few freeware programs which are good for simpler graphics. A good example is the Google Fusion Tables: www.google.com/fusiontables/Home/.

Figure 4.27   Newspaper mogul Rupert Murdoch as depicted by cartoonist Steve Bell (Copyright © Steve Bell 2011/2012 – all rights reserved)

Some of the new generation of interactives are stunning. Watch nine years of CIA drones in Pakistan with this excellent interactive timeline from Pitchinc's team.

CARTOONS

A cartoon is a piece of art, commenting on a news event, usually humorous in intent.

This usage dates from 1843 when *Punch* magazine applied the term to satirical drawings in its pages, particularly sketches by John Leech. The first was Leech's 'Cartoon no. 1: Substance and Shadow' (1843), which satirized preparatory cartoons for frescoes in the Palace of Westminster, creating the modern meaning of 'cartoon'.

Cartoons are found almost exclusively in news publications and news websites. Although they also employ humour, they have a more serious purpose of encapsulation, commonly using irony or satire to make the point. The art usually acts as a visual metaphor to illustrate a point of view on current social and/or political topics. Editorial cartoons often include speech balloons and, sometimes, multiple panels. Editorial cartoonists of note include Alex, Matt, Steve Bell, Garry Trudeau, Vicky, Giles, David Low, David Brown and Gerald Scarfe.

The images here are both from Steve Bell (b. 1951), who is an English political cartoonist. He is probably best known for the daily strip called 'If ...', which has appeared in the *Guardian* newspaper since 1981. Since the mid-1990s he has also been the *Guardian*'s principal editorial cartoonist.

>>Summary<<

1   In the world of convergence journalism the reporter needs to know how to think visually and be able to lay out a page using a range of digital images and text so that the user will want

(Continued)

(Continued)

    to keep browsing through the site. Learn to read pages and identify how your eye 'reads' a page.

2 Photographs are very effective for grabbing the reader's attention and place the story in context. Photographs never represent pure unadulterated reality – the photographer always imposes their own personality and agenda on the photograph (Berger 1972; Evans, 1997).

3 Infographics enable us to simplify complex information in an attractive and easily readable form. There are an increasing number of programs that help us create infographics. Where possible use interactive graphics to engage the user.

4 Many news sites are very serious and sometimes it is important to have a mix of information that can give us light and shade. Cartoons can be about very serious issues but still make us laugh. Cartoons can insert insight and irony into the page which is a nice counterpoint to factual news stories.

5 If you can learn to use images and lay them out effectively you can greatly increase your audience and your own professional satisfaction.

EXERCISES

1 Identify three cases where news photographs have been used in a misleading way in the last week.

2 Look on a major news website and identify how many of the day's stories are text led and how many are dependent on images. See how cartoons are used. How effectively are the graphics used? Pulling all these different types of digital image together enables us to have a palette of colours to improve the look of the page. Photographs can tell us in a fraction of a second something important. Graphics can reduce huge amounts of information into easily understood images. But most important is the content.

FURTHER READING

Bell, Steve. 2010. *If ... Bursts Out*. London: Jonathan Cape.
    Steve Bell is one of the great UK cartoonists and this is a good primer to his work.
Berger, John. 1972. *Ways of Seeing*. Harmondsworth: Penguin/London: BBC.
    John Berger revolutionized the way a generation looked at pictures and his book, while a little dated, still makes you think about the way you, as an individual, look at images.
Evans, Harold. 1997. *Pictures on a Page: Photojournalism, Graphics and Picture Editing*. London: Paladin.
    This dates back to the 1970s, but this updated edition is a key text for the visual journalist, even if there is not much about online journalism.
Evans, Jane and Hall, Stuart. 1999. *Visual Culture: A Reader*. London: Sage.
    The best overall guide to theory of images. Stuart Hall has done more than anyone to develop a framework to explain how journalists use images to convey messages.

CHAPTER 5

Using Audio and Podcasts

INTRODUCTION

Audio is an exciting medium for journalism as it requires the audience to engage and use their imagination. This creates a special bond between the journalist and the listener. The key difference between audio and other news media is that it is the 'theatre of the mind' and allows you, the journalist, to paint pictures in the listener's head. No other medium has quite that privilege. We have a range of tools with which to create aural painting, including interviews, commentary, eyewitness accounts, background sounds, music and archive. BBC producer Chris Ledgard told us that he believes there is something special in the way that audio delivers to its audience. 'The power of the human voice is really strong and if you have voice coming out at you and saying something which is interesting and spikes your curiosity, then it's a way of drawing people into your story. We are all drawn to the human voice.'

Online audio is delivered in two main ways – as a downloadable file (e.g. in MP3 format) or streaming (for example: streaming audio radio stations via BBC iPlayer, iTunes and Spotify). Online audio packages are often referred to as podcasts, a term based on the Apple iPod. Podcasts have the advantage that they can be streamed from a website or downloaded if the audience has access to RSS feeds, iTunes or similar software. With the rise in the use of mobiles, tablets and iPads, the podcast is a very convenient 'time shift' format to download and listen to when convenient.

Internet audio stations and podcasts may be relatively new but the art of making good audio packages is not. For 80 years pure audio has almost exclusively come to us via the radio and many of the conventions of the radio news journalist can translate to the new world of converged media. In this chapter we look at the tradition of high-standard professional audio journalism but we also encourage you to experiment and try new techniques. Online news sites are much better for experimentation than if you are working for long-standing radio news organizations. As with all journalism each generation has a different take on audio and they will change the way it is delivered. An example is that radio stations are increasingly being enjoyed on digital TV and via Internet streaming through apps on tablets and mobile phones.

>>OBJECTIVES<<

In this chapter, you will learn how to:

1. record audio on location;
2. improve your listening skills;
3. write a script and make a package;
4. edit using different sound sources;
5. deliver podcasts and streamed content.

Figure 5.1   The audio studio. (Source: Paul Lashmar)

AUDIO JOURNALISM

The human imagination is extraordinary. If a reporter says, 'The packed airliner skidded off the runway and crashed into a hangar bursting into a ball of flame', immediately you can see that in your mind. It is generally agreed that the audio-only listener is much more engaged than the online reader, the video news viewer or the print reader, as the listener really does have to use their imagination. This is what makes writing for audio so exciting. By clever use of words and sound the audio package can be really evocative and engaging. But it does have to be written differently even from its near relative video. Audio is much more descriptive because, in absence of pictures, the reporter has to make sure that everything is described, or use background sounds, music or archive to convey the story. If you want to see an example of how this works watch a football match on TV with the sound down and have BBC Radio's 5 Live commentary on. Notice the difference in approach from the usual commentary.

AUDIO IN A CONVERGED WORLD

Audio is part of the world where no platform dominates and audio production is a skill set needed by all news reporters. In the converged world of journalism, editors will expect you to be able to make a professional standard audio package and put it online. It may be a stand-alone news package or it may be an element of a multimedia piece of reporting. Jon Smith (2007) points out 'the ability to work with video and audio has become a highly-prized asset among editors looking for new journalists'. Sarah Niblock (2011) also highlights these changes in the approach to journalism when she says, 'Newsrooms are being reorganized and re-fitted to reflect the arrival of new media forms; traditional roles and job descriptions are becoming outmoded and redundant as editorial staff are required to work across two or more media simultaneously'.

Once upon a time the reporter working in audio had to lug around a large reel-to-reel tape recorder called an Uher with lots of batteries and tapes and a microphone. Now nearly every reporter walks out of the office with a mobile phone that records sound. The professional may take out a dedicated and digital audio recorder like those made by Zoom or Sony which is light and fits comfortably into the hand.

The advance of technology means that audio is now wide open as a medium and the possibilities endless. 'It's an experiment, really,' according to Christopher Lydon (cited in Hammersley, 2004), the former *New York Times* and National Public Radio journalist, a pioneer in the field of audio journalism. 'Everything is inexpensive. The tools are available. Everyone has been saying anyone can be a publisher, anyone can be a broadcaster,' he says. 'Let's see if that works.'

However forward looking we are, we must also look to how we arrived at where we are today. Audio may have great potential but the standards we judge it by are set by how news has been and is delivered. We need to understand how those professional standards have been achieved before we start to break the rules and find new ways to deliver the news in the audio medium.

A SHORT HISTORY OF AUDIO

As in all broadcasting in the UK, the history and benchmarks tend to come from the BBC. The BBC started broadcasting by radio in 1922, but the rapidly growing BBC radio audience didn't get a lot of news in the early days.

It was in the United States where the potential of radio was first most clearly shown. Nearly every student of audio journalism will have been told the story of and listened to the scratchy recording of Orson Welles's dramatization of H.G. Wells's science-fiction novel *The War of the Worlds* in the US because it remains the most compelling example of the power of radio.

Figure 5.2   BBC Broadcasting House. (Source: Flickr © R/DV/RS)

The arrival of the TV age in the late 1950s resulted in much soul searching as to whether radio was dead. Believe us when we say that music radio in the UK in the 1950s and early 1960s was dull and all delivered by a very worthy but patronizing BBC. Then a major challenge came in 1964 when ten pirate radio stations started broadcasting from just outside UK territory, often using wartime forts or anchored ships. This was mainly about changing music radio. Young people tuned into these stations bored by the fuddy-duddy nature of much BBC radio output still stuck somewhere in 1943. Why would you listen to crooners when you could listen to the Beatles and the Rolling Stones? However, this was a great period for talk radio and many of the shows that remain classics come from this era, especially when it comes to comedy. This is the time of *The Goons*, *The Navy Lark* and *Round the Horne*, as well as the early days of *Desert Island Discs* and *Woman's Hour*.

The UK government passed a law in 1967 outlawing the pirates and only one, Radio Caroline, hung on for a while. In response to the challenge, the BBC did modernize its output setting up new stations, including Radio 1 aimed at the audience that had been listening to pirate radio. It hired a lot of the former pirate radio station disc jockeys. In 1972 the government opened up radio frequencies so commercial companies could set up radio stations. First out of the blocks was London Broadcasting Company (LBC) with its 24-hour talk radio.

Since radio was liberalized in the 1970s it has been a tumultuous experience. It is not an easy business to make money in especially where news delivery is required. The dominance of the BBC also makes it tougher for commercial companies to flourish. On the one end of the spectrum are the large radio businesses trying to reach the largest audiences possible, others like Jazz FM and Classic FM with an expanding niche market, through to local radio stations and ultimately the not-for-profit community radio stations. The casualty rate is high with radio companies closing down and stations being sold or rebranded constantly.

For a timeline of the history of commercial radio in the UK, follow this link.

Radio is booming in the UK as figures from RAJAR (Radio Joint Audience Research Ltd) show: 90 per cent of the UK adult population tuned in to their selected radio stations in the fourth quarter of 2012. This was up by approximately 340,000 adults on the same quarter of the previous year.

The total number of hours listened to radio is 1.04 billion, up marginally year-on-year. There are over 300 radio stations broadcasting in the UK and most have websites.

Why we like to listen

'I regard radio as the hottest of all mediums,' says Simon Jenkins (2010), the media commentator. 'The power of radio is the power of speech.' He quotes the late media theorist Marshall McLuhan who divided the media into hot and cold mediums. 'McLuhan said if you want to stage a revolution use radio; if you want to suppress it, use television. If you go on radio people listen to what you say. If you go on television they say, what is the colour of your shirt?' Jenkins continues: 'Radio forces the listener to engage. You have to listen, the other senses are set aside. You have to listen, listen to the words.'

According to McLuhan's (1964) theory, hot media usually, but not always, provide complete involvement without exercising other stimuli. Print occupies visual space and uses visual senses, but can immerse its reader. He said hot media favour analytical precision, quantitative analysis and sequential ordering, as they are usually sequential, linear and logical. They emphasize one sense (for example, of sight or sound) over the others. For this reason, McLuhan thought that hot media also included radio, as well as the lecture and

Total number of BBC national radio stations	11
Total number of regional BBC radio stations	4
Total number of BBC local radio stations	39
Total number of national commercial radio stations	15
Total number of local commercial radio stations	224

Figure 5.3   Radio in the UK in numbers. Source: RAJAR

| | | | DECEMBER 2012 RELEASE SUMMARY OF LISTENING | | | | | |
| | | | Survey Period 17th September 2012 – 16th December 2012 | | | | | |
	Survey Period	Adult (15+) Pop'n '000	Weekly Reach '000	Weekly Reach %	Average Hours per head	Average Hours per listener	Total Hours '000	Share of Listening %
All Radio	Q	52352	47015	90%	19.8	22.1	1037158	100.0%
All BBC Radio	Q	52352	35190	67%	10.9	16.3	573178	55.3%
BBC Local Radio	Q	52352	9138	17%	1.6	9.0	82288	7.9%
BBC Radio 1	Q	52352	11091	21%	1.5	6.9	76774	7.4%
BBC Radio 2	Q	52352	15109	29%	3.5	12.1	182948	17.6%
BBC Radio 3	Q	52352	2061	4%	0.3	6.5	13302	1.3%
BBC Radio 4 (including 4 Extra)	Q	52352	11012	21%	2.7	12.7	139456	13.4%
BBC Radio FIVE LIVE (inc SPORTS EXTRA)	Q	52352	6272	12%	0.9	7.6	47395	4.6%
BBC 6 Music	Q	52352	1891	4%	0.3	7.8	14737	1.4%
1Xtra from the BBC	Q	52352	1044	2%	0.1	5.1	5324	0.5%
BBC Asian Network UK	Q	52352	453	1%	0.1	6.8	3078	0.3%
BBC World Service	Q	52352	1462	3%	0.2	5.4	7877	0.8%
All Commercial Radio	Q	52352	33223	63%	8.4	13.2	438978	42.3%
All National Commercial	Q	52352	16244	31%	2.5	8.1	130791	12.6%
All Local Commercial (National TSA)	Q	52352	26410	50%	5.9	11.7	308187	29.7%

Figure 5.4   Radio listening figures from September 2012 – December 2012. Source: RAJAR

photography. Whether this is now true in the era where we have audiences who are often engaged with multiple media at the same time is an interesting research question.

News has always been important to radio stations. Stations tend to run on a shoestring. Those of our former students who are now radio journalists, often tell us they run one-person, one-shift newsrooms. To make the sector more financially viable governments have relaxed the rules. In too many cases local radio isn't really local any more as once independent commercial radio stations have been bought by more successful rivals they use the same newsroom and team to broadcast on different stations.

Through the internet we have access to thousands of audio channels at any time. The traditional radio stations are now all on the internet but so are thousands of others.

PODCASTING

Podcasts are pre-recorded programmes which are normally downloaded by the user in MP3 format. This is different to internet streaming where radio stations will broadcast live over the internet. Indeed, some radio stations are internet only – that's to say they broadcast exclusively online instead of via old fashioned FM radio or more modern DAB (digital audio broadcast).

A podcast is a type of digital media consisting of a series of audio files subscribed to and downloaded through RSS or streamed online to a computer or mobile device.

The term 'podcasting' was coined by Ben Hammersley in the *Guardian* newspaper in February 2004. Content can be accessed using any computer that can play media files and not just portable music players. Use of the term 'podcast' predates the addition of native support for podcasting to the iPod, or to Apple's iTunes software. Podcasting is now massive and tens of thousands of downloads are made every day. If you are a user of Apple 'i' devices, you may well have download podcasts through the iTunes store which compiles a top ten chart of the most downloaded podcasts in the country. The BBC, the *Guardian* and *Telegraph* usually dominate the iTunes chart of the most popular podcasts. The fact that relatively few independent providers have found fame through podcasting in the UK is a shame as in the early days many thought that podcasting could allow for a more diverse range of voices to be heard outside the limitations of mainstream media. Great podcasts from independent providers and amateurs are out there and they are well worth seeking out on iTunes.

Duncan Geere (2012) of Business Radio Bunker, citing the UK radio ratings body RAJAR figures released in June 2012, says: '… podcasts are enjoying a renaissance in popularity. 7.8 million people have downloaded a podcast, and 4.2 million say that they listen to podcasts at least once a week.' For example the *Guardian* podcasts Football Weekly and Football Weekly Extra were attracting 300,000 downloads a week each and were becoming attractive to advertisers. According to RAJAR, a third of the UK population listened to internet radio – some 16.9 million people, up 5 per cent since October 2008. The RAJAR data release on radio audience figures as of May 2012 shows that internet radio listening has reached an all-time high with the UK population listening for 42 million hours per week, and 17 per cent of UK adults listening to radio via their mobile phone.

Audio is becoming a force in internet content, well beyond music and radio streaming. SoundCloud CEO Alexander Ljung told the 2011 French internet conference 'Le Web': 'Sound will be bigger than video.'.

Online journalism expert Jim Colgan (2011) says Ljung is most likely right:

"

You might expect those words coming from the head of a company that relies on wide adoption of audio for its business, but his argument was convincing. Recording audio is less intrusive than recording video. Everyone who has a smartphone doesn't just have a camera in their pocket, but a microphone. And unlike video, you can listen to audio you and others create when you're doing other things.

"

MAKING AN AUDIO PACKAGE

- Do think: 'Theatre of the mind'.
- Do think: 'Let me tell you a story.'
- Do think: 'Let me take you on a journey.'

An important part of learning to make good audio is to listen to how the professionals do it. We have all heard thousands of radio news bulletins in our lifetimes. The important thing to do is stop listening merely as a news consumer and start to listen as an audio professional. The way to start doing this is to record a news bulletin and then listen and make notes (or more simply use the BBC iPlayer). Deconstruct how the bulletin is made. Think about the subject of each report:

- Why did the reporter make the decisions they did?
- What is special about this news item that makes it easy for the radio listener to hear?

It is hard to over-estimate the importance of deconstructing packages made by the professionals as a method for learning how to make good audio packages. Once you have heard a BBC online bulletin, listen to an Independent Radio News (IRN) bulletin and compare and contrast. Listen to a longer BBC news package. Listen to the way the reporter has put the package together. Now tune into one of the very

contemporary music radio stations aimed at listeners in the 16–25 year age group. Listen to their radio news and analyse that too. How long is the bulletin? How many stories does it include? Does it have sport? Does it have weather and traffic at the end? Does it only have a presenter because they do not use reporters' voices? Does it use music?

Top journalists are surprisingly willing to talk about what they do and give early career journalists advice. Catch them if they are visiting your university as guest speaker, or email to ask them whether you might ask for their advice.

Writing for audio

Simon Cadman (2008), former deputy editor of IRN, has a simple formula for success in writing for audio news: 'Tight, bright but not shite, that's my mantra for writing for broadcast.' He says: 'Brevity is at the core of good writing for broadcast, but without any loss of authority. If you lose facts as you write tight then you are failing.'

'Most audio news stories are quite short: just 30 or 40 seconds, so you have little time to play with. Remember that most people speak at three words a second. That makes an absolute maximum of 90 words for a 30-second report,' he says. Cadman demanded high-quality writing from his reporters. 'The writing style should help the listener understand the story. Sentences should be digestible sound bites for the ear,'

Figure 5.5   Simon Cadman. (Source: Simon Cadman)

he says. He points out the word 'that', saying that it should almost never appear in audio scripts. 'It's completely useless, takes up time where every second counts.'

Thompson (2007) makes the point: 'Facts have much more power than vague adjectives inserted to try to make the story seem bigger than it is.'

The most important thing to remember in audio production is that your listeners cannot see anything. You are their eyes and you must therefore describe what is going on, provided it adds to the story. If you are interviewing you might describe the interviewee, or what they are doing, or where you are and why they are significant. Or you might describe the scene of an event. You are there to paint pictures in people's minds. That is the privilege of radio – it is the one medium where the audience will readily use their imagination to understand the story. Boyd et al. (2008) say: 'In print, shades of meaning are conveyed with choice adjectives and skilful prose, but the spoken words make use of a medium, which is altogether more subtle and powerful – the human voice.'

Writing and structuring a script for audio is different from writing for other media. You do not have the luxury of being able to edit a piece from the bottom up like when you are working in text journalism. A script must sustain interest, and key points should be spread in the package. Thompson (2007) says stories should 'start by attracting your attention, then quickly develop your interest, and progress to either a conclusion or a question about what will be the next chapter'.

Boyd et al. (2008) say, 'Writing for broadcast can mean throwing away literary conventions, including the rules of grammar, so the words make sense to the ear, rather than the eye'.

Remember: the same principles of accuracy, balance, fairness, impartiality and relevance apply to all forms of multimedia journalism.

TIPS FOR WRITING FOR AUDIO

1 Grab interest in the first line.
2 Write scripts for audio in the present tense whenever possible.
3 Write as you would speak – clearly and conversationally. Use everyday spoken English as if you are talking to a friend, not the more formal style of writing for a newspaper.
4 In audio reports use simple conversational contractions where it feels natural so 'they have' becomes 'they've', 'we will' becomes 'we'll' and so on.
5 Avoid too much alliteration – it can be very hard for you or a presenter to read. Two classic but extreme examples of alliteration are: 'She sells sea shells by the sea shore' and 'Peter Piper picked a peck of pickled peppers'.
6 Use short punchy sentences.
7 Don't use colloquialisms or slang.
8 Avoid using clichés, e.g. 'At the end of the day'. For a list of clichés to avoid follow this link to the companion website.
9 Use active voice rather than passive voice.
10 Don't forget to say who you are.
11 Avoid commas.
12 Don't use the word 'that'.
13 Check your facts.

The cue is also known as 'the lead in'. For some formats where there is a presenter,
the reporter usually has to write the presenter cue as well as their own report. A typical audio package can be constructed as follows.

Getting the intro to a story right is a test of the journalist's ability. In professional radio bulletins it is tougher because the reporter's intro should not repeat what the presenter has just said. As with all news writing the first sentence – 'the top line' – should sum up the story. The second sentence should give extra facts or a context to enable the listener to learn more about the story or realize the significance of the first sentence. The third (or last) sentence sets up the report that will follow.

It shouldn't use the same phrases (or even words) as the next piece of sync (recorded voice). For example:

Presenter: 'A major oil spill is threatening the coast of Devon after a tanker was in collision with another ship off Plymouth. Emergency services are fighting to contain the leak. Our reporter John Smith is at the scene.'

Bad practice: Reporter: 'An oil spill is threatening the coast of Devon near Plymouth after a tanker was holed.'

Good practice: Reporter: 'The Good Hope, a 30,000 tonne tanker was badly holed in a collision off Start Point last night at about 10 o'clock. An estimated 20,000 gallons of crude oil has spilled into rough seas …'

Remember the job of the reporter is to bring an eyewitness account of events wherever possible. It's not possible in every case but even when the reporter cannot be on the scene their job is get there and gather together eyewitnesses to give the best possible account of events. It's because they are on the scene that the reporter is important. This brings authority and authenticity to the report. It also can be a good way to avoid repeating the presenter's cue.

For audio news online it is likely that you will not have a presenter. You may present and report alone. This is known as a 'stand-alone'. You might utilize agency clips if your company subscribes to an agency feed like IRN. This means the conventions for the cue can be discarded and you will need to tell the story from the off, either in your own voice or through the use of what your interviewees say.

Do not use quotes when writing commentary (that's what the reporter says) for broadcasting scripts. If you want your listeners to hear the words as they were spoken, record them and use them as clips. This facility to hear people speak is one of the great benefits of broadcasting.

Also, quotes in broadcasting do not work as they do in print where the readers can see the quotation marks. It is just as effective to turn quotes into reported speech.

INTERVIEWING FOR AUDIO PACKAGES

If you are recording an interview for audio editing it needs pace and concision. The first thing you must do is work out what you need from the interview. You will have a rough list of questions. Then how you are going to handle the interview? You must be in control.

So what do the professionals look for in an interviewee? Experienced radio reporter Sutish Sharma (2012) told us:

To me a good interviewee is someone that should tell us something new or should confirm something we are trying to say. I like to give a clip that gives you a bit of a reaction or a headline. A good interviewee has to be a good speaker, they have to be interesting and they have to have some knowledge about what they are talking about.

Figure 5.6   The studio mixing desk. (Source: Paul Lashmar)

If you hand over control to the interviewee then you will not get the interview you want. Empathy is everything. Many people you will interview will not be used to being recorded. Imagine how you would feel in their place. Make them feel comfortable. Offer them a drink if possible. Have a little chat before you start.

Sutish Sharma agrees:

> I think it is important to offer direction. You must look at it from the point of view of the interviewee. They may or may not be used to being interviewed. They may not have done this before. What you shouldn't do is tell them what to say. You can offer encouragement and you can tell them why we are interviewing them and why it is important to get their views on board.
>
> I don't think there is any harm in having a quick chat with them before hand and put them at ease and say – this is the kind of question I am going to be asking. Sometimes the answers you want they have got it but they are not used to being interviewed. They are not used to giving you the answers in a concise form.

Then start gently. Record. If you are not sure you got a good answer to a question, try again. If they stumble in replying to a question, politely ask it again. If they give an answer that is too long, explain that you will not be able to use it at that length and ask if they could do it again more concisely. Look your interviewee in the eye and engage them in a conversation. You set the pace of the interview. Don't stick rigidly to your questions if their answers are taking you somewhere more interesting. Listen to what they say and adapt accordingly. Thank them afterwards.

The basics are:

- Tell the interviewee who you are, your job and who you are working for.
- Always take control and be confident.

Questions you should ask in your research include:

- Does this person know about the subject?
- Are they articulate?
- Do their replies tend to be too long or too short?
- Do they have a personal agenda?
- Are they likely to say anything that might cause legal problems?
- Think about audio backgrounds for the interview.

Before you start:

- Understand why you are doing the interview.
- Make sure you know what result you want.
- Make the interviewee comfortable.
- Explain how the interview will be used.
- Think about how you are get the best out of the person.
- Have a rough list of questions.
- Check the audio environment (is there too much background noise?).

During the interview:

- Listen to what the interviewee said.
- Listen to make sure the interviewee gives a succinct answer to the key questions.
- Ask again if the interviewer fluffed a key question.

Afterwards:

- Get a contact number.
- Say when the piece is to be broadcast.
- If necessary get a release form signed.

RECORDING DIGITAL AUDIO

Using a mobile phone to record calls

The iPhone is designed to prevent you recording your calls because there are restrictive laws in the United States and that's the iPhone's main market-place. But there are a growing number of ways around that and you can find some apps here: www.journalism.co.uk/skills/how-to-record-calls-on-an-iphone/s7/a551745/.

There are also a number of apps for mobile smartphones to allow you to record audio and upload to the web in a couple of clicks.

SoundCloud

SoundCloud is one of the dominant sound applications. Until recently it was mainly focused on music content. But the platform has moved into the spoken word and is keen on encouraging journalism.

SoundCloud is an audio social media platform as it has usernames, contributors to follow, items to favourite and comments to share. The SoundCloud smartphone app is essentially just one big record button that lets you add a title and a picture before uploading and sharing.

SoundCloud is a useful tool for a wide range of users, for example an editor at a major audio programme, looking for new ways to distribute output. The site lets you upload a total of 120 minutes at any one time, but you can pay a yearly subscription for more space (anywhere from £25 to £450 a year, converted).

SoundCloud has emerged as the 'go-to-place for anything audio,' says Adam Curry (cited in Locke, 2012), the former MTV video DJ who created the world's first podcast and founded Podshow, and the start-up that developed the technology for iTunes' podcasting platform.

Figure 5.7 SoundCloud's smartphone app which is used to record audio for easy upload to the web. (SoundCloud)

AudioBoo

AudioBoo is audio equivalent of Twitter to SoundCloud's Facebook. AudioBoo is an app that lets you record short clips and share them on Twitter, Facebook or its website, AudioBoo.fm.

Figure 5.8   The Audioboo app interface on an Android smartphone. (Source: AudioBoo)

Figure 5.9   Digital audio recorder Zoom H4N. (Source: Paul Lashmar)

The site is free with the three-minute limit, but for £60 you can get 30 minutes recording time and some enhanced sharing and podcasting features.

You are more likely to find AudioBoo on British news sites like the *Guardian* and regional BBC radio stations; AudioBoo says 53 per cent of 'listens' come from the US.

DIGITAL AUDIO RECORDERS (DARs)

It is common to see audo journalists use smartphones to record interviews. The Apple iPhone is particularly popular and you can attach a professional external microphone to it, although you may need an adapter. For the professional it is a good idea to have a digital audio recorder to maximize control over your recording. Currently the Zoom H4N is an excellent recorder (see Figure 5.9). It has a range of recording qualities right up to 24bit/96Khz which is high-quality audio. It's light and has a built-in stereo microphone but also an external microphone socket (and the vital headphone socket so you can monitor as you record). Its strength is that it is easy to do the basics but there are a whole bunch of extra functions available that do not get in the way of simple recording. The display is also very clear.

The DAR records either in .WAV or MP3 format onto an SD card. In normal situations, when you want even just a little better quality, it's best to record in WAV format. However, if you're recording outside, you will probably want to record for an extended time. For this situation, MP3 may be best. MP3 recordings are about one-tenth the size of WAV recordings (at 128 kbps).

Recording levels

First set the recording level. For normal everyday volumes, such as interviews, setting the mic sensitivity to HIGH is best. You can do level checks by putting the H4N into recording standby during the pre-interview chatter. Make sure the AGC (Auto Gain Control) is off. This automatically raises or lowers the recording level to match the loudness of the sound but it makes it harder to edit.

To test that you have set the record volume at the right level, enter recording standby mode, then press the record (REC) button while the main screen is showing. The REC indicator blinks showing the unit is in recording standby mode. Get the interviewee to speak into the microphone. The level meter indicates the loudness of the input.

Adjust the volume

Adjust the input volume gradually by pressing the input level button while the sound is playing.

Wind noise is a major problem if you are interviewing or recording outside. If it is a windy day try to get out of the line of the wind. But if that is not possible try turning on 'low cut' located on the H4N. Because the wind sounds produce low frequencies, you can reduce the noise by cutting out the lower frequencies during recording.

You can also use a 'wind sock' on your microphone to help reduce wind noise. This is usually a piece of foam designed to fit over the business end of a microphone.

Figure 5.10 Level settings should be the highest input level (volume) that has no distortion.

Download your recording

If your computer has a card slot, take the SD card out of your DAR, put it into you computer and drag and drop the recording into the right location for editing. Don't forget to give the file a new name that tells you what it is, e.g. MP interview 30 May 2013.

The DAR can also connect to the computer using a USB cable. When 'Insert the disk for this file type?' is shown on the PC, click on cancel. After a while, the DAR is recognized by the PC, and the USB screen is shown in the DAR's display.

Select the files to copy and then drag them to an appropriate location.

Figure 5.11 Waveform of a voice. It should not touch the top or the bottom as that will be distorting. (Source: Paul Lashmar)

EDITING YOUR AUDIO USING AUDACITY

There are a range of different programs for editing audio, including Adobe Audition, Total Recorder, Roxio audio and Pro Tools.

Audacity

For editing audio we recommend using the Audacity program as it is free to download and use (its open source). But it is not as good as Pro Tools or Audition, both of which offer free trials. This means that you can download on your own computers and work at home as well as on workplace computers in the newsrooms. Audacity is developed by a group of volunteers and distributed under the GNU General Public License (GPL). To download follow this link.

Audacity is available for Mac OS X, Microsoft Windows, GNU/Linux and other operating systems. Audacity 2.0 was released in March 2012.

Audacity is easy to use. A slight problem with Audacity, as with some of the more expensive programs, is that it does not have proprietorial rights to use either .MP3 or .WAV files. This means it saves files to its own .aup format. These files do not play on other systems. So you have to convert the working file into an .MP3 or .WAV when you finish editing.

> " Audacity project files are saved in a special format that only Audacity can open. To open your project in another program or burn it to CD, firstly open the .aup file in Audacity if you have already saved one (if you saved it recently it will be in the File > Recent Files menu). Then use the export commands further down the File menu to save the audio in a standard format like WAV or AIFF. "

For general help on Audacity see:

For Audacity manual read online see:

To download in PDF (156 pages) see:

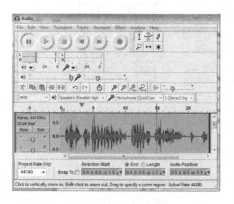

Figure 5.12   Audacity editing screen. (Source: Paul Lashmar)

When you have finished your interviews we would recommend the following way to construct your package.

Write a short opening script of say four pars (sentences). Identify what exactly you think the angle is on the story now you have done all the preparation, research and interviews. Summarize this in four to six words and put it at the top of your draft script (this keeps you focused).

Listen through to all your recorded material, making notes. Listen again whilst logging so you know which bit you want and where they are. We would normally expect to hear some interview clip by the fifth par (sentence) of your script. Then edit the clips and put them into a rough order. Just listen through to that – it will give you an idea of how many links you will need. Think whether any other items from the sound palette, background sounds, music or archive would help your package. Now script and record your commentary.

Edit all the parts together. Listen through and tidy up.

Choose sections which have a 'clean' in and out, sounding natural and with a natural intonation, falling towards the end. If you are recording an interview consider asking the same question in different ways to obtain a variety of clips. The simplest form of package is some commentary (the link) and an interview (the clip). This is known in radio news as a clip-link. Remember above all that it's important that the reporter acts as the eyes of the listener. Mervin Block (1997) emphasizes: 'No one writes exactly the way he talks or talks the way he writes. So writing for broadcast is a compromise. But keep in mind you're writing for people who can't read your script. They only hear it. And they hear it only once.'

Improving your voice

The voice is a tool and most of us need to train to use our voice to its best potential. We have some tips on improving your voice on the companion website.

TIPS FOR EDITING

1 'Wild track': When you are out on an audio job record lots of extra material. Wild track is the sounds in the background and not of your interviewees speaking. First, it could be something that is happening as part of your story – if there is a street demonstration then record dramatic sounds. Second, record the general ambient background sounds where you did the interview as this is helpful in avoiding sudden sharp edits when you put the package together. Record at least one minute of wild track background sounds in every situation where you record. You can lay the wild track on a separate track in the editing program.

2 Use dead air – where nothing is heard – carefully. You can cut two pieces of sound too tightly, especially if they are interview voices, and make it sound unnatural. Don't forget most of us breathe between sentences!

3 Always use headphones to edit. If you just use computer speakers you will not notice important details and sounds.

4 Cut out as many ums and ahs from your interviewees as you can. Try to remove repetitions as in when people start a sentence, falter and start again.

5 If you rearrange interviewees sync to make the sentences more coherent – make sure you do not change the meaning.

6 Never forget to make sure you have the entire five Ws and the H: who, what, when, where, why and how.

7 When you have finished your script *read it out aloud.* Ted White and Frank Barnas (2002) say that reading aloud makes it clear 'when words should be contracted, which words should be emphasized, how clear the sentences are and how well the copy flows from sentence to sentence … the ear, not the eye, is the best judge of well-written broadcast copy'. Kristina Beanland, one of our former students (and now a professional journalist), reinforces this point: 'I found the advice of reading my work aloud conducive to good copy, and this carried over into my print work as well. Speaking words to hear how the sounds hit the ear was a revolutionary moment in my writing, and saw many sentences that would have been suitable for print in my written script altered.'

INTERVIEW: SUTISH SHARMA, EXPERIENCED RADIO REPORTER

Sutish Sharma loves making audio packages:

The first thing I ask3 myself is, 'What is the story I want to tell here?' I think that is important. I'm not a great fan of other styles of package-making where you just go out first, record everything and then decide.

I think as a journalist you should have an idea of the story and what you want to tell from the start. From there I start building it. I ask myself: Who do I need to help me tell the story? What kind of sound effects do I need to put together? Or what kind of wild track do I need to put together? From there I write a skeleton script – which is ever changing right to the last moment. I don't think a story miraculously appears – you have to have an idea. I'm not a journalist who writes on the back of an envelope. I like something that has a structure to it, a running order. From then on your story starts to take shape. It must have truth behind it – 'Is this a true account of what the story is about?' **"**

INTERVIEW: CHRIS LEDGARD, BBC PRODUCER

Figure 5.13   Broadcast producer Chris Ledgard.
(Source: Chris Ledgard)

Chris Ledgard is a highly regarded audio producer whose distinctive style is naturally intimate. He spent many years as a regional and then national radio reporter working across Radio 4 and Radio 5 Live. He makes great use of tantalizing interview clips to hook his listeners in. He has a gentle and intimate programme style. He is a very modest reporter and only uses his voice when necessary, preferring for his interviewees to tell the story.

As you become more skilled in packaging you can look for different ways of telling the story. Ledgard says don't always start with a standard intro and that you should be looking for innovative ways to tell a story if you can. 'It is like when you are teaching little children and you say to them don't always start with "Once upon a time...". Think about whether you start in the middle. Can you start with something dramatic? Then recap.'

Someone once identified the essence of radio by saying: 'Radio is your friend.' It works best as an intimate personal medium. Ledgard says the human voice on its own is what makes audio unique. 'In radio you have the strength of the human voice and of other sounds like music or things happening, but particularly the human voice. Basically it's all storytelling but your weapon is the recorded human voice, which is a strong one I think.' With a greater length you can make greater use of interviews. It's worth remembering that a brilliant interviewee can carry a whole package, while poor interviewees can leave you struggling.

Here's a good example of a strong interviewee with powerful emotional content from the BBC. It's a great example of what can be done in just three minutes. Presenter Zubeida Malik spoke to Joan Almond, the daughter of John Stafford, a British soldier who was left for dead for two days in the Somme before being rescued.

You can also use other sounds more effectively including music. Ledgard is cautious in the use of music. He says: 'Try to avoid the obvious. If it's about the economy, Abba's 'Money, Money, Money' isn't the thing. I've used music many times but don't splash it around too liberally. It can distract people.'

If you are in an environment where the background sounds set the scene for the listener then use it. The simplest is to combine the sound of seagulls with the sound of waves hitting the beach to conjure up a picture of the seaside for the listener. Birds twittering and cows mooing tell us that we are in the country. A creaking door in an echoey room may help us imagine a haunted castle, and the roar of the crowd a sports event.

Sound archive is another tool in the audio reporter's box. Most radio stations have access to archive from past sound recordings. There is some nice archive to be found online but sometimes it needs to be purchased. Ledgard says:

> I'm a big fan of archive. Textually it's very nice. It often has a slightly different texture from the stuff you are recording. It gives the listener a nice place to rest for a minute rather than being constantly battered with what you are doing. It helps the listener and gives nice contrast. It's a good way of doing history without explaining it yourself. It's a good radio tool, a strong colour in the palette.

Ledgard describes how you go about making a package in a busy news environment where time is at a premium. 'Am I making a three-minute piece, a five-minute piece or a seven-minute piece? That makes a big difference. This is obvious but that is the first thing I think.'

He then asks himself the normal journalistic question: 'What's the line? What is the line at the top and what are the paragraphs that come underneath it?'

Chris says that too much subtlety in the package may lose the listener. 'You might put a lot of work into the package and understand why all the elements are there – the person who is listening is doing the washing up or getting the tea for the kids. You have got to make your point clear.'

The ability to have your audience grasp exactly what you are saying in your news package is the skill most admired by experienced audio reporters, says Ledgard. 'The Holy Grail of all of this is clarity but maintaining your lightness of touch. Trying to make what you are saying really clear but not laying it on with a trowel and making it too ploddy.'

A good example of a programme presented and produced by Chris Ledgard is the brilliant but gentle, multi-faceted *The Poppy Factory*:

Audio

Background information

UPLOADING AUDIO TO THE WEB

When you have completed your package you will want to upload it. In the first instance it depends where you want to keep the file. Uploading an audio file to a website is no different from uploading a digital photo. You will either upload the audio file, which should be in .MP3 format, via FTP or use a web-based file-uploading tool that comes with your CMS. There are many free media player plugins for WordPress and Joomla! that allow your users to play your audio directly off the page.

If it is not part of a news package presentation then it is always a good idea to provide a text link explaining what the audio is. Don't force your users to click on the audio file to find out what it's about.

If you want to run a series of podcasts then using iTunes is a good method. You can upload, and using a RSS allows you to find an audience. iTunes supports podcasts and will help you make your podcast work for you. How to do this is explained here:

>>Summary<<

1 The human voice is a powerful tool when heard without any distraction. It is a fundamental part of being human to react strongly to other people's voices. Use that potential in your audio packages.
2 Radio has been at the birth of audio journalism and through much of its growing up period but audio journalism is now spreading, thanks to the internet, into lots of different and innovative formats. There is strong audience demand for audio news journalism as it can be listened to in places where other news media would be inconvenient.
3 Audio is the theatre of the mind and the only media that allows you to paint pictures in the minds of your audience. You have to become the eyes of your audience. It is very demanding to do well but hugely pleasing if your audience likes what you have done. Writing for audio is different from writing for text or even video. You need to describe what is going on.
4 There is no such thing as silence. There is always some sound. Learn to listen to what is really around you. Then record and use the sounds you hear when on location to give your audience a strong sense of place.
5 Always record your interviewees. You never know when someone is going to tell you something important or emotional and if you have a recording of it, it is great way to deliver the story to your audience. Always check your recording equipment before you start.

EXERCISES

1 Take a newspaper report and work out how you would make a stand-alone news package of the story. Who would you interview? What sounds would you record and use to bring the package alive. How would you script the package for 30, 45 or 60 seconds?
2 Silence may be golden but it's rare. The first thing we do when we teach audio is ask the group to be perfectly quiet for one minute. We would like you to try the same thing. Can you hear anything in those 60 seconds? The answer is usually yes. In most university rooms there will be the sound of air conditioning. There is often the sound of someone drilling a wall nearby. There may be students in a nearby corridor talking and someone mowing a lawn. As your ears' condition to the silence you can hear more. A roomful of computers will have the low hum of their internal fans. Someone will cough and another will open a bottle. Oh yes, there's a mobile phone ringing and the ping of an email arriving on a nearby computer.

There is always noise of some sort. Now we would like you to go outside and listen for 60 seconds. We bet that there will be noise! The human ear is very good at filtering background noise when in location. It's amazing how we can hear what someone is saying even if we are in a noisy club. However, if you record someone speaking against a noisy background and then play it back in a quiet place, the ear, mysteriously, doesn't filter out the background noise so well. There is nothing worse than trying to listen to a radio report with a lot of background noise. Try not to record when there are loud variable background noises.

3   Make your own news bulletin – a two-minute bulletin consisting of an intro, two headlines, six stories and a sign-off. Decide the news outlet and audience you are making the bulletin for. The length of each of the stories can vary. (One might be 45 seconds another might be 20 seconds.) Try to include a interview clip or a vox pop in the bulletin. When you have finished listen to the way you have used your voice and also the pauses between each element – does it sound right and hang together as a bulletin? Is there popping on the microphone? Have you clipped a word in the edit? Listen to the news outlet you are copying and see how your bulletin compares to theirs.

FURTHER READING

Boyd, Andrew. 2005. *Broadcast Journalism*. 5th edn. Oxford: Focal Press.
    This is the best basic guide to audio journalism.
Crisell, Andrew, and Starkey, Guy. 2009. *Radio Journalism*. London: Sage.
    A guide to the history, current scope and theory of radio journalism.
Crook, Tim. 1998. *International Radio Journalism*. Oxford: Routledge.
    An excellent look at how to make audio for an international audience.

Useful links:

This American Life archive. This is our favourite non-BBC audio online site with lots of great stories.

Sound Women. This is a network of over 700 inspirational women working in audio who are committed to raising the profile of the women who work in the radio and audio industry, and celebrating their achievements.

CHAPTER 6

Working with Video

The potential power of mobile-phone journalism was shown during coverage of the 2011 London riots. Using just an iPhone, Sky News journalist Mark Stone captured some of the most striking footage of the riots. His confrontations with the looters engaged viewers and the impact of his work was immediate: his footage led bulletins on Sky and was used by rival TV networks across the globe. Online he was trending on Twitter within an hour of the video being filmed. Within 24 hours his video material had been viewed by nearly a million people online. You can see his video at:

Stone's reporting earned him a lot of admiration. Here are some of the Twitter responses to his reports:

- 'Have to say, what a great job Mark Stone is doing tonight. Very courageous journalism' – @skynews via @HayleyRockss
- 'Mark Stone is super brave. He's reporting from all over with his bike and camera phone' – via @6inchstilettos
- 'Love it, my colleague @stone_skynews is currently trending worldwide on Twitter for his reporting' – Mark Stone via @fieldproducer

In this chapter we look at how to put video news online. To work effectively with video you need to bring a range of skills together. You need to be able shoot video, record sound effectively, record a 'piece to camera', script, voiceover and edit. Most importantly you need to bring words and pictures together to tell the story in the most compelling and informative way.

While production standards in video outside the mainstream national media are often quite low we encourage you to adopt a high standard in your video-making as there is no doubt this is the way the news industry is going. To be a competent video journalist (VJ) takes a lot of effort, but the reporter with good video skills opens many career opportunities. Not only is the ability to make a video news package essential to working in TV news, it also opens the way to current affairs, documentary and factual programming. Researchers for TV are expected to have good video skills.

Learning the TV news model – those well-established practices that make television news eminently watchable – is the most effective learning method for the VJ. Watch and analyse how TV journalists deliver the news engagingly with a synthesis of words, pictures and sound.

>>OBJECTIVES<<

In this chapter, you will learn how to:

1 use a video camera;
2 record sound for package including voiceover;
3 write to pictures in a script;
4 use a video-editing software program;
5 include user-generated content.

VIDEO JOURNALISM FOR ONLINE

> **"** There is no doubt that video is an incredibly engaging format for information, news, and entertainment – well, for anything really. A video can much easier explain a complex topic than text alone as people can see and repeat what you do. You can show instead of just telling or hoping people read what you painstakingly wrote. (Christian Heilmann, Mozilla, 2012) **"**

Figure 6.1   A video camera is best held on a tripod to avoid shaking. (Source: Dreamstime)

In the UK we have some of the highest professional standards for producing video news in the world. Look at any news programme on a major channel and you will see brilliantly made news packages.

Online video journalism versus TV journalism

There is a running debate about online news websites copying the TV model. The American new media guru Jeff Jarvis (a visiting professor at London's City University) (2012) says that online sites should not copy TV. He believes they should innovate with new forms of video delivery:

I think they are still making a big mistake in trying to imitate old time TV. They are trying to do stand-ups. They are trying to do B rolls [the supplemental footage intercut with the main shot in an interview or documentary] and establishing shots because TV did it. There is no reason to. **"**

The basic concept of the VJ is of a reporter who goes out on their own, with a camera, and shoots, scripts and edits their own work. News teams working on websites tend to be smaller than their equivalent in traditional media. However, the introduction of video journalism online has been gradual. It is mainly a resources issue as most websites operate on very tight budgets. Even with modern hardware and software a video package takes longer to prepare than its text or audio or even a photo-gallery equivalent. It also requires some training and this has deterred many local newspapers.

The rise of the VJ

About ten years ago the video journalism revolution in the UK started in the traditional media – in the then well-funded BBC TV news. The BBC believed that one person making news packages could be more flexible and productive. It began training reporters to be video journalists, mostly on regional news teams for TV news. Hundreds have now been through the training scheme. Some journalists became video journalists as they found making their own videos was the best way to persuade news desks to broadcast the stories they covered. Many video journalists love the freedom of working on their own. David Heathfield (in Heathfield et al., 2011) from NATO TV says: 'I like to work myself and camera, making the whole thing from start to finish.'

Karen Thayer, Multi Media Journalist and Change Manager at the BBC (in Heathfield et al., 2011), says: 'Where I'm coming from, video journalism is about the storytelling and unless you have something to say don't pick up the camera. The more difficult thing is to work out what I have to say, what is the story I want to tell.'

Connected TVs arrive in the living room

One thing is certain: video will become more and more important as audiences become more and more interested in visual delivery. We are witnessing the rise of digital streaming media players – using digital set top boxes, such as Apple TV, games consoles and a new breed of smart TVs. These allow users to watch online video on their living-room TV sets from sites such as YouTube, Vimeo, BBC iPlayer and Channel 4oD, which mean there will be more demand for content in video format. We are also witnessing the rise of specific title video channels. The US-based *Wall Street Journal* now has a very effective video channel featuring high-quality business news. The video journalist might also be delivering text, photographs and audio versions of the story, and may also provide stories by social media as well as online. Sometimes the video will be the only medium used to deliver the story. On other occasions the journalist might decide not to use video at all.

By comparison to TV news, the quality of video on the websites of most regional and local papers is still often average and sometimes very poor, consisting of a wobbly interview shot by a reporter on an iPhone with barely audible sound. A growing number of newspapers like the idea of using a fuller interview on a video as part of the online presentation of the news story if only a few quotes were utilized in the actual news piece. The interview gives added value to those members of the site's audience who are really interested in the story.

Editors are very conscious of low professional standards of the video on their website and are requiring new reporters to have video packaging skills. It is worth noting that the National Council for the Training of Journalists (NCTJ) – the body which sets the training standards for reporters based on industry requirements – now has a video for online unit in its new diploma. These modules require aspirant reporters to be able to shoot, script and edit a news package that achieves a standard very similar to what one might find on a regional TV news bulletin. There is convergence of the newspaper reporter and the VJ of regional TV news. In both cases the reporter is a one-man band who has to record, script and edit as well as deliver a purely text version of the story.

We were told by the then head of the *Guardian*'s multimedia team, Tom Happold (2012): 'I am sure that if you are applying for a job on the *Guardian* as a news reporter and you have the ability to shoot and edit video, this will give you the edge in getting the job. It is important to us.'

User-generated video content

Video news doesn't just come from staff and freelance journalists. Members of the public will offer video to you. Members of the public frequently film dramatic events and this is known as user-generated content (UGC). If you watch any of the numerous 'fly on the wall' documentaries about policing, for example, you will notice at any late-night fracas bystanders busily capturing events on their mobile phones. They are very often happy to share their video with you. Steve Punter, a freelance VJ (in Heathfield et al., 2011), says: 'I think we are about to enter a golden age of new media, but whether it is TV, I doubt it. It will be mobile, it will be on the web, it will be pro-am and completely disruptive of ownership.'

HOW NEWSPAPERS USE VIDEO

There are a growing number of sources of video material to use online. There are agencies that supply basic clips of any event. ITN is one of these. The staff journalist can then use the material and edit it into a package. There is a wide range of different types of footage online. At its most simple the reporter might edit and upload footage shot by a member of the community without any voicing. For many news reports, the reporter simply writes and voices a script to the pre-supplied pictures.

Here is an example from the *Southern Daily Echo* where the reporter has written a script to pictures supplied by the local emergency services: www.dailyecho.co.uk/video/87129/.

Another example of scripted footage from one camera is: www.dailyecho.co.uk/video/87076/.

One of the simplest versions of a package is a short script that the newsreader or presenter reads 'out of vision' to accompany a sequence of shots. In TV this is known as 'an OOV'.

Figure 6.2 A reporter at the *Daily Telegraph* newsroom presents a video report. (Source: Steve Hill)

They are often used for scripting 'found' footage. This is footage provided, for example, by the police as in a piece of CCTV of a crime taking place or by a reader. It may also be a jolly, if embarrassing, piece of video in the spirit of 'You've been framed'. Here's an example of CCTV footage from a shop recording a theft: www.dailyecho.co.uk/video/107716/.

Figure 6.3   Emergency services rescue crane driver after crane collapse in Southampton docks. (Source: *Southern Daily Echo*)

Figure 6.4   Man threatens to jump from 120 foot high crane. (Source: *Southern Daily Echo*)

CCTV footage works well for local newspapers as it is cheap and often very popular – particularly footage of bank robberies and late-night pub brawls. It also allows local newspapers to 'cross-promote', for example from a text report in a newspaper to an associated video on its website. It's an increasingly common practice.

Another technique used on online sites is to link to free pre-packaged content on YouTube or similar hosted site. This takes little effort on the part of the journalist. This video content is often very popular with users, even though it is not at all exclusive content. It is sometimes more popular than painstakingly produced video packages made by a journalist.

With the proliferation of CCTV and the ubiquity of mobile phones there is a wide range of video available and much of it is free. If you are working on a news desk the editor will expect you to be able to create and utilize video to enhance the website and grab the attention of users. The news editor will want you to make sure that the footage belongs to the person who is providing it to you. They will also want to make sure you consider privacy issues – for instance was the video recorded in a private place and did the person who recorded it have permission to be there. Here's an example of a high-quality piece of a trainee journalist's work that has been used on a professional newspaper site: www.buckinghamshireadvertiser.co.uk/south-buckinghamshire-news/local-buckinghamshire-advertiser-news/2012/03/14/why-people-feel-so-strongly-about-hs2-82398-30535893/.

FINDING THE STORY

Finding a story is a skill. We know at first, many trainee journalists find this hard. Often student journalists lack confidence and find it hard to speak to people they do not know. With effort that reticence is overcome. First, think through what is the most topical aspect of an event and what is the best way to tell the story. Something has happened but there will be different 'angles' to the story. An 'angle' is the particular way you choose to tell the story. You want to tell the one that is most topical, or is most important or is most dramatic. But you must not bend the truth to get your angle. Accuracy is a keystone in good journalism. Think about it.

WRITE TO PICTURES

Writing for video is different from audio and pure text. The same basic rules of news-writing apply as we detailed in the early chapters. But writing for broadcast (known as writing to pictures) is a synthesis of words and pictures. You still have to deliver the basic news information. The pictures can do a lot of the work and reduce the need for everything to be explained in the words. Like all news, every video story needs a different treatment but there are some basic rules. These rules are well proven and if you want to break them you need a good reason to, and you should be sure that you have found a better way of telling the story. Writing for video is not a question of writing a script and then adding pictures. Neither is it a case of just getting pictures and then writing the words. It's about creatively bringing the two elements together to the best effect. That takes a bit of getting used to and is a matter of practice.

Sometimes the picture does most of the work and you need few words. For example, a story about a train being derailed at high speed with pictures of the derailed train lying on its side does not need a script that says 'a train has been derailed', because it's obvious to anyone viewing. Use what you write in the script to complement the pictures. Tell the audience who was injured, how many were in the train, how fast it was going, where it was travelling from and to. Use your script to add information, not to repeat to the audience what they can already see.

A very simple example of writing to pictures was on the BBC1 10 o'clock TV news on 26 April 2012, in an item about Culture Secretary Jeremy Hunt's controversial links with News Corp over the BSkyB bid. It opened with a picture of Cabinet Minister Hunt who was out jogging. The commentary started: 'He can run but he can't hide.' Simple but effective writing to pictures.

Video lends itself to the great interviewees. Sometimes rather than the reporter opening the piece with their intro lines setting the story, the interviewee does it better. Starting with the interviewee in this way throws the viewer right into the story.

One major difference between TV news and online video packages is the way they are introduced. Think of all the TV news you have watched. On screen throughout the news you will have one or more studio-based presenters. Their job is to introduce the news. Typically they will introduce a story with two or three sentences, ending with something like 'Our reporter Jane Smith is at the scene'.

Figure 6.5   The police will often supply CCTV footage to local newspaper websites. It is a good way of catching criminals and generates traffic to the website. (Source: *Southern Daily Echo*)

Figure 6.6   Luke Karmali's video. (Source: Trinity Mirror)

CREATING PACKAGES WITH DIFFERENT LENGTHS

For most online reports the video will be stand-alone, delivered by the reporter alone. This means the reporter has to find a way to explain the story from the start. There is no help from a presenter. As a reporter working for the main TV channels you will be required to produce 'reversion' – a range of different format packages from one story. Say you are sent out to cover an armed robbery. You may be required to make the following versions:

- A 90-second version for the main evening news TV bulletin. This will need a cue written for the presenter. This might include one piece to camera (PTC).
- A three-minute stand-alone version for the online site. This might include two pieces to camera.
- A 45-second version for a short news bulletin.
- An audio version for radio news. This might be 30, 45 or 60 seconds.
- The reporter will also have to write a short text link for the online page to encourage browsers to watch the video version.

While the reporter can use much of the same information, each package will need to be scripted slightly differently and a range of editing decisions made. The experienced reporter will know that they are likely to have to re-edit their story for a range of formats so they will think carefully about how to make sure they have all the right material available. They will do this before they start filming. The professional might shoot too much material to give themselves room for manoeuvre.

As a journalist you need to learn to make packages of different lengths. You should be able to make packages of one, two and three minutes. In our experience, one of the biggest problems trainee journalists give themselves is not recording enough material rather than recording too much.

If you are asked to cover a news event and produce a video package there are a range of possible basic ingredients:

1 interviews;
2 vox pops;
3 general views (known as GVs) – shots that show the place or person at the centre of the story;
4 commentary (known as COMM) – this is the reporter voicing the story;
5 reporter talking on screen ('piece to camera', PTC) – this is another method of delivering the script;
6 found footage – someone might have recorded dramatic footage of the event you are reporting; and
7 graphics.

Remember the job of the reporter is to bring an eyewitness account of events wherever possible. It's not possible in every case but even when the reporter can't be on the scene, their job is to get there and find eyewitnesses to give the best possible account of events. The reporter's 'piece to camera' at the scene is important as it brings authority and authenticity to the report.

INTERVIEW: KURT BARLING, BBC LONDON REPORTER

Kurt Barling is a highly experienced reporter working for BBC London News. His main outlet is television but he also services other platforms. 'BBC London News has 1.5 million viewers a day and so that has to be our paramount focus.' He has access to other London BBC platforms. 'Quite often you will see a good line coming off the television item which could be used as a talking point on the radio station 94.9FM.' He will do a radio package from his material. Then he looks to online. 'If the story has more layers and can afford more context you might also do something online like a 750-word treatment for online, and the benefit of online is that you give your television work a secondary market.' Kurt likes the fact that once you get a video package online, 'It stays there in perpetuity', unlike the ephemeral nature of television. He often gets feedback on packages he made online from people who have only just seen it many months later. As a BBC reporter, he says, 'You are always alive to the possibility that your piece can thrive and survive across all three platforms.'

How does Barling choose his stories from all those that come into the BBC London news desk every day? 'First thing you ask is whether there is a story there. Sometimes a story comes in and you look at the lines and there is no story there.' But every day there is a story that will work. He used as an example the on-going story of the shooting of the young north Londoner Mark Duggan by the police in controversial circumstances which sparked off the 2011 riots. 'An obvious public interest story, an obvious story for me to do because I have very good connections in London's minority communities. It is an area in London I know particularly well as I have done a lot of work there in the last

Figure 6.7　BBC reporter Kurt Barling. (Source: Kurt Barling)

25 years. So it's a natural place for me to go and look at the story.' What does he do next? What questions does he ask himself?

> ❝ What are the lines of the story? Well the obvious lines of the story are the who, what, when, where, why and how of the story, starting off with Mark Duggan. Who shot him? Where did they shoot him? When did they shoot and why did they shoot him? And trying and explore all those fundamental questions. And in order to animate those questions you have a number of different potential sources. Clearly you have a number of official sources although in a shooting like that the officials will clam up pretty quickly and just give you the official line.
>
> Then you might find yourself with eyewitnesses in the community who can offer you some insight into what they saw. So you're reporting directly what they saw in the incident. Then you can turn to other people in the community who have their own pathways of intelligence. They can give you a little bit more insight into who saw what and when although you would have to be careful how you report that because it is not necessarily 100 per cent accurate. You will go to the scene and gather pictures of the scene, of that incident from whichever vantage point you can get to. In the end television is about pictures. No pictures – very difficult to tell the story. ❞

Barling says it is very hard to keep a video story alive if you don't have fresh pictures.

> ❝ The one thing you had with Duggan is that you constantly had fresh pictures. You could go to the family to get a new line. You could get the family at the coroner's inquest for a new line. And that new line was constantly pushing that story along. The inquest was a fresh line. ❞

He summed up the method:

> In terms of going out and gathering material, though, you identify the key lines of the story, the key characters who are going to animate that story and get their story on tape. Any story for television needs pictures, that's self-evident. I would hasten to add, many times, it doesn't stop a story because you don't have fresh pictures, but the story gets tired very quickly if you don't have pictures.

LEARN TO REALLY SEE

In Chapter 5 we emphasized that you have to learn to listen to make good audio. With video you really have to learn to see. When you are filming, what is it you really see? What will your pictures really say to the viewers? What is the background?

Have you seen video footage where the interviewee appears to have a lamp-post growing out of their head? This happen when we don't look carefully and think 'What does this say to the viewer?' and 'Does this look OK?' If you are recording someone on screen, avoid situations where something distracting is going on in the background.

Be careful not to let the words and pictures contradict each other. You might be writing a story saying that a council fell behind with rubbish collections over Christmas causing a build-up of rotting rubbish in some streets. If that is true, don't show just a couple of bags of rubbish in the street as that undermines your story-line. You need a large pile. Don't show refuse collectors picking up the rubbish as that will contradict visually what you are saying in the commentary. If you are talking about a hosepipe ban being introduced because of a drought don't start your package with a reservoir of water. You can bring that in later in the story, perhaps to explain that the reservoirs are only half as full as they should be. But don't use that shot at the beginning. At the beginning you need something that signposts drought – perhaps cracked earth or grass that has gone brown or crops that are dying.

For example, if your editor tells you to produce a video package about a council that has withdrawn subsidies to a rural bus service, you will need the following video material:

General views (GVs) of one of the bus services that are threatened as a result of the cuts. This footage should make it clear that the bus is a rural service. So a good shot would be a shot that swings around from fields to a bus stop as the bus draws up.

Interview 1: perhaps with a family from an outlying village that relies on the bus to get them to the nearest major town and will be cut off without it. It might be a mother and son. The boy might tell you he uses the bus for school and to see his friends at weekends. The mother might say she cannot afford a car. A good place to film the interview would be on the bus.

Interview 2: optional – perhaps with an elderly person who relies on the bus to take them on weekly visits to the hospital or to do their shopping.

Interview 3: with the councillor who is responsible for the decision to cut the subsidy. This is important to make sure the story is correct and to make sure that it is balanced. The council may be under tremendous financial pressure to cut back and would have to cut back other vital services if this subsidy is not cut.

Interview 4: with a spokesman from the bus company, who might explain that without the subsidy the service is not financially viable. They might have some surprising information perhaps disclosing that only a handful of passengers actually use the bus service in question.

Vox pops: You might get some vox pops from people at the bus stop.

Piece to camera (PTC): A sense of authenticity will be conveyed if the reporter reports from the scene. A good place to report would be from the moving bus where you can see the background is of the countryside. You would prepare some script for the piece to camera so you can learn it and deliver it. On the BBC College of Journalism site, reporter David Shukmann (Shukmann, n.d.) says he does not write and learn the script. He writes some rough notes and then records a spontaneous piece to camera. He believes this makes his PTCs very easy to listen to and prevents them from sounding rehearsed. We think this is great, but only for the experienced reporter or for the reporter who finds talking to a camera very natural. Most people don't at first and a script is generally the best way to look and sound professional.

When you come back to the newsroom with your recorded video you are looking for the best way to tell the story. You will have written the top of the story – the intro that outlines the story. That might be:

> Rural bus services in the West Darley area are likely to be severely cut following the council decision to remove £1m worth of fare subsides. Arriva – the bus company running the services – say that at least ten routes will have to go if the subsidies are withdrawn.
>
> A spokesman for the council says they were necessary in order to protect the provision of elderly people's care.

You then develop the narrative. You might choose to broaden the story to other cutbacks in transport in the whole area. Or to explain which other cuts they may be considering.

SIGNPOSTING

Certain shots are what we call signposting shots. A signpost shot reinforces the words and is a visual representation of a key point of the story. The first shot is often known as an 'establishing shot'.

If you are talking about cutting back bus services it is usual to show a bus.

CHOOSING A VIDEO CAMERA

A journalist should always carry a video camera even if it is just your mobile smartphone. As we have seen with Mark Stone's riot footage, the video camera feature on a smartphone can produce gripping content. This material was technically not really broadcast quality but was used for broadcast as they were the only images from the scene that were available. When you are in this situation, sound quality and camera shake are likely to be your two biggest problems.

A suitable video camera will have manual settings – especially focus and exposure. This enables greater control in difficult conditions such as poor light. We have all been in rooms where blinding natural light floods in and yet some parts of the room remain relatively dark. Manual exposure helps you keep the image in a constant light. Automatic exposure may dim and brighten making the video difficult to watch.

In busy streets an automatic focus camera may respond to an event peripheral to your subject. It might try to focus on a bus moving behind your interview subject. Sticking to manual focusing really helps.

The iPhone 5 is capable of video recording HD (1080p) up to 30 frames per second with audio. This is a great improvement and other smartphones are very good. Camera phones are OK but because of their thin size lack the ability to give a good depth of field (DOF), as well as some other important features. Depth of field is the distance between the nearest and farthest objects in a scene that appear sharp and clear in an image. Although a camera lens can focus at only one point in the distance at a time, the decrease in sharpness is gradual on each side of the focused distance, so that within the DOF, the lack of sharpness is imperceptible under normal viewing conditions.

In some cases, it may be desirable to have the entire image sharp, and a large depth of field is appropriate. In other situations a narrow DOF may make for a more powerful image, emphasizing the subject while de-emphasizing the foreground and background.

Flip cameras are also improving. These look like mobile phones but are dedicated cameras using the extra physical space (not having to have telephone electronics) for additional features. They have many of the elements that more expensive video cameras have. Phones and flip cameras are not good on stability. If you are going to use a camera phone – for interviews – we recommend you buy a camera stand. It will make a significant difference to the quality of the video you capture.

We strongly recommend a reasonable quality dedicated camera. Canon DSLRs are very good, and in particular the Canon EOS 600 DSLR at around £500. This has a much higher resolution than a mobile phone and is capable of capturing good-quality HD video as well as superb 18 megapixel digital still images. It is important that the camera has an external microphone input and headphone socket so you can monitor the sound. It is also important that the sound quality is good. You will know from audio recording that it is important to get the microphone close to the source of the sound. When interviewing, the microphone needs to be close to the interviewee's mouth – usually a few inches below.

Stability is a key issue. A larger camera is easier to hold steady and fit onto a tripod. There is a very good guide on how to shoot and edit video for the web when using an iPhone, iPad or iPod out in the field or covering breaking news on Journalism.co.uk (www.journalism.co.uk/skills/how-to-shoot-and-edit-video-on-an-iphone/s7/a545443/

Before you set out there are a number of things you need to do. Make sure the equipment is all working properly. Are the batteries in your equipment fully charged? Do you have spare batteries? Is the microphone working? Are the leads working well? A dodgy microphone lead can ruin your sound. Professionals still find themselves with equipment problems. It is almost a rite of passage for a trainee video journalist to come back and discover that a vital interview was not recorded because of a flat or low battery.

CAPTURING GOOD VIDEO

Video rules are very similar to those for using a stills camera in Chapter 4. If outside, don't film into the sun.

Rule of thirds

If interviewing use the rule of thirds to frame the interviewee. You make sure the person's eyes are located in the place one third from the top and one third of the width from the side. It can be either left or right but it is good to have interviewees on different sides.

When recording a piece to camera, it is usual to place the reporter in the centre. But when you film an interviewee you should offset them to the right or left. Their eyes should be one third from the top and one third from the side of the frame. Alternating interviewees right and left is very useful in editing to keep the video visually interesting. The interviewee should be looking at you – slightly to the side of the camera – and not looking directly at the camera.

As Stephen Quinn and Vincent Filak (2005) explain, the rules for video are similar to that for stills photographs: 'You should usually avoid placing the subject in the centre of the frame. People read left to right so their eyes are conditioned to naturally go to a point about two-thirds up the page.'

Allow yourself some footage to play with in the edit so let the camera run for a few seconds before you or your interviewee speaks – likewise at the end.

When you start filming keep the camera still – don't start panning or zooming until you have practised and can make this type of shot work.

Know where your material is going to appear

If it is going to be a small format, low-resolution online format or for mobiles, shoot close shots especially of interviewees. The closer the shots are, the better they'll look on a computer screen as wide scene-setting shots tend to get lost on a small screen.

Camera techniques: distance and angle

Wide shot (WS) – shot which shows all or most of a fairly large subject (for example, a person) and usually much of the surroundings.

Medium wide shot (MWS) – with an interviewee, the lower frame line cuts off his feet and ankles.

Extra Long Shot.jpg   Long Shot.jpg

Medium shot (MS) – in such a shot, presenter of interviewee and its setting occupy roughly equal portion of the frame. In the case of the interviewee, the lower frame passes through the waist. There is space for hand gestures to be seen.

Medium Long Shot.jpg   Medium Close Up.jpg

Medium close shot (MCS) – the setting can still be seen. The lower frame line passes through the chest of the interviewee.

Close-up (CU) – a shot that shows the interviewee's face so that it fills the screen.

MCU (Medium close-up) – head and shoulders.

Close Up.jpg   Big Close Up.jpg

BCU (big close-up) – forehead to chin. Close-ups focus attention on a person's feelings or reactions, and are sometimes used in interviews to show people in a state of emotional excitement, grief or joy.

Figure 6.8   A range of distance shots. (Source: Paul Lashmar)

Camera moves

A pan or zoom can be visually very effective. You might have a vicar talking about his church – you can pan down the church and move to him as he speaks and that is a much more interesting shot than a static frame. When you pan and zoom you need to work out the timing of what is going to be said in that shot. You should always begin and finish statically. Cutting into a moving shot when you edit is ugly and unprofessional. Don't jerk your body around when filming. If you decide to pan, use a steady motion so you aren't giving your audience a headache. As you become more skilled you can use movement shots. It is generally agreed that viewers like dynamic news footage. Even where the story does not lend itself to moving shots you can inject energy by panning and zooming. If you are shooting piles of rubbish in a street try to have some movement, even if it is of passing cars or pedestrians. White and Barnas (2010) say about filming, 'avoid zooms and pans unless there is some important reason to zoom or pan on to something … it is better to cut from one shot or another'. Avoid 'hosepiping' – do not move your camera backwards and forwards or shoot and move. Movement shots should start statically, move evenly then stop. When using a camera which has an electronic zoom, use your body to zoom in. Don't use the actual zoom unless you absolutely have to as the footage gets more pixelated the more you zoom in.

Why that shot?

When you shoot think about how you are going to edit the video footage. Think about editing and about creating sequences so the footage works together and has a harmony.

EDITING

At the simplest level there are a range of very basic video editing packages like Apple's iMovie, or Windows Movie Maker. Sometimes they come pre-installed on your computer. One of the benefits of using iMovie is that it has pre-settings for both YouTube and Vimeo uploading. They are for the home-users and lack some elements that we feel are important in a professional context. We have found accurate editing can be difficult and frustrating.

There is a range of high-quality editing programs on the market for a reasonable price. Very popular is Final Cut Pro which is only for Apple computers. Another is Pinnacle Studio. Pinnacle has incorporated the Avid system which is well regarded in the TV industry.

It is often worth getting some basic training on these programs. They appear dauntingly complex but for most news packages you only need a few functions.

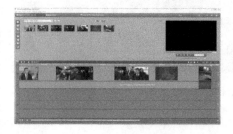

The first move is to upload your footage onto the computer so that your editing software can access the material. View the material and log your best material. If GVs, which are good clear stable shots? Which are useful for signposting the story? What are the timings on your pans and zooms? Once you have the pictures logged, look at any interviews – what are the good quotes? Draft a rough on the basis of what you have seen.

When editing you should know that every story needs a different approach. There are rules but you need to develop the confidence to know when to break them. Always think – what is the best way to tell the story?

Figure 6.9   Pinnacle editing screen. (Source: Paul Lashmar)

The sequence

A news video package will consist of a number of sequences. Where you need to use a range of images to tell a distinct part of a story you might construct a sequence. (A sequence expresses one of the thoughts that together make the story.) You need to think in sequences to plan your shots. For instance, the reporter may be at the opening of a new sports stadium. You will want to shoot video that shows them moving through different parts of the building. They may be reporting to camera but talking about another part of the stadium. You need to shoot video of that part of the stadium so you can put them together to tell the story well.

Example of sequence

If we take the West Darley bus service cuts story – one sequence will be about the family we are interviewing. So our sequence might be:

1 Camera on path in front of bus stop. Wide shot: bus pulls into bus stop family gets on board.
2 Camera on bus. Wide shot: family getting into bus and finding seats.
3 Medium shot: interview with family.
4 Camera outside at town bus stop. Wide Shot: family gets off.

Cutaways

You will also need some shots to act as cutaways for when you edit the interview. These shots allow you to cut interviews without nasty jump cuts. What you do is edit out what you don't want. This usually means joining two sentences. To hide the edit you use a shot that 'bridges' the sound edit. One important rule of cutaways for editing interviews is that you should not be able to see the face and especially the mouth of the interviewee. Typically, you video them from the back or perhaps you shoot a close-up of their hands gesticulating. Never 'clip' a sound edit – that's where you cut into a word. Sound edits should always be clean – between words.

Make every shot count. BBC guru Vin Ray (2003) counselled, 'never use a shot – any shot – as "wallpaper". Never write about pictures as though they weren't there'.

Captions

The caption should usually be located across the bottom quarter of the screen and be big enough for the viewer to read easily.

SOUND

Recording the voiceover is quite a simple process and is essentially the same as you learnt in Chapter 5. Most editing

Figure 6.10 How a caption should look. (Source: Steve Hill/Solent University)

packages have the capability to record sound so all you have to do is plug the microphone into the computer, check your levels and record the commentary of your script. This is often referred to as a voiceover. When you are using a mix of voiceover, interviews, general views and pieces to camera it does get more complex. The better-quality editing programs usually have four or more audio tracks so you can put the voiceover on a different track which makes it easier to edit.

An important don't: when you cut between shots it is often a good idea not to allow the sound to cut so dramatically. You might let it run for a fraction of a second into the new shot. Or you might run some 'wild track' across the edit to smooth out the sound.

Wild track

As with audio you should always record at least 30 seconds of wild track. This is recorded at the end of filming at each location to get the background sound or ambience and is an important tool for smooth sound edits. Wild track can also be recorded sound that 'places' the story, e.g, the sound of Big Ben to suggest the House of Parliament or seagulls to suggest that the story takes place at the seaside.

Sound effects can be useful to develop a story. There are a number of places online where you can get sound effects free. We list a number on the companion website, plus some useful links explaining how they can be best used.

GRAPHICS

Graphics can help. In the case of the bird-watching story the reporter uses graphics to help liven up the story. Bear in mind this is a BBC breakfast news programme so it can be quite light-hearted. The reporter turns to his advantage the fact that he has no footage of the rare bird by getting the graphics people to superimpose the graphic of the bird wherever he goes: in his hand, in the local pub and local grocery store where businesses have boomed since the bird arrived. The reporter is having fun.

Graphics, used with care, can help visualize a story in all sorts of ways. You might use the occasional graph or fact or quote. Typing large screeds of text onto the screen is a no-no. Keep it simple as in the example below.

UPLOADING VIDEO TO THE WEB

When you have finished editing you will need to 'render' your edit. This brings it together as a finished package to either upload online or to broadcast. The usual choices are usually either to use .avi format or .MP4. The .avi uses a lot of bytes and is high quality. Mp4 uses compression (see below) to reduce the amount of bytes used and is good if you need the material to be seen on iPhones. Part of the decision will depend on how your media organization presents video online. Some use YouTube or Vimeo to act as a remote server. You then take the link offered and embed it into a news page, so it appears alongside any text or still images you have. If your organization hosts video on its own server then you will need to upload onto the server and link onto the page. It is always better to use a system that has the video immediately visible on screen rather than requiring you to click and download before viewing.

Embedding your video

Most online news sites need a text caption on the page explaining what the video is about. Search engines can't read the content of the video itself, so you will need to describe what is in the video. Embed tags – these could be names of people interviewed, places, etc. – in your web page to explain what is in the video. These text tags can be read by search engines and are easy to create in popular CMSs.

The latest versions of Final Cut Pro (this is version 10 or X as we write this) and iMovie include the best settings for a range of video outputs (including YouTube, Vimeo, mobile, tablet computer or TV). These can be found under the 'share' heading in the main toolbar. It is normally best to stick with these headings.

If you want the option to be able to show your video at full screen you will probably need to render to high quality .avi. Unless you have a very powerful computer and fast broadband connection, optimizing for the web and then uploading even a relatively short video to YouTube can take up to 30 minutes. YouTube is a popular site and at busy times videos can take another 30 minutes or so to appear online.

If you want to host the video on your own server and keep it simple – use Quicktime or Adobe's Flash. Flash has been hampered by the dispute between Apple and Adobe – which means that it does not work on iPad. This is a problem for news outlets that use Flash.

The great thing about YouTube is that it is very simple. You can choose whether you want all or some YouTube viewers to see your video by selecting the suitable privacy controls. If you want viewers only to see it on your media site you can use the private setting.

The downside of Flash video

One of the reasons that online video news has been slow to take off is that it has had a negative reputation – mainly because it was often slow to load and choppy. Flash video, embedded on the page, certainly made things easier. But Flash of course needs a free browser plugin (the Flash Player) which needs constant updating.

HTML5 looks promising, and includes new ways to stream video for mobile. In November 2011 Adobe announced that it will discontinue development of Flash for mobile devices and reorient its efforts towards developing tools utilizing HTML5.

HTML5 may do away with the need for any extra browser plugins, and video will be much simpler to watch. You will know if your package works. If the story flows and the words and pictures work together you will feel a great sense of professional delight that you have done the job well.

>>Summary<<

1 Video journalism is a dominant form for delivering the news. Mastering video skills is vital for anyone entering the news industry. *Guardian* reporter Paul Lewis (2012) emphasized the importance of video for all media. The *Guardian*'s coverage of the London riots in 2011 won awards. Lewis says it was the two news videos of the riots the *Guardian* placed online that had the greatest impact with their audience.

2 You can't make one video news package and expect to be a video journalist. Video journalism is a complex set of skills that need a lot of practice. Repetition is everything in learning journalism skills.

3 Writing to pictures is not a case of writing a script and then adding pictures. Nor is it a case of laying the pictures and interviews and then writing words to match. You need a synthesis of words and images that work hard without repeating. Ask yourself: What is the best way I can tell this story?

4 In Chapter 4, we reminded you of John Berger's *Ways of Seeing*. It is easy to get complacent about the familiar and fail to notice things we can see. Ask yourself: What do I really see?

5 Never go out without a camera. Know the rules but be prepared to break them and innovate. That stimulates your imagination, keeps you creative and is what makes being a journalist such great fun.

EXERCISES

1 Filming: Find a friend or classmate and record an interview with each other outside on a subject of mutual interest. You should record enough to get a good one-minute sequence. Make sure you get some cutaway shots and some 'wild track'. Then look at the footage and listen to the audio. How professional is it? Now edit into a one-minute video.

2 Filming: There has been a huge rise in scrap-metal thefts as prices rise. To get used to filming general view shots, film a wide range of metal street furniture including bollards, manhole covers, war memorials, cables and so forth. Try to make the pictures as interesting as possible.

3 Package: Find a local scrap-metal story. You should be able to use the footage you recorded in Exercise 2. The minimum you need is:

   o a scrap-metal story with an example of theft, preferably recent and topical;
   o at least one interview with someone key (e.g. a person who has suffered a theft, police, British legion rep, local) – you need expert opinions, so do not interview a student or a friend;
   o a drafted script; and
   o a piece to camera with you as reporter.

FURTHER READING

Boyd, Andrew, Stewart, Peter and Alexander, Ray. 2008. *Techniques of Radio and Television News*. Sixth edn. Oxford: Focal Press.
   This is the best basic primer for making video news.

McAdams, Mindy. 2011. Reporter's Guide to Multimedia Proficiency: www.jou.ufl.edu/faculty/mmcadams/PDFs/RGMPbook.pdf

This free download has useful practical tips on all forms of online video journalism.

Ray, Vin. 2003. *The Television News Handbook*. London: Macmillan.

This book is very orientated to television, but is written by one of the best exponents in the BBC.

Thornburg, Ryan. M. 2011. *Producing Online News*. Washington, DC: CQ Press.

This guide to multimedia journalism has an excellent section on online audio and video.

BBC College of Journalism: www.bbc.co.uk/academy/collegeofjournalism

This BBC training site has video tutorials and plenty of advice on good news package technique.

CHAPTER 7

Doing Investigative Reporting

INTRODUCTION

In the middle of the chaos of the anti-capitalist G20 demonstrations in London in March 2009, Ian Tomlinson, a 47-year-old newspaper vendor, collapsed and died. According to the official police version of the day, he had died of natural causes. Almost immediately allegations were posted on the internet that the police version was misleading. Paul Lewis, a reporter with the *Guardian*, was keen to discover what had happened, but how could he get eyewitness accounts? Tracking down witnesses from a crowd of 10,000 that had long dispersed would not be easy.

All that was known about Ian Tomlinson in the 48 hours after his death was that he had been wearing a Millwall football club T-shirt. Lewis began pursuing two separate lines of inquiry. One involved the old school 'shoe leather' method – re-reading reporter notepads to find names of anyone who may have been in the area who could identify Tomlinson from press photographs (of him lying unconscious on the ground). This yielded one useful eyewitness,

Figure 7.1   Ian Tomlinson moments before falling to the ground after being pushed by a police officer. (Source: Paul Lewis)

who had photographic evidence of Tomlinson alive – with images of him walking in apparent distress 100 yards from where he would eventually collapse. Lewis (2012) then turned to social media – a newer ground-breaking method of investigating. Lewis put pictures of Tomlinson's last few minutes online both through *Guardian* stories and Twitter:

> We became part of a virtual G20 crowd who had coalesced online to question the circumstances of his death. In this environment, valuable contributions to the debate, which were more sceptical in tone than those adopted by other media organisations, worked like online magnets for those who doubted the official version of events. Twitter proved crucial to sharing information with the network of individuals who had begun investigating the death of their own accord.

Lewis had signed up to the social media website two days before the protest and became fascinated with the pattern of movement of 'newsworthy' tweets. For example, two protesters who had witnessed Tomlinson's collapse and who strongly disputed police claims that officers treating him were attacked with bottles uploaded their account of events onto YouTube. Lewis says: 'Through Twitter I discovered there were Flickr albums with hundreds of photographs of the vicinity of this death, and dissemination of blog-posts that speculated on how he may

Figure 7.2   Paul Lewis of the *Guardian* who reported the Tomlinson story. (Source: Paul Lewis)

have died.' Lewis eventually connected with an investment fund manager from New York who had been passing by the demo at the crucial moment and who had been sufficiently interested by the drama to film it. He handed Lewis a video showing Tomlinson being hit from behind with a baton and forcefully pushed to the ground by a police officer. Similar evidence emerged and at the inquest into his death, the coroner ruled that Ian Tomlinson had been 'unlawfully killed'. Later, the police officer identified as pushing him was charged with manslaughter. After a trial he was then found not guilty but was then dismissed from the police for gross misconduct. Lewis utilized the power of public knowledge, eyewitnesses and the sharing ability of social media as a new style of investigative tool now dubbed 'crowdsourcing'.

At its best, journalism has an important role to play in society by, for instance, holding those in power to account. Investigative journalists conduct broad, deep and systematic research to unearth new information of value to the public. Such journalists have often overcome significant obstacles to find worthwhile stories. You may not have thought about becoming an investigative journalist, but the chances are that investigative journalism techniques will play a role in your work at some point and it may be important to know what such reporters do.

An investigative journalist must have an analytical and incisive mind with strong self-motivation to carry on when all doors are closed, when facts are being covered up or falsified. Above all the investigative journalists must the prepared to ask difficult questions. Such journalists develop the expertise to expose the rich and powerful who may be taking advantage of the weak and powerless.

>>OBJECTIVES<<

In this chapter, you will learn:

1 what investigative journalism is;
2 key moments in investigative journalism;
3 key concepts of investigative journalism;
4 what skills investigative journalists use;
5 the impact of new technology on the way such journalism is carried out.

INVESTIGATIVE SKILLS

It is very useful for journalists to have the range of skills described in this chapter as well as the enthusiasm, motivation and sheer bloody mindedness needed for investigations. One of the most important characteristics of the investigative journalist is a particular attitude – it's the journalist who is always sceptical, always questioning. This is jokingly summed up by journalists in the dictum: 'Why is the lying bastard lying to me?' Or equally sardonic the question: What do we investigate? 'If your mother says she loves you, check it out.' So, check your facts and assume nothing. This state of mind can be applied to the most simple of journalistic tasks. For instance, as a reporter you will see hundreds of press releases each designed to persuade you, the reporter, to see something in a particular way and to publish it. Always ask: Why do they want me to see things this way? It may appear to be the simple act of promoting a new product but it may also be to distract you from the real story. Government departments send out press releases drawing your attention to what appears to be their successes but a closer look at the overall report or statistics from which the press release is drawn may reveal a less than rosy picture overall. A lazy journalist will take a press release, cut and paste and publish it, without checking anything. A good journalist will check out the story and think: Are the people sending me this press release trying to distract me from a more important story? What is the real story?

So what is investigative journalism? Investigative journalism is notoriously hard to define and is worth stating what it is *not*. In the first instance, it is the opposite of 'churnalism'. This term, coined by the journalist Nick Davies (2008) in his book *Flat Earth News*, captures the practice of journalists in cash-strapped and time-pressured newsrooms spending too much time rewriting press releases and agency copy and too little time phoning or meeting people. There is no serious attempt to question facts and information, and so material that now goes out as 'news' is material concocted by press officers to give the best impression of their organization. So can we tell you what investigative journalism *is*? There are a number of definitions of investigative journalism and we think the best one is as follows:

> **❝**
>
> An investigative journalist is a man or woman whose profession it is to discover the truth and to identify lapses from it in whatever media may be available. The act of doing this generally is called investigative journalism and is distinct from apparently similar work done by police, lawyers, auditors and regulatory bodies in that it is not limited as to target, not legally founded and closely connected to publicity. (de Burgh, 2008)
>
> **❞**

A SHORT HISTORY OF INVESTIGATIVE JOURNALISM

In his excellent book on investigative journalism Hugo de Burgh (2008) traces the roots of investigative journalism back to government inspectors in China in 700 sent to report on economic and social conditions in the empire. In the UK it goes back at least as far as to the seventeenth-century pamphleteers, William Cobbett and Charles Dickens. There is not enough room here for a detailed history of the vast amount of brilliant investigative journalism carried out in modern times, but the following key investigations illustrate the impact it can have.

Washington Post and Watergate

Modern investigative journalism is often epitomized by the 1970s Watergate scandal, which illustrated the important role journalism can play in society. Bob Woodward (2006) and Carl Bernstein, two reporters on the *Washington Post*, investigated a break-in at the Democratic Party election campaign headquarters in the Watergate building in Washington.

Figure 7.3   The DVD cover of the famous Watergate film (Source: Paul Lashmar)

They uncovered what turned out to be a huge 'dirty tricks' operation designed to discredit the Democratic Party and get the then President Richard Nixon, a Republican, re-elected. Woodward and Bernstein discovered that Nixon had known about the break-in and condoned it. Their work ultimately forced the President to resign. At the core of their inside investigations was a high-level source of inside information known by the pseudonym 'Deep Throat' (a joke using the title of a contemporary popular porn film). The term has since become commonly used for a high-level dissident source.

That a newspaper investigation could reveal the personal corruption of a President of the most powerful nation on earth and force him to resign showed what journalism at its best could do.

Sunday Times 1970s heyday

From the 1970s the *Sunday Times,* under editor Harry Evans, was regarded as the centre of newspaper investigative journalism thanks to investigations such as the Thalidomide scandal where the paper fought legal suppression to publish the facts about the drug, which was responsible for terrible birth defects in children whose mothers had used the drug to reduce sickness in pregnancy. The case has been called Britain's Watergate and ended in victory for the paper via a judgment in the European Court of Human Rights. At that time the *Sunday Times* led a new wave of journalism that inspired many other journalists across the media, and investigative journalism was seen as central to good journalism.

That was some 40 years ago and may sound a little dated, but investigative journalism has continued and there have been more recent high-profile examples.

Private Eye: A must read

Private Eye is a UK fortnightly satirical magazine which sells over 226,000 copies. The editor is Ian Hislop, whom you might know from the BBC TV panel show *Have I Got News for You*. *Private Eye* has been published since the early 1960s and has a great track record for investigative journalism. It will often report stories other media are afraid to make public and has fought off hundreds of legal actions by the rich and powerful. It's become a public institution much read by other journalists and is enjoying a resurgence. Sales of the magazine increased by nearly 10 per cent to the year 2012. Hislop put the magazine's continuing sales success down to its on-going investment in investigative journalism. Hislop (cited in Wilson, 2012) says that while the Leveson Inquiry and the Queen's Diamond Jubilee helped bolster sales, the real driver was that the magazine was 'trying to buck the trend and do investigative journalism, rather than say it is expensive and nobody is interested, because I think they are'.

If you have never read it we recommend you go out and buy yourself a copy.

PHONE HACKING

Perhaps the best-known recent investigative reporting in the UK is Nick Davies's work on the phone-hacking scandal. (He was also instrumental in the *Guardian's* release of the WikiLeaks material on US diplomatic correspondence: see below.) Besides being an exceptional example of investigative journalism the story is made all the more dramatic because of its exposure of appalling behaviour by fellow journalists from the tabloids. In the summer of 2009, Nick Davies and Amelia Hill's article in the *Guardian* made a series of allegations that the phone hacking at the *News of the World* published by News International went far beyond a few cases of intercepting the voicemails of a number of members of the royal family for which the paper's royal editor Clive Goodman was jailed in 2007.

The *News of the World* denied the *Guardian's* claims. The *Guardian* was persistent and on 8 July 2009 reported further evidence of *News of the World* journalists using private investigators to access mobile-phone voicemail accounts. Contrary to denials made by *News of the World* senior management, the *Guardian* alleged that phone-hacking activities were known to a range of senior staff at the tabloid including its then editor Andy Coulson. By this time Coulson had left News International and was Director of Communications for the Conservative Party and one of David Cameron's most trusted advisers. The Conservative Party initially stood by Coulson, who later resigned when a stream of allegations became too embarrassing for his political employers. This story has run and run and led to the Leveson Inquiry into press conduct.

Since then Nick Davies, his colleagues and the *Guardian* have won a string of awards for their pursuit of the hacking story. They were awarded 'Scoop of the Year' for their 'Milly Dowler's phone hacked' story at the

Figure 7.4   *Private Eye*: the satirical magazine is a must-read for investigative journalists. (Source: Private Eye)

Figure 7.5   The journalist that exposed the phone hacking scandal – Nick Davies. (Source: Nick Davies)

Press Awards 2012. This revelation transformed phone hacking from a minor issue to one which led to the closure of the *News of the World*.

WIKILEAKS

The distinctive image of Julian Assange has featured repeatedly in the world's media over recent years. Holder of an Australian passport and mega computer buff, Assange was a founder of the WikiLeaks website. The premise of WikiLeaks is to act as a global online repository for previously secret, classified or private documents about significant subjects (usually governmental, corporate or other) from any country, allow them to be published and made freely available. WikiLeaks has no physical base, but is an informal network of like-minded individuals – usually with high levels of computer literacy – spread across the world. In theory, WikiLeaks' international and online existence protects it from prosecution.

WikiLeaks launched its website in 2006, and claimed a database of more than 1.2 million documents within a year of its launch. WikiLeaks was to achieve world fame in 2010 with a series of disclosures.

In April 2010, a classified United States military video of a 2007 helicopter mission in Baghdad was released. The footage showed a cannon attack against a group of men including two Reuters employees. The Americans mistakenly thought the two men were carrying weapons, which were in fact cameras. The 17-minute sequence is shocking not only for displaying people being obliterated but the casual attitude of the US military involved in the attack.

Figure 7.6   Julian Assange. (Source: www.new-mediadays.com/Peter Erichsen)

Three months later, WikiLeaks released 92,000 documents related to the war in Afghanistan between 2004 and the end of 2009 to the *Guardian*, the *New York Times* and *Der Spiegel*. The documents revealed a huge amount of detail of individual incidents including friendly fire and civilian casualties.

In October 2010, around 400,000 documents relating to the war in Iraq were released. Media coverage focused on many new revelations including evidence that the US government had ignored reports of torture by the Iraqi authorities during the period after the 2003 war,

On 28 November 2010, WikiLeaks and the five major international newspapers started to simultaneously publish the first of 251,287 leaked confidential (but not top secret) diplomatic cables from 274 US embassies around the world, covering 44 years from 28 December 1966. At the time Assange explained that such partnerships with the media gave WikiLeaks' activities more impact than if it simply posted material online and waited for people to seek it out.

The documents provide a worm's eye view and, cumulatively, provided facts that challenged the carefully constructed official narrative. One of the most revealing stories to come out was that US forces kept civilian body counts, despite many denials to the contrary. In 2002 US General Tommy Franks categorically stated: 'We don't do body counts.' As a result of the release of the war logs civilian casualties are now known to be much higher than previously thought. They showed that troops on the ground filed secret field reports over six years of the occupation, purporting to tot up every casualty, military and civilian. These detailed more than 100,000 people killed in Iraq following the US-led invasion, including more than 15,000 deaths that were previously unreported. The mass of leaked documents provided the first detailed tally of Iraqi fatalities by the US military.

Wikileaks produced many insights:

- Saudi Arabia put pressure on the US to attack Iran. Other Arab allies also secretly agitated for military action against Tehran.

- Washington is running a secret intelligence campaign targeted at the leadership of the United Nations, including its Secretary-General Ban Ki-moon and the permanent Security Council representatives from China, Russia, France and the UK.
- Details of the round-the-clock offensive by US government officials, politicians, diplomats and military officers to curb Iran's nuclear ambitions and roll back its advance across the Middle East.

Julian Assange

WikiLeaks was to become itself the story and not just the means of delivery. WikiLeaks founder Julian Assange was accused of sexually assaulting two women while visiting Sweden. Assange fought and lost an extradition order in the UK and then sought asylum in the Ecuadorian Embassy in London. He claims he does not want to go to Sweden as he feared being extradited to the United States to face spying charges. In the United States the American soldier Bradley Manning who was alleged to have leaked all the military material to WikiLeaks was tried but there was no result at the time of writing.

But is WikiLeaks a news media outlet, and is Assange a journalist? Canadian academic Lisa Lynch (2010) says of WikiLeaks:

In a moment when investigative journalism is recognizably in crisis, WikiLeaks has emerged as something of a strange bedfellow to a beleaguered industry, one that holds itself up as a champion of principles many journalists hold dear – freedom of information and the sanctity of the source – yet embeds these principles in a framework of cyber libertarianism that is frequently at odds with the institutional ethics of journalists and editors. Though these ventures seek, like WikiLeaks, to use new technologies to transform the way in which investigative work is produced and distributed, they are firmly committed to traditional journalistic values and see themselves as preserving an industry at least as much as reshaping it. How WikiLeaks fits in along this spectrum of new online ventures and whether the investigative journalism and the industry as a whole will be reshaped or revolutionized in the process is yet to be determined.

THE DEATH OF INVESTIGATIVE JOURNALISM?

It is often suggested that in an era when the accountant is the dominant figure in the media hierarchy, expensive investigations are on the wane. John Mair (in Mair and Keeble, 2011) a journalist and lecturer, says of investigative journalism in 2011:

Its death has been much predicted and is long in coming but Investigative Journalism in Britain is still in rude health.

In the last year alone we have seen Rupert Murdoch catapulted to crisis by 'Hackgate', (FIFA's) Sepp Blatter forced into a corner and Jack Warner out of FIFA, a policeman prosecuted for the unlawful killing of a bystander at the G20 demonstrations in 2009, a quarter of a million previously secret diplomatic cables released by WikiLeaks, Winterbourne View, a 'care' home exposed and closed by 'Panorama' and more wrongdoers brought to justice all thanks to the diggers of the journalistic world.

The Daily Telegraph, not renowned for its anti-Establishment positions, did splendid work on the MP Expenses Scandal in 2009 where it simply bought the purloined data from an insider and exploited it on the page slowly surely and deliberately. Six Members of the Mother of Parliaments are serving or have served prison sentences as a result of those revelations.

The power of the internet has breathed new life into investigative journalism. Online expert Paul Bradshaw (2011) thinks that we may finally be moving past the troubled youth of the internet as a medium for investigative journalism, whereby observers looked at this ungainly form stumbling its way around journalism, and says: 'It will never be able to do this properly.'

Now the internet is growing up, he says,

finding its feet with the likes of Clare Sambrook, Talking Points Memo, PolitiFact and VoiceOfSanDiego all winning awards, while journalists such as Paul Lewis (the death of Ian Tomlinson), Stephen Grey (extraordinary rendition) and James Ball (WikiLeaks) explore new ways to dig up stories online that hold power to account. As these pioneers unearth, tell and distribute their stories in new ways we are beginning to discover just what shape investigative journalism might take in this new medium.

Many reporters work on both diary and breaking stories but also manage to undertake major investigations. One is Ronke Phillips who is correspondent for ITV London, specializing in crime and social affairs. Starting on her school magazine, then university student newspaper, she has been a journalist for 25 years and has worked in print, radio and television. She secured a major exclusive when she found out the real identity of the 'Torso in the Thames' child known as 'Adam'. The resulting film recently won an Amnesty International Award, was shortlisted for a Royal Television Society Award and won three different ITV regional and national awards. In 2002 she won a Royal Television Society Award for her coverage of the verdicts in the Damilola Taylor trial. Phillips (2013) believes that those who want a career in journalism have to be highly motivated:

This is a profession for those who are obsessed by news and current affairs. If you're not waking up thinking 'what is happening today?' If you are not waking up to the *Today* programme, or reading a newspaper, then this is not the profession for you because it is one of those professions where you are expected to a know a lot about everything. It is a drug, news is a drug. Most of the people, the kind of people I admire, male and female are obsessed by news generally, constantly reading books and everything. It is a profession for people who want to absorb knowledge.

She has identified the trait necessary for journalists who do the difficult investigative stories: 'I look to see what the best reporters I know share in common, and I think what it is, is tenacity.'

Figure 7.7   Ronke Phillips, ITV News correspondent. (Source: ITV)

↘TIP

Paris-based journalist Mark Lee Hunter describes the basics of his method of investigative journalism using the slogan, 'Publish it!'

- We discover a subject.
- We create a hypothesis to verify.
- We seek open source data to verify the hypothesis.
- We seek human sources.
- As we collect the data, we organise it so that it is easier to examine, compose into a story, and check.
- We put the data in a narrative order and compose the story.
- We do quality control to make sure the story is right.
- We publish the story, promote and defend it.

His team has drawn up an excellent free guide to hypothesis-based investigative journalism, which complements this chapter by taking you to the next level of investigative skills. It can be found at this link.

KEY CONCEPTS

Key concept 1: fourth estate

A key concept in journalism is the fourth estate and it is particularly relevant to investigative journalism. In media theory the role of the media in a liberal democracy is often characterized as that of the fourth estate. In this journalists are seen as the guardians of the public interest. In the first written reference, Carlyle (1841) quoted the earlier philosopher Edmund Burke as having said: '... there were Three Estates in Parliament; but, in the Reporters' Gallery yonder, there sat a Fourth Estate more important far than they all.' In this context, the other three estates are those of the States: the church, the nobility and the townsmen. The fourth estate concept tasks the media to hold the errant state and powerful to account.

The media draws heavily on its fourth estate role for legitimacy, seeking privileges and exclusions from legislation on the basis of this function. The genre of journalism known as investigative journalism is frequently seen to exercise a fourth estate function. Professor Hugo de Burgh (2008) reminds us:

Investigative journalism has helped bring down governments, imprison politicians, trigger legislation, reveal miscarriages of justice and shame corporations. Even today, when much of the media colludes with power and when viciousness and sensationalism are staples of formerly high-minded media, investigative journalists can stand up for the powerless, the exploited, the truth.

Professor Steve Barnett (cited in Allan, 2005) observes that a vigorous journalistic culture – in particular challenging investigative journalism – is vital for a healthy democracy. He says:

 Without it, executive or corporate wrongdoing will not only continue but can eventually corrupt the body politic. I believe that this process of investigative journalism – of breaking important stories rather than simply reporting or recycling public relations handouts – is under serious threat.

Key concept 2: public interest

A defining feature of much good investigative journalism is that it is in the public interest and is information someone in power does not want published. Victorian politician Lord Acton's famous dictum 'Power tends to corrupt. Absolute power tends to corrupt absolutely' encapsulates why there will always be a need for probing journalists to protect the public interest. Journalists will sometime use methods that would otherwise be described as dubious or even illegal to get information – methods which can only be justified if they serve the public interest.

Defining the public interest for journalism is not easy. It is not the same as what interests the public. The public interest is most simply seen as important information that should be available to the public to help them make informed decisions in a democratic society. Revealing corruption among the rich and powerful comfortably fits this category.

The phone-hacking scandal has resulted in close scrutiny of the more unseemly practices of investigative journalists and led to calls for a much clearer definition of public interest. Editor of the *Guardian* Alan Rusbridger says in his 2011 Orwell Lecture:

 Why is this agreement over 'the public interest' so crucial? Because, in the end, the public interest, and how we argue it, is not only crucial to the sometimes arcane subject of privacy – it is crucial to every argument about the future of the press, the public good it delivers and why, in the most testing of economic times, it deserves to survive.

METHODS

A characteristic of investigative journalism is that it is not usually driven by the daily news agenda. Unlike general news reporters, investigative journalists tend not work on the daily news diary but are freed to follow up their story leads. A good investigative journalist will produce a story that *makes* the news agenda.

THE IMPORTANCE OF RESEARCH

Gavin MacFadyen of the Centre for Investigative Journalism identifies in-depth research as a key feature distinguishing investigative journalism from other reporting. He says UK investigative journalists have to be particularly diligent in their research: 'Because of the severity of the UK libel law, the standard required proof and the fear of prosecution are significantly higher than in many other metropolitan countries.' (in de Burgh, 2008)

Another vital ingredient is that this research should result in a highly accurate piece of journalism, usually containing information that someone, typically in a position of power, does not want made public. It should stand the test of time and be in the public interest.

Jonathan Calvert (in de Burgh 2008) a highly experienced investigative journalist, says:

> Some stories you make five calls on, some twenty. When you are making a hundred, that's investigative journalism. The story may land in your lap – it's the substantiation that makes it an investigative story, because when you realize people are lying to you, blocking you, then you have to find different ways of getting hold of information and it can take a lot longer. Also you have to be careful when you are making serious allegations against people, then the evidence really matters.

Investigative journalists will tell you it is one of the most difficult forms of journalism but also the most exciting and satisfying. They will tell you there is nothing like turning the results of a meticulous and difficult investigation into a big story which everyone including their media rivals talks about.

A fantastic example of what can be done with assiduous research is that of 'Brown Moses', who exposed Syrian arms trafficking from his front room. Brown Moses in the online name for Eliot Higgins, a Leicester-based blogger, whose monitoring of weapons used in conflict has been taken up by media and human rights groups. As an unemployed finance and admin worker his expertise lies in compiling spreadsheets. He has broken some of the most important stories on the Syrian conflict. His analysis of Syrian weapons, which began as a hobby, and is based on analysing the pictures from video and online, is now frequently cited by human rights groups and has led to questions in parliament. Higgins's discovery of a new batch of Croatian weapons in the hands of Syrian rebels blew the lid on a covert international operation to arm the opposition. To read the full story follow this link.

UNDERCOVER REPORTING

In the contemporary world the corrupt, the immoral and criminal are much more careful than they used to be. Many years of effective investigative reporting have made the wrongdoer ever more cautious about talking to reporters. Such people are also much more careful about creating documentation that would expose their activities. One technique for getting round this is to send a reporter posing as someone who the target might be candid with – perhaps posing as another arms buyer to trap an illegal arms dealer. This is known as undercover reporting.

Perhaps one of the best-known and the most controversial UK undercover reporters is Mazher Mahmood, who spent 20 years working for *News of the World*. He has been dubbed 'Britain's most notorious undercover reporter'. The *News of the World* claimed Mahmood has brought over 250 criminals to justice although this has been challenged as inflated. Mahmood is also known as the 'fake sheikh', alluding to the disguise he adopted as a sheikh in order to gain his target's trust.

His most famous exposés include posing as an Indian businessman to expose a match fixing by members of the Pakistan cricket team. In 2010 he recorded a bookie Mazhar Majeed naming Pakistani cricketers Mohammad Amir, Mohammad Asif, Salman Butt and Kamran Akmal as having committed spot-fixing during Pakistan's 2010 tour of England; the team was accused of deliberately bowling three no-balls. Mahmood's targets have included society figures, Sophie, Countess of Wessex in 2001 and more recently Sarah, Duchess of York in 2010. In normal reporting you must always identify yourself as a reporter and state that anything said to you could be published. We talk about this in Chapter 14. Undercover reporting should not be done by the inexperienced or without the support of a major news organization because you must have a robust reason that will stand up in court and in front of regulators. Taking such a course is usually agreed by an experienced group of journalists and an in-house lawyer.

Undercover reporting can carry a lot of risk. If the reporter is caught with undercover equipment they can be put in a very vulnerable position. The decision to go undercover is always carefully thought about and the risk assessed by experienced editors and journalists.

There's a good site in the US about undercover reporting at this link.

FREEDOM OF INFORMATION

The Freedom of Information (FOI) Act is an excellent journalistic tool that affords access to information held by thousands of public bodies in England, Wales and Northern Ireland. Scotland has its own FOI Act, which is very similar. Freedom of Information is the presumption that the public is entitled to all information produced by government about the way it goes about its business, except where there is an exceptionally good reason not to provide it. Journalist Heather Brooke is the doyen of FOI users, best known for helping expose the 2009 parliamentary expenses scandal which culminated in the resignation of House of Commons Speaker Michael Martin. Since 2004 Brooke had been using the FOI not to request the release of MPs' expenses. The House of Commons authorities resisted but, in May 2008, were forced into full disclosure of MPs' second homes allowances after Brooke won a case in the High Court demanding such information be made public.

The material effectively resulted in the jailing of six MPs and the discrediting of many more, and has had an enormous impact on the public perception of the work of Parliament. In 2010, BBC Four broadcast a dramatized account of Brooke's campaign for disclosure of MPs' expenses entitled *On Expenses*.

The FOI Act creates the right to ask any public body for all the information they have on any subject you choose. In theory, unless there's a good reason, the organization must provide the information within 20 working days. Anyone can make a request for information – there are no restrictions on age, nationality, or where the requester lives. You can ask for any information at all – but some information might be withheld to protect various interests which are allowed for by the Act. If this is case, the public authority must tell you why they have withheld information.

How to make a request

Write to (or email) the public body and include:

- your name;
- an address where you can be contacted; and
- a description of the information that you want.

The system is not perfect and there are problems with its administration. Heather Brooke (2012) suggested ways of improving it:

> Firstly, it must be made easier to conduct public interest investigations. It should not take five years of a person's life to find out the most basic facts of how public officials spend the public's money (MPs' expenses). And here we find in the UK, the crucial ingredient necessary for responsible journalism missing: easily accessible public records.

An excellent guide to freedom of information is Montague and Amin (2012).

SOURCES AND WHISTLEBLOWERS

Lots of people give you information. Sometimes they are well placed, knowledgeable and provide information over a period of time. These are called sources, and are vital to journalism. They often want to remain anonymous. 'Go to jail rather than reveal your source' is the one immutable rule of good journalism. It's the fixed point on the ethical firmament to which all other journalism principles are anchored, and reflects the highest aspiration of reporting – to inform the public whatever the personal cost to the journalist. As media commentator Tim Luckhurst says: 'The legend of Deep Throat runs deep and, to British journalists, it conveys a solitary absolute: Confidential sources must never be identified while they are alive.'

But what exactly is a source, why do some journalists take the 'go to jail' stance, and how do you protect sources? Most are best described as a 'confidential source', to distinguish from other sources of information.

Sources can vary from a police officer telling you about corruption within their force, to a civil servant revealing a cover-up, to a worker telling you about health and safety breaches in the company they work for.

Guardian reporter Paul Lewis (2012) makes the point that in the pre-internet age journalists mostly sought sources, now with social media, sources can seek out journalists. He does warn that people who approach you via social media are not sources, as often you have no real idea who they are. 'They are only online entities. They don't become sources until you have met them.'

There are also whistleblowers. Gomez-Mejia et al. (2007) define whistleblowing as an occurrence in which a current or former employee discloses illegal, immoral or illegitimate practices under the control of the employer to persons or organizations that may be able to take corrective action.

Some go public and some remain anonymous knowing that if they get caught they will be sacked and find it hard to get another job. Whistleblowers are rare, in our experience, as most people worry about their mortgage which stops them whistleblowing even when they are angry about something their organization is doing. In certain situations, especially in some countries, whistleblowing may result in jail or even death. It is never to be taken lightly. It is rare for someone to blunder into whistleblowing as US soldier Bradley Manning appears to have done with WikiLeaks. Finding and 'running' a confidential source is one of the most difficult tasks facing a reporter. Often whistleblowers have a complex relationship with the journalist, it can be both symbiotic and adversarial. On the one hand, they serve as sources of story ideas and information which can end up as high-profile exposés, and some whistleblowers feel empowered by media exposure to pursue justice in cases of institutional wrong-doing. On the other hand, journalists are often suspicious of whistleblowers' claims and self-interest in the case. They in turn are often concerned about how revelations might affect their personal and professional lives (Lewis, 2004).

The journalist's right to protect confidential sources is a principle recognized in European and British law. If your source has provided you with good information, and your story has been splashed, assume that someone will investigate. They might be an unscrupulous private investigator, the police or even the security services. The first thing any of these agents will do is try and access your phone records to see who you have been phoning and texting. Next they will be after your emails.

Protecting your source

If there are compromising contacts between you and your source then this is high risk. Even Googling your source's name to check them out can leave corroborative evidence. There are some simple tips: try to avoid electronic communication with your source; meet face to face; turn off both of your phones long before meeting (otherwise your phone can be used to approximate your location using the location of the phone cell area you are in); and try to meet away from CCTV cameras. If you do use phone or email, do not use names. The best method of communication is to use two pay-as-you-go phones that are not traceable. Give one of the phones to your source and explain that the phone should only be used for communicating with you. If you use email, create anonymous Hotmail-style accounts, but not on your personal computer. To find out more read Lashmar (2008b).

It is vital that journalists protect their sources. Every source revealed will put other potential sources off talking to the media.

Two excellent articles on whistleblowing in the UK are:

TIP

Investigative journalists record everything as they find out about the story and make copious notes. Write down everything, however unimportant it may seem at the time. If you cannot write your notes immediately, write them as soon as possible. Record every conversation you can.

COMPUTER-ASSISTED REPORTING

Computer-assisted reporting (CAR) is widely used in America. Exactly when journalists started using databases is hazy. Some say it dates back to 1952 when US TV channel CBS used experts with a main-frame computer to try and predict the outcome of the presidential election. Others say that it didn't really take off as a technique until 1967.

In the UK it has only taken off relatively recently. In the US, government and non-governmental organization (NGO) data is released in such a way that it can be easily analysed using programs. In the UK, data is often piecemeal and incompatible with earlier datasets. The constraints imposed by the Data Protection Act do not help and sites such as data.gov.uk, whilst useful, do not always contain key information. Often the only way to obtain really useful data is to use the Freedom of Information Act or to collect it yourself.

One of the authors of this book was an early adopter of CAR. According to a 2010 article in *Television* magazine:

The original pioneers of computer assisted reporting in the UK are two well respected invest-igative journalists: Paul Lashmar and Richard Oliver who in 1998 and 1999 earned a number of front page stories on the *Independent on Sunday* and *The Observer* by conducting the first comprehensive comparison of local council performance. It was an incredible accomplish-ment given that the Freedom of Information Act was yet to come into force.

So what role can CAR play in investigative journalism, the writer of the *Television* article Elena Egawhary (2010) asked. 'The answer is simple: it might not be sexy, it might not always be visual, but it is a source, and like all sources of information you just don't know how explosive the information they hold might be until you choose to examine it.' Computers are now absolutely integral to successful investigative journalism and CAR is closely linked to data journalism, which we talk about in Chapter 1. Computers and datasets have given us the opportunity to explore new areas that were once beyond the resources of investigative journalists.

CROWDSOURCING: THE INSIGHT OF CROWDS

At the beginning of this chapter we gave an example of a reporter tapping the knowledge of the public on-line to crack an investigation. It's a technique that has been dubbed 'crowdsourcing'. Using the resources of the public – or as author James Surowiecki (2004) put it, 'The Wisdom of Crowds' – is a 180-degree turn from the classic idea of the investigative journalist as the solitary figure working behind the scenes in great secrecy to find out what has happened in controversial events. Surowiecki proposed that groups of people can bring together information and experience that result in decisions which, he argues, are often better than could have been made by any single member of the group.

During the 2009 MPs' expenses scandal the *Guardian* asked the public to help it sort through nearly half a million documents released by the House of Commons in an effort to establish what individual MPs had claimed and whether such claims were legitimate. The *Guardian* had 458,832 pages of documents. Over 33,000 *Guardian* website users reviewed 226,170 pages and gave useful information. An excellent example of what can be done comes from journalist and lecturer Paul Bradshaw.

HelpMeInvestigate

Paul Bradshaw is a founder of the helpmeinvestigate.com website which uses new investigative techniques including crowdsourcing to help with its investigations. Bradshaw has suggested the model shown in Figure 7.8 for successful online investigative journalism. It has certainly worked on his website.

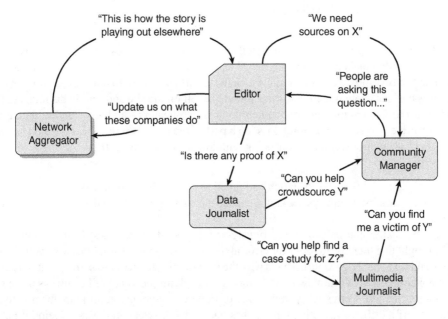

Figure 7.8   The online investigation team. (Source: Paul Bradshaw)

One of the many highlights of the 2012 Olympic Games was the Olympic torch being taken through many of the UK's cities. The torch carriers – we were told – would largely be chosen from people who had done something exceptional and altruistic for the community and by way of public recognition. In June 2012 Bradshaw revealed on the site that a man called Rupert Soames would have the opportunity to carry the Olympic torch through Wandsworth. It turned out that he is chief executive of the company supplying energy to the 2012 Games (see http://helpmeinvestigate.com/).

Concerned that this did not seem in keeping with the ideals of the Olympic Games, Bradshaw dug a little deeper. It turned out Soames was one of four of the company's seven executive directors to be found among the list of Olympic torch-bearers – although not one mentioned the company in their nomination story. Another colleague was also a torch-bearer. Bradshaw pointed out that Olympics Minister Hugh Robertson was on the record that the Olympic organizers LOCOG had written to sponsors and 'discouraged them from allowing executives to run with the torch and encouraged them to find as many local champions as possible'. Bradshaw described the Olympic torch-bearer data as a data journalist's dream. There were over 6,000 torch-bearers listed on the London 2012 website, with 5,500 nomination stories. This made it one of the best places to compare the claims of the organizers with the reality on the ground. So, with the help of the website Scraperwiki, Bradshaw grabbed data from thousands of pages on Olympic torch-bearers. From the early days of planning for the torch relay, organizers LOCOG had said that there would be 8,000 torch-bearers all with 'inspirational' stories, and 90 per cent of those 8,000 places would be open to the general public. The rest would be allocated by the International Olympic Committee (IOC), British Olympics Authority, and 'core partners' – sponsors. Bradshaw opened the data to the public to see if they could help identify corporate torch-bearers.

Bradshaw's team found many stories of torch-bearers who could not be defined as 'inspirational' but, rather, came from a commercial background.

> The data alone wasn't always enough to tell these stories: in many cases, the work moved into identifying individuals and verifying their identity. We received anonymous tip-offs through the Help Me Investigate Olympics site which led to further stories. In one case, a photographer who was curious about one torch-bearer found himself on the site and sent in his images. This sent me off to find photographs of other corporate torch-bearers – and this wonderful image of two executives exchanging a 'torch kiss' on a part of the route where a local boy had recently been told his torch-bearer place was being withdrawn. (Bradshaw, 2012)

The local newspaper and BBC radio station had failed to pick up on who they were. It is a clear example of how a good journalist is always looking beneath the surface for the real story. That's investigative journalism.

We take investigative journalism very seriously as it is one of the toughest forms of journalism. You have to get it right and there is no room for error in investigative journalism, otherwise your news organization may end up in the High Court. That's why the tone of this chapter is so serious. But it is also one of the most enjoyable forms of journalism, as doing a very difficult job very well is always more satisfying than doing a routine job. Let us tell you that one of the great moments in all journalism is to be found when you pull off a difficult investigation that has taken blood, sweat and tears – seeing it published is the most exhilarating act of journalism.

NEW INVESTIGATIVE JOURNALISM MODELS

This chapter has explained the basics of investigative journalism and revealed some of the new techniques that are increasingly being used by organizations such as the following:

- ProPublica: www.propublica.org. Founded by the philanthropists Herbert and Marion Sandler. ProPublica is an independent, non-profit newsroom that produces investigative journalism in the public interest 'that shines a light on exploitation of the weak by the strong'.
- Spot.us: http://spot.us. This is an example of an open-source crowd-funded project where members of the public can fund reporters to investigate an issue. Stories begin with tips from the public or pitches from journalists about issues they would like to cover.
- Bureau of Investigative Journalism: www.thebureauinvestigates.com. Founded in 2010 in the UK with a start-up fund from The David & Elaine Potter Foundation. The Bureau produces investigations for press and broadcast media with the aim of educating the public and the media on the value of honest reporting. One of its many big hits was an investigation into the lobbying firm Bell Pottinger, published in the *Independent*.

>>Summary<<

1 Many journalists will not become and perhaps have no interest in becoming investigative journalists. A very small percentage of journalists do. However, it is important to know why investigative journalist exists and what they do.
2 Investigative skills may be something you use rarely but it is good to know about them.
3 Investigative journalism acts to monitor the rich and powerful, protect the weak, deter corruption and inform the public, and is therefore the highest form of journalism.
4 But there are negatives: investigative journalism can be expensive to undertake and even more expensive in the law courts if you get it wrong. It can anger powerful people and may leave the journalist threatened with prison or worse.
5 Investigative journalism has not died out despite predictions. New technology is being used to revitalize this kind of journalism with new approaches. We hope that wherever you practise your journalism you keep in mind the spirit of investigative journalism and remain prepared to ask that difficult question or probe for the real story behind a press release.

EXERCISES

1 Identify three recent investigation-based stories where social media played a major part in cracking the story. Do not use any examples from this book. Then compare the cases and suggest which situations benefit most from using social media.
2 Go onto the website Helpmeinvestigate.com. Find a story that interests you and see if you can help by finding information that will help that investigation be published.

FURTHER READING

Bradshaw, Paul, Online Journalism Blog: www.onlinejournalismblog.com
   A constant source of new information about investigative journalism online and data journalism.
Davies, Nick. 2008. *Flat Earth News: An Award-winning Reporter Exposes Falsehood, Distortion and Propaganda in the Global Media*. London: Chatto & Windus.
   Excellent, controversial discussion of the state of journalism by the *Guardian* newspaper reporter who exposed phone hacking.
de Burgh, Hugo (ed.). 2008. *Investigative Journalism: Context and Practice*. Oxford: Routledge.
   The core textbook for investigative journalism.
Grey, Stephen. 2006. *Ghost Plane: The Inside Story of the CIA's Secret Rendition Programme*. London: Hurst & Company.
   One of the best investigations in recent years.
Hunter, Mark et al. 2011. *Story Based Inquiry: A Manual for Investigative Journalists*: http://unesdoc.unesco.org/images/0019/001930/193078e.pdf
Pilger, John (ed). 2000. *Tell Me No Lies: Investigative Journalism that Changed the World*. London: Pan.
   John Pilger continues to produce some of the best investigations for ITV, *New Statesman* magazine and the *Daily Mirror*.
The Centre for Investigative Journalism: QR Link www.tcij.org/
   This is what it says on the packet – the centre for good investigative practice in the UK. It runs a series of courses in investigative journalism.

SECTION 3

Building Communities, Interaction and Entrepreneurship

Social Media and Building Online Communities   141

Blogging and Participatory Journalism   160

Freelancing and Entrepreneurial Journalism   178

Outputting for Web, Smartphone and Tablet   196

CHAPTER 8

Social Media and Building Online Communities

INTRODUCTION

It was during the Arab Spring of 2011 that American journalist Andy Carvin realized the importance of Twitter as a reporting tool. Carvin curated user-generated content published on social media sites from dozens of activists and citizens in the Arab world. He outputted this to provide a real-time commentary of events to his thousands of Twitter account followers. Social media site Mashable (Peters, 2011) described this a game-changing moment in news reporting:

> What set Carvin apart was not only his volume of Tweets—his record is 1,200 Tweets in 48 hours, according to The Guardian—but also his recognition of fellow Twitter users as experts. He wouldn't hesitate to Tweet unverified information and ask his Twitter followers to help him determine its accuracy.

The press dubbed the Arab Spring the 'Twitter revolution', a rather simplistic headline for a complex chain of events. It is certainly true that Twitter became one of the main tools to share information in the region, so much so that various governments tried to prevent citizens from accessing it.

In contrast to government supporters, pro-democracy groups in the Arab region were led by young and technically literate students. They soon realized the impact of having videos of their protests, which often ended in violent suppression by security forces, broadcast by the world's media. Mainstream media, particularly the BBC and CNN, were closely monitoring Twitter for stories about the protests.

Protests were happening in many cities across the Arab world simultaneously. News organizations, finding their resources stretched, were often unable to get their reporters into the countries. They welcomed the free video footage supplied by the pro-democracy groups.

Other news stories where social media provided journalists with valuable content include:

- Mumbai terrorist attacks (2008);
- G20 protests (2009);
- Hudson River plane crash (2009);
- Iran elections (2009);
- UK Summer riots (2011);
- Woolwich murder (2013).

How do journalists use social media sites like Twitter, Facebook, Google+ and YouTube?

- Social media is a tool for news distribution. It acts as a tool of personal recommendation and for the sharing of news. We can see it as an extension of Negroponte's (1995) concept of the personalized newspaper – the 'Daily Me'.
- Social media is a wonderful research tool. It allows journalists to make connections with the communities that they write about (although we should not assume all social groups use it).
- Social media allows our users to feel a sense of involvement in the newsgathering process. It is a good way to build loyalty to a media brand.

Social media trends change very fast and it is worth reflecting on the social sites that you use today and the devices you use to access them. It is worth carrying out a small survey of colleagues or classmates to find out what sites they use and how they are used. It is worth thinking about the balance of content creation to content consumption – some people use social media exclusively just to read what others produce. To what extent do they use it to read news and what topics of news are most popular? Are these stories in text, video or audio formats? Do they share or chat about the news with friends? There is plenty to consider in this developing area of journalistic and academic research.

>>OBJECTIVES<<

In the chapter, you will learn:

- what social media is and how it relates to terms such as Web 2.0 and citizen journalism;
- how the news is now a two-way conversation between journalists and users;
- how to set up a social media page to interact with your users;
- why information obtained on social media sites must be carefully verified.

SO WHAT *EXACTLY* IS SOCIAL MEDIA?

Social media is a broad group of websites and internet-based applications that allow for the creation and sharing of content.

Most definitions of social media highlight two key elements:

1 *Participation*: There is a multi-directional flow of communication where users may produce as well as consume content.
2 *Community*: People gather in communities based on shared interests. Status or social importance is a key ingredient in any community. We can achieve importance by cultivating a long list of friends or followers. Content, such as a link to a story or funny video, can act as social capital when shared among a group of friends who find the content significant. If your friends re-post the link, that only enhances your status within a group. When content is widely shared on the internet, it is said to go viral.

As journalists we don't just use social media as a tool of personal communication or reading news shared by our friends, but we must actively take part in communities of shared interests.

The social and community elements run deeply through network technology. The roots of current social media sites, like Facebook, can be traced back to a time before the invention of the web in the early 1990s. Text-based message boards, known as Usenet newsgroups, and Internet Relay Chat (IRC), where people chatted in real time, were massively popular in the days before the web:

- *Newsgroups*: These text-based public message boards acted as forums for public debate and criticism. Newsgroups were a method of asynchronous communication, meaning that participants did not have to be online at the same time to communicate.
- *IRC*: Internet Relay Chat is a form of synchronous (simultaneous) communication – that's to say that participants need to be online at the same time. Conversations occur in real time and move fast, so early IRC users used abbreviations which are also used in SMS text-speak today – LOL (laugh out loud), GR8 (great) and POV (point of view). It was used in 1991 to discuss a breaking news story of a coup d'état in Moscow, Russia.

Modern social media sites, like Facebook, offer a range of ready to use, community tools – such as chat and message boards which share similarities with many of the pre-web tools discussed above. Social media sites can be divided into five broad groups. In each case it's worth considering what modes of communication are represented in each, and how and why users participate in them:

- *Content communities*: Multimedia content sites such as YouTube (video) and Flickr (photos) allow for the upload and sharing of UGC. In 2012, 60 hours of video was uploaded every minute to YouTube. That is one hour of video every second!
- *Collaborative projects*: These include text-based wikis and collaborative journalism. The most famous and largest wiki of them all is the free online encyclopaedia Wikipedia.
- *Friendship community sites*: These include profile-based sites such as Facebook and Google+.
- *Location-based services*: The GPS function on phones uses satellite technology to recognize where in the world a user is located. This is used in many social media applications, mostly to allow people to find friends who are in their local area.
- *Virtual worlds*: Many multiplayer online virtual games, particularly on the PlayStation games console, contain a social element where players can talk online with each other.

Social media as a term is closely associated with UGC and with:

- *Web 2.0*: loosely defined as web applications that allow for sharing of content, participation or collaboration, e.g. content communities such as Blogger.com, photo sites such as Flickr or video sites such as YouTube include technology that allow for sharing of content. These sites include technology that is Web 2.0 as well as often being social communities.

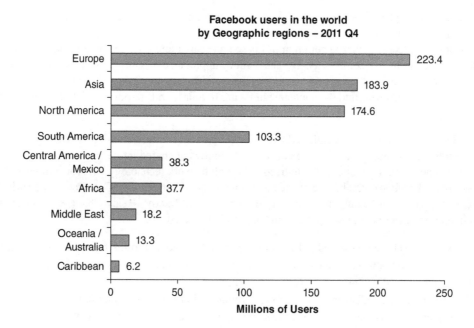

Figure 8.1　Europe and Asia have some of the largest numbers of Facebook users. (Source: Internet World Stats)

- *Citizen journalism*: when amateurs carry out roles normally associated with professional journalists, e.g. a reporter or video journalist role. The concept of citizen journalism is highly contested. To say that members of the public, without any formal training, can assume the role of journalist is highly controversial. In reality, many amateurs producing content online don't purport to act as journalists. A more accurate phrase is that of pro-am (professional amateur) or amateurs with media skills.

HOW DOES SOCIAL MEDIA RELATE TO JOURNALISM?

We all know that there is a lot of rubbish on social media that has little news value. The first reason why we need to take an interest in social media is simply that it is where our users are. From a business perspective, we can't afford to ignore the fact that these sites are very popular with our users.

　　Social media is a major aggregator of news content, particularly among the young. The 18–24-year-old readership is traditionally one of the most difficult groups for newspaper to reach. That's to say social media has become the primary way that large numbers of people consume and share news whether this is news about their friends' personal lives or news about the world around them.

Social media as horizontal media

We can view social media as being a form of horizontal media where information is shared from user to user as part of a global network without the need for traditional media. Jay Rosen (Bartlett, 2011) describes the 'great horizontal', where people are connected to others 'as effectively as they are connected up to big media.' This is in contrast to mainstream media that is traditionally viewed as being vertical media, where journalists 'pass down' information to an audience consisting mostly of passive receivers of content.

With horizontal media, communication is globally fragmented and dispersed. It lacks centrality – that's to say that there is not a central point where content is produced. This can make social media a confusing environment to study.

Social media challenges the role of journalists and editors as information gatekeepers

Social media content often bypasses the traditional information gatekeepers – that's the journalists who work in mainstream media who, at one point, were the main controllers of the flow of information to the public. Social media can be viewed as being more democratic than traditional media as any user can publish news and respond to what people have posted.

Traditionally, newspapers operated in a manner where roles were clearly defined:

- reader: the consumer of content;
- journalist: the producer of content;
- editor: the selector of content and arbitrator of quality control.

With social media, users switch between different roles at different times.

It allows users to scrutinize the news publishing process

The Economist (2011) states: 'Thanks to the rise of social media, news is no longer gathered exclusively by reporters and turned into a story but emerges from an ecosystem in which journalists, sources, readers and viewers exchange information.' It's now common for journalists to use social media in a range of situations to communicate with their users. Dan Gillmor, author of *We the Media* in 2004, commonly regarded as the classic text on the rise of citizen journalism, described the news agenda as becoming 'conversational' and 'open to question'.

To take part in a conversation online we need to develop listening skills, something that may not come naturally to some journalists. 'Journalists need to give up their self-adoration as the authority on the topics they write about,' said Michele McLellan, a journalist and consultant (in Lavrusik, 2010). She adds: 'Members of any community are the experts in what they are experiencing and seeing on given topics.'

In October 2011, the *Guardian* newspaper began an extraordinary experiment where it published its editorial news list for all to see. The news list is the stories a newspaper is researching or planning to run and is normally kept a closely guarded secret. You may wish to think about the risks and rewards of seeking help from our users in this way. One risk was that rival journalists could pinch the *Guardian*'s ideas.

Social media is used as the 'second screen'

Academics have become interested in the interplay between various media platforms. Social media is now being used as what's known as the 'second screen'. People multi-task, watching a live TV show, while simultaneously taking part in a live debate about what's happening on Twitter, using tablets and smartphones, all from the comfort of their armchair.

Figure 8.2   Zeebox: the iPad app allows multi-tasking TV viewers to chat in real time. (Source: ZeeBox)

Media theorist Aleks Krotoski (2010) highlights how online interactions occur around live television broadcasts: 'Pre-Web, if we weren't all watching the TV or the event in the same physical space, we would have waited until we ran into friends at the water cooler the day after to talk about it … Now, because of online tools, we are able share and receive instant, real-time feedback to something with a lot of people.' Tablet and smartphone apps, like ZeeBox (www.zeebox.com), allow those watching live TV shows to chat and discuss it in real time. In this respect, we can view such technology as bringing people together around the virtual water cooler in online communities of interest.

A 2010 study by social media company Live Talkback of free-to-air TV found that ITV's *The X Factor* talent show was the most tweeted TV programme in the UK, accounting for 3.7 million of the 38.7 million tweets over a four-month period in 2010.

Social media is *not* mass media

Some journalists are rather fond of criticizing the content that appears on social media sites for its supposedly amateur nature. It is certainly true that much of the content is very poor quality – photos and videos may be poorly shot, gossip replaces fact, and writing may lack basic spelling or grammar skills. However, the reality is that social media is *not* like mass media. Most of the content that appears hasn't been created by media professionals for general consumption or with the purpose of being viewed by a large audience. They are 'private conversations' that are aimed at a few friends – the kind of gossip that is shared in pubs and bars across the land. Of course, depending on the social media site used, these 'private conversations' can be very public indeed.

Clay Shirky warns us (2009) that to view social media as being similar to mass media is to miss the point. He states: 'Most of what gets created on any given day [on social media] is just ordinary stuff of life – gossip, little updates, thinking out loud.'

Shirky says prior to the internet, when we talked about media we were talking about two different things: broadcast media and communications media. He says:

> Broadcast media, such as radio and television but also newspapers and movies (the term refers to a message being broadly delivered from a central place, whatever the medium), are designed to put messages out for all to see (or in some cases, for all buyers and subscribers to see). Broadcast media are shaped, conceptually, like a megaphone, amplifying a one-way message from one sender to many receivers. Communications media, from telegrams to phone calls to faxes, are designed to facilitate two-way conversations. Conceptually, communications media are like a tube; the message put into one end is intended for a particular recipient at the other end.

He continues: 'Most user generated content (UGC) is created as communication in small groups, but since we're so used to communications media and broadcast media being mixed together, we think that everyone is now broadcasting. This is a mistake.'

Clearly, only a tiny fraction of UGC that appears on social media sites represent, in any way, traditional journalistic news values. However, that is not to say that social media is irrelevant to us as journalists. Twitter and Facebook users will share news from the mainstream news sites that they find significant with their lists of friends or followers.

Eyewitnesses at the scene of a news event may share content with their circle of friends or followers on social media. Journalists now monitor social media as big stories develop for photographs, video and eyewitness accounts posted to sharing sites such as Flickr, Instagram, YouTube, Twitter and Facebook. They also use social media to proactively post requests for help with news stories.

Social media is a great way to build an audience for your journalism. It is essential for any trainee who seeks a career in TV news to post video to YouTube and create a channel. They often publicize their work by posting links to their videos on Facebook and Twitter in a deliberate attempt to have it go viral (become widely shared) and generate a large online following.

HOW JOURNALISTS USE SOCIAL MEDIA

Social media is a great communication tool as it can allow our users to understand more about the news production process, the stories that we are working on and can encourage user involvement. To achieve this, it requires a degree of personality, fun and authenticity in the way we communicate in social media which is very different to how we write as journalists.

As journalists, we have authority and a level of trust in the public domain which makes our use of social media potentially risky. 'Post in haste and repent at leisure' is perhaps the best warning when it comes to using social media sites to express personal opinions on controversial topics.

The views we express on social media may be confused with those of the publication or broadcast outlet that you work for. It's important to state clearly on the social media account whether it's being used for personal or professional reasons. Many media companies have policies on how social media is to be used. The *New York Times* in its Facebook Ethics Guide advises its journalists (Koblin, 2009):

> Anything you post online can and might be publicly disseminated, and can be twisted to be used against you by those who wish you or *The Times* ill—whether it's text, photographs, or video. That includes things you recommend on TimesPeople or articles you post to Facebook and Digg, content you share with friends on MySpace, and articles you recommend through TimesPeople. It can also include things posted by outside parties to your Facebook page, so keep an eye on what appears there. Just remember that we are always under scrutiny by a magnifying glass and that the possibilities of digital distortion are virtually unlimited, so always ask yourself, could this be deliberately misconstrued or misunderstood by somebody who wants to make me look bad?

Social media needs to be embedded in the news production process at every stage from researching stories to output. However, while is an important reporting tool, it shouldn't become a distraction. Traditional ways of getting information – principally getting out into the community and talking to real people face-to-face – remain as important as ever.

News tip-offs

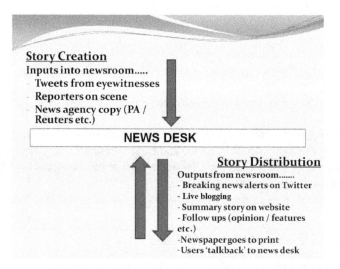

Figure 8.3   Twitter is used in addition to traditional sources of information to help journalists cover breaking news. Journalists use Twitter to break stories and respond to feedback in a two-way flow of communication to and from the news desk. (Source: Steve Hill)

A Social media story: A fire at a university halls of residence

1   The tip-off: A Twitter user posts a message to his followers about a fire at a university hall of residence. As journalists we must be aware that Twitter is first a personal media and users don't automatically assume that their posts are news or will be of interest to media. Spotting a story like this, in the vast amount of content posted online, is very challenging and it relies on journalists monitoring their patch closely. We also don't know much about this story yet (or whether it is news). We don't know if it's a large or small fire. Has someone just burnt their toast? We could message the user to find out more and monitor other channels.

Figure.8.4   A Twitter user posts a message to his followers about a fire at a university hall of residence. (Source: Twitter/Jimmy Norval/Alex Loughlin)

2 A photo tweeted: A Twitter user has now posted a picture that appears to show a small fire in a building. As journalists, we will need to verify the authenticity of the image. How we go about doing this is discussed later in this chapter.

3 A search using Twinitor: Twinitor (www.twinitor.com), a twitter search engine, allows us to search the text of recent tweets. This reveals a large number of tweets about the fire mostly from students who have been evacuated. We can post messages to make contact with Twitter users at the scene. A large number of tweets on the same incident can help us corroborate the story, although no official sources, such as the emergency services, have commented.

4 A statement from the university who run the halls posted on Twitter: 'The University can confirm there has been a fire. No one has been harmed and the university is working to re-home those affected.'

5 A statement from the fire service. The local fire authority has posted the following information on their website:

   o A call was made to emergency services at 20:29 tonight.
   o A fire was on the 5th floor.
   o It was in a kitchen and bedroom area of student accommodation.
   o Five fire appliances and one specialist unit attended .
   o It involved 25 fire officers and four senior officers.
   o Fire services left the scene at 21:50 (1 hour and 20 minutes on the scene).

6 News coverage: BBC local news and the *Southern Daily Echo* in Southampton cover the story.

Figure 8.5   An eyewitness tweets an image of the fire. (Twitter/Danielle King)

Figure 8.6   The *Southern Daily Echo* site reports the story. (Source: *Southern Daily Echo*)

INTERVIEW: ZOE KLEINMAN, TECHNOLOGY REPORTER, BBC

What are the most useful social media sites for journalists?

I think Twitter is an incredibly useful tool for journalists. It is instant, accessible and succinct. It's the closest platform to a free-for-all grapevine at the moment.

Figure 8.7   Zoe Kleinman, Technology Reporter, BBC. (Source: Zoe Kleinman)

Are hoaxes a problem?

Fortunately most hoaxes aren't very good. But I think the key is to never accept a tweet or a status as a genuine source. It is only a lead, a nudge to go and check something out. If, for example, you are an entertainment journalist and suddenly the death of a celebrity starts trending on Twitter, contact their agent. Don't assume that a Twitter account in their name is necessarily them – it could well be a fake or fan site.

What tips do you have for journalists looking to improve how they use social media?

Stick with it – it's a slow burn and you are unlikely to generate hundreds of followers overnight. Talk to others and get conversations going – that way you are getting your name out there through word of mouth.

What is the future of social media?

Don't be dazzled by Facebook. It may seem like the star of social networks but not necessarily on a global scale. At the time of writing it's not accessible behind the firewall in China, which cuts it off from an enormous potential market.

FINDING STORIES ON SOCIAL MEDIA

You will need to keep abreast of the news as it breaks on social media and what people are talking about. Searching for contacts and information about breaking news stories is the core of what journalists do on social media, but we need to develop skills in identifying useful information. As we saw with the fire at the halls of residence, among the useful tweets, video and images was a huge amount of junk tweets. Often these were re-tweets or personal conversations that had little in the way of news values. Luckily, there are a large number of tools that can help filter content on social media.

If you work on a regional newspaper

You will want to have searches set up, so you are alerted to mentions of town and cities in your patch. If you are a specialist reporter you will want to have searches set up for the companies, sports teams, celebrities, politicians you write about regularly. TweetDeck (www.tweetdeck) is a desktop and mobile tool that allows you to monitor Twitter and Facebook for mentions of subjects and people in real time.

Locating social media accounts

You will also want to follow the social media accounts of news-makers. During a recent government re-shuffle, some politicians broke the news of their new positions – promotions, resignations and demotions – via Twitter the evening before Number 10 officially released the information. England cricket player Kevin Pietersen got into trouble for leaking that he was furious about being dropped by the squad in 2010. Despite immediately deleting the tweet, the announcement made headline news.

Twitter advanced search (www.twitter.com/search) allows you to search by words, people or places. Independent sites like Snap Bird (http://snapbird.org) provide more search options for Twitter. Facebook Search (www.fbsearch.us) allows you to search across posts, photos, people, pages, groups and events without the need to login or even have a Facebook account yourself. If they are sensible, most people keep their Facebook profiles private and as journalists we won't be able to search these. However, Facebook pages and some groups are usually searchable.

Take care in becoming 'friends' with contacts on Facebook or LinkedIn – to outsiders this could suggest some sort of personal connection and may will lead users to question your partiality. When it doubt, make it clear that you don't endorse the views of friends or the people you follow.

Following Blogs

For material that appears on YouTube, Flickr, as well as blogs and other websites, Google Alerts (www.google.com/alerts) allows you to be emailed on a daily basis when new information is listed on Google, based on your search terms.

HANDLING HOAXES

Any information supplied on social media needs to be thoroughly checked out, as you would with any source. Ideally you need at least two independent sources, maybe even three, to corroborate the story. In the cases below, how would go about verifying these stories before you published them online?

a   A 'shooting' on Oxford Street, London: In January 2011 a rumour spread via social media that a gunman was on the loose in central London. Some Twitter users claimed police had issued 'official warnings' of the incident. Panic spread and some office workers in the area were advised by their employers to stay indoors. It was a hoax which was based on rumours when news of a genuine police training operation in the area became public knowledge. A tweet about a fashion 'photo-shoot' in the area added to confusion.

b   The 'polar bear' washed up on a beach: In September 2010, ITV's West Country regional news bulletin reported that a polar bear was washed up on a Cornish beach. Video footage, shot by a member of the public, purported to show the 'bear' which was eventually identified as a dead cow.

c   'The death of Margaret Thatcher': In August 2012, the fake Twitter account @officialSkyNews reported the death of former British Prime Minister Margaret Thatcher. The news was re-tweeted thousands of times, her Wikipedia entry had been altered to corroborate the hoax and had a few journalists fooled. Thatcher really died eight months later.

As with any story, you need to ensure you corroborate information sourced from social media. Check out the social media accounts of the person giving the information. Check the information with official sources (these are often government bodies, emergency services, etc.) and also consider what damage is caused if you report false information.

It's always best to do an interview with the source in person or over the phone. The Twitter profile page of the user may reveal their occupation and personal website – you will want to investigate these to see if they appear genuine. If they claim to work for a large company, you could try to call them at work. Alarm bells should start ringing if the source lists themselves as comedians, performance artists or similar professions. It is easy to see if a Twitter account is new or has very few followers. What have they tweeted in the past? If the person claims to live in a particular town or city, is there any evidence they have tweeted about their location before? Do they have followers that live in the area?

Followerwonk (https://followerwonk.com) provides powerful tools to search for contacts on Twitter. Its 'social authority' rating tells you how influential the contact is in the social media world and when their accounts were created.

Twiangulate (http://twiangulate.com) allows journalists to authenticate the reliability of Twitter accounts.

PeerIndex (www.peerindex.com) is used by marketing companies to identify influential bloggers and social media users, but the site is also useful to journalists in identifying contacts.

You should always ask the source for any pictures they may have. However, you'll need to do a little detective work to make sure they are genuine.

It is worth asking some basic questions of any user who submits content:

1   What sort of mobile phone do you have?
2   We are very interested in using this – is that still OK with you?
3   Why did you take these pictures? They look very professional.
4   On what day did you take the photo? (You can check the weather.)
5   Where were you located?

If people have taken a photo with a mobile phone, the image may contain GPS information that may reveal the location of the user on a map. Digital images may have EXIF (Exchangeable Image File) data embedded which photo image editing software packages can read.

EXIF data includes a massive amount of information that may potentially be helpful if there are doubts regarding an image:

- date the image was taken;
- date the image was modified or edited;
- camera used;
- exposure;
- aperture;
- focal length;
- flash.

FACEBOOK PAGES

Facebook launched in 2004 as a tool for university students to connect with one another. Facebook pages launched three years later as a way for media publishers, such as magazines, newspapers and TV shows, to interact with the site's users. If you run a newspaper, magazine or other media brand, pages are a great way to promote your content online and interact with Facebook users.

1 Facebook pages are public facing: Unlike Facebook's personal profile pages which most users only allow their friends to view, pages are created by media companies, are public facing, and can appear in search listings.
2 Media publishers use pages to engage with their users: Any Facebook user can like or subscribe to your Facebook page. You don't have to approve them first and there is no limit to the number of people that can like a page. Users who have liked the page will be updated when the page posts breaking news or other content.
3 Facebook pages are not the same as Facebook Groups: Facebook pages are different to Facebook Groups which provide a private forum for small groups, who usually know each other, to collaborate on a project. Groups can be an efficient way to help manage an editorial workflow for a newspaper or magazine as they contain many different communication tools.

BBC Breakfast

The Facebook page of *BBC Breakfast*, the UKs most popular breakfast TV programme, has 32,000 'likes'. The page is set up in addition to the official *BBC Breakfast* webpage at www.bbc.co.uk/breakfast which contains video clips from past shows and profiles of presenters.

Users who 'like' *BBC Breakfast* on Facebook receive updates about the show as part of their Facebook newsfeed.

It also has a Twitter page which can be accessed at twitter.com/bbcbreakfast with just over 40,000 followers. Presenters encourage viewers to interact and ask questions during the live broadcast.

The site includes many requests for help with stories. One reads:

> When you go for your regular dental check-up, you might expect a pep talk on the benefits of flossing – but how would you feel if you had to fill out a detailed questionnaire on your alcohol intake? Dentists are being urged to monitor their patients for alcohol misuse, in a paper published by the Royal College of Surgeons' Dental Journal. But is it taking the health message a step too far?

On the companion website we show you how to set up a Facebook page.

ENCOURAGING USERS TO SHARE NEWS CONTENT

It is generally believed that lighter content tends to be 'shared' the most on Facebook. This is because the majority of people use Facebook as a tool for keeping in contact with friends. It helps to have a sense of humour and an ability to poke fun at ourselves. People are fascinated by how the media works and usually love to hear 'insider gossip' about what is happening in the newsroom and the stories that you are working on. This is important as it builds loyalty among users. Other social media sites, such as Twitter and LinkedIn, work best for more serious news.

Pew Research Center's Project for Excellence in Journalism (2010) gathered a year of data on the top news stories shared. It came to two key conclusions – first, the stories and issues that gain the most traction in social media differ substantially from those that lead in the mainstream press; and second, different types of stories led different social media. The most shared videos on YouTube were the 'Hey, you've got to see this' type content, i.e. videos which were funny or shocking and had a strong visual appeal. However, on Twitter, the report states: 'The mission is primarily about passing along important – often breaking – information in a way that unifies or assumes shared values within the Twitter community.'

Nic Newman (2009) found that the most shared stories from mainstream news organizations on Twitter were:

1 disasters and deaths;
2 latest news on breaking stories;
3 quirky and funny stories;
4 provocative comment and analysis;
5 original and distinctive content (e.g. an exclusive interview that no other no news organization had).

The most shared stories also tended to generate a mood among the users. Shock (usually caused by some death or disaster) was a big driving force for sharing content. News stories that were considered funny or weird also did very well. One of the most interesting areas of future research is into whether the likelihood that a story will be shared impacts the stories that are covered by mainstream news organizations. If so, we can expect news to focus far more on disasters and death which produce which much valued 'shock and share' reaction.

When posting content to social media, timing really does matter. Most people can't access the web for fun during working hours and some companies strictly forbid social media access. So people often access it via their mobile phone while commuting or at home in the evening while watching TV. If your site is aimed at sports fans, consider publishing on Saturday when users tend to be thinking about sport. Websites aimed at teens find they get a spike of activity between the hours of 4–6 p.m. directly after school, but before children sit down to do their homework. Software such as Tweetdeck (www.tweetdeck. com) allows you to schedule messages to be posted at pre-defined times.

LEVELS OF ENGAGEMENT WITH SOCIAL MEDIA

The BBC (Wardle, 2010) gathered together a group of 20 Londoners aged 19–39 who described themselves as light or heavy social media users and asked them how they used social media for news. It found:

The first theme that emerged was that they all saw comment and discussion as a key component of enjoying news on Facebook. They shared and posted stories they were interested in, sure, but also so they could make a point or start a conversation. But the vast majority really only wanted to have that conversation within their own group of friends, partly because that was where they felt comfortable. Partly, though – and this was a real Homer Simpson 'D'oh' moment – because if they commented elsewhere, on a group or page, they would be inundated with notifications in their email inboxes of responses to their comment from people they didn't know. And why on earth would they want that! A second theme was that they were 'only interested in the news they were interested in' – not what they thought they ought to be interested in, or what news organizations thought they should be interested in.

99

Perhaps one of the most startling findings of this report is how popular Facebook was. This is supported by data from analyst firm Social Bakers which tells us that there are over 30 million UK Facebook profiles or approximately half the UK population. We don't know how many of these profiles are dormant and how many are active, but at the time of writing, no other social media site comes close in terms of popularity in the UK.

Still, 'It's a great leap to presume that the availability of digital networked technologies turns everyone into active participants,' warns academic José van Dijck (2009). Referencing technology editor Charles Arthur of the *Guardian*, van Dijck says: 'An emerging rule of thumb suggests that if you get a group of 100 people online then one will create content, 10 will "interact" with it (commenting or offering improvements) and the other 89 will just view it.'

Van Dijck poses a key question – if it is true that there are relatively few active creators of content, what do we mean when we talk about participation? Citing research by Forrester Research, van Dijck says that users can be divided into six levels on a 'participation ladder':

- *Active creators* – people actually producing and uploading content such as blogs, videos or photos.
- *Critics* – which means they provide ratings or evaluations.
- *Collectors* – a term referring to those who save URLs on a social bookmarking service which can be shared with other users.
- *Joiners* – people who join social networking sites such as MySpace or Facebook, without necessarily contributing content.
- *Passive spectators* – those who perform activities such as reading blogs or watching peer-generated video.
- *Inactives* – those who do not engage in any of these activities.

You can probably guess that the passive spectators and the inactives were the two largest groups. So perhaps a more realistic analysis is that the majority of users are perfectly happy to spend most of their time simply consuming online content. However, despite this, they do welcome opportunities to engage in news online when they have the time or inclination.

ACADEMIC CONCERNS ABOUT SOCIAL MEDIA

Authenticity of content

Verification is at the heart of journalism. A critical element of modern social media sites (particularly profile-based friendship communities) is the importance placed on authenticity, i.e. that a person is who they say they are, rather than someone pretending to be them. However, in the days of Usenet newsgroups and IRC it was case of 'on the internet, no one knows you're a dog' as users went by creative nicknames and pseudonyms rather than their real offline identities.

Iran 2009 #iranelection #neda

The disputed Iranian elections of June 2009 demonstrated the power of social media. The most shocking story related to video footage shot on a mobile phone of the death of a young womam, Neda Agha-Soltan, an innocent bystander to the protests. The video was posted to YouTube and went viral around the globe and the Twitter hashtag #neda became a rallying point for tweets by pro-democracy supporters.

Mobile phones and digital cameras were widely used by pro-democracy activists to film demonstrations that were often violently suppressed by government forces. The videos were then uploaded to YouTube in the hope they would be broadcast by foreign media. Eventually, the Iranian government restricted internet access to such sites, so activists emailed videos out of the country for supporters to upload. YouTube spokesman Scott Rubin told the BBC (Shiels, 2009): 'Iranian citizens are having their voices heard, their faces seen and their story gets told around the world without filtering. The real story of this election is being told by the citizen.'

Newman (2009) warns that during these elections:

> There was a huge amount of noise and false information generated by these networks, some of which was deliberately placed to influence the debate. There was very little balance on Twitter and other social networks: conversation was overwhelmingly in favour of opposition candidate Mir Hossein Mousavi, who tended to attract the support of younger, more computer-literate Iranians, as well as activists in the West.

There is a valuable lesson that we should never assume that the views expressed on social media are always representative of the views of the population at large.

Online identity

There is some evidence that social media users appreciate the improved trust that knowing who you are talking to online brings. The anonymous nature of the internet is sometimes blamed for the rise of internet trolling – the posting of abusive comments online which are designed to upset the recipient. But a lack of anonymity reduces the ability to experiment with online identity which early internet users enjoyed. It can also raise privacy concerns as all those embarrassing photos from our university days can come back to haunt us much later on in life.

Young people living declarative lifestyles

In the real world, we present ourselves differently based on who we are talking to and where the conversation takes place. The classic example is the difference between how you present yourself for a job interview and how you present yourself when chatting with friends in the pub.

But some, particularly the young, live online declarative lifestyles where very little appears to be off-limits. As journalists, we have to be careful about how we use content that we find on social media. When an individual posts a photo to their private profile on Facebook they are making it accessible to only a select group of people who make up their list of Facebook friends. They won't expect such photos to appear in a newspaper or magazine. However, it's relatively common when an individual is involved in a news story to find their Facebook photos leaked to journalists or re-posted on public forums. It is essential for social media users to understand precisely what personal information they are sharing on the internet and what should remain private.

The situation with other social media sites is different. With the exception of the direct message facility, communication on Twitter is held entirely in public. You may argue that users of social media sites have to take responsibility to keep information that they don't wish to be shared private. While it is usually legal to use personal pictures taken from social media, some may regard it as an invasion of privacy. It's certainly important to consider the original intention of the person publishing the picture, video or text. Consider whether the content was posted on an open site or shared with just a few friends on social media? What are the likely consequences of publishing the material for the individuals concerned? What is the public interest in publishing the pictures?

The case that is most commonly cited in academic discussion is the usage of content taken from social media sites following the shootings at the campus of the US college Virginia Tech in 2007, where journalists from the world's media trawled blogs and social media sites looking for images of the deceased.

BBC editorial guidelines: Pictures from social media sites

The BBC issues this guidance to its journalists; follow this link for more details.

The growth of social media has undoubtedly created a generation of people who are willing to make personal information about themselves available online, and much of that information may be considered to have been placed in the public domain – but the fact that material has been placed in the public domain does not necessarily give us the right to exploit its existence, disregarding the consequences.

Whilst some in the media might argue that, once an individual has begun a declarative lifestyle, opening the door to their personal lives by putting private information into the public domain of the internet, they cannot expect to be able to set limits on that. People making content for the BBC should ask themselves whether a door that is only ajar can justifiably be pushed further open by the media.

Despite the fact that a generation of primarily younger people are sharing personal information and pictures online, there is research that suggests they still place a high value on privacy. And it

(Continued)

(Continued)

should be considered that the use of social media content by the BBC often brings that content to a much wider public than a personal website or social media page that would only be found with very specific search criteria.

Consequently, when the opportunity arises to use pictures from social media and personal websites, without first seeking the consent of those concerned, we should pay due regard to the context in which it was originally made available online and media responsibilities in its re-use – balancing our considerations with any public interest the pictures may serve.

>>Summary<<

1 The following types of sites all have social elements to them: content communities, collaborative projects like wikis, friendship community sites, location-based mobile apps, and online virtual worlds.
2 Some of the above sites contain UGC and citizen journalism that has news value to professional journalists.
3 As with any information from sources, extreme care needs to be taken if we use content pulled from social media sites as it must be authenticated and carefully verified. While some people live declarative lifestyles we must also respect the privacy of users.
4 News is a conversation and it is important that journalists don't just use social media as a marketing tool to promote their content. Social media challenges the role of the journalist as 'information gatekeeper'.
5 Setting up a Facebook page is a cheap and easy way to engage with users and generates leads for stories.

EXERCISES

1 Join a Facebook page for a TV or radio programme you enjoy. During the live broadcast, visit the page and note the following:

   o How many people have 'liked' the page at the start of the show? Does this figure increase during the broadcast?
   o How do the programme's creators use the Facebook page to communicate with their users? Can you see examples of where journalists have posted requests for help with stories? Do they provide behind-the-scenes gossip? Do they share video/images?
   o Do they make links from their page to other social media such as YouTube for video content or Twitter for discussions?

2 If you are working on producing a website, newspaper or magazine or similar project, set up a private Facebook Group for your editorial team. Facebook Groups can only be seen by those invited to join so

you can use it to schedule an online virtual editorial meeting using the Facebook chat facility. You can also use it to post editorial deadlines, send out reminders to reporters and chase up any missing work.

3   Select three social media sites and examine how members achieve 'status' or 'authority' within the online community. Who are the dominant members who appear most frequently? What type of content do they post? Is it funny or serious? Status is usually achieved through having large numbers of 'friends' or 'followers'; however, it can be achieved through other more subtle methods like posting links to funny stories. Using PeerIndex.com try to identify a number of influential users in the area you write about – these may be journalists, celebrities, bloggers or politicians.

FURTHER READING

Gillmor, Dan. 2004. *We the Media: Grassroots Journalism by the People, for the People*. Beijing; Farnham: O'Reilly.
   This highly influential text takes an extremely optimistic view of how citizen journalism can improve public discourse and professional journalism.
Newman, Nic. 2009. *The Rise of Social Media and Its Impact on Mainstream Journalism*. Reuters Institute for the Study of Journalism.
   A wide-ranging study into how Twitter and other social media sites are used for newsgathering.
Shirky, Clay. 2009. *Here Comes Everybody: How Change Happens When People Come Together*. Updated edn. London: Penguin.
   The New York University professor looks at how social media crowdsourcing tools make it easier and cheaper than ever before to bring people together.
Shirky, Clay. 2010. *Cognitive Surplus: Creativity and Generosity in a Connected Age*. New York; London: Penguin.
   For decades technology encouraged us to be passive consumers of content, but today people are increasingly using their spare time in new creative ways.

CHAPTER 9

Blogging and Participatory Journalism

INTRODUCTION

The blog, a shortened version of weblog, grew in popularity in the late 1990s as a tool for self-expression and participatory journalism. Blogs raise numerous interesting practical and theoretical issues for academics and media professionals alike. Academic Alan Knight (2008) writes: 'Blogging has reshaped globalized communications and in doing so has demanded that journalists re-evaluate and reform their practices.'

Knight continues:

> Freedom of speech threatens to become universal, empowering bloggers to articulate, advocate, proselytise, and sometimes mis-inform, dis-inform, vilify, threaten and subvert, all of the things journalists once had pretty much to themselves. So where does this explosion of unmediated information leave journalists who previously enjoyed privileged access to mass communication?

Knight reflects how the rise of blogs presents challenges to the way we operate as journalists, as well as providing new opportunities to better inform our users.

Blogs were once best known as a tool for online diary-keeping or 'life-streaming', as it is commonly known. Most of us won't be interested in telling the world what we had for breakfast. You do? Well, if life-streaming is your thing then blogging probably isn't for you. Things move on and technology is always changing. Many of the former life-streamers have closed their blogs and switched to Facebook and the microblogging platforms Twitter and Tumblr which makes it even simpler to post short status updates.

So why do you need a blog? First, it is a great way to learn the principles of content management systems (CMS). As we will see in Chapter 11, most large news sites also are CMS-based.

If you see a gap in the market or a subject that few journalists are covering, why not set up a blog? Successful independent news blogs have been bought up by big media players and made their founders wealthy. The most obvious blogging success story has been that of the liberal political site the *Huffington Post*. Founded in 2005 by the newspaper columnist Arianna Huffington, it was bought by AOL in 2011 for $315 million. We look at more examples of successful blogs in Chapter 10 on entrepreneurial journalism.

A blog, alongside active use of social media, allows a journalist to build up a personal following of online users. Editors certainly take notice of bloggers with large audiences, which can lead to further job opportunities. This is particularly common in the area of political journalism where successful bloggers on the left, such as Laurie Penny of Penny Red (www.penny-red.com/), and on the right, such as Paul Staines, who blogs under the pseudonym Guido Fawkes (http://order-order.com/), have obtained national newspaper columns through blogging. Blogging is also a wonderful way to test ideas for stories. In Twenty Reasons Why It's Kicking Off Everywhere (www.bbc.co.uk/blogs/newsnight/paulmason/2011/02/twenty_reasons_why_its_kicking.html), Paul Mason of BBC *Newsnight* blogs story ideas. This influential post tested theories about what caused the protests of 2011 in the Arab region and around the world. The post eventually provided enough research for a book with the same title.

>>OBJECTIVES<<

In this chapter, you will learn:

1   what a blog is and how the word is used as a noun and a verb;
2   the importance of curation and aggregation of content;
3   how to set up a blog in WordPress CMS;
4   how to moderate user comments;
5   why some people don't consider blog content to be journalism.

WHAT IS A BLOG?

The word 'blog' is a mash-up of two words – 'web' and 'log'. Most literature suggests it came into existence about 1997, although the idea of an online diary or journal almost certainly existed before then. Blogger.com was one of the first free software tools. Launching in 1999, it soon became popular with journalists. It made it easier than ever before to create a website, without needing to learn programming languages such as HTML or CSS.

How the word 'blog' is used:

- As a verb – 'to blog', i.e. to write or edit a blog post.
- As a noun – a blog is a media platform and software, e.g. Blogger.com and WordPress.com. A blog is a media platform which produces web pages that have a broadly similar layout and design. Content is arranged in the format of a series of dated posts or entries. These are presented in a reverse chronology where the most recent updates appear at the top of the page. The best-known feature is the comment box that automatically appears beneath blogs posts – this turns a blog into a conversation.

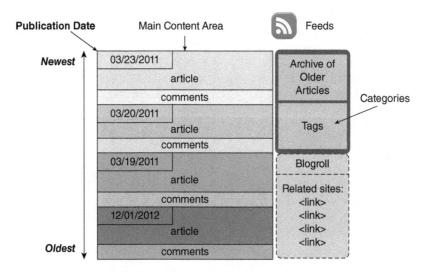

Figure 9.1   The traditional layout of a blog page – including the RSS newsfeed and modules such as the blogroll (links to sites). (Source: WordPress.org)

- Style of writing – the word blog is often associated with opinion or comment based articles written in a lively or conversational style. However, the type of content which appears on modern blogs is incredibly varied. It has moved away from personal online diaries to include news, photography, video and features. Blogs are also used for content aggregation and curation.

If this distinction between 'content' and 'platform' sounds just a tad pedantic, its relevance will become more obvious when we discuss that ongoing question of whether 'blogging is journalism'.

The phrase 'the blogesphere' suggests a unified entity of bloggers, yet the blogging community is highly fragmented in terms of who authors blogs and the topics they cover. After the terrorist attacks of September 11, 2001, journalistic or punditry style blogs began to emerge from the USA. A new genre of war blogs, often critical of mainstream media's coverage of the terrorist attacks and the subsequent wars in Iraq and Afghanistan, began a trend for bloggers to position themselves as critics of mainstream news coverage.

During the 2003 invasion of Iraq, a blog titled 'Where is Raed?' was launched, focusing on disappearances of people under the Saddam Hussein regime and the invasion of Iraq by the US and allied forces. It was authored by a young architect Salam al-Janabi (AKA Salam Pax) who became internationally famous as the 'Baghdad Blogger' for his lively reports of bombings near his home in the Baghdad suburbs. Mainstream media constantly raised doubt about the authenticity of the blog until a newspaper located al-Janabi living in Baghdad.

BLOGS AS CITIZEN JOURNALISM

The Baghdad Blogger was an early example of online citizen journalism. It was Dan Gillmor's highly influential 2004 book *We The Media: Grassroots Journalism by the People, for the People* that highlighted how new technology has enhanced the role of the citizen journalist. Once a passive consumer of media content, Gillmor described how the citizen reporter takes part in activities normally associated with professional journalists, providing a voice for ordinary people.

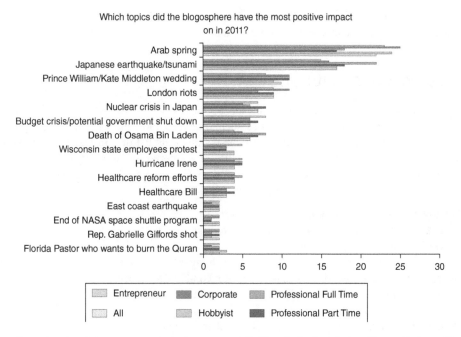

Which topics did the blogosphere have the most positive impact on in 2011?

Figure 9.2 Blogs played a role in many news stories in 2011, most significantly the Arab Spring. (Source: Technoratti)

It was hoped that blogs could lead to pluralism in media – not just in the range of outlets, but in the number of voices that take part in the public debate. Blogs created by amateurs could fill a gap in the market where there are few other outlets. In the UK, examples include hyper-local blogs that offer in-depth, often street-by-street, coverage of a local area. Where regional or local newspapers have closed, independent blogs have sometimes stepped in to take over their role as scrutinizers of local decision-making.

In countries where mainstream media is restricted, blogs are used by pro-democracy activists to communicate alternative views. Bruce Etling et al. (2010) say: 'Around the world, in open and repressive nations alike, Internet-based communications challenge the traditional regimes of public mass communication and provide new channels for citizen voices, expression of minority viewpoints, and political mobilization.' Of course, the flipside is that they also provide opportunities for racists and bigots to find a platform.

Blogs had grown rapidly in popularity from 2001 to 2005, but by 2007 a backlash against such ideas was emerging. This was typified by the release of another book with an unnecessarily long title: Andrew Keen's (2008) *The Cult of the Amateur: How Today's Internet Is Killing Our Culture and Assaulting Our Economy*. He writes:

66 The blogosphere is a sideshow, all eyeballs and no real relevance, a poker game played with fake chips. Bloggers are very rarely sued or prosecuted because the government and corporations don't seem to really care what they write. As a result, they aren't held accountable for their work in the way that real reporters are. In contrast professional journalism matters. Companies sue newspapers' and reporters' get sent to jail. Professional journalism is hardball. **99**

Modern academic theory highlights the weaknesses in the value-laden term 'citizen journalism' when many bloggers do not view themselves as a replacement for professionally produced journalism.

DO BLOGS EXPAND THE PUBLIC DEBATE?

Blogging communities exist in many interesting subject niches. There are particularly active communities in the often highly partisan arenas of politics, technology, religion and sport where bloggers tend to have polarized opinions. *Total Politics* magazine breaks down its list of political blogs into numerous niches including political standpoint (left-wing, right-wing, libertarian, non-aligned), regional politics (Welsh, Scottish and Northern Ireland) and by who blogs (local councillors, Members of Parliament, etc.). This is a list of *Total Politics'* top ten political blogs:

1   Guido Fawkes (right) – http://order-order.com/
2   Left Foot Forward (left) – www.leftfootforward.org/
3   LabourList (left) – http://labourlist.org/
4   Conservative Home (right) – www.conservativehome.blogs.com/
5   Spectator Coffee House (right) – www.spectator.co.uk/coffeehouse
6   Political Scrapbook (left) – http://politicalscrapbook.net
7   Liberal Conspiracy (left) – http://liberalconspiracy.org
8   Political Betting (non-aligned) – www.politicalbetting.com/
9   Dale & Co (right) – www.iaindale.com/
10 Labour Uncut (left) – http://labour-uncut.co.uk/

More choice: long tail theory

We have mentioned earlier that the rise of blogs have been related to pluralism or the expansion in the number of media outlets. There has also been an increased expression of a range of opinions, which could not be supported by mainstream media. This idea is closely aligned with a theory of economics devised by technology journalist Chris Anderson. He argues the internet has vastly expanded the types of informational products sold by online retailers and this has been dubbed 'long tail theory' (2006). He says that the large e-commerce sites, such as Amazon, can provide a vast inventory of informational products that are of a niche or minority interest. This is because distribution costs are far lower than selling through a high street, brick and mortar retailer. This is especially true as books, films and music are now available to download in digital formats. 'Non-hit' items, such as an album by an obscure death metal band, can be sold alongside music from the big name artists. This leads to almost unlimited choice available to consumers. How can you apply this theory to blogs? We need to think about the wider range of choices of media outlets now available online. Blog readers are often attracted to intellectual and in-depth news and commentary on specific topics which is often missing in other media. Mainstream media, with their broad brushstroke approach to news, can only offer generalized coverage.

Some blogs, like a band that plays in your local pub or bar, have very small audiences, perhaps even tiny. But in aggregate blog audiences can add up to many millions of people and present a serious challenge to mainstream media.

However, there are limitations to this in terms of the impact of blogs in the public debate. Kevin Wallsten of University of California (2005) attempted to correlate mainstream media political discussions with those of political blogs in the USA. He aimed to see if the political blogosphere is merely an 'echo chamber' for the messages of political elites that were reported in the mainstream media. That is to say, issues discussed in political blogs closely echo or mimic the issues discussed in the mainstream media, i.e. more media coverage on an issue leads to more discussion of that issue in the political blogosphere. The results of studies vary, but clearly if a majority of blogs are simply repeating the same stories that mainstream media are covering and producing very little content themselves, then this may result in very little improvement in public discourse.

Encouraging ditto-head mentality

Some people may only read blogs containing what is known as self-confirmatory content, i.e. that is likely to agree with their pre-existing political viewpoints. The concept of the 'ditto-head' refers to callers to the US radio talk show *The Rush Limbaugh Show*. Fans who called to agree with Limbaugh's right-wing views were affectionately known as ditto-heads. Indeed, some callers just phoned in to say 'ditto' and then hung up. The journalist and academic Aleks Krotoski (2010) expanded this definition to describe 'people whose reference for new information becomes narrower and narrower as they selectively consume what content they'll pay attention to'. For example, those with extreme political views may choose to only consume news from sites that support their views and increasingly drop out of consuming mainstream media sources. This trend appears to be increasing as we become more selective in the news content we consume.

The end of journalism 'club'?

Journalism has often been considered an exclusive club. As Tim Cushing of TechDirt (2012) explains the story goes something like this:

> You can get into the club in many ways, but all of them are equally difficult. You've put the time in, done the training, had the lucky breaks, struggled and finally made it. Once you are actually in the club then life is easier. You have a name, you are a part of a network and you work with a lot of the same people year in year out.

Those that have invested the time, money and effort in training to be a journalist are perhaps understandably wary about large number of amateurs creating journalistic content and competing for jobs. Cushing says: 'Many who are "in" [the club] quietly believe that they have to keep many more people "out" in order to hold on to what remains … A reduction of difficulty in getting into the club threatens to increase its size many times over.' In an era where 'anyone can publish' online there has been an increase in competition for journalism jobs.

Aggregation and curation are important terms to understand in modern journalism and these are discussed on the companion website.

SETTING UP A BLOG

We all need to build an internet presence whether that's a blog, independent news website, social media or all three. It's a great way to showcase your work, engage with and build an audience of people who like your work and demonstrate your knowledge and expertise. Also most potential employers will Google you to find out what you've been up to before commissioning you, so it's essential to have built up an online portfolio.

What is a CMS?

A CMS is a content management system and is nothing more glamorous than a large online database which stores digital assets. This is editorial content created by journalists, i.e. text, images, audio and video. A CMS is a program that resides on a server at a web host and you access it via an internet-enabled device. This is in contrast to desktop software, such as Microsoft Word, that resides locally on a computer hard drive.

One of the most useful things about all CMSs, and why most news and blog sites use them, is that the graphic design of a page (specifically the template or theme containing banners, navigation, etc.) is separate from content (e.g. the blog posts). If all goes well, once a template has been correctly set up, journalists working on a site can focus on creating content rather than worrying about design issues. It is also easy to re-design a site, without having to re-create older stories. You just change the theme of the site and the content remains unaltered. This is a key benefit of using a CMS.

Based on rules you have set up in your CMS, when a user clicks on a particular link on your blog the CMS will go and 'pull' the content from the database and present it to the user. Once the user clicks on another link on your site, the first bit of content is returned to the database and the next bit of content will be pulled from the database to replace it.

We describe such content as being 'dynamically generated', rather than old-fashioned static HTML pages where design and content is mixed together in a single page. It's obviously important that content is filed correctly in the CMS, so it can be found when a user requests it. Many CMSs use a system of categories which allows for the orderly filing of content. We suggest that you set up a series of categories early on in the process when setting up a webpage.

Which CMS is best for you?

Decisions, decisions, decisions ... there are many blog tools on offer and the good news is that most are free to use. The contenders we will look at include:

- Blogger.com: www.blogger.com. Founded in 1999 by Pyra Labs, Blogger.com is one of the oldest blog tools and is now owned by the mighty Google. Many of the popular blogs that are around today started life on Blogger. It is available as a free-hosted service only.
- Moveable Type: www.moveabletype.org and www.movabletype.com. Moveable Type was launched in 2001 by Six Apart. You can self-host the CMS – just download the software from the .org site. A paid-for hosted version is available at MoveableType.com.
- WordPress: www.wordpress.org and wordpress.com. Launched in 2003 WordPress is free, open source and one of the world's most popular CMS. A free-hosted solution is available at wordpress.com or you can host it on your own server.
- Tumblr: www.tumblr.com. Launched in 2007, Tumblelogs are a tool aimed at life-streamers. This cross-over tool offers a combination of light blogging (short text posts), mobile phone and social media tools. Available as a hosted service only.

If you are designing a site which will have a limited life-span, you don't want to get bogged down in the technicalities of blog design, Blogger or Tumblr are very easy to learn. Those who are looking to set up larger blogs and don't mind a small learning curve will like the flexibility provided by WordPress.

There are some advantages of going the hosted route – this is where the service offers both the CMS software and hosting in one. For the non-technically minded, who don't want to get involved in installing software updates or paying a separate hosting company for space this may be a good solution. But hosting the service yourself gives you much more customization choices. (The hosted WordPress.com offers over 180 themes as part of its free-hosted service and a small range of pre-installed extra modules (plugins) that extend the CMS's functionality.)

SETTING UP A BLOG ON WORDPRESS

WordPress is an advanced CMS tool that is used for blogs. Increasingly it is also being used for larger news sites and in doing so it is becoming a competitor to more complex CMS, like Drupal and Joomla!, which are discussed in Chapter 11. WordPress provides a rich set of powerful features, although it is still relatively easy to learn.

Installing WordPress on a server

As we have said, you can use the free-hosted solution at wordpress.com or you can choose to host it on shared hosting space provided by an external company. Shared hosting space, where your blog will be hosted on a server alongside many other sites, is relatively cheap on hosts such as the US giant GoDaddy (www.godaddy.com) or British-based Heart Internet (www.heartinternet.co.uk). The hosting company will take you through the process of installing WordPress. It involves creating a database password, a folder on your web host and setting up an administrator's username and password.

Figure 9.3   The 'Settings' section in the WordPress CMS allows you to set up basic features like the site's title and tagline (slogan). (Source: WordPress CMS)

Going into WordPress for the first time

Once the install is completed, you'll be given a web address where you can log in to the CMS. It will take the format: www.YourDomain.com/wp-login.php.

Using the administrator login password that you set up earlier (you remembered to write it down?), you'll gain access to the CMS login page. This is known as the back-end of the CMS. The front-end is the blog that is publicly available on the web.

Basic settings

In the WordPress dashboard go to 'Settings-General'. Here you'll find a range of options that need setting before you can begin posting content.

Site title and tagline

Give your blog a site 'Title' and 'Tagline' (a brief explanation of what the site is). You can also set time and date formats – these are set in American formats by default.

Figure 9.4   The default theme for a WordPress blog – you'll probably want to change this. (Source: WordPress)

If you click on the name of your blog in the top left corner of the page this takes you to the live publicly facing site.

Privacy settings

The privacy settings allow you to determine who can see your blog. If you are using WordPress as a tool for personal or professional reflection, you can password protect the entire site or just individual posts. If the site is publicly facing, you can set it so that search engines can find your site to add to their databases.

Permalinks

Permalinks, as the name suggests, are intended to be permanent links to your content and it's worth setting these up before posting any content. The default URLs produced by WordPress look ugly. They contain question marks and lots of numbers and are no good for SEO. The best option is to change the custom URL to either one of the following:

- Day and name: http://YourURL.com/2012/06/10/headline-here/
- Month and name: http://YourURL.com/2012/06/headline-here/

In Chapter 11, we have look at why it is important to get SEO keywords in the headline of an article and early in the body copy of the stories. By changing the Permalinks, you'll even be able to get keywords into the website URL.

Installing a theme

While the hosted version of WordPress gives you a choice of 200 or so themes (this is what WordPress call page templates), one of the benefits of hosting WordPress yourself is that you can download around 2000 or so free themes at http://wordpress.org/extend/themes. The WordPress theme gives the blog a consistent look and feel. Installing a theme is simple – you download the theme files to your desktop (they normally come as a compressed .zip folder) and then 'upload' it to WordPress in the 'appearance' section. WordPress will automatically unzip (expand) the theme files into the correct folder. You then need to apply the theme in the Appearance section.

Changing the header

A university lecturer blogs about online journalism education in the UK

Figure 9.5   The header in WordPress acts as the site's branding. (Source: Steve Hill)

Whatever theme you choose, you will probably want to change the themes existing header (banner or site logo) to reflect your blog's branding. An image-editing tool like Photoshop allows you design your own header. It is usually important that the size of your new header is precisely the same size as the existing one that you will replace in the theme. Web designers measure image sizes in pixels (px) rather than millimetres or centimetres. Once you have a great looking header upload it to your site host: go to Wp–Content–Themes–Images–Header.

WRITING YOUR FIRST BLOG POST

To create a new post go to: Posts–Add New Post. The key elements of a new post are the following.

Give the post a title

The headline of the article you are posting. It's well worth reading the section on SEO in Chapter 11 to understand the best way to write headlines.

Using the text editor

You do not need to know any HTML to write a blog post as the Word-Press text editor. You'll find many familiar looking icons to format text here: bold, italics, bullet points and font styles. The icon that looks like a chain is used to insert hyperlinks.

Figure 9.6   The Edit Post is the section journalists use most in WordPress CMS. The text editor is basic, but very easy to use. (Source: WordPress CMS)

If you are looking to add multimedia (images, audio and video) you need to click the Upload button just under the title bar.

A word of warning – you must avoid pasting text into the editing area directly from other applications (for example MS Word or InDesign). These applications put in codes and formatting that causes all kinds of havoc on a live website. The latest version of WordPress has a special text-pasting button that automatically strips imported text of any strange formatting codes.

Posts and pages

When adding content to your blog you will normally start by creating a post. Posts are what appear in a reverse chronology on the home-page. Posts are not to be confused with pages. Pages live outside of the normal blog chronology, and are often used to present timeless information such as contact details.

LINKING

Hyperlinks, normally known simply as links, form the basis of how we browse the web and move from page-to-page. Just about all modern CMS allow you to automatically insert links at a click of a button – look out for the 'chain' icon in the editor of WordPress.

Journalists create links to external sources of information on the net for many reasons. These include the following.

It helps to provide extra detail

Jonathan Stray (2010) highlights how hyperlinks work to add context and depth to our articles. He says:

> 66
>
> In theory, every statement in news writing needs to be attributed. 'According to documents' or 'as reported by' may have been as far as print could go, but that's not good enough when the sources are online. I can't see any reason why readers shouldn't demand, and journalists shouldn't supply, links to all online resources used in writing a story.
>
> 99

Journalist and media analyst Patrick Smith (2010) says that linking is very efficient: 'Linking – sometimes referred to as "in-line linking" – has a fundamental role: it conveys information faster and more efficiently than writing it all out again from the original source'.

Links are used by search engines

Academic Han Woo Park (2003) states that the number of links *into* a website (i.e. the number of sites that link to it) reflects its trust, prestige, authority and credibility within the internet community. If a respected news site links to your site this will not simply generate new traffic for you, it will improve your search engine ranking. Google and other search engines will measure the quality of your site by looking at other high quality sites that link to it.

It is a form of gatekeeping

It is traditional to links to other blogs within your subject area. An editorial filtering process is taking place when a blogger makes links to sites she or he feel will be of benefit to users. In this respect, having another blog link to you is a big vote of confidence.

What is the best way to link out to content online? Users need to know where they are going and what content they are likely to find when they click on a link. So simply typing 'click here for more' (typically the word 'here' is the link) should be avoided. Try making the linked word something more descriptive.

The web was built on a system of navigation by shared links, yet some news websites and blogs have a bizarre policy of not linking out to other sites. This is often done in the hope that they can keep users on their site for longer and generate more ad revenue. In reality, not linking out just reduces the depth of coverage and frustrates users.

CATEGORIES AND TAGS

A category determines the main topic of the blog post. Categories are a useful navigation tool for both your human users and for the computers that search engines use to crawl your website. They take the format of:

- Name: The name is how it appears on your site.
- Slug: The URL-friendly version of the name. It is usually all lower-case and contains only letters, numbers and hyphens.
- Parent: Categories can have a hierarchy. A local news blog may have a category called 'sport' which then has children categories for 'football', 'rugby', 'cricket' and so on.
- Description: Some WordPress themes allow you to give more details about what kind of content is in the category.

Tags are clickable, comma separated, keywords that allow you to describe what is in individual posts in more specific terms.

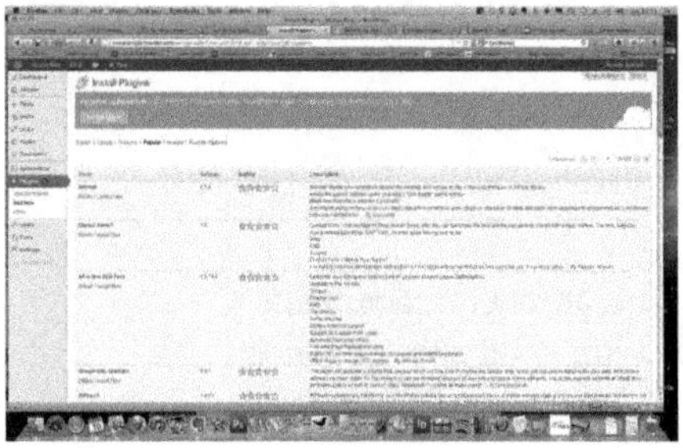

Figure 9.7   You can add extra functionality to a WordPress blog by installing add-on modules and plugins – most are available for free. (Source: WordPress CMS)

PLUGINS AND WIDGETS

Add-on modules, what WordPress calls plugins, provide extra functionality and you will be able to download plugins to do just about anything you want. Thousands are available to download via http://wordpress.org/extend/plugins/ and most are available for free. A smaller number can be installed if you have hosted your site for free at WordPress.com though, which is yet another reason to host it independently. Installing a plugin is a three-stage process – download the plugin to your desktop, upload the zip files to WordPress and then activate them within the plugins section (quite a few people forget that last stage!). Widgets are WordPress Plugins that appear in the sidebar. The following widgets are installed and are showing on your live website by default – a search box, recent comment from users and categories box. These can be removed or re-positioned on your site.

Some recommended plugins for WordPress are at this link.

- Viper's Video Quicktags: http://wordpress.org/extend/plugins/vipers-video-quicktags/. As we discuss in Chapter 6, it's often best to host your video on a sharing site such as YouTube or Vimeo rather than on your own server due to their size. This plugin allows you to easily embed videos into your posts.
- All In One SEO Pack: http://wordpress.org/extend/plugins/all-in-one-seo-pack/. Make your blog SEO compliant and it automatically generates tags to describe your content.
- WordPress Database Back-Up: http://austinmatzko.com/wordpress-plugins/wp-db-backup/. Back-up your site regularly, particularly before making any big changes like changing your theme.
- Sharebar: http://devgrow.com/sharebar-wordpress-plugin/. Include a vertical box next to your posts containing buttons to allow users to share your content on a range of social media sites.
- Post Types Order: www.nsp-code.com. WordPress was originally designed for blogs, where content appears in a reverse chronology; however, for news sites the most important story isn't always the most recent. This plugin allows you to order your stories easily.
- Zemanta: www.zemanta.com. Put simply, it matches text within any blog post you write to publicly available content. This makes linking to content on other blogs and news sites very easy.

HOW TO COPE WITH COMMENTS

In WordPress under Settings–Discussion in the main menu, you can control how comments are displayed on your site. A comment box, which allows users to express their opinion on what you have written and appears automatically beneath every post, is a key characteristic of a blog. It turns it from a one-way form of communication to something far more interesting. There is a theory that a 'blog' that does not give users the opportunity to post comments is not really a blog at all.

Allowing comments to appear on your blog is both a blessing and a curse.

- Spam comments: Spammers will post links that contain viruses or offensive material in comment boxes. Automated programs, known as spambots, will target your site and can leave hundreds of messages in a single day.
- Trolling: These are bullying comments from users. As these posts are written by people, rather than computers which generate spam, they are far harder for your blog filters to catch. These comments

can raise legal issues as they may be defamatory, false or misleading, abusive, obscene, racist, sexist or homophobic in nature.

Journalist Helen Lewis-Hasteley highlighted the problem of trolling or internet bullying of female bloggers in a *New Statesman* article in 2011:

 The sheer volume of sexist abuse thrown at female bloggers is the internet's festering sore: if you talk to any woman who writes online, the chances are she will instantly be able to reel off a greatest hits of insults. But it's very rarely spoken about, for both sound and unsound reasons. No one likes to look like a whiner – particularly a woman writing in male-dominated fields such as politics, economics or computer games. Others are reluctant to give trolls the 'satisfaction' of knowing they're emotionally affected by the abuse or are afraid of incurring more by speaking out.

Julia Hobsbawm (2011), media analyst, writes on the Dale & Co political blog:

 The public who are encouraged to leave comments at the end of their authored articles often do so with a level of viciousness which is often breathtaking. By all means let's have more members of the public contributing well-argued, passionate, fact-based, opinion-rich comment which adds seriously to the debate. But let's not pretend that masked, anonymous bile masquerading as free speech is helpful, right, or particularly readable.

 There are more tips for managing comments on the companion website.

TAKING YOUR BLOG TO THE NEXT LEVEL

To maximize your chances of success as a blogger, it's worth following a few simple tips:

Aim to cover a single topic in-depth

Blog users are attracted to what they view as intellectual and in-depth news and commentary. Follow the rule of the 'long tail' and aim to be quite specific in your choice of topic. Remain focused on your target user base and avoid going 'off-topic' even if you feel it will generate a one-off burst of Google traffic.

Develop a network model

A proven trick is to launch multiple blogs covering a series of niche topics. It sounds like a lot of work, but there are economies of scale to be exploited: you'll use the same CMS software and hosting for all your sites. And, of course, all your blogs can be used to cross-promote each other which will improve your position in the search engine rankings. AOL, the American internet service provider giant, runs a network comprising dozens of blogs. The company has spent the last few years buying up successful independent blogs including Engaget (consumer technology), Autoblog (car industry), TechCrunch (technology start-ups) and the Huffington Post (liberal/left politics).

Post short articles, but post often

Creating a successful blog is really hard work. Gawker.com, the successful New York-based media gossip blog, created by British Journalist Nick Denton, has a team of writers posting around 50 to 70 articles per day online. The posting of relatively short but frequent blogs posts are the key to success in building traffic and bring in the advertising revenue.

Don't forget you are in the media business

You need to decide on your goals right the start. Is the blog simply to showcase your work? Will you be happy if you make enough money from advertising revenue to pay your server expenses or do you want to make blogging your full-time career? Running a profitable blog usually means operating a highly efficient media operation. When British journalist Nick Denton started Gawker Media it was run from his apartment at home to cut down on the costs of office space. Hosting and software costs are usually very cheap, so your biggest costs will be your time. You may want to invite guest writers to blog for you and you could return the favour by writing for their blog. Some sites pay writers based according to how many posts they write each week, page views or even the amount of advertising revenue their posts generate. The Huffington Post is famous for not paying its contributors.

KEY ACADEMIC ISSUES IN BLOGGING

Here are some of the most common academic debates:

Is blogging journalism?

This is the big one and is the issue that dominates the debate regarding blogs. It is a perennial debate that pops up with alarming regularity. Of course this is a bit of a trick question – can you guess why? As we mentioned in our introduction, a blog is essentially software. It creates sites with a shared design characteristic and layout, although even this is changing. So a similar question to ask is whether a paper diary is journalism? No, it is just a series of printed pages, with dates and, usually, a useful calendar at the back.

But let's assume the people who constantly debate whether blogging is journalism are talking about content that appears online, rather than the blogging software used. Unfortunately, the varied nature of content that appears on blogs is very difficult to categorize. It is common to hear critics accuse bloggers of lacking editorial standards, mixing news with comment, lacking in original reporting and mixing editorial with advertising in a way that undermined public trust. That's certainly true of some bloggers, but equally it also applies to some journalists who work in mainstream media.

One of the authors attended a conference in 2006 where a senior editor working at a mainstream TV news company ridiculed the rise of citizen journalism. Banging his hand on the table, the editor declared that his company had the 'trust of the viewers'. To vocal agreement from the assembled audience, he said that viewers were as likely to trust a 'citizen journalist' to accurately tell them the news as they would a 'citizen doctor' to fix their broken leg!

However, increasingly mainstream outlets such as the BBC, the *Guardian* and Sky News encourage their journalists to blog. Journalist Felix Salmon (2011) writes: 'There's convergence going on—news organizations are becoming bloggier, and blogs are becoming newsier—and that process works to the benefit of both, even as it makes the status of "blogger" less interesting or meaningful.'

Newspapers increasingly use weblogs as sources, especially in their coverage of politics and technology. 'The findings of this study indicate the possible existence of a continuous or repeating source cycle between the traditional media and weblogs,' write academics Marcus Messner and Marcia Watson DiStaso (2008). 'It seems as if the traditional media report on an issue, which directly reaches the public. The issue is then picked up by weblogs, who use the traditional media as their sources.'

Messner found that while weblogs were used only rarely as sources by the traditional media in the early part of this decade, they have clearly gained legitimacy with journalists between 2003 and 2005. 'This is not only stressed by the use of weblogs as sources, but also by the regular mention of weblogs in reporting contexts. Weblogs, which were initially considered an alternative news format, have moved into the mainstream by heavily relying on other media sources.' Mainstream news organizations now closely monitor the blogosphere for topics and opinions on a daily basis.

The political blog the Huffington Post has been criticized by its rivals in mainstream media for being a mere aggregator of original journalism found elsewhere and doing very little boots-on-the-ground reporting. But it recently startled its critics by featuring a series of original reports on the struggles of wounded American soldiers returning home from Iraq and Afghanistan, which won its military correspondent, David Wood, a Pulitzer Prize in 2012.

But while citizen journalism has not replaced professional journalism, it has become harder to define what a journalist is. 'The line between professional and personal has blurred amid an overwhelming tide of interlinked news sources and outputs. Terms like old media, new media, social media and blogging have become less and less useful in defining value or quality,' states Nic Newman (2011).

Alan Knight (2008) says professional journalists are increasingly questioning their position:

> **"** Journalists were once defined by where they worked; in newspapers, or radio and television stations. The Internet promises everyone can be a publisher. But not everyone has the skills or training to be a journalist; defined by their professional practices and codes of ethics. Such journalists will continue to authorise information, providing signposts for discerning audiences. So who in the future should be called a journalist? Anyone applying professional practices within recognised codes of ethics will be differentiated from most bloggers as well as our friends at Fox News. What will they be doing? Seeking to create non-fiction, buttressed by transparent sources . . . News. **"**

Is aggregation and curation *really* journalism?

It used to be said that content is king – that's to say original, ideally exclusive, journalism is at the heart of what we do. However, some people say that curation is also important. Perhaps not quite at 'king' status, but perhaps a duke or duchess?

Content curation is sorting, categorizing and presenting information from a wide range of sources in a format that is easy for the user to digest. Sayid Ali, owner of NewsFlick.net (cited in Sternberg, 2011), says that curation 'gathers all these fragmented pieces of information to one location, allowing people to get access to more specialized content'. In this respect bloggers take on the role of sense-makers of material from a wide variety of sources.

Daniel Tynan (2009), American technology journalist, accused bloggers of stealing stories written by professional journalists. He writes:

> Kind-hearted conscientious bloggers will write a one paragraph summary and link to the story, citing the source where they found it (though not necessarily the original source). Some will add their own commentary or expertise, though this is pretty rare. Others will lift the story wholesale, but retain my byline and some notion of where they originally found the story. And some evil bloggers will lift the content and claim it as their own, the bastards. From all of this I get exactly bupkis.

In the media eco-system a debate exists about whether blogs are parasites that suck the life out of original journalism and eventually kill off their hosts or, is the relationship complementary or biotic?

Data from the Pew Research Center (2010) in the US shows that bloggers take a disproportionate amount of content from mainstream media, even when compared to some social media sites.

> While social media players espouse a different agenda than the mainstream media, blogs still heavily rely on the traditional press – and primarily just a few outlets within that – for their information. More than 99% of the stories linked to in blogs came from legacy outlets such as newspapers and broadcast networks. And just four – the BBC, CNN, the *New York Times* and the *Washington Post* accounted for fully 80% of all links.

Are blogs losing popularity?

Some have said the rise of social media sites has led to the 'death of blogging'. As evidence, they point to the slow growth of blogs in recent years compared to the boom years of 2001 to 2005.

The State of the Blogosphere report by blog search engine Technorati (2011) highlights that those looking for simple tools for life-streaming have largely moved to social media. It states:

> In 2011 we are seeing bloggers updating their blogs more frequently and spending more time blogging. The type of information influencing blogging has shifted from conversations with friends, which was the primary influence in 2010, to [comments made about] other blogs, which for 68% of bloggers are having more of an influence in 2011.

Jodi Dean, author of *Blog Theory* (2010), writes:

> The most frequently invoked blog killers were large social networking sites. Rather than orientated around daily or even weekly posts on a regular set of themes or from a particular perspective, these large social network sites rely on brief, frequent updates to user profiles, lots of photos, and ever-growing lists of friends...Contacts matter more than information, angle, or opinion.

However, Dean says that social media does not replace blogs. Instead they 'traverse, extend and include them'.

As blogs started to gain large audiences for their authentic communication they attracted the attention of the PR and marketing industry. The rise of flogs (fake blogs) are seen as leading to a reduction in the quality of blogs and a renewed doubt regarding trust. They have also been accused of killing blogs. Flogs are blogs that often appear authentic and credible, indeed they will trade on having an amateur looking appearance, yet they have been set up by a company who uses them to promote their products.

Paul Boutin (2008) writes in *Wired* magazine: 'The blogosphere, once a freshwater oasis of folksy self-expression and clever thought, has been flooded by a tsunami of paid bilge. Cut-rate journalists and underground marketing campaigns now drown out the authentic voices of amateur wordsmiths.'

>>Summary<<

1 A blog is a technology platform, although it is commonly used as a verb – to 'blog' (meaning to write or edit an opinion article). In reality a blog posts may contain news content, photos, video and other forms of content and are often not just the opinions of the author.

2 Bloggers often link to sources, aggregate and curate the news content produced by others. News sites from mainstream media outlets such as the BBC have become 'bloggier' by including similar content.

3 Blog platforms, such as WordPress and Blogger, have their own particular jargon. It is important to understand the meaning of words like: pages, posts, users, blogroll, tags, categories, plugins, widgets, permalinks and themes.

4 A key feature of blogs is the comment box that appears beneath posts. This turns a blog post into a conversation with users, rather than the traditional model of journalism where information is passed down to a passive audience.

5 A criticism of some blogs is that they rip off content from mainstream media outlets, often without adding original comment to the story and providing no credit to the source.

EXERCISES

1 Constructive criticism from our users can provide us with valuable feedback, but some users may post comments that cause offence. Write a list of house rules for your website to act as a code of acceptable behaviour for users. Research what house rules your local newspaper website, a national news broadcaster and a social media site have in place.

2 Curate content for a story you are working on using a curation tool such as Storify (www.storify.com). The best stories to curate are often events where there is a large amount of material on social media that can be brought together.

3 The process is straightforward:

   o Log in to Storify (www.storify.com) and click 'create a story' – you can log in using your account details of any major social media sites that you use.

   o Enter a headline for your story (e.g. 'Demonstration in Southampton') and a description (paragraph summary of the story).

   o Get curating – using Storify you can search a vast range of social media sites for text, video, audio or still images that can be brought together to create a narrative.

4 Blogs can be used for personal or professional reflection. Set up a password-protected private blog on WordPress to document how you went about researching, writing, producing and outputting your next story. Consider what sources you decided to interview (as well as who you didn't interview) and the challenges you faced. Take a look at Paul Mason's Twenty Reasons Why It's Kicking Off Everywhere post for inspiration.

FURTHER READING

Beck, Jessica. 2012. *WordPress*. 2nd edn. Berkeley, CA: Peachpit.
  This visual guide provides tutorials for creating blogs using the world's most popular content management system.
Dean, Jodi. 2010. *Blog Theory: Feedback And Capture in the Circuits of Drive*. Cambridge: Polity.
  Dean explores the ways new media practices like blogging and texting capture their users in networks of enjoyment, production and surveillance.
Keen, Andrew. 2008. *The Cult of the Amateur: How Blogs, Myspace, YouTube and The Rest of Today's User-Generated Media Are Destroying Our Economy, Our Culture, and Our Values*. Rev. edn. London: Nicholas Brealey.
  Despite its impossibly long title, this is a very readable and scathing attack on the 'techno-utopia' surrounding the rise of blogs.
Singer, Jane et al. 2011. *Participatory Journalism: Guarding Open Gates At Online Newspapers*. Oxford: Wiley-Blackwell.
  A look at how the internet presents challenges to the traditional model of gatekeeper journalism.

CHAPTER 10

Freelancing and Entrepreneurial Journalism

INTRODUCTION

In May 2012 journalist Martin Lewis sold his website MoneySavingExpert (www.moneysavingexpert.com) for £87 million. Lewis was a BBC journalist before launching the money advice site in 2003. He used a mix of fact, analysis, journalism and advice to develop money saving expertise into a valuable commodity. The site generates revenue from affiliate marketing – a process whereby a website (the affiliate) is paid according to how much traffic it sends to recommended websites (the retailers). This raises ethical issues if users are not aware that sites generate revenue through this method. However, MoneySavingExpert makes it clear which links it makes money off at the bottom of each article. The site cost only £80 to set up, but after nine successful years, he was offered and accepted a takeover from MoneySupermarket.com, which runs an online price comparison service. Lewis once told the *Guardian*, 'I'm more motivated by ego than money', but claimed that the site 'is far bigger than the man who founded it', and that 'MoneySavingExpert' had replaced 'Martin Lewis' as the more popular internet search term. (Osbourne, 2012)

As every viewer of TV's *Dragons' Den* and *The Apprentice* knows, being an effective entrepreneur attracts a lot of kudos. The two words entrepreneur and journalist rarely appeared together until recently. But with the great historical shifts that are occurring in the media it is now becoming commonplace as media innovators find new ways to deliver journalism and make money.

There is a notable group of media experts dubbed the 'future of news' (FON) school mostly based in the United States, including Professor Jeff Jarvis of City University of New York, Jay Rosen of Studio 20 at New York University, Henry Jenkins and Clay Shirky, who have been the leading proponents of the idea that there is an emerging breed of online journalists who have nothing to do with the old-fashioned mainstream media and believe the MSM will die off to be replaced by a brave new world of new media innovators. To them we are witnessing the last days of the traditional media dinosaurs. 'The hallmark of revolution is that the goals of the revolutionaries cannot be contained by the institutional structure of the existing society,' Shirky wrote in *Here Comes Everybody*, his 2008 popularization of network theory. 'As a result, either the revolutionaries are put down, or some of those institutions are altered, replaced or destroyed.'

Jeff Jarvis (2009) captured this idea as: 'The future is entrepreneurial not institutional.' He says:

> I believe journalists must become entrepreneurs. They don't all need to be sole proprietors of hypersomething blogs. But they need to make smart business decisions when they decide where to put their effort. They need to sense and serve the market. They need to work with innovators. They need to see a future for journalism that looks different – better, even – than its past.

'Future of News' media guru Clay Shirky has made the point for the media: 'If the old model is broken, what will work in its place?' he asked rhetorically. 'The answer is: Nothing will work, but everything might. Now is the time for experiments, lots of and lots of experiments' (in Starkman, 2011). This can all seem very daunting but it is also very exciting as a new generation of journalists explore new frontiers.

Mark Briggs (2013) says:

Figure 10.1 MoneysavingExpert.com website. (Source: MoneySavingExpert)

> Journalists must now take on the urgent responsibility of building the future of news. That work is more likely to happen in new, entrepreneurial ventures than through continuing to try to right the unwieldy old ships of media. In these new enterprises, our task is not only to serve society but to find a sustainable ways to do so – efficient, economical and profitable ventures that fully leverage new technologies. We journalists must create new business models.

We often cite the *Guardian* in this book as it is at the forefront of changes as the first UK print media to go 'platform-neutral' and 'digital first'. Reporter Paul Lewis (2012) says they have a policy of 'Open Journalism' at the *Guardian* not to be stuck in the past glory days of print journalism and to see that the future is online – 'to embrace what the internet can add (to journalism) rather than distrust it'. He says the crisis in the economy and journalism 'has pushed the *Guardian* to be more entrepreneurial and looking for different funding streams'.

In this chapter we are going to examine the impact of new technology on the business of journalism. We are then going to look at three elements that together you can describe as entrepreneurial journalism:

1 The journalism entrepreneur – the self-employed journalist who seeks to find new markets for journalism, create a business and make a profit.
2 The freelancer – now a high percentage of journalists are freelance, working for one or more organizations. This section looks at what makes a successful freelancer.
3 The employed entrepreneur – the journalist who can spot revenue opportunities in their organizations.

>>OBJECTIVES<<

In the chapter, you will learn:

1 to understand the business of online journalism and journalism-based blogging;
2 to think entrepreneurially and understand markets;
3 how to create a financially viable online website or blog;
4 to understand how to work as a freelance journalist.

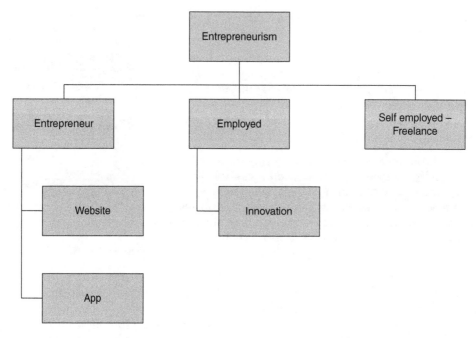

Figure 10.2   The different types of entrepreneurism by journalists. (Paul Lashmar)

WHAT IS AN ENTREPRENEUR?

Entrepreneurism is a state of mind, a way of looking out at the world and constantly watching for opportunities. You attune your mind so you look at every situation and evaluate for its business potential. It is not something you do for eight hours a day but all the time you are awake. You look for opportunities. It fits nicely with journalism because good journalists spend all their time looking for stories. Many successful entrepreneurs started by providing a service that they themselves wanted but found missing. If you can identify a service you need but can't get, the chances are that there's a lot of people who also want that service. Sarah Karam is a young Lebanese entrepreneur and says the main work of an entrepreneur is to make things happen. 'A lot of people have great ideas, but it's about actualising those ideas and not just talking.' She adds: 'Some of the best ideas are the most simple. Just fixing a problem or finding a gap in society that is not being met, and that can even be delivering food. It doesn't have to be about re-inventing the wheel' (in Tavakoli-Far, 2011).

Second, when it comes to entrepreneurial journalism, the relationship between risk and rewards is very important. Can you afford to lose all or part of your money on some project that may or may not work out? It's often said that it's better to be an entrepreneur when you are young – the simple reason is that you have less to lose. By the time you are 30, you may have children, a mortgage and perhaps a comfortable job paying a decent wage which you may not wish to jeopardize.

Americans with their market-driven culture can teach a lot about entrepreneurism. A start-up culture exists in the US, emanating from Silicon Valley – that area close to San Francisco which houses large numbers of high-tech internet businesses. This culture encourages innovation, experimentation and calculated risk taking in business. In the UK stuffy high street banks are traditionally very cautious when it comes to lending money to new businesses. The shame of bankruptcy still puts many people off from starting businesses in the UK. In Silicon Valley culture it's considered acceptable, perhaps even desirable, to have a few failed ventures along the way before you finally manage to succeed. Journalist Shaun Nichols wrote on technology site V3.co.uk:

> Fifty years ago, starting a small business meant either opening a restaurant or a local retail shop. A handful of people were able to expand those operations into regional outfits, and even fewer were able to go national. But when the web exploded, so did the prospects for entrepreneurs. Now, starting a new business can be as easy as purchasing a domain and placing your code online. No longer do college students dream of landing a mid-level position with a large company and climbing the corporate ladder. Now, an ambitious individual can build his or her own corporate ladder from the top down.

In British universities entrepreneurism was once only mentioned in the business school – a part of the university then shunned by other disciplines. That has changed dramatically. Business schools are blooming and other disciplines have now seen the light. In response to the austere financial climate that prevailed after the crisis of 2008 most departments in universities now encourage entrepreneurism and there are university entrepreneurial societies. Now it is common to hear talk of on campus 'enterprise zones', 'development pods' and 'entrepreneurial societies'. Many universities provide 'seed capital' – grants or low-interest loans – to allow students to develop their bright ideas into new businesses. Many also have developed links with successful local entrepreneurs and business angels who provide all-important mentoring advice. 'Universities can be seen as entrepreneurial spaces where students and staff engage creatively and collaboratively in testing boundaries of knowledge and understanding; where students can take risks they could not take in a workplace,' say David Baines and Ciara Kennedy (2010), two journalism educators.

HOW TO BE AN ENTREPRENEUR

So what's the difference between a journalism entrepreneur and a freelance journalist? Multimedia guru Adam Westbrook says that:

> this talk about journalists-as-entrepreneurs recognizes a distinction between freelance journalism and entrepreneurship.
>
> Yes, if freelancers run themselves as mini businesses there is some similarity, but I think it's also about embracing the entrepreneurial spirit, looking for new markets and opportunities to exploit – seems a bit anti-journalism but that's the game I think.
>
> And the ultimate journalism start-up is the one which cuts a profit and self sustains (ideally not through advertising alone), rather than living off grants or donations. (In Townend, 2009)

Paul Bradshaw (cited in Townsend, 2009) says the new approach does go beyond traditional methods; it's a form of entrepreneurial journalism 'that seeks to find new business models for journalism, rather than existing freelance journalism models. That could be anything from new forms of advertising, public funds, or platforms like iPhone apps etc.' So while there are overlaps there is a distinct difference between the freelance journalist and the entrepreneurial journalist. Entrepreneurial journalists usually work for themselves. Perhaps they set up a website with a unique selling point (USP). The freelance journalist, as we see further on, while self-employed, tends to work for organizations on an ad hoc basis. It is perfectly possible to be both. These days you need to be flexible and opportunistic and follow the idea. Many successful entrepreneurial projects we are aware of started as journalism-based ideas but the journalism becomes less central as the ideas develop.

Mark Briggs (2013) says:

> Entrepreneurial journalists recognise the potential pitfalls and conflicts of interest in running a news-based business. Most find that the slope is not as slippery as they'd feared. Smart ethical professionals with good values, who practice serious journalism, can build trust with an audience, just as corporate news companies once did.

Example: *Little White Lies*

Little White Lies is an independent film magazine produced by the Church of London. Issue zero was created as the final degree project of co-founder Danny Miller in 2001. The first issue was released in February 2005, printed in an edition of 2500 and distributed only in a chain of bookstores.

According to the *Guardian*:

> Danny Miller conceived Little White Lies with his school friend Matthew Bochenski aged 17, and they carried the dream with them through university and into their first jobs at skate and snowboard magazine Adrenalin. When the independent publishers behind Adrenalin collapsed, he put together the first issue of Little White Lies with Bochenski.

> In 2008, *Little White Lies* won its first major award: Best Designed Consumer Magazine of the Year at the Magazine Design & Journalism Awards. A website, littlewhitelies.co.uk was launched in 2006. A major redesign took place in 2008, followed by the addition of a digital back-issue archive in 2009, and an online forum in 2010.

Figure 10.3   *Little White Lies* website. (Source: *Little White Lies*)

Rationale

The magazine's rationale is set out under the 'About' heading of littlewhitelies.co.uk:

> Because movies don't exist in a vacuum, we venture beyond the boundaries of the big screen, exploring the worlds of music, art, politics and pop culture to inform and illuminate the medium we love. Bold, beautiful and unique, LWLies is a magazine on a mission – to reshape the debate across the movie landscape.

LEARNING TO FAIL WELL

 Anyone who has never made a mistake has never tried anything new. (Albert Einstein)

One of the great myths about entrepreneurs is that they are always successful. Most of the famous entrepreneurs have been involved in failures before they became successful. Some have been bankrupted by one venture only to return to make their fortune in another. That is how entrepreneurs learn. The art of entrepreneurism is to keep spotting possibilities and trying them. Failure often brings a sense of shame, embarrassment and damage to one's pride. But an article in *The Economist* (www.economist.com/node/18557776/) titled 'Fail Often, Fail Well' suggests we learn a lot when we fail at something:

 Success and failure are not polar opposites: you often need to endure the second to enjoy the first. Failure can indeed be a better teacher than success. It can also be a sign of creativity. The best way to avoid short-term failure is to keep churning out the same old products, though in the long term this may spell your doom. Businesses cannot invent the future—their own future—without taking risks.

Dame Stephanie Shirley (2012) known to friends and colleagues as Steve – arrived in Britain as a child refugee. She started her business career in software with £6, which built to a fortune of £150 million. She then proceeded to give a lot of it away. Speaking to the *Today* programme, she explained that she sees a link between success and failure. 'People remember entrepreneurs because of our successes but ... it depends far more on how we deal with failures,' she says.

When we 'fail' we analyse what went wrong, learn from the error, make changes and then try it again. *The Economist* says:

 Students of entrepreneurship talk about the J-curve of returns: the failures come early and often and the successes take time. America has proved to be more entrepreneurial than Europe in large part because it has embraced a culture of 'failing forward' as a common tech-industry phrase puts it: in Germany bankruptcy can end your business career whereas in Silicon Valley it is almost a badge of honour.

Colleen McMorrow (2012) of the leading accountancy firm Ernst & Young says:

 A willingness to take risks is often cited as a core characteristic of entrepreneurial leaders. While many companies won't take risks, even when they're close to failure, entrepreneurs are more nimble and more willing to take a chance. Culture also plays a role in how entrepreneurial leaders see risk, as different cultures celebrate or stigmatize failure. Early business failures should be worn as a badge of honour as they provide vital experience for future successes.

Some of those experiments will work and some have worked making their entrepreneurs millionaires. Jeff Jarvis (2009) says that investment rather than grants will create healthy new forms of news media.

For investors, the entrepreneurial worldview says not only that it's time to get their money out of old media companies – that, given their market caps and bankruptcies, has already happened – but also that it is time to invest in new and innovative ventures. That requires investors to believe, as I do, that there is a robust and growing market demand for news and that there are new opportunities to meet it efficiently and profitably. But until we start proving that, investors will be shy. This is why I wish that the capital that has gone into not-for-profit news ventures in cities across the country had gone instead into creating for-profit enterprises: so we can prove the market, so we can learn how to make news sustainable. That is god's work.

Figure 10.4   Mike Butcher, European Editor,
TechCrunch.com. (Source: Mike Butcher)

INTERVIEW: MIKE BUTCHER, EUROPEAN EDITOR, TECHCRUNCH

Mike Butcher is the European Editor of TechCrunch (www.techcrunch.com), a US-based website covering the world of start-up technology companies. It runs GeeknRolla, an annual conference to bring together Europe's technology start-ups to network with investors and talk about how they create and build themselves.

1 What have been the most successful start-ups that you have covered for TechCrunch?

   Skype was the one most people refer to. Right now one of the most successful is Moshi Monsters.

2 What is the worst idea you have seen?

   The most depressing thing is a really enthusiastic person pitching you a business idea that had already been tried and ultimately failed. Sometimes it's a reflection of how little research they've done.

3 What are the key skills needed to be an entrepreneur:

   - Personal: Tenacity, people skills, the ability to tell your story and the ability to hustle.
   - Technology: The more technical you are the better. This is ultimately the tech business, not show business.
   - Business: This is about high growth companies. So it's not just ordinary business skills they need but knowledge of how funding rounds work, how business angels and venture capital works.
   - Think mobile: Have a good feel for the disruption happening in mobile and hardware.

4 How does the UK compare with the rest of the world in terms of capital funding available for new tech ideas?

   It's about two things: money and talent. The UK has both – though it could be argued that often start-ups are too under-funded when they start out here.

GOING NICHE AND HYPERLOCAL

Whenever one hears discussion about online news journalism the words niche and hyperlocal come up time and time again.

Niche means that you identify an unfilled need for information in a group of people with a specialized interest. Here's a good example – a website dedicated to revealing pictures of prototype cars (see Figure 10.5).

Hyperlocal is where a very identifiable but relatively small area is covered. Hyperlocal tends to be smaller than the old local newspaper areas. Across the country are a range of successful hyperlocal websites serving communities. Many have been missed out by the local newspaper. Having seen the success of independent hyperlocal sites, many local papers have divided their own areas in hyperlocal sections. In some cases they assign a reporter to the area. In others they recruit local people to act as correspondents often for small payments or no payment at all. This is one of the developments of citizen journalism.

An example of a hyperlocal news site is the *Caerphilly Observer* launched by Richard Gurner in July 2009, which acts as a local news and information website for Caerphilly County Borough. The site is one of the growing number of financially viable hyperlocal websites.

Figure 10.5 Autospies website. (Source: Paul Lashmar)

ONLINE LOCAL NEWS

Stewart Kirkpatrick, who runs an online newspaper called the *Caledonian Mercury*, argues that journalism education should now focus on preparing students for life as an independent freelancer/entrepreneur and not as a staffer (writers are becoming the brands), so they need to know:

- WordPress;
- Creative Commons;
- podcasting;
- how to provoke and handle user-generated content;
- analytics;
- sales;
- advertizing networks;
- business skills.

Figure 10.6 *Caerphilly Observer.* (Source: Paul Lashmar)

He also suggests students should be encouraged to identify specialisms early on, since specialist knowledge is what people pay for. This could be an aspect of business, a niche aspect of sport or fashion, or a geographical area. There are very many niches and people are finding new ones all the time that users will pay for.

Example: EuropeBudgetGuide (www.europebudgetguide. com/europebudget/)

Kash Bhattacharya runs EuropeBudgetGuide, which focuses on budget travel in Europe, offering tips and advice for readers. He earns around £900 per month through 'advertorials', site banners and has a few affiliate links. Bhattacharya started writing his blog when he was unemployed but has found other work through blogging. He says:

> I don't intend my blog to be my main source of income. I see it as a platform for my individual talents and for my personal brand. I've learned about social media through blogging which led to me being recruited for my current job and I'm acting now as a social media consultant for travel brands. In short, the blog has opened doors to many possibilities in life. (Wren, 2011)

Example: KYEO TV (www.kyeo.tv)

Two students – Steve Noble and Job Corbett – who graduated from Sunderland University went into traditional journalism jobs and didn't like what they were doing and wanted to be their own bosses. With a friend called Andrew Fenwick, they set up an online TV station serving the North-East of England called KYEO TV – it stands for Keep Your Eyes Open TV – covering arts, culture and society, and they promise 'a new approach to what being a local journalist means'.

They say on their website:

> With over 6 million hits a year, 36,000 unique users and over 50,000 page views per month, the website is aimed at demystifying the arts scene in the North East – helping people understand creativity in the region isn't for 'those kinds' (arty types), but something that can be of value to all.

HOW SITES GENERATE REVENUE

While some news websites make money by charging users a subscription for content, it's relatively rare unless your content is deemed as being extremely valuable. Examples of valuable content may include video highlights of football matches and some business information. This means that websites are restricted to more limited ways of generating revenue.

Adverts

Pay Per Click (PPC) is an advertizing programme in which ads are placed on your blog and you are paid whenever your visitors click on the ads. The downside is that visitors hardly ever click on adverts unless adverts are particularly enticing, so another measurement is used.

Cost Per Thousand (CPM – 'M' is the roman numeral for a thousand) is an impression-based advertizing system (it is sometimes known as cost per impression). These relate costs that companies will pay you to show their adverts to 1000 viewers. Google Adsense (www.google.co.uk/adSense) is one of the most popular advertizing networks.

Takeover advertizing is when an advertizer takes all the advertizing spots on a website on a given day. This obviously generates lots of revenue for the site, but it comes at a cost as it associates the website with one particularly company and can impact the look and feel of the design. There is usually considerable damage to brand and independence of a site, although sites need to weigh up the pros and cons. Advertizers can attempt to exert influence on the news agenda.

Advertorials

An advertorial is an advertizement in the form of an editorial. The term 'advertorial' is a portmanteau of 'advertizement' and 'editorial'. But they are controversial as they blur the distinction between editorial material and advertizing, once seen as a no-no in journalism.

Affiliate marketing

We have mentioned earlier that perhaps the most lucrative process for earning money online is by using your blog to recommend useful and relevant products to your readers. The best examples are seen by the many bloggers linking to ebooks and other products. The best thing about affiliate marketing is that you are only marketing the product and not selling it. Just make sure the product is relevant and not over-used. Similar to advertorials, there are ethical issues you should consider. MoneySavingExpert.com, which owes its success to affiliate marketing, makes it clear which links it makes money off at the bottom of each article. Commission Junction is one of the biggest names in Affiliate Marketing (http://uk.cj.com/)

Email Newsletters

These are becoming extremely popular. The purpose of the email newsletter is to build up a mailing list of email addresses and then use the emails you send to drive traffic, sales, or income in a variety of ways. Magazine giant Bauer, publisher of *Zoo* and *Heat* websites, uses ExactTarget (www.exacttarget.co.uk) software for its permission-based email marketing. It is refered to as 'permission-based' because web publishers must get users to 'opt-in' to receive email newsletters. They don't want to spam users with unwanted junk email.

Selling products

A lot of sites do this. It might be information – perhaps very specific financial information – but equally it could be branded T-shirts and baseball hats. CafePress (www.cafepress.co.uk) allows you to design and sell your own branded merchandise.

GOOGLE'S ROLE IN ONLINE ADVERTIZING

Google, along with Facebook, is the dominant name in online advertizing and if you wish to promote your website there is a good chance you will at some stage work with them. Google runs two main systems – AdWords is Google's main source of revenue and it allows you to advertize your site by taking targeted adverts which are linked to what people type into Google.

If you run a news site or blog, you can also carry adverts on your site for other companies through a system known as Google AdSense. You simply insert a bit of JavaScript code into your web page and Google will serve an ever changing stream of ads which are related to your content. Google shares a proportion of the revenue generated based on clicks and page views, although you'll need a very large number of visitors to make even modest amounts of money through AdSense.

WRITING A BUSINESS PLAN

It is a really good idea to write a business plan that explains your business aims, the reasons why you think they can be achieved and the plan for reaching those goals. This has a number of useful applications. First, it requires you to concentrate your mind and write down what you are trying to do. Your project may look very different once it is written down and you will have a clearer sense of your aims. Business plans are really useful to show someone who is going to invest in your business that you mean, well business. When planning a new venture, a three–five-year business plan is a good idea. Make the plan concise, but include enough detail to ensure the reader has sufficient information to make informed decisions and can see you are serious.

Given that the plan's writer usually has a significant role to play in the running of the business, the plan should reflect a sense of professionalism, with no spelling mistakes, realistic assumptions and credible projections of turnover.

If possible the entrepreneur should estimate the size of the potential and accessible market, its predicted growth path and how they will gain access to this market. Internally focused business plans target intermediate goals required to reach the external goals. They may cover the development of a new product, a new service, a new IT system, a restructuring of finance, the refurbishing of a factory or a restructuring of the organization.

Though business plans have many different presentation formats, they typically cover five major content areas:

1 background information;
2 a marketing plan;
3 an operational plan;
4 a financial plan;
5 an executive summary of the key points of the business plan – it should define the decision to be made and the reasons for approval, though the specific content will be highly dependent on the core purpose and target audience.

Useful links

This article describes ten of the most common mistakes that occur in business plans: 'Business Plan Mistakes to Avoid' by Alan Gleeson.

THE FREELANCE JOURNALIST

Journalist Jemima Kiss (2006) says:

> **❝** Be in no doubt about it – freelance journalism is a very tough gig. In theory, anyone can call themselves a freelance journalist because there are no rules or qualifications for entry. Generally though, talent will prevail and those with the appropriate experience and skills are most likely to succeed. **❞**

Some journalists seek to be freelance, as they like the freedom it gives them. When the economy is good, journalists will leave their staff jobs to go freelance as it will usually allow them to make more money and give them the freedom to write for a much wider variety of publications and on subjects of their choosing. If you are good, the sky can be the limit in terms of how much you can make. Others become freelance after cutbacks in news organizations, often investing their redundancy cheque in a new business, but freelancing is not an easy life. It requires:

1 a bulging book of contacts – you need the details of every commissioning editor in your area of specialism in both big and small publishers;
2 up-to-date skills – as a freelancer you can't ignore your training needs, particularly when technology is changing rapidly;
3 experience – editors need to know you can produce high-quality work on time;
4 the ability to promote yourself – many freelance jobs are obtained by word-of-mouth and personal recommendation, but you need to be proactive in getting your name out there and attend regular networking events.

Being paid by what you produce can be stressful when work is scarce, but also incredibly liberating as you are effectively your own boss.

Many starting journalists turn to freelancing in the absence of a staff job or, in some cases, because they struck a good set of relationships within the industry while training. The percentage of freelance journalists compared to staff journalists in the traditional media has gradually increased. It is one thing to leave the mainstream media with a lot of experience, a reputation and a lot of contacts and survive as a freelance. It is an entirely different matter if having left your university journalism course you start up as a freelancer. It is tough but it can be done.

There are many variations of the freelance journalist. We will not go into every aspect but concentrate on what the newly trained journalist needs to know as a freelancer. One route that the new journalist will find is working shifts while trying to get a staff job. Typically a newly trained journalist with good radio skills will approach a local radio station to get a job. As few editors will take on an unproven journalist you will have to show your worth. You have to be prepared to take on anti-social 'graveyard' shifts perhaps in the very early morning or late at night. If you want a staff job then it is no good just delivering what the editor asks. If you want a job you have to be seen to be willing to go the extra mile, perhaps by finding your own stories. We have known many young journalists who started this way and gradually got their break. Many are now on staff on major media organizations and to be heard broadcasting on national and regional broadcast news or their bylines are familiar to millions of readers of online sites and newspapers.

INTERVIEW: FIONA WEBSTER, FREELANCE JOURNALIST

Fiona is a 'portfolio' freelancer, she edits a bi-monthly mag, writes freelance features for the *Daily Express* as well as some other titles. She has an excellent website that enables potential commissioning editors to see what she does: http://fionawebster.co.uk.

She says:

These days it is very important to market yourself. That's why I have a website and use social media like Twitter. It's important for the freelancer to get their name out there. Take every single opportunity you can to get your name known. If you are interested in writing about food look on the net for all the cookery websites. Write for them, and that will help you get noticed by editors in other media.

Figure 10.7   Fiona Webster, freelance journalist. (Source: Fiona Webster)

It can be hard to get in touch with commissioning editors, these days a lot work part-time, but persist. If possible get to meet them even for a few minutes, perhaps over coffee. Face-to-face is much better than an email or phone calls. Make sure you have examples of your work with you when you meet them.

It is really important to know the kinds of stories the media outlet you approach wants and the style of writing they like. Don't go to see the commissioning editor without looking at what they do very carefully so you know what they might like. Freelancing can lead to regular, well paid work and commissions – my features have appeared in a range of titles including the *Daily Telegraph*, *Sunday Times* and the *Mail on Sunday*'s *You* magazine. Being published in magazines and newspapers and my name becoming known led to my being offered my own opinion column in the *Daily Mirror*. I also wrote a regular column for the *Daily Mail* and one of the Sunday supplements.

A lot of young journalists say that they don't have contacts but I say 'What about your family or friends?' Often they then say my auntie has a friend who works in the BBC. So there you are, contact them!

How does Fiona get ideas for articles? She says:

I look at the news all the time, I read online, I read different newspapers every day, the *Telegraph* one day, the *Mirror* the next, I watch TV news. You might spot a story you can develop. If, for instance, there is a report saying sugar is good for you and salt is bad then suggest a feature where you get three people to eat sugar but not salt for the week and say how they felt about it. It's that kind of thing.

Use what you know, i.e. if you are a rugby fan/player, try getting a few stories published in specialist magazines, websites or on your own blog, you'll be writing with some authority and credibility and building a portfolio you can show to commissioning editors, plus making contacts. Feature ideas: Look for 'hooks' in the news and think creatively to progress an idea or news item, i.e. when a report came out on the health benefits of rationing, I lived on a wartime diet for a week for the *Daily Mail*, writing about what it was like to prepare rabbit stew, the cost and health and benefits, etc.

You can still get shifts on some newspapers and that's a good way to make contacts. Some of the Sunday newspapers have shift journalists on Saturdays. IPC hire people to fill in on their magazines when staff are away.

Freelancing is a tough old world but you can crack it if you are determined. **,,**

COMMISSIONING EDITORS

It might seem obvious but before you try to sell a story to a commissioning editor make sure that the story or the issue has not been recently covered by that media outlet or their rivals. If you are offering a story about a family that has triumphed over a rare genetic illness make sure that they have not covered it before. If they have you have just made a bit of a fool of yourself. Work to build up a relationship with your first commissioning editor. Then start to work on another commissioning editor. Very few freelancers survive on income from one media outlet. There is no set number because every freelancer will need to work in a slightly different way. But a typical freelancer might have three key commissioning editors that they work with regularly and four or five they work with occasionally.

What commissioning editors are looking for is a simple professional delivery. They want you to offer ideas. If they commission they want the material to arrive well written or scripted, to length and on time. You make sure you establish what images they want and help to deliver them. Commissioning editors are rarely interested in excuses. Once you have been identified as reliable, the process becomes easier. While the world has gone virtual it is good, where possible, to meet the commissioning editor from time to time in person. Virtual relationships are easy to break. When you meet face-to-face relationships tend to sustain. If you visit the outlet you might be introduced to other commissioning editors who are in a position to offer work. You know you have really broken through when the commissioning editor rings you up and asks you to do a story that the editor, not you, has discovered. It is usually best to start with something a bit more modest. Build up a portfolio so when the time comes to approach a national outlet you have something to interest a high-level commissioning editor.

One thing that surprises us is how few journalism students take advantage of their time on course to start the process of approach commissioning editors. It is a great time to learn the art of dealing with commissioners when you are not in a position where you are desperate for income.

FREELANCE FINANCES

Our advice is that wherever possible make the financial arrangements by telephone as it is easier to negotiate in person than by email which is a brutal form of communication that lends itself to the 'take or leave it' approach. Before you have the conversation, think about what you will need to fulfil the commission. Do you have to travel anywhere? Do you have to go out to interview anyone? Who will take visual material? How many interviews will it take? Do you have to get hold of people who may not be easily available? Factor those in and then work out what the story is worth. Do you incur expenses? Can you charge them to the media outlet?

Then decide a figure for your fee which you would think is reasonable. Then think of the fee that would be too small to make it worthwhile to do the piece. Then ring up the commissioning editor and negotiate. You have to be both tough and flexible. Let the commissioning editor do the pushing downwards. Don't volunteer yourself for a lower fee and don't agree to do it for less. Some organizations only pay by the number of words they use. This is a tough approach as if the piece gets cut down, so does your fee. This is not all one sided in favour of the commissioning editor though. Journalism is a commodity and if you have a story that is very interesting and unique then you can negotiate strongly. Commissioning editors usually have flexibility to negotiate.

Getting Paid

Journalists tend to be creative people and they want to do what they love – reporting rather than chasing invoices. Yet one of the commonest reasons why new businesses fail is cash-flow – that's people who you have worked for not paying up on time. As soon as this happens your debts start to mount. Send an invoice with the completed job and on your invoice state that you need to be paid within a set period of time (perhaps 30 days). After 30 days is up, the company concerned will become a late payer and you will need to contact the company's accounts department (assuming they have one). Be assertive and contact them by phone. You may want to threaten to charge interest on the debt (after all, the money is sitting in their bank account accumulating interest when it should be with you).

Here comes the taxman

Book-keeping may be the most boring and time-consuming part of the freelancer's job. But here's the essential bit of advice for any freelance journalist or entrepreneur: never ignore letters from the taxman – that's Her Majesty's Revenue and Customs (HMRC) to you and I.

If you're not making much money, then you won't need to pay much tax. But you still must notify HMRC that you are self-employed. Once you're registered with HMRC, you'll receive a Self Assessment tax return to complete each year so that you can provide details of your earnings and any other income you get during the tax year. The tax years runs from 6 April to 5 April. The deadline for Self Assessment each year is 31 October if you do a paper return – this allows HMRC to do the calculations for you, or a later date of 31 January if you do an online submission. Missing this deadline incurs penalty charges.

Keep a safe record of all paperwork relating to your work and HMRC advises that you should keep records for six years This will include the invoices that you sent to media companies that you have worked for and all your expenses (credit card bills, receipts, mobile phone bills, etc.). Save everything as you'll need this when you file your tax return.

When you start out, you may not be making much money because your start-up costs (computers, desks, printer cartridges, business cards, etc.) can be partially set against the income from your journalism (and any other sources). This will (legally) reduce your tax bill. You can claim back reasonable expenses that aren't paid by your employers. You can claim for a range of things including travel, telephone, internet costs, stationery, part of heat, lighting and water in your home.

You should also approach National Insurance and tell them you are self-employed and want to be registered as Schedule D. HMRC is the body that looks after National Insurance. We all have to pay National Insurance contributions and you pay by direct debit (though we should say there is a threshold where you if you do not earn much you can defer payments). If you aren't making much money you can apply for a Certificate of Small Earnings Exception for the period concerned.

Accounting for your money

Do you need an accountant? An accountant can't help you find those missing invoices (try behind the sofa!). If you've got your paperwork in order, completing the actual tax return can be pretty straightforward. If you file online, the system does all the calculations for you. Taking a DIY approach to your accounts mean that you will truly understand where your money is going.

WHY ALL JOURNALISTS NEED TO LEARN ABOUT BUSINESS

There are many reasons why journalists need to learn business skills. Most journalists will have times where they are freelance and self-employed and other times when they have work for larger media companies. Journalists need to be adaptable and understand how journalism content makes money whether we are working for ourselves or as part of a large organization.

One of the most forceful UK critics of the old journalism/business divide is the former *Birmingham Post* editor Marc Reeves. He now edits the West Midlands branch of TheBusinessDesk.com and recalls the old days of the strictly divide newspaper industry:

> From my side, the inhabitants of the advertising department seemed strange and bestial, whereas I and my colleagues viewed ourselves as passionate and heroic. Heaven only knows what a bunch of pompous prigs we must have seemed to the commercial teams ...
>
> I've worked with generations of hacks to whom the very idea of passing on a sales lead was regarded as a murderous betrayal of the memory of CP Scott. No wonder so many didn't see the meltdown coming. To all of you who are saying, 'Sorry I'm just a journalist, I don't sell advertising or organize events ...' I say, tough, that's just the way it will be from now on. We tried it the other way and it broke. (In Greenslade, 2010)

As journalists it is important we understand the latest trends. In 2008 the apps industry did not really exist. The rise of the iPhone and iPad changed all that. The entrepreneurial staff in the media who picked up on apps early created major revenue boosts for their companies. Apps have made mainstream media much more accessible and some people are prepared to pay for the ease of access of high-quality news. Journalism has learnt to evolve to survive and so have journalists. Employers are very keen to have journalists who can find new revenue streams. Newly hired journalists, perhaps fresh out of university but knowledgeable about new technology and with an entrepreneurial state of mind, will shine in the eyes of employers.

>>Summary<<

1. Entrepreneur is no longer a dirty word in journalism. Everyone recognizes that someone who can think of ways to create new revenue streams is an asset.
2. Try to think how you might be able to get revenue for your work. Create a website or blog and see whether it can produce income. Get a sense of how easy or difficult it is.
3. Start to build relationships with commissioning editors. Think of stories and offer them. Don't wait until you need a full income. This is the time to take risks and try things out.
4. If you are going to freelance then try to attend a freelance training session. The NUJ for example organizes these on a regular basis. Experienced freelancers give you tips and tell you how best to manage your time
5. Keep records of all your professional income and expenditure. File your tax return on time. Don't let companies owe you money for long periods.

EXERCISES

The aim here is to try to come up with an idea for a content-based website that really has the potential to earn income.

1. Start by looking at a successful online business with a journalism element and deconstruct it. You should research the website to provide a good analysis of the site. Look at the key ways it generates revenue. Does it use online techniques to enhance its value (search engine optimization, social network sites, etc.)? What improvements would you make to the site?
2. Start to think about developing your own website or mobile app. What are your primary business objectives? What social demographics will you target (try to target a specific age range, gender and social class) for your site and why will they use it? What rivals are out there in the market already? What is your USP (unique selling point)? The internet is a noisy environment where large numbers of online businesses compete for exposure, so how will you promote your site so people hear about it and you generate some online buzz?
3. Using software such as Photoshop, do a mock-up of what your website or mobile app will look like and ask a group of target users to give their views on your plans. You could conduct a focus group or carry out a survey of your users.

FURTHER READING

Briggs, Mark. 2013. *Entrepreneurial Journalism*. London: Sage/CQ Press.
     This is currently the best book on the subject but is very US orientated.

Dawson, Tim. 2013. *Help Yourself: New Ways to Make Copyright Pay:* www.nuj.org
  In this book, two national newspaper journalists showcase 11 widely contrasting real-life case studies of writers who are making a living by innovative means.
Flying Start Online: www.flyingstartonline.com/public/home
  A website designed to encourage young entrepreneurs which is very comprehensive.
Glasgow, Faith (ed.). 2008. *Small Business Finance All-in-One for Dummies.* Chichester: J. Wiley & Sons.
  A practical guide to running a small business.

CHAPTER 11

Outputting for Web, Smartphone and Tablet

INTRODUCTION

Setting up your own news sites can be an exciting and slightly intimidating prospect. Perhaps you have caught the entrepreneurial bug we talked about in the previous chapter or maybe you have been asked to set one up as part of a class project that may involve working together with other trainees; whatever the case, the process is much the same. It involves managing deadlines, other people and computers – all of which can be stressful and fail at the most inopportune moments.

American Journalist Tom Foremski (in Schneider, 2009), who left his job in journalism to work on his own site, says:

> It's a tremendous amount of hard work. If you want a nine-to-five job don't do it. Advertising won't be able to support you unless you have very high traffic and that will take time to build. The noise level is huge and getting louder, it is ever more challenging to stand out and build traffic.

Laura Rich of Recession Wire, an independent news site which helps people get jobs after redundancy, says:

> Do it! But have a good plan for keeping the site fresh. Either consider posting several times a day with smaller bits, or post even just once a day with something meaty. Having a good structure for content – categories of topics, regular feature types (we have regular features like Recession Concessions, Recession Lexicon, The Recession Will End ...) – will help organise your thinking about stories. (in Schneider, 2009)

In many respects, setting up a news site is a similar process to setting up a blog, albeit on a much larger scale. Unlike with a blog where you may be the only contributor; you may be working as part of team of journalists on a news site. Increasingly, news sites output to a range of online devices including PC, smartphone and tablet. Running a news site is a tremendous amount of hard work and you'll need persistence, but there are plenty of opportunities to build a mini media empire from scratch.

>>OBJECTIVES<<

In this chapter, you will learn:

1 how to set up a digital newsroom;
2 the role of the digital workflow;
3 the importance of search engine optimization (SEO) for your website;
4 why developing an editorial and design style guide is essential to produce a professional-looking website;
5 how to create a mobile app for a smartphones and tablet computers.

THE DIGITAL NEWSROOM

In 2006 the *Daily Telegraph* moved into a new digital newsroom based in the Victoria area of London. It is a giant space and by far London's largest open-plan newsroom. The purpose-built editorial floor is based around a 'hub and spoke' layout, where the editor and a team of section editors are seated around a large round table in the centre of the newsroom. Radiating from the 'hub' is a series of desks where journalists file content for print, web, smartphone and tablet editions throughout the day. Aside from areas for making video and editing audio material, the newsroom is entirely open plan. The move has been deemed a success and has been much copied. In 2008, the *Guardian* moved to new premises in King's Cross in North London. Once, *Guardian* journalists sat according to the outlet they worked on – the *Guardian*, the *Observer* or the website (known then as Guardian Unlimited). In the new converged structure, journalists sit in areas based around subjects such as sport or features.

Figure 11.1 The *Daily Telegraph* newsroom is based on a 'hub and spoke' layout. At the central hub, editors meet around a large round table. (Source: Steve Hill)

The integration of online media with other outputs such as print and broadcast is often fiendishly difficult, although it is a very valuable class exercise to think how you would do it.

Here are some questions to get you started:

How many people are working in your editorial team?

A large set-up may include an editor, deputy editor, website section editors, production editor, sub-editors, reporters and specialists in images, audio, video, data journalism and web design. Increasingly, reporters have to do more of the work traditionally associated with that of the sub-editor. Reporters may have to import their copy to the CMS, add hyperlinks, do basic spell and style checks, include SEO data, write image captions and even draft headlines. Editors, who are increasingly handling many more stories than in the past, may demand that copy arrives to them in as near as publishable format as possible. Some sites only proof a story once it is live (published on the site) – sometimes known as a 'right first time' model of working.

Communication

You need to consider every journalist's role and who they will interact with on a day-to-day basis. Most newsrooms are open plan where everyone sits in the same room which aims to improve communication. Often the editor will wish to be positioned in the centre of things, as she or he usually needs to speak to the most number of people. You may well be thinking that by the time you become an editor you will get your own office – after all you wouldn't want to mix with the riff-raff! Sadly, the days when newspaper editors had large offices of their own, complete with chaise longue and drinks cabinet, are fading. Most editors work side-by-side with their editorial teams.

It also helps to have a place to hold editorial meetings. We've worked for companies where meetings have occurred in the local pub, but we don't recommend it. You need a room with a large table and enough seats so everyone can share their ideas.

A smooth production

The digital workflow refers to the system which ensures that digital assets – editorial copy, images, audio and video content – move through the production process in an efficient and smooth manner to ensure quality and accuracy of output. Content comes into the newsroom in various formats. An image that is in high-resolution 'raw' format needs converting to the compressed jpeg file format to appear on a website. There are numerous video and audio files – some of which may be fine for broadcast output, but will need converting for online.

On the output side you may be creating content for one or more of the following: print, broadcast (radio/TV) and online (web, smartphone, e-reader or tablet). Production and design work for these various outputs involve numerous software packages and compatibility issues frequently arise.

Anjali Mullany (in Zak, 2012), social media editor at technology magazine *Fast Company*, says:

I'm a strong believer that workflow and technology changes the kind of journalism you put out. If you have a CMS that doesn't make it easy for a reporter when they file to include a link in their story, that will actually change the output. If the reporter isn't the person who is able to put that link in, the editor who ultimately is prepping that story and putting that story up isn't going to go back and hunt down that link. **"**

HEADLINES AND DEADLINES

Most CMS software allows the scheduling of content. It automatically publishes content (and removes it later on, if required) according to a schedule defined by the editor. Mobile users consume news during the rush hour commute and content can be scheduled to be published during these times. So you need to factor in the lifestyle habits of your users.

Commercial CMS often include sophisticated tools to monitor the digital workflow and the progression of stories through the production process. You can improvize using spreadsheet software like Microsoft Excel or Google Spreadsheets (https://drive.google.com/) which will allow you to monitor the stories currently being worked on, who the reporter is, who will sub it and the deadline to go live on the site, etc. A traffic light colour code system of red (it's late), yellow/amber (being worked on) and green (done/ready to publish) can be used to highlight the status at each given point in the production process.

Diary stories are any newsworthy events you know will happen in advance, as opposed to breaking news, which, by its nature, is unexpected. Typical diary events include press conferences, arranged interviews, photo-ops and other arranged events that need to be covered. The dates of which should be inserted into the traditional paper diary or, even better, in an online or cloud-based calendar such as Google Calendar. This will allow everyone in a team to view it, add dates to it and be sent email reminders. Although often dreary, diary news provides the bread and butter material for most news websites.

INTERVIEW: JAMES FYRNE, CO-FOUNDER, INDEPENDENT NEWS WEBSITE SOGLOS (WWW.SOGLOS.COM)

1   When was SoGlos founded and what were the aims?

Following a full year of research, planning and development, So-Glos was launched back in 2007. We spotted a gap for a quality arts and entertainment publication in our home county of Gloucestershire, and knew that the demand was there from both a readership and commercial point of view. The whole market was shifting online, so that was the natural choice.

2   What business tips do you have for journalists starting an independent site?

Figure 11.2   James Fyrne, co-founder, SoGlos.
(Source: James Fyrne)

- Be great – set out to fulfil a niche and be the best at what you do.
- Be specific – know your market and products and be very precise about who your target readership and potential advertizers are.
- Be on the ball – respond and develop quicker than any large publishing house could hope to.
- Be innovative – content is still king, but fresh innovations keep SoGlos current and relevant.

3   What technology tips would you have for journalists starting an indie news site?

Good old-fashioned journalism and search engine optimization go hand-in-hand. Students should perfect writing in a hierarchical style, and Google will thank them for using a simple headline, standfirst and body copy structure. Learning a little HTML won't do any harm either.

4   What are the key challenges?

If you're selling advertizing or other services to fund your site, take on someone dedicated to the commercial side of the business as soon as possible. There are lots of great publishing and blogging platforms available now, but you'd do well to make friends with a web developer and designer too.

SETTING UP A NEWS SITE

Often the first job when launching a site is to choose its name. Aim to register your name in two formats: first, the international Top Level Domain .com, e.g. www.bbc.com; and, second, as a country-specific domain, such as .co.uk for Britain (e.g. www.bbc.co.uk or Guardian.co.uk) or .fr for France (e.g.www. lemonde.fr), etc. It is better to change your site's name rather than register the more obscure domains such as .name, .info, or .biz which are not well known with users.

A CMS is referred to as being collaborative software, also known as groupware. It is designed to categorize and publish the masses of text, audio and video that a group of journalists are likely to produce in a given day.

Selecting a CMS that fits your needs is one of the most important decisions in setting up a news site. For many small and medium-sized news sites, a free, open source CMS may be more than adequate. WordPress, Joomla! and Drupal are considered open source because the source code is freely available to download and, if you want, you can change it. An online community of developers and users support the CMS and provide advice in help forums.

Larger news sites may wish to look at commercial products and the most popular ones used by large news organizations include: Vizrt Escenic (*Daily Telegraph*, the *Guardian* and others), Mediaspectrum ContentWatch (*Daily Mirror* and others), ATEX Polopoly (Johnson Press and others). Commercial CMS are often expensive, but provide flexibility where journalists can output content to web, smartphone, tablet and e-reader devices, often at a click of a button.

A news story may have several different headlines and lead texts depending on where the story appears on a website or mobile device. Images also need to be scaled according to different presentation layouts for numerous different outputs and this is an area where a free CMS may struggle. Commercial CMS usually integrate with other programs such as Photoshop, Final Cut and MS Office which journalists tend to use frequently. This integration is often crucial in the smooth running of a digital newsroom.

OPEN SOURCE CONTENT MANAGEMENT SYSTEMS

W3Techs (2012) looked at a sample of sites that used a CMS in 2012. WordPress is the most popular CMS in the world, powering just over half of the world's CMS-based sites:

1 WordPress – 54.2%
2 Joomla! – 9.0%
3 Drupal – 7.0%
4 vBulletin – 3.7%
5 Blogger – 3.2%

WordPress

WordPress is best known as a blogging tool, but is increasingly used to power many small and medium-sized news sites. Traditionally blogs present their content in a linear reverse chronology, with the latest blog post appearing at the top of the page. In contrast, a news site has the most important news, not always the latest, in the most prominent position. So you will need to tinker with the design of your site (the theme) to make it look like a news site. For more advice about setting up a WordPress site see Chapter 9.

Case study: A student site created in WordPress

Solent News, a student news website, was created in WordPress and is based around a free theme from Der Prinz (www.der-prinz.com). A large number of plugins have been installed to make the WordPress environment more suitable for journalist students. Edit Flow (http://wordpress.org/extend/plugins/edit-flow/) is a plugin that allows editors managing a news site to manage the flow of copy through the production process. Zone Manager (http://wordpress.org/extend/plugins/zoninator) allows editors to prioritize stories not just by the latest news, but by importance and subject matter. The AudioBoo for WordPress plugin (www.audioboo. fm) embeds audio into news stories.

Figure 11.3 An example of a news site developed using WordPress. (Source: Steve Hill)

Joomla!

Joomla is an English spelling of the Swahili word 'Jumla', meaning 'all together'. Joomla! files 'articles' (new stories) in 'sections' and 'categories'. Its core – the package that you install – is just a mere skeleton of a CMS and doesn't even provide comment boxes beneath stories by default. However, Joomla!'s power comes from the nearly 10,000 extensions – the plugins, modules and components that extend the CMS's functionality and allows users to tailor their sites to individual requirements. It is a great choice for medium to large news sites, where groups of journalists are working collaboratively on a site.

Drupal

Drupal is the most flexible CMS on the list and has a reputation for being an intimidating environment for new users. Luckily, as with WordPress and Joomla!, there is plenty of technical support in online forums. The administrative screens for configuring a site have a huge number of options and settings, making them harder to interpret. You may require a professional developer to at least help you set up a basic site. But once you are set up, Drupal can cope with very large and complex content-based sites.

Case study: *The Economist* uses a free open source CMS

The Economist magazine (www.economist.com) selected a free open source tool as its CMS, proving that expensive commercial CMS are not always best. Moshe Weitzman (2010), who developed the site, says:

> *The Economist* evaluated several open source CMS and proprietary solutions aimed at media publishers. In the end, *The Economist* chose Drupal for its vibrant community, and the ecosystem of modules that it produces. *The Economist* will be adding lots of social tools to its site over time, and doing so on its existing platform was too slow and inefficient.

Figure 11.4   Video is embedded into the website of *The Economist* (© *The Economist* Newspaper Limited, London, 2013)

SETTING UP A NEWS SITE USING JOOMLA!

Installation on a web server

Figure 11.5   A mock-up news website set up in Joomla! (Source: Steve Hill)

You can host Joomla! on just about any server that supports PHP and MySQL (see below for definitions). Many commercial hosts offer 'one-click' installation through script libraries such as Fantastico. If your host doesn't offer this, download the compressed file from www.joomla.org/download.html to your desktop and then upload it to the public_html folder on your host and then unzip the files. During the installation process, you will be asked to enter a username and password for the MySQL database, name your site and provide a username and password for the Joomla! administrator.

Controlling the design and layout

Once installed, go to www.YourDomain.com/administrator and login to the back-end (the non-public) area of the CMS. Once in, you'll see the Joomla! Control Panel. Take note of the Preview link in the top right corner; this allows you to see your front-end (the live public site). Joomla! gives you a free template, but you'll want to change this. Those who have a good understanding of HTML and CSS can design a template in a web authoring package such as Adobe Dreamweaver. Joomla24 (www.joomla24.com) has over 4000 templates available to download for free. Once you have a template go to Extensions>Install/ Uninstall in the top menu in Joomla! to install.

The importance of planning a site

Before you start working in the CMS, it's important that you think about site navigation. Website usability is an approach to web design that makes a site easy to use for a web user. Jakob Nielsen, an American usability consultant, has written extensively on the topic and he believes that navigating the web is a source of great frustration to many web users. We've all been in a situation where we know a bit of information we are seeking is probably on a website, but we just can't find it. These problems are often caused by bad design, for example buttons in menu systems are often labelled in such a way that they don't explain what content is contained in each section of a site. Nobody sets out to design a site providing poor usability; it's often simply down to poor planning, particularly as the site expands in size. The example in Figure 11.7 is a plan of the NME.com site and shows how a logical approach to labelling menus can help users find what they want.

It's important to understand how Joomla! files content in its database. 'Articles' (news items) must be filed under both a 'section' (these can be viewed as drawers of the filing cabinet) and 'categories' (file folders within a drawer) – see Figure 11.7 for an example of a 'football' section on a sports site. It is worth creating all the main Sections and Categories you are likely to need in Joomla! early on, even though you won't always fill them with article content immediately. This will mean that content will be filed in a logical and systematic way which is very useful as the site grows in size.

These are set up in the section manager or category manager part of Joomla! News stories (known as 'articles') must be filed in an appropriate 'section' *and* 'category'. Joomla! won't allow you to save an article to the system unless it has been filed somewhere – so that's another reason why you should plan ahead and set up a logical navigation system. The sections you choose usually appear in the primary navigation bar of the site.

Adding extra functionality

The power of Joomla! is in its Extensions and these come in three different types known as modules, plugins and components. These add extra functionality and allow you to tailor Joomla! to your own requirements. Running a news site you will want to add extensions that allow you to add photo galleries, embed audio and video into articles, online voting, list of most popular articles on the site – the choice is endless. Most extensions are available for free on the internet from the Joomla! extension site (http://extensions.joomla. org). Once downloaded they can be uploaded to your site via Extensions>Install/Uninstall.

Figure 11.6   Inserting an image into a news story in Joomla! (Source: Steve Hill/Joomla!)

Working in an editorial team

Joomla! has a 'user manager' section which allows you to keep track on who has access to what on a site – these are known as user privileges. If you set up the site you are the self-appointed 'super administrator'. You may want to appoint your fellow journalists as managers. This allows them access to content creation tools at the back-end and they can do most things apart from access the mechanics of the site such as changing the template and installing new extensions.

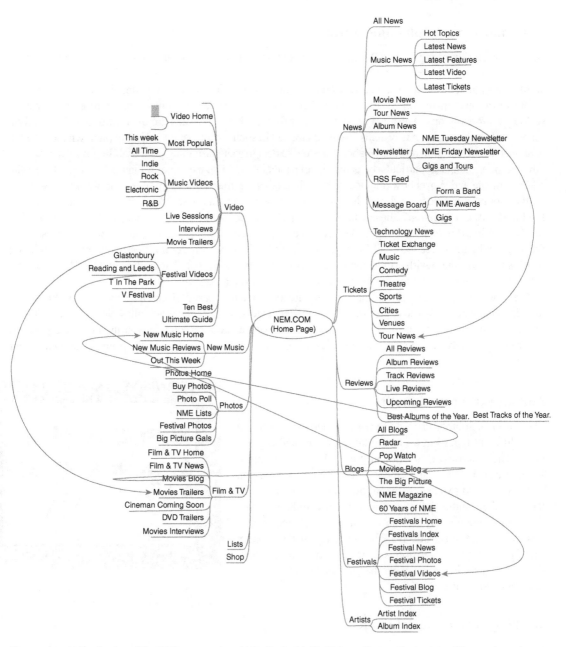

Figure 11.7   A visualization of the NME.com music website. Content is filed into sections and categories. (Source: drawn by Steve Hill)

Section (parent)	Category (child)	Article
Sections are normally linked to the primary navigation bar on the website's homepage.	Every category must appear in a section. Categories that are on the same level (e.g. results and transfers) are known as 'siblings'.	Content, such as a news story, is known as an 'article'. Articles should be filed in both a section and category.
Football	Results	Manchester Utd 3-2 Arsenal QPR 5-2 Derby etc.
	Fixtures	Fixtures tables
	Transfers	1. Arsenal selling Van Persie & Song was 'a big mistake', says Eduardo. 2. QPR and Real Madrid agree Ricardo Carvalho loan deal. 3. etc.
	Match reports	1. Saints win League Cup Final.

Figure 11.8 A football 'section' on a sports site will be divided into 'categories' where news 'articles' are filed in Joomla! (Source: Steve Hill)

	Front-end Groups					Back-end Groups		
	Un-registered	Registered	Authour	Editor	Publisher	Manager	Administrator	Super-Administrator
View 'public' content	yes	yes	yes	yes	yes	yes	yes	yes
View 'registered' content	-	yes	yes	yes	yes	yes	yes	yes
View 'special' content	-	-	yes	yes	yes	yes	yes	yes
Create new content	-	-	yes	yes	yes	yes	yes	yes
Edit own content	-	-	yes	yes	yes	yes	yes	yes
Edit all content	-	-	-	yes	yes	yes	yes	yes
Publish new content	-	-	-	-	yes	yes	yes	yes
Access the Administrator page	-	-	-	-	-	yes	yes	yes
Create new users	-	-	-	-	-	-	yes	yes
Install extensions	-	-	-	-	-	-	yes	yes
Change the template	-	-	-	-	-	-	-	yes
Change site settings	-	-	-	-	-	-	-	yes

Figure 11.9 Joomla! is flexible enough to allow you to determine the publishing rights for members of your editorial team in the 'user manager' section. (Joomla.org)

PROGRAMMING LANGUAGES

As a journalist you will spend most time creating articles in the Joomla! text editor, which is like writing text in a word processor. You won't need to learn how to code. Text editors are WYSIWYG (what you see is what you get). But it helps to have a basic knowledge of key terms and both Joomla! and WordPress allow access to the code so you can make changes to the template and news articles if required.

Key jargon

The following are some basic terms you need to know.

Hypertext Markup Language (HTML)

This is the language used to create web pages. It was devised by Sir Tim Berners-Lee, inventor of the World Wide Web. Joomla! uses templates which are collections of HTML, CSS, JavaScript (see beneath) and image files which are used as a means to present content.

HTML5

As we write this, the latest version of HTML is still in development. The key aim is to improve how sites run on low-powered mobile devices. It also integrates audio and video without the need for extra plugins, such as Flash.

CSS

Cascading Style Sheets (CSS) is a style sheet language and its most common use is to style web pages written in HTML. CSS is designed primarily to enable the separation of document content from its presentation so each can be updated separately. It's heavily used in WordPress and Joomla! themes and templates.

PHP

PHP originally stood for 'Personal Home Page'. This is a server-side scripting language commonly used by open source CMS. It is 'server-side', as it works with the website's hosting server rather than being part of the web page (the client-side).

MySQL

MySQL – pronounced My S-Q-L – is a relational database that is used by many open source CMS to store content including Joomla! as well as social media sites such as Facebook and Twitter.

Java

This has nothing to do with coffee, an Indonesian island or, indeed, JavaScript (see beneath). It is used in mobile app development among other things.

JavaScript

JavaScript, a scripting language, adds interactivity to HTML pages and is usually embedded directly into HTML pages.

Flash

Flash, developed by Adobe, has been around since 1996 and is used to add animation and video to sites. Increasingly video sites are using the more flexible HTML5. Controversially, Flash is not supported on iPads or iPhone devices.

Python

Fear not, this programming language won't kill you. It is particularly used in data journalism for scraping – a process by which data is automatically pulled from another source for analysis e.g. statistics from a government website.

 So you want to learn how to code? Find out how on our website.

EDITORIAL ISSUES IN WEBSITE PRODUCTION

When setting up a new site it's easy to get wrapped up in the technology. No matter how well designed the site is it will be doomed to failure without high-quality editorial content. You should create editorial and design style guides so that all journalists working on a website produce copy, images, audio and video of a consistent quality, style and length. A style guide is a live document that is updated as and when questions over style arise. Style guides range in both size and the amount of detail they contain. We have worked for media publishers where the style guide was just two pages of A4. Increasingly, style guides are stored on a newsroom server.

The editorial style guide

Most websites have an editorial style guide which journalists are expected to follow closely. The aim is to give consistency. The last thing any editor wants is a rogue journalist who decides to choose their own way to spell things.

Large media organizations such as the BBC, the *Guardian*, *The Times*, *Daily Telegraph*, *The Economist*, Associated Press and the online portal Yahoo! make their style guides publicly available online or in printed format.

An editorial style guide gives guidance on areas of writing such as spelling, capitalization, grammar, punctuation and many other areas. Some areas are open to question. The militant Islamist network may be spelt al-Qaida, but it could also be spelt al-Qaeda or punctuated al-Qa'ida in the media.

The design style guide

Your website will have a template or theme which contains various positions for images and other media. An image that hasn't been resized correctly can seriously mess up the layout of a site and make pages look ugly. Journalists working at the BBC Online use Photoshop Elements to resize images for the web. It is set up so that all the journalists needs to do is click a few buttons to optimize images according to the precise dimensions of images (measured in pixels – px) and resolution (in ppi – pixels per inch). Similarly, journalists must write headlines to specific lengths. The CMS won't allow a journalist to publish copy live to the BBC site unless it obeys these precise word counts.

A design style guide, alongside the CMS theme or template, will set out the various colours, sizes, word counts and styles for page elements such as:

- story headlines;
- tasters;
- subheads;
- captions;
- hyperlinks.

There is a lot to think about when writing a design style guide. A strict style guide will ensure your site has a consistent appearance where all news pages look the same; however, this does mean that web design becomes rather boring and lacking in creativity.

SEARCH ENGINE OPTIMIZATION (SEO)

Most users are not loyal to one single news website. Instead they access news content at an individual story level. They may follow links that are shared on social media or they simply use a search engine to find their news. A lot of users search Google using keywords – the names of celebrities, places (such as news about their home town) or company names for instance.

If you've gone to the trouble of writing a great story, then you'll want users to be able to find it and this is the point of SEO. When a user types in specific search 'keywords' to do with a news story into a search engine – such as Google – the aim is to make sure they see your site or news story first.

Shane Richmond (2008), former head of technology for the *Daily Telegraph*, argues that SEO skills are as important as the five Ws that every journalist learns. He states that the skill is in coming up with not just search keywords that people are likely to enter into a search box, but also word associations. In other words, Richmond describes these as:

> **“** keywords that the search engine knows are commonly associated with the search term. So if someone types 'credit crunch' into a search engine, the computer knows that an article about the credit crunch often contains other words, such as 'financial crisis', 'bail out' or 'bailout', 'banks', 'recession' and so on. **”**

When a user types in a search string into Google (such as 'Guildford pub bombing'), it crawls or spiders its database searching for sites and articles. These are returned in order of what it believes are most relevant to the user.

To get listed on a search engine you first need to submit your site address for compilation in their databases. Search engines spend their days automatically crawling the web looking for new sites and new content to include in their databases, but you should not assume that they will automatically find you.

There are companies that will automatically submit your sites to many search engines in one hit, but these sites are commonly used by spammers. We recommend you submit your site manually to the leading search engines – Google, Bing, Yahoo! and Ask – via the 'submit your site' links on the individual search engine pages.

Once you have submitted your site, it may take a few days for your site to appear but you can't rest there. It is important that you make the news content on your site search-engine friendly.

The precise way that individual search engines work is normally kept a closely guarded secret as they don't want spam sites or flogs to abuse the system.

But we know that search engines read the following elements of a news story:

- the page title – words that appear in the title bar at the top of the browser. this is often the same as the story headline, but longer with more keywords;
- the headline – this should stand alone. Never rely on an image to explain a headline;
- the first paragraph of body copy;
- the last paragraph.

Use keywords in all of these elements. You have to be more specific than you would when writing for print. Good keywords are people, places and organizations. Write in full where possible – don't just write 'the Council', but 'Southampton City Council'.

The following are some other tips for good SEO.

Ensure articles are filed correctly and logically

If you use Joomla! or WordPress make sure content is filed in appropriately named sections and categories. You should 'tag' your stories using appropriate keywords from your article. The most useful tags are the names of people and places mentioned in the story.

Install a site map plugin

As the name suggests, a site map makes it easy for the search engine crawlers to see the complete structure of your site and retrieve it more efficiently. Google XML Site Map (Wordpress) and Xmap (Joomla!) work well.

Include keywords in editorial content (without sounding silly!)

Get keywords in the intro paragraph. Take care: don't write nonsense intros such as, 'Young men, such as Harry Potter star Daniel Radcliffe, are increasingly driving eco-friendly cars like the Toyota Prius'. We work in journalism, not PR! Google can't watch video or listen to audio content (it would be great if it could!), so you need to explain what it is in text format using a short description and tags.

Use special SEO creating plugins and extensions

SEOSimple for Joomla! and All In One SEO Pack for WordPress automatically generates metadata based on your content. Metadata – data about an individual web page which is stored in HTML tags – is read by search engines.

But SEO has its critics. Charlie Brooker (2008) in *The Guardian*, writes that it is 'the journalistic equivalent of a classified ad that starts with the word "SEX!" in large lettering, and "Now that we've got your attention . . ." printed below it in smaller type.'

He continues: 'There's something uniquely demented about slotting specific words and phrases into a piece simply to con people into reading it. Why bother writing a news article at all? Why not just scan in a few naked photos and have done with it?'

A lot of focus is placed on the 'dark art' of SEO, but original content, with genuine news value, that has relevance to your users and is kept up-to-date will always appeal to users and search engine crawlers.

Encouraging sharing of your content on social media

After search engines, social media is an important driver of traffic to news sites. So it pays to promote your content on social media and encourage your users to share content they like on your site with their friends. There are many plugins that automatically insert 'share this' social buttons beneath news article. Just do a search on http://wordpress.org/extend/plugins/ or http://extensions.joomla.org/.

CREATING APPS FOR MOBILE SMARTPHONES

We need to ensure that our journalistic content is available on all the major media platforms. Before you even think about app development, you'll need to create a mobile website. This is relatively straightforward as WordPress Mobile Pack plugin will automatically convert a news site into a lightweight, quick to load, mobile version. Mobile Joomla! extension does a similar thing for Joomla! sites.

Some media publishers see pound or dollar signs when they think about apps as it is commonly viewed as an easy way to monetize news content (generate revenue online). While a 'culture of free' has developed on the desktop PC, a culture of payment exists online which was brought about by paid-for ringtones and games. *The Guardian*, for example, charges £3.99 for a six month subscription to its iPhone app.

App creation is very different to web design as smartphones have navigation systems which are very different to desktop computers. They use touch screens and are controlled by finger gestures such as swipe, tap, pinch and reverse pinch. It is time-consuming and expensive to create apps for all of the mobile operating systems out there. At time of publication, Google's Android and Apple's iOS are the most commonly used mobile operating systems and these are probably the ones to begin creating apps for.

Figure 11.10   WordPress Mobile Plugin automatically re-purposes your website for easy reading on a small mobile phone screen. (Source: Steve Hill)

Requirement:	Google Android App	Apple iOS App
Computer needed:	Mac or PC	Mac only
IDE (Integrated Development Environment) (see below):	Eclipse	Xcode
Programming languages:	Java / XML	Objective-C
SDK (Software Development Kit):	Android SDK	iOS SDK
App store:	Google Play Store. Developer account required (cheap one-off fee).	Apple App Store. Developer account required (expensive annual subscription). Apple enforces strict quality controls.

Figure 11.11: Tools needed to design apps for Google Android and Apple iOS. (Source: Steve Hill)

Figure 11.11 shows what you need to start developing an Android and iOS app.

INTEGRATED DEVELOPMENT ENVIRONMENTS

An integrated development environment (IDE) is software for the development of computer programs. For Android you'll need a program called Eclipse and for Apple you need Xcode.
IDEs include:

- A source code editor – which allows you to edit the computer code.
- A debugger – a way to test and remove bugs or errors in code which may lead the app to crash.
- Compiler – which converts source code into a fully fledged application (executable) for viewing in the iOS simulator or the Android Emulator and eventually uploading to the app store, Google Play or Apple App Store.
- A simulator or emulator – as you create your app you will want to see how it looks on a phone screen using the software's simulator. You can even attach your own smartphone to your computer to see how your app looks.

Xcode

Xcode, Apple's free IDE software, has a polished interface which looks a bit like iTunes. The bad news is that you need a Mac to run Xcode, as at the time of writing there was no PC version. It's available to download through the Apple store. The source code is written in Objective-C, a complex programming language and new users are better off using one of the many online app developers for the creation of the source code such as BuzzTouch (www.buzztouch.com). You will then import the file produced by BuzzTouch into Xcode for testing on a simulator, compiling and sending to the Apple App Store. The bad news is there is no other way to get your app to the public, you have to go through the Apple App Store.

Eclipse

Compared to the polished Xcode interface, Eclipse, the recommended IDE for Android, looks like an amateur program. But Android apps are coded in Java and XML which is a more common computing language than Objective-C. Eclipse is used for a wide range of software development tasks, so to start with you need

to install two extensions – the Android SDK Manager (software development kit which includes the Android APIs) and Android Virtual Device Manager. These can be downloaded from http://developer.android.com. Eclipse manages your Android project and compiles the application into an app for upload to the Google Play store.

HOW TO DESIGN AN APP

Designing an app UI (user interface) can feel like a world away from designing a website.

Plan ahead

Most apps have a home screen which is a menu of options which give access to other screens. Themes and Tabs control how your applications look, feel, their functionality and performance. Only one app can be in the foreground, i.e. active and visible, on screen at any given moment.

Figure 11.12   Magazines have to decide how content will be presented on mobile phones. (Source: MagPlus/ICON)

Think about using the GPS facility

It's good to know where our users are so you can offer them content tailored to their location. You may want to begin tracking the user's location using GPS, but it's essential to obtain the user's permission before switching on the GPS. App stores may even insist on this before they will publish your app.

Will you allow rotation?

The accelerometer feature of a phone monitors movement of the device. Most content style apps look and perform better when only portrait orientation is supported and you change the control setting to prevent landscape viewing.

Selling your app

Apple has a rigorous quality control threshold which means that it rejects many apps developers submit. It doesn't matter if you sell your app or give it away for free, there is no other way to get on to the iPhone other than through the Apple Apps Store. If the company rejects your app, it's back to the drawing board. This makes publishing on iOS a potentially frustrating experience.

IPAD AND OTHER TABLET COMPUTERS

For the first time in its 190-year history, the *Sunday Times* published a digital-only edition on Christmas Day 2011. The reason? To target all those people un-wrapping shiny new tablet computers. In fact Christmas Day has become a new battleground for media publishers to showcase their digital content.

iPads certainly offer new and interesting user experiences:

It's a highly individualized experience

Users download their favourite apps which personalizes the user experience. Carolina Milanesi of technology analysts Gartner (cited in Preston, *Observer*, 2010) writes:

> Media tablets have much more in common with a smartphone than a PC. The usage model is closer to what consumers do with a smartphone on the go than what they do on a PC at their desk. It is about running applications, playing games, watching video content, reading books and magazines, surfing the web, updating your status on your social network of choice and checking email.

It provides a tactile computing experience

The touch screen shows off photos, videos and maps in all their glory. The 9.7-inch iPad screen is large and portable enough to make it easy to read long-form journalism. Users spend longer reading journalism content delivered via iPad apps compared to browsing newspaper websites. Newspaper apps, like the *Guardian*, encourage readers to sit down and work through the content in a similar way as people read a newspaper or magazine. The *Guardian*'s Janine Gibson (cited in Andrews, 2011) describes an app as 'more of a closed, finite reading experience'. In contrast, web browsing on a PC was 'an infinite, take-you-anywhere experience'. For many people the desktop PC is associated with work, while tablet computers are for fun.

It can generate revenue

When the iPad tablet computer launched in 2010 some heralded it as a new way of delivering journalism digitally which, at some stage, could even replace the printed newspaper. However, not everyone agreed. 'Publishers are fooling themselves if they think it circumvents the current problem of persuading people to pay for something they have grown used to getting without paying,' writes Roy Greenslade (2010a). However most newspapers charge for content delivered via tablet apps and evidence suggests that some users are willing to pay for the convenience of reading content on a tablet computer.

CREATING MAGAZINE CONTENT FOR THE IPAD

There are number of different ways to design content for the iPad. One of the most important decisions is to decide which order to do things. Print is a more open-ended and flexible medium. Designs that look great on glossy printed paper can look poor on an iPad screen. It is therefore usually best to design your magazine or newspaper for a tablet first and then convert the design for the less restrictive print output, unfortunately this is the opposite approach taken by many magazine publishers where digital output may still play second fiddle to the printed magazine. This approach also allows you to think creatively about the interactive possibilities provided by tablet computers, which includes embedded video and links, which cannot be replicated on paper.

MagPlus (www.magplus.com) allows users to build pages using Adobe's InDesign (CS4 or later) desktop publishing package. It's free to develop an iPad magazine or newspaper and preview pages on your iPad, but you just have to pay to publish it.

Design considerations include the following.

An infinite canvas

The shape of the template is a vertical rectangle – this is because iPads provide an 'infinite canvas' where users scroll text up using touch and swipe gestures.

Will you allow rotation?

Users hold their iPad either in landscape or portrait mode. As an app developer you can insist that content is viewed in particular formats – this is particularly common for gaming or video apps where the view is most commonly 'locked' to landscape mode. However, most people prefer to read text in portrait mode.

Figure 11.13: Designing an iPad interactive magazine in MagPlus. (Source: MagPlus)

Fat finger syndrome

iPad users have problems selecting individual lines of texts
with their fingers on a touch screen. MagPlus has a tool that allows for a selection of a 'hotspot area' – a larger area of the page that can easily be clicked.

Add sound or video

Video, particularly when in HD, looks stunning on tablets – so try to include some. You can show movies as part of an app design layout or allow users to click the video to go full screen. Video can be streamed from another site (e.g. YouTube). Streaming keeps your app file size down, but users need to have net access to stream video over the net. The alternative is to embed a video file as part of the page. This will raise the file size of your publication, but will mean users can access video offline.

KEY ACADEMIC ISSUES IN THE DIGITAL NEWSROOM

Displacement and cannibalization

Do you think the following statements are true or false:

1 People who use the internet have less time to read newspapers in print.
2 People who read a newspaper's website won't want to buy the printed newspaper.
3 People who watch videos on YouTube or Vimeo watch less television.

If you agree with these statements then you probably subscribe to what is known as displacement effect theory, i.e. the use of one medium (e.g. newspapers) decreases as another medium (e.g. online) grows in popularity. Similarly, the idea of cannibalization, a business theory with a cool name, suggests that newspapers that give away content for free online are stealing readers from their print products.

Academics Jack Herbert and Neil Thurman (2007) state:

> From a theoretical point of view, concerns about cannibalisation are reasonable. Although online newspapers are producing an increasing amount of their own content, most content still comes directly from the print edition, so it would seem that the two products are substitutes. If this is true, offering the online content for free would remove the incentive for anyone to purchase the printed newspaper, thus eroding print sales.

The reality of how displacement and cannibalization works is quite complex. Some studies suggest that use of one medium simply complements use of another, rather than displaces it. The numbers of people who are interested in news remains constant – people are just getting their content in different ways and over different devices. Websites are also good at picking up new overseas users. The *Guardian* newspaper and magazine and website publisher Future Publishing are just two examples of British media firms picking up new readers abroad, particularly in the USA. So the internet allows us to reach a larger audience than ever before. Net users also tend to be younger than print readers.

Should we blame the internet for newspapers' ills? Newspaper sales are certainly in decline in many developed nations, but it is not true in all countries. Rodney Benson (cited in Fenton, 2009) states:

> Since 2000 when internet competition could conceivably have played a major factor in any decline, while US and UK per 1,000 circulations fell 9 and 18 per cent respectively, from 2000 to 2006. In the 'developing' world, including the former USSR states and Eastern European satellites, circulation increases have been substantial.

Should you take a converged approach when creating newspapers and websites?

Not all newspapers have taken such a radical approach as the *Guardian* or *Telegraph* groups to integrating their media outputs. The *Daily Mail* news site, one of the world's most popular content websites, runs the newspaper and website as separate entities. On the web it runs far more celebrity stories than it does in the newspaper and the reverse is true for political stories. A survey of DailyMail.co.uk users (cited in Herbert, 2007) found that most users did not view the website as a substitute for the print edition; and that the presence of the website had not affected the frequency with which they bought the printed newspaper.

Most people agree that long-form journalism, such as magazine features, don't work well on the web. So some publications only publish these in print format or for their tablet apps. They keep their websites for breaking news and shorter articles. You'll need to think carefully about the approach you take for your own site.

>>Summary<<

1 A smooth digital workflow is at the heart of news production. We must consider how online media integrates with other outputs such as print and broadcast.
2 Journalists often worry about cannibalization, i.e. that by giving away content online (often for free) you are killing print sales. But research presents a complex picture. The web often expands the numbers of people who enjoy our content, bringing in younger and overseas users.
3 The fields of journalism and computer programming are moving closer together. Having just a basic understanding of HTML, CSS and Javascript – the most important computer languages – is very useful in journalism.
4 There are a huge number of CMS around – both free and commercial. Joomla! and WordPress are two of the most popular. Most work in similar ways and they are not difficult to understand.
5 Mobile devices (smartphones and tablets) are becoming the primary way people access news content.

EXERCISES

1 As we have highlighted in the chapter, designing a mobile application is a completely different skill to website design and one that takes forward planning. Begin by deciding what functionality and content your app will provide users. Draw a plan for the design by hand, using trusty paper and pen, or one of the many design tools like iPhone Mockup (http://iphonemockup.lkmc.ch).
2 Write a proposal for a news website on the topic of your choosing. The main areas to think about are content (what are the key sections of the site?), staffing (how many people will you need to employ and what are their roles?), technology (what hardware and software do you need?). Can you keep costs down by using open source (free) tools? Take a multidisciplinary approach by getting advice from friends who have skills in business, computing and web design.
3 Take a free course to learn how to code – Code Academy (www.codecademy.com) offers free courses in JavaScript and other languages – and blog about what you learn.

FURTHER READING

Holzner, Steven S. 2011. *Joomla! for Dummies*. 2nd edn. Hoboken, NJ: Wiley.
   This practical book offers a how-to guide to setting up a site using the free and open source Joomla! content management system.
Marsh, David. 2007. *Guardian Style*. London: Guardian Books.
   Creating an editorial style guide from scratch can be a daunting prospect, so it can be useful to start by consulting existing style guides on the market. *The Times*, BBC news, Yahoo! and *The Economist* also publish their guides in print or online.
Stevens, Chris. 2011. *Designing for the iPad: Building Applications that Sell*. Hoboken, NJ: Wiley.
   A practical guide to launching an app – from sketching out the app to selling the completed app in the Apple App Store.
Wolber, David. 2011. *App Inventor: Create Your Own Android Apps*. Beijing; Farnham: O'Reilly.
   Written specifically for non-computer geeks, this shows how to build an app for a smartphone.

SECTION 4

Becoming a Thinking Journalist

Ethics and Good Practice   219

Law and Regulation   236

How the Internet Transformed Journalism   256

CHAPTER 12

Ethics and Good Practice

INTRODUCTION

There can be no higher law in journalism than to tell the truth and to shame the devil. (Walter Lippmann)

Ambitious young reporter Richard Peppiatt was delighted when he got a job at the *Daily Star*, his first on a national newspaper. But he became appalled at what he experienced there: what he considered to be very dubious professional standards were rampant and they required him to engage in poor practice if he was to keep his job. He resigned and went public. He told the Leveson Inquiry:

> The truth (and by this I mean a moral, as opposed to legalistic truth) is treated with such flippancy, and their motivations so capitalistic as opposed to journalistic, as to be a prime example of the gross irresponsibility that has engulfed this country's tabloid press, and for which I am ashamed to have been part.

Journalism can be tremendous fun and very satisfying but it is a serious profession and a journalist has to be careful about what they publish as it can have serious consequences for those you write about. In return for the excitement there are responsibilities: what you do as a journalist can have a big impact on other people's lives. Media academic James Curran (in Curran and Seaton, 2009) says:

Figure 12.1 Richard Peppiatt resigned from the *Daily Star* over ethical issues. (Source: Richard Peppiatt. Photographer Steve Ullathorne)

Figure 12.2   How you portray ethnic groups is a key ethical issue. (© Photographer: Andy Blackmore)

> **"** The media absorb over thirty hours a week in the average person's life. They are central to the democratic life of Britain. They are a vehicle through which different social groups connect to each other, and join in the shared conversations of society. They are also major sources of pleasure and cultural fulfilment. How the media are organised and regulated matters. **"**

To grasp the role of the journalist it's important to have an in-depth understanding of our chosen profession taking in key concepts and ethics. Practitioners, lecturers and trainees spend a lot of time thinking about the moral foundations of journalism. You have to be able to think deeply about the world, your journalism, and your specialism. There is also the big picture: as we have discussed elsewhere, without high-quality journalism a democracy cannot survive and that means that journalism has to have ethics at its heart. Like Richard Peppiatt you may have to, at some point, make a stand to maintain the moral standing of the profession of journalism.

This chapter will encourage you to develop your critical analysis, and to be a professional who is alive to the contested ideas and issues that surround journalism. We are also entering a new world of challenges. Ethics in the traditional media are well debated but the frontier world of online journalism presents a range of new challenges for the journalist. Throughout the book but particularly here we encourage new journalists to the ability to be reflective by comparing and contrasting real-life journalism with ideas and theories relevant to journalistic practice. Thus the distinguishing hallmark of this book is that theory and practice are beneficially interconnected, to help produce better journalism. That is thinking journalism.

>>OBJECTIVES<<

In this chapter, you will learn:

- the key journalism concepts;
- how ethics impact on professional practice;
- to take advice from more experienced colleagues;
- what to do if you are asked to do something unethical by your editor.

JOURNALISM CONCEPTS AND IDEAS

There are a number of key concepts that underpin any discussion of journalism. We have already touched on some in earlier chapters, for instance public interest and fourth estate in Chapter 7 on investigative journalism where these concepts are vital.

Freedom of expression

At the heart of journalism's role in society is the concept of freedom of expression that allows everyone to communicate publicly through a range of methods including electronic media. This freedom implies the absence of interference from an over-reaching state; its preservation may be sought through constitutional or other legal protections. The Universal Declaration of Human Rights states: 'Everyone has the right to freedom of opinion and expression; this right includes freedom to hold opinions without interference, and impart information and ideas through any media regardless of frontiers.'

'Journalism is the exercise by occupation of the right to free expression available to all citizens' (Robertson, 1983). Experienced radio reporter Tim Crook (1998) from Goldsmith's College, University of London, concisely sums up the higher aspirations for journalism:

> The journalist has a role in any society to report truthfully and to convey information to fellow citizens about events which offend against human decency. There is a moral obligation on the part of journalists to expose abuses of power, injustice illegality, and wrong doing. This role will inevitably force the journalist to confront authority and challenge powerful forces within society. In any democracy there is a constant war being fought between the forces of journalism and the forces of censorship and control. Information is power. In a genuine democracy journalists should be allowed a wide discretion to disseminate information as a service to fellow citizens.

Freedom of expression is great but inevitably there are areas where it is contested. Should you quote people who make racist statements and justify it on the grounds of freedom of expression? Should you allow your interviewees to incite violence? Should you identify a child that has been the subject of a sexual attack? Most people would say no to these questions, but not everybody. There has to be consensus of what can and cannot reasonably be said.

Ethics expert Chris Frost (2011) identifies eight particular areas where it is important for the journalists to understand the importance of the limits of the freedom of expression:

- coverage of criminal proceedings;
- protection of individual honour (defamation);
- protection of commercial confidentiality;
- invasion of personal privacy;
- security and defence;
- the public good (decency and good taste);
- public order;
- prevention of terror.

To be able to exercise 'freedom of expression' requires a space or forum and the media is one of the providers of 'the public sphere' where discussion can take place in an open society. German theorist Jürgen Habermas defined the notion of the public sphere as a 'virtual or imaginary community which does not necessarily exist in any identifiable space, made up of private people gathered together as a public and articulating the needs of society with the state'.

Grant Greenwald (2012) sums up the inherent dilemma of freedom of expression.

> Nothing tests one's intellectual honesty and ability to apply principles consistently more than free speech controversies. It is exceedingly easy to invoke free speech values in defense of political views you like. It is exceedingly difficult to invoke them in defense of views you loathe. But the true test for determining the authenticity of one's belief in free speech is whether one does the latter, not the former.

Privacy

In the 'public interest', is a term that is used to describe the right to put into the public domain the knowledge, that every citizen should have to make informed decisions; what interests (some members of) the public (some of the time) in the more salacious activities of film and TV stars, footballers and celebrities does not usually come under the public interest concept. Unless, of course, they are doing something that is unlawful or immoral outside of their private life. And what is private and what is not? Are footballers entitled to privacy if they have affairs outside of their marriage? You can see already why public interest is hard to define. Unscrupulous journalists have tried to extend the 'public interest' defence in law to justify their activities when in fact the stories concerned have nothing or very little that is high minded about them and are most clearly there to titillate the readership. Public interest and privacy are two very closely related concepts.

Journalists need to be clear whose interest journalism serves by publishing a given story. As academic Silvio Waisbord (2001) neatly summarizes the problem: 'Does the press fulfil its social responsibility in revealing wrong-doing? Whose interests are being affected? Whose rights are being invaded? Is the issue at stake a matter of public interest? Or is individual privacy being invaded when no crucial public issue is at stake?

Objectivity versus subjectivity

That journalists should seek objectivity has been a core mantra of journalism professionalism for a long time, and described by US media academic Michael Schudson (2003) as 'a kind of industrial discipline [for journalists]'. Journalists have realized for a long time that they can never be totally objective but the general agreement was that it was part of the professional standards to strive for objectivity. Indeed with the rise of online journalism it is the way that traditional journalists have sought to distinguish themselves from the broader church of online journalism. Matthew Kieran (1998) says:

In journalism, as distinct from fiction, there is a truth of the matter and this is what objectivity in journalism aims at. Where reporting turns away from the goal of truth and journalists treat events as open to many interpretations, according to their prejudices, assumptions, news agenda or the commercial drive toward entertainment, the justification and self-confessed rationale of journalism threatens to disappear.

Professor Ivor Gaber, a former BBC TV journalist, has been at the forefront of critiquing objectivity (cited in Townend, 2009b):

It must surely be self-evident that objectivity is, and has always been, a meaningless concept. That is because all journalists – subject to official confirmation – are human beings. That means they have a gender, an ethnicity, a family, a social background, a personal history, a set of prejudices etc. etc. that afflict us all.

Objectivity was a possible stance to maintain when journalism was a homogeneous profession where its inhabitants were drawn from one culture, one ethnicity, one recruitment process and similar outlets. In the modern multicultural, global world, objectivity looks threadbare. You only have to look at the way UK journalists report the deaths of the soldiers of their nation, which is very different to the way those deaths will be reported in neutral or hostile media elsewhere, to realize that objectivity is a very moveable feast. Online journalism doyen Paul Bradshaw (2012) says:

 Objectivity is one of the key pillars of journalistic identity: it is one of the ways in which we identify ourselves as a profession. But for the past decade it has been subject to increasing criticism from those (and I include myself here) who suggest that sustaining the appearance of objectivity is unfeasible and unsustainable, and that transparency is a much more realistic aim.

Ivor Gaber (2009) has offered his own 'Seven Pillars of New Journalistic Wisdom' – applicable to journalists and bloggers alike where objectivity is replaced by a much more viable model.

1   Thou shalt recognize one's own subjectivity.
2   Thou shalt strive to be fair.
3   Thou shalt strive to be accurate.
4   Thou shalt strive to be thorough.
5   Thou shalt seek verification.
6   Thou shalt strive to be transparent.
7   Thou shalt be accountable.

One way forward, suggests US media guru Jay Rosen, is to abandon the ideology of viewlessness and accept that journalists have a range of views; to be open about them while holding the reporters to a basic standard of accuracy, fairness and intellectual honesty; and to use transparency, rather than objectivity, as the new foundation on which to build trust with the audience. He cites the memorable phrase coined by David Weinberger, a technology commentator, that transparency is the new objectivity. In part, this can involve journalists providing information about themselves.

For example, on AllThingsD, a technology-news site owned by Dow Jones, all the journalists provide an ethics statement with information about their shareholdings, financial relationships and, in some cases, their personal life (e.g. a journalist who is married to an employee at a large technology company they are reporting on should declare the relationship).

People are more likely to trust you if they know where you are coming from. Transparency also means linking to sources and data, something the web makes easy. Bloggers have long used the technique to back up their views. Ezra Klein, a blogger at the *Washington Post*, has suggested that news organizations should publish full transcripts of interviews online. WikiLeaks's Julian Assange, who claims he is a proponent of radical transparency, has made a similar argument. 'You can't publish a paper on physics without the full experimental data and results. That should be the standard in journalism,' he says. Weinberger observed on his blog that transparency prospers in a linked medium: 'Objectivity is a trust mechanism you rely on when your medium can't do links. Now our medium can' (*The Economist*, 2011).

Gaber (2008) proposes that 'fairness' is the single most important of the pillars.

 For fairness, unlike impartiality, neutrality and so on, is not something that can be established, or experienced, objectively. By its very nature it is felt. As a broadcasting journalist, even working under extreme time pressure, there was always a sense of ultimately how 'fair', or otherwise, one was being.

He says that sometimes that awareness only came to the fore as one watched or listened to the programme on transmission.

> The overwhelming majority of journalists set out to be fair; but in the rough and tumble of a news story subjective judgments come to be made about 'good guys' and bad guys'. Being aware of such judgments is the key to transcending them. This is done by seeking to attain fairness in the editing which sometimes is achieved and sometimes is not – but the important thing is to be aware when it has not.

Moral panics

The news media are quite often accused of creating a 'moral panic' over the way a particular controversy is reported. The accusation is that the reporting of the issue is disproportionate and designed by the media to wind up the public and then force politicians to create hasty and pointless laws. Theorists describe a moral panic as the intensity of feeling expressed in a population about an issue that appears to threaten the social order. Stanley Cohen, author of *Folk Devils and Moral Panics* (1972), who coined the term, said a moral panic occurs when a 'condition, episode, person or group of persons emerges to become defined as a threat to societal values and interests'. Those who start the panic when they fear a threat to prevailing social or cultural values are known by researchers as 'moral entrepreneurs', while people who are seen as a threat to the social order have been described as 'folk devils'.

The media have a reputation for acting as agents of moral indignation. The murder of Jamie Bulger in 1993 has become a classic example in the moral panics canon as a story refocused by the media, from a legitimate issue about children falling through every safety net which should have stopped them from becoming killers, into a moral panic about (a) 'video nasties' and (b) 'evil children' (Barker and Petley, 2001; Petley, 2011; Thompson 1998).

To count as a 'classic' moral panic the media's reporting of the issue in question has to be in some way disproportionate. It also has to be stirring up moral concerns aimed at bringing about some form of change in the law. In this vision of things, the media are seen as moral entrepreneurs who, often in collusion with other moral entrepreneurs, put public pressure on politicians to act; bombarded with the message that 'Something Must Be Done', politicians push through hasty and ill thought-out legislation. The Dangerous Dogs Act 1997 is often used by moral panic theorists as an example of this process at its worst. A few cases pulled together, media pressure on politicians results in flawed legislation that has made little difference tackling the problem.

There is no doubt that some media organizations are disproportionate in their report of some events. However the phrase 'moral panic' has all too often become a form of coded shorthand to criticize the media as well as, on occasion, other primary definers. The question then arises: is this intellectual laziness, or the actions of individuals with a political or ideological agenda (Lashmar, 2013)?

What is news?

One of the most important issues under discussion is how journalists make news selection decisions. Journalists have tended to take a Zen-like approach to their news judgements claiming they don't have to think about the selection of material *they know*. And most often they do. It's not a random throw of the dice – it is based on experience and skill. Machin and Niblock (2006) researched how journalists set the news agenda:

" News journalists often describe their thinking as so instinctive that it defies explanation. Split-second decision-making, gut instinct, curiosity and a 'nose' for news are highly prized attributes for any reporter or editor working in a fast paced news environment. The editor of a leading international news agency says that 'with experience that thought process happens in about one and a half second'. "

Machin and Niblock point out that digital technology is changing the staffing needs of newsrooms, the internet is providing a greater variety of news voices and debate, and over the last two decades waves of deregulation of the market have placed news production under increased commercial pressures. They write that there is an urgent need to examine and update our understanding of how news journalism functions and impacts on our society. 'If, as journalists claim, newsgathering and production is conducted not through intellectual tools but through experience, tenacity and gut feeling, how do we respond to countless theoretical discussions about news that have emerged since as early as the nineteenth century?'

GATEKEEPING THEORY

Gatekeeping is a long-standing concept used in journalism theory. It's the idea that journalists filter and select information for their audience, thus having a powerful control over information flow.

Gatekeeping was applied to news in 1950 when researcher David Manning White looked at the factors an editor takes into consideration when deciding which news will make the paper and which news will not. White (1950) observed the editor of a morning paper. He had the editor retain all copy that he rejected from the paper. After the editor's shift he made notes on why that story was rejected. White found that rejections could be classified in two ways: 1) rejection based on not being worthy of being reported or 2) rejection based on duplicate of other reports on the same thing.

Gatekeeping has been one of the media's central roles: people rely on mediators to transform information about large number of daily events into a manageable number of stories. For a long time journalists decided what news reached the public. The gatekeeping simile though is increasingly seen as irrelevant in the age of the internet where the information flow is now so complex that the journalist can hardly been described as a gatekeeper. Axel Bruns (2003) has been suggested that the term should be changed to 'gatewatching' where the journalist watches the flow of information and culls some for their news outlet.

COMMERCIAL PRESSURES

A thinking journalist follows good ethical practice, even when working to the tightest of deadlines. As journalists we face ethical dilemmas every day. These may include:

- Speed versus accuracy: As we discuss in Chapter 3, online news moves as warp speed where pressure to get the story online and beat the competition is greater than when working to print deadlines.
- Commercial imperatives versus the public interest: American celebrity gossip blog *TMZ* (www. TMZ.com) had few misgivings about publishing on its website naked pictures of Prince Harry covertly taken with a mobile phone. To the frustration of some national newspaper journalists, the British press agreed with requests from Buckingham Palace not to publish them as they were taken without the Prince's permission (until the *Sun* newspaper decided to break the agreement claiming it was an issue of 'the freedom of the press'). The case highlights how some blogs

and news sites do not necessarily work to the same ethical codes as those working for national newspapers. The test has to be: Is what you are doing in the public interest? Is the good achieved much greater than the harm done? For example, it is one thing to obtain and read someone's private emails if you are certain that they are from a politician who is taking a bribe. It is quite another if it is merely to show that a well-known footballer is having a sexual relationship with a model.

- The former audience knows as much as we do: In some cases users know more about the topics that we are reporting on and we should use their expertise. It is common courtesy to credit and thank sources that have helped us in our research – you may even want to link to their site if they have one. We need to remind ourselves that we should treat sources as we would expect to be treated. In many cases, these people are not just sources, but they are also our website users, so being polite is good for business. It's called good online etiquette.

HOW DO PROPRIETORS INFLUENCE NEWS?

For the ethical reporter there can be the tricky issue of how to work for news organizations where their proprietors influence the news agenda. The UK has a long history of press barons and their interference in editorial matters is legion (see Greenslade, 2003a). The most powerful media baron now is Rupert Murdoch, the head of a family that owns hundreds of news organizations across the world. In the UK he owns the *Sun*, *The Times*, *The Sunday Times* and SKY.TV. He closed down the *News of the World* in 2011 as a damage limitation exercise following the phone-hacking scandal (see also Chapter 7). It is widely believed that Murdoch has used his power to further self-interest and the politics of every country he operates in. His support for the Conservatives in 1979 and Labour in 1997 is seen as important in Margaret Thatcher and Tony Blair coming to power. But he denies this influence. Rupert Murdoch gave one of the most remarkable performances at the Leveson Inquiry when he claimed that he had never used his media empire to influence politicians. He says he has 'never asked a prime minister for anything'. He also claimed he had never used his newspapers to further his business interests. Steve Barnett (in Barnett and Brevini, 2012) says it was a startling claim because there 'are so many examples of him doing exactly that'. Barnett pointed out that *The Times* newspaper ran three consecutive editorials attacking any increase to the BBC's licence fee. The Murdochs see the BBC as a major obstruction to the expansion of their media empire in the UK and want it emasculated.

Do journalists and editors chose stories that suit their proprietors? Rupert Murdoch repeatedly claimed he had never influenced editorial direction. The obvious riposte is that he didn't need to. Rupert Murdoch owned 175 newspapers in the world at the time of the Iraq invasion in 2003 (Greenslade, 2003a). Rupert Murdoch favoured the invasion. Every single one of his papers supported the invasion. There is no evidence that he told his editors what position to take – *they knew*. The concept of 'anticipatory compliance' sums up the mechanism. A working journalist should be aware of the issues around confirmatory bias and anticipatory compliance.

Figure 12.3   War reporting raises many ethical dilemmas. (Source; © Photographer: Andy Blackmore)

REGULATION

Different media are subject to different regulation and regulators – Ofcom, for instance, regulates commercial broadcasters. The print media have largely been self-regulating, using different bodies to regulate different parts of the media. In some areas the law is the effective regulator, for example, where a journalist is accused of libelling another person or accused of certain crimes (as in phone hacking). The media always tries to avoid state regulation on the basis that freedom of expression should not be hampered by the state. The abuses of the tabloid press have put great strain on self-regulation. By the time you read this there will be a new regulator body for newspapers as a result of Lord Leveson's Inquiry into ethical standards. The Press Complaints Commission (PCC) did much good work mediating in disputes between newspapers and the public, but it was too close to those that it regulated and too weak to hold them to account. It failed to take the phone-hacking scandal seriously until it was too late. At the time of writing, a new body, which will be much tougher, is being set up underpinned by a Royal Charter.

Media regulator Ofcom ensures TV and radio audiences are protected in areas such as taste, decency, fairness and privacy. But Ofcom only has control over material broadcast over an analogue or digital TV signal. There are moves to tighten up regulation of news output on the internet, which is a concern for many freedom of speech activists. There is growing case law for regulating the mainstream media in the UK that categorizes their online output as part of their overall publication. The PCC has adjudicated against newspapers that have breached the PCC code on material published only online and the body that replaces it will do the same and may extend to online only new outlets.

ETHICS ONLINE AND OFFLINE

Ethics was not a widely discussed topic in many parts of journalism until relatively recently. If anything journalists made light of it as this famous quote by Nicholas Tomalin in the *Sunday Times* from the 1960s shows: 'The only qualities essential for real success in journalism are rat-like cunning, a plausible manner, and a little literary ability.'

You cannot hope to bribe or twist,

thank God! the British journalist.

But, seeing what the man will do

unbribed, there's no occasion to.

(Attributed to Humbert Wolfe in the 1920s but disputed)

In the 1980s, Kelvin MacKenzie, then editor of the *Sun*, famously made a joke about ethics playing on a pun with the word Essex. 'Ethics is a place to the east of London where the men wear white socks.' This quote is seen to reflect MacKenzie's flippant view of the role of ethics in journalism.

Over the last decade and mostly profoundly since the phone-hacking scandal, journalists have taken ethics much more seriously especially as there is a need to rebuild trust with the audience. Professor Chris Frost (2010) says journalists acting responsibly is at the heart of journalism and its relationship with its audience: 'Trust, and an understanding of what it means, is important as an ethical concept and it separates professional journalists from bloggers.'

'ROCKING THE BOAT'

Journalism expert Professor Steve Barnett told the Leveson Inquiry:

Figure 12.4   Lord Justice Leveson's Inquiry has revealed extensive journalistic malpractice. (Leveson Inquiry website)

> There's an abundance of people who are keen, eager, quite idealistic about their view of what journalism can do, what they can achieve as journalists, the role of journalism in a democratic society. But when they entered the workplace they were told that if they did not do what was asked of them they could be replaced by other 'young, willing recruits'. I'm talking specifically now about the kinds of national tabloid newspapers where a lot of these problems have occurred. (BBC, 2011)

The newly trained journalist will find that many news desks have a sense of camaraderie that their team are better at getting the news than their rivals. This is perfectly healthy and fun. But the commercial pressures on the news media mean that reporters can, as Steve Barnett says, come under pressure to cut corners.

> A free press can be good or bad, but, most certainly, without freedom a press will never be anything but bad. (Albert Camus)

HOW CORRECTIONS AND CLARIFICATIONS SHOULD BE HANDLED

It is important to correct any errors or misinformation that you have published on your site. The *Washington Post* has good advice as part of its online publishing guidelines.

ONLINE ETHICS

There has been plenty of discussion about the ethics of the national press (even if they do not always follow their own rules.) Professor Frost says the internet introduces a lot of different problems including:

- crossing national boundaries;
- mixing media – print, audio and video;
- the ability to search and filter;
- the ability to access semi-private information.

Frost says that widespread use of mobile phones raises ethical questions for the journalist:

> The ubiquitous mobile phone camera now means we're more photographed than ever before; Every night out is now plastered over several websites as friends load up their Facebook pages. The ability to send instant messages and take pictures & video of news events as they happen has revolutionized news gathering. (Frost, 2010)

Using this material is full of ethical issues. So, how do we work out a framework for good ethical journalism?

As with all rights come responsibilities. We do recommend joining the National Union of Journalists – not only is it a trade union but also an ethical professional body. It lays down a code of conduct and has an ethical committee. It protects journalists who act ethically.

NUJ CODE OF CONDUCT

The National Union of Journalists (NUJ) Code of Conduct has set out the main principles of British and Irish journalism since 1936. The code is part of the rules and all journalists joining the union must sign that they will strive to adhere to it.

Members of the NUJ are expected to abide by the following professional principles. A journalist:

1 At all times upholds and defends the principle of media freedom, the right of freedom of expression and the right of the public to be informed.
2 Strives to ensure that information disseminated is honestly conveyed, accurate and fair.
3 Does her/his utmost to correct harmful inaccuracies.
4 Differentiates between fact and opinion.
5 Obtains material by honest, straightforward and open means, with the exception of investigations that are both overwhelmingly in the public interest and which involve evidence that cannot be obtained by straightforward means.
6 Does nothing to intrude into anybody's private life, grief or distress unless justified by overriding consideration of the public interest.
7 Protects the identity of sources who supply information in confidence and material gathered in the course of her/his work.
8 Resists threats or any other inducements to influence, distort or suppress information and takes no unfair personal advantage of information gained in the course of her/his duties before the information is public knowledge.
9 Produces no material likely to lead to hatred or discrimination on the grounds of a person's age, gender, race, colour, creed, legal status, disability, marital status, or sexual orientation.
10 Does not by way of statement, voice or appearance endorse by advertisement any commercial product or service save for the promotion of her/his own work or of the medium by which she/he is employed.

11 Shall normally seek the consent of an appropriate adult when interviewing or photographing a child for a story about her/his welfare.
12 Avoids plagiarism.

A BLOGGER'S CODE OF CONDUCT?

There is a debate over whether a blogging code of conduct should exist (see Cenite et al., 2009). A survey of bloggers' ethical beliefs and practices says: 'Whether an ethics code is necessary, desirable or feasible for such a large, heterogeneous group as bloggers has been debated' (Kuhn, 2007). Usually, ethical codes are developed for the professions such as medicine or law or journalism, whose status as a profession is disputed, not for a recreational activity such as blogging. Despite such objections, several commentators (including some bloggers) have recommended blogging ethics codes, in part because many blogs are public and are similar to journalism. No quantitative study has investigated whether bloggers themselves see a need for a code.

HOW YOU PORTRAY PEOPLE IS AN ETHICAL ISSUE

As a journalist you have a lot of power as you can portray people in a positive or negative light. You must consider the impact of your decisions. You may be stereotyping an ethnic group or a group of people who do not have the power to confront you. You may portray people in a way that is not fair. This can be much about the image you use of a person as what you write. Experienced journalist and lecturer Rachel Sharp (2013, interview with author) points out that the police sometimes hand out to reporters mugshots of people who have died in tragic circumstances. The fact that someone has been killed may have nothing to do with the mugshot which just records an earlier arrest. 'Families are often upset when they see a mugshot used to illustrate the death of a loved one as it implies that criminality might have had something to do with the death,' she says. 'It is not the kind of picture you would use to remember a loved one.' As a reporter in north-west London she made a point of visiting the families of the dead person, explaining the situation and requesting a better photograph, a practice she required of her reporters when she was editor.

Winston Silcott was charged with the murder of a police officer after the Broadwater Farm riots in Tottenham in 1985. A photograph was taken by police on his arrest which is hardly flattering and exacerbates Silcott's image of criminality. The Silcott family and friends grew to intensely dislike the mugshot, as it was endlessly used by the media, even when Silcott was freed on appeal. The family offered and sent portrait photographs of Winston Silcott to the media that represented him in a more relaxed and ordinary pose. The media ignored these photographs and continued to use the mugshot. The implication is that the Silcott mugshot had become iconic and that that is how the media wanted their audience to 'read' Silcott, i.e. in a negative light. The question is: is that ethical?

BASIC ETHICAL QUESTIONS

We've already dealt with some ethical issues in other chapters, for example whether you can alter a photograph using software such as Photoshop. Or what happens if a court tells you to reveal a source's name. Here we look at some more very basic questions that journalism students have asked us. We do not intend to try to answer all ethical issues as there are entire books devoted effectively to this issue by such luminaries as Professor Chris Frost (2010) and Professor Richard Keeble (2008).

Q: Can I refuse an assignment that I believe is unethical?

A: This is exactly the kind of situation where your own moral compass might be the only thing to guide you. Richard Peppiatt, who we quoted early in this chapter, was required to make up and falsify stories but eventually he decided to resign and expose his employers, the *Daily Star*. Remember you are as responsible for the reputation of journalism as any other reporter. Acting unethically hangs over you and does not make you feel good. If you find yourself in this situation, before making the decision, you might consult the National Union of Journalists (NUJ) or even an old hand whom you trust. There is no doubt it is a tough one. The NUJ has been pressing for the 'conscience clause' in all journalists' contracts where they opt out of any assignment that they have reason to believe is unethical. 'The NUJ believes a journalist has the right to refuse an assignment or be identified as the author of editorial that would break the letter or spirit of the code. The NUJ will fully support any journalist disciplined for asserting her/his right to act according to the code.' Employers have resisted the clause. The conscience clause was highlighted again with new vigour at the Leveson Inquiry.

Q: Is it OK to make up quotes?

A: No, never. It sometimes happens when you have conducted and finished an interview and you are going over quotes you realize the interviewee was poor at expressing themselves. You read back the quotes and realize that without quoting large chunks the key quotes do not make sense. You know what the person meant because you heard the whole interview. There is a long-standing debate about whether you change a person's quote to make them mean what the interviewee clearly meant. Some small changes may be acceptable. The best method is to take the quote and rewrite it as you believe the interviewee meant to say. You then contact the interviewee and say, in a very polite way, often by saying you are short of space and would they check your version is OK. If they agree the new words that is a perfectly professional practice. It's more difficult with editing audio or video. Its common practice to remove ums and ahs out of an audio interview clip but that's about as far as you can go. In the case of audio and video you really have to get the interview right the first time. Re-ask the question until you get a concise and coherent clip.

Q: Can I cut and paste what other people have written and re-use quotes?

A: Depends on the circumstances. As Nick Davies points out in *Flat Earth News* (2008), a disturbingly large proportion of the material put out by news organizations is taken from new agency material or press releases. Agency reporters write the basic story and do interviews and take quotes which are sent to subscribers. Press releases are often written so the journalist can use them with the minimum of effort. In both cases it is permissible to use the material and quotes.

Reusing quotes is a delicate matter and an effort should be made to show that the quote was not given to you, the reporter. One method is to put it in the past tense: 'As Ann Smith has said in the past…' The working principles for journalists should be: a) write your copy/script in your own words; b) do your own interviews wherever possible and if you don't, try to indicate where the quotes originally came from; and c) don't put agency stories under your own name.

Figure 12.5   Johann Hari. (Flickr: internets-diary)

THE CAUTIONARY TALE OF JOHANN HARI

Johann Hari was once a youthful and fast-rising star of journalism. In 2000 at the tender age of 19 he was joint winner of *The Times* Student News Journalist of the Year award for his work on *Varsity*, the Cambridge University student newspaper. He left King's College with a double first in Social and Political Sciences and joined the *New Statesman*. At the 2003 *Press Gazette* Awards, he won Young Journalist of the Year and was made a columnist by the *Independent's* then editor Simon Kelner. In 2008 he won the Orwell Prize for his work. There appeared to be no stopping his extraordinary career.

Suspicions arose about Hari's ethics over a period of years and in 2011 bloggers highlighted what appeared to be plagiarism where he picked up material from other journalists' work and passed them off as his own.

At first Hari said that this was not plagiarism. In July 2011, Hari was suspended from the *Independent* for two months pending an investigation into the allegations. Also in July 2011, Hari was accused of inventing an atrocity for his Orwell Prize-winning article on the Central African Republic.

In September 2011, Johann Hari announced that, though he stood by the article which won the Orwell Prize, he would be returning it as an act of contrition for the errors he had made elsewhere.

In the months leading up to the accusations a Wikipedia account in the name of David Rose had attacked a range of people including writer Nick Cohen, who had also had a fall-out with Johann Hari. In September 2011 'David Rose' was shown to be Johann Hari.

The *Independent* reported in September 2011 that 'Johann Hari, the writer and columnist for the *Independent*, has admitted plagiarism allegations'. Hari published an apology and admission of misconduct and admitted to using a pseudonym to add positive material to the Wikipedia article about himself and negative material to Wikipedia articles about people he had had disputes with. Hari said he would take unpaid personal leave of absence and seek training in journalistic ethics at his own expense.

Chris Blackhurst, the editor of the *Independent*, said in evidence given at the Leveson Inquiry in January 2012 that Hari had 'severely damaged' the paper. Shortly afterwards Hari said, following his move to the US, he had decided not to return to his job at the *Independent*, because he was going to write a book.

So Hari, who thought he was such a high-flyer he could take ethical shortcuts, was caught and it is unlikely that this once member of the glitterati will return to journalism. Ethics do matter.

FINAL ETHICAL QUESTIONS

It is now easier than ever for a journalist or any writer to check the internet to see if their copy has been plagiarized by using Google search.

Q: Should you always identify yourself as a journalist?

A: As a general principle the answer is yes. In most situations where you are interviewing someone or intend to quote them you should say you are a journalist. This applies as much online as it does offline. If you are using Twitter, Facebook or any message board to contact people you should make sure you say you are a journalist and may well quote what they say or write. There are obvious sensible exceptions to this. If someone says something in public you do not need to identify yourself. After the England football team's disastrous penalty shoot-out performance in Euro 2012, the next day a train driver announced over the PA system on his train 'This is the 7.19 to London Bridge but because I am called Ashley this train will be arriving at Liverpool Street'. A journalist on board quoted him and that was fine as it was a public statement. The one time you can use quotes given to you in private without you disclosing that you are a journalist is when you use subterfuge perhaps working undercover. Then you will have already got approval from senior editors and perhaps the organization's lawyer because you are operating in the public interest.

Q: Can I record people without telling them?

A: If you are recording to broadcast or upload to your website you do have to tell people. If you are recording people as an 'aide memoire', perhaps on a telephone conversation, in the UK, you do not have to ask. It would be polite to ask. In the US and some other countries you cannot record people without their permission. That's why a lot of mobile phones, built with the US market in mind, have that annoying bleep every 30 seconds when you use the record facility. It's to tell the person at the other end that you are recording. There are exceptions about not recording someone without permission where wrong-doing is suspected. This again would be subject to your editors and lawyers.

Q: Can you use subterfuge?

A: Subterfuge is the use of pretence to get the target to admit things that they would not have revealed to a journalist. Perhaps the reporter is pretending they are someone other than a journalist. It might be pretending to be a criminal to get another criminal to admit illegal acts.

Andrew Gilligan (2011) famous for the BBC's infamous 'sexed-up' dossier story in 2003 and now working at the *Daily Telegraph*, says: 'As a journalist I have lied, I have received stolen goods, and for these things I have won two of the top awards in the profession.'

Journalist Heather Brooke (2011) has correctly observed:

> " The pursuit of this high-minded ideal is not exclusive to reporters: a lot of academic and scientific research fits that bill. But journalism is different because as a rough trade it deals with the ugly realities of human nature: sex, scandal, crime, corruption – all the emotional vagaries that make up the 'crooked timber of humanity'. It's not about peddling pretty pictures; that's public relations or propaganda. Because of those ugly realities journalists have to use subterfuge or deception to dig out the truth. "

Figure 12.6 Journalist Andrew Gilligan. (Source: *Daily Telegraph*)

The *Guardian*'s former investigations editor David Leigh says he had once pretended to be an arms dealer in a successful attempt to prove that Mark Thatcher had entered into a business deal with a Middle Eastern businessman. He argued that was a legitimate technique because the story was in the public interest.

'I don't think journalists should break the law,' Leigh says. 'I don't think they should break the criminal law, at any rate. Sometimes … we challenge the law and sometimes it's difficult.'

David Leigh explained at the Leveson Inquiry: 'Journalists on public interest investigations have to use a certain amount of guile,' he says, pointing out that reporters cannot arrest people, or compel individuals to appear before a court.

'We have to find out things often from powerful people who are anxious to conceal them,' he added. 'There are many powerful organizations in society who want to keep things quiet for their own reasons, and that includes newspaper corporations too.'

Leigh criticized the *News of the World* and the tabloid press in general. 'The tittle-tattle [they publish] is being got illegally, intrusively and sometimes cruelly,' he says. 'It does bring our trade into disrepute,' Leigh added. 'It's very upsetting; because they failed to clean up their act it makes it more difficult for people like me on serious newspapers to do worthwhile things.'

Because of the high-minded motives of public interest, journalists can claim some protection from the law when pursuing it. Journalists justify some of their methods, such as invasion of privacy but which can carry out exemptions if carried out in the public interest.

We will end with a prescient 20-year-old quote from media correspondent Ray Snoddy (1993):

> **"** In the end, talking about and encouraging high standards and ethics in newspapers – tabloids as well as broadsheets – is not some sort of self-indulgence for amateur moral philosophers or journalists with sensitive psyches: it is a very practical matter, involving customer relations, product improvement and profit … Unless such issues are taken more seriously, future generations could be reading about many of today's newspapers in the history books, rather than actually reading the papers themselves. **"**

>>Summary<<

1 Keep up with the ethical discussions that always surround journalism. Think what you would do in any controversial situation. Always remember the power you have over people because you can access a large audience and act responsibly.

2 When in doubt about an issue, consult a senior colleague or the house lawyer.

3 Keep all your notes and recordings – you never know when you might need them.

4 Never try to avoid correcting an error once it is made. If you make a mistake, come clean quickly to your editor. Then discuss how best to remedy the problem. Cover-ups destroy more careers than mistakes do.

5 Journalism is a worthy profession so you should never do anything unethical. Join a professional group that has an ethical code. Unprofessional and unethical behaviour has resulted in journalism having a low reputation.

FURTHER READING

Curran, James, and Seaton, Jean. 2009. 3rd edn. *Power without Responsibility.* London: Routledge.
    The classic text on the role of the media.
Greenslade, Roy. 2003. *The Press Gang.* London: Pan.
    This has been the key text for many years on all theoretical issues surrounding journalism and is updated
    from time to time.
Lashmar, Paul (ed.) 2011. *Journalism: Cutting Edge Commentaries on the Critical Issues Facing Journalism at the
    Practical, Theoretical and Media Industry Level.* The Marketing & Management Collection, London: Henry
    Stewart Talks Ltd.
    A series of augmented audio podcasts covering ten of the big issues of recent journalism.

CHAPTER 13

Law and Regulation

Andy Chatfield

INTRODUCTION

The web has frequently been compared to the wild west – a vast, borderless place, where, from the comfort of their PC, anonymous cyber-outlaws can ride into town, outrage the decent citizenship by saying what they like, and vanish again into the desert. In his report into press ethics, Lord Leveson described the internet as an 'ethical vacuum' (Leveson, 2012). For libertarian proponents of free speech, this vision is an anarchic paradise. But to others it is less welcome. In the words of one analyst, 'territorially-based law-making and law-enforcing authorities find this new environment deeply threatening' (Johnson and Post, 1996).

Well, at the time of writing at least, civilization has survived and the web is far from lawless. There are lively debates about who precisely does control the internet (see, e.g., Goldsmith and Wu, 2008) and how rules from the 'non-virtual' world can be adapted to cope with it. But there is no doubt that the rapid expansion of the web and multimedia journalism continues to raise fundamental new challenges for journalists, regulators and the justice systems of the world – not to mention the many millions of people who publish words online every day via tweets, blogs, status updates and so on.

Laws which have evolved to apply to a particular country, or jurisdiction, are now being applied internationally, and international regulations are fast evolving too. Codes of conduct devised to regulate print or broadcast journalists are proving outdated. Judges – whom we might like to think consume their news via only *The Times* and BBC Radio Four – are having to decode the alien jargon and multiplying complexities of electronic networks.

If you are a journalist launching your first blog, knowing the legal and ethical boundaries is important for establishing your credibility, even if your limited profile means you are unlikely to face serious legal threats.

If you are professionally responsible for content on a news website, this knowledge is essential to ensure your choices are well informed.

A single chapter cannot cover every aspect of relevant law (some texts which do are recommended at the end). Rather, the focus here is on the particular legal challenges for online journalists.

AN UNCERTAIN UNIVERSE

Social regulation within modern society has developed within physical bounds of time and space. But the development of cyberspace distances its inhabitants from local controls and the physical confines of nationality, sovereignty and governmentality, leading to regulatory solutions which conduce to a divorce from the old paradigms and the prominence of such features as self-organization and social interaction rather than institutional authority. *(*Akdeniz et al., 2000: 5)

New challenges for law makers range from the logistical (e.g. how can wrong-doers be traced in the 'wild west' of cyberspace?) to the conceptual (e.g. in what sense and where is something 'published' online?).

These are challenges for journalists too. We have always needed to know the law, but now have to monitor a fast-changing legislative landscape, where the ability to publish instantly to the world puts pressure on traditional editorial processes. There is often less time to consult, check and reflect before publishing.

Newsdesk memo: Speed, yes, but safety too

Jason Collie, Head of Content for the *Oxford Mail*, its sister titles and all their websites, takes the leading role in his newsroom on negotiating legal dangers, in print and online. He believes that the medium in which you publish is fundamentally irrelevant: 'If you're wrong in print, you're wrong on screen.'

But he has some particular advice for those using more instant forms of publication than newspapers:

> Don't let the time pressure of the web alter the key point that you have to get it right first time, every time, be it web or paper. Better to be a few minutes late and right than throw legally unsound copy up online – particularly as in the modern world your web copy is more likely to be seen by more people like judges, barristers, solicitors and local authority and private company press officers now so will be what gets you in trouble. And don't let reporters upload direct to the web – everyone makes mistakes so every bit of copy needs second eyes.

Figure 13.1   Jason Collie, Head of Content, *Oxford Mail* website. (Source: Jason Collie)

Journalists' growing involvement with the web in all its forms has raised intriguing new questions:

Whose rules apply?

If a journalist in London libels a businessman in New York on a website whose HQ is in Germany but whose server is in Sweden, who and where might he sue? And if your work is truly multimedia, do you follow press or broadcast regulations? Or an exotic combination of both?

Who is a publisher?

If a posting on a forum breaches a privacy injunction by revealing the name of an adulterous footballer, who is liable? The original author? The website hosting the message board? The host's ISP? The search engine delivering a link to the page? And what about the 100,000 users of Twitter who spread the name within 24 hours?

When is something published?

Is it when it is uploaded (once) or downloaded (perhaps a million times on YouTube)? Is an article sitting quietly in an online archive still being 'published'? And who has the right to 'unpublish' it?

Who is a journalist?

Some laws give special protection to 'journalistic' work. But who is a journalist? Only paid editorial employees of media companies? Anyone with a journalism qualification? Every blogger and tweeter on the planet sharing 'news'? Or to put it another way: 'You don't need to be employed by a newspaper or broadcaster to commit an act of journalism' (Butterworth and Johannes, 2009). And if a blogger gets protection in law, should she or he also get a press card?

What about naughty readers?

A precious dimension of news online is the interactivity with readers, but few know much about media law. Is their misbehaviour your problem? How can you control it?

...And *who* are they anyway?

A bank robber tries to stay anonymous by donning a mask, but clues to his identity might lie in CCTV footage, a witness's memory of his voice, a fingerprint, DNA in a strand of hair. Online, we can all (including some conducting journalism) wear 'masks' of made-up usernames – whether for fun, convenience, security or deliberate subterfuge. But what if a law is broken by @CustardCreamFan, @BolshevikMuppet or @GodIsDead? Who and where are they? Are they adults or children? Are they even human (see, e.g., dogsontwitter.com)? The evidence may lie in a database you control, even if it is simply the IP address of a subscriber to your website. When should you tell the police?

Courts and governments worldwide have begun to answer some of these questions.

The sections below explore four principal areas of media law, but space excludes many (notably the growing impact of legislation controlling hate crimes and terrorism). Although the focus is on the situation in England and Wales, an international perspective is unavoidable at times. Not only do European laws and court decisions have a direct application to British media rules, but high-profile decisions made by courts in one country are often referred to by judges wrestling to frame new principles in others.

DEFAMATION

Overview

An expensive libel action is a serious threat for journalists, whether part of a big news organization or freelance. But it is rare for journalists to end up in the dock. The greater danger may be the so-called 'chilling effect' on freedom of expression such laws impose, making editors play it too safe for fear of costly consequences. Long-promised reforms in the UK, outlined in a box below, are imminent and expected to have a liberalizing effect.

Whatever the impact of the reforms, there has been a growing sense in the UK, at least, that 'privacy is the new libel' because high-profile public figures are finding it easier to use the developing privacy laws to muzzle the media or win damages (see the section 'Privacy' below). There are signs too that the justice system is beginning to take a more sophisticated approach to the often casual nature of online communication. One judge compared reader comments at the foot of a *Daily Mail* article to mere 'pub talk', refusing to rule they should be identified for damages to be sought (*Clift v Clarke* [2011] EWHC 1164 (QB)).

According to one report (cited in Dodd, 2011), the number of UK libel cases, in all media, only rose from 83 to 86 in the year to May 2011 – a modest number given the explosion in communication tools. However, the same report said the number of *online* libel cases had doubled.

The basics

Defamation laws protect people's reputations. In England and Wales, it is a civil matter – that is to say, one party sues another.

A statement about a person will be considered defamatory in law if it 'tends to'

- lower the person in the estimation of right-thinking people, and/or
- expose the person to hatred, contempt or ridicule, and/or
- lead others to shun or avoid the person.

The statement must refer to someone living and must be published to a third party – someone other than the victim. The statement does not have to have actually caused provable damage to the person's reputation (though this will soon change).

Journalists defame people all the time. Indeed, it is part of their job to dent or even destroy reputations when it is deserved. For instance, every murder conviction you report defames the murderer – 'right-thinking people' are very likely to think less of him. Every serious error by a politician tends to lead to ridicule, not least in satire. A negative film review may explicitly or implicitly defame someone, such as the director or writer, and lead others to avoid employing them – i.e. shun them.

Free speech and public debate of all kinds would be impossible if these things could not be reported. But of course they can and are. Legal problems arise when the publisher has no *defence* for reporting such things, most obviously when facts are wrong or lies have been told.

Until the new Act comes into force, the injured party (the claimant) only needs to prove that the words that have upset them refer to them, are defamatory and have been published to at least one other person. The burden is on the defendant to shield himself with a suitable defence. This is why sound knowledge of the possible defences, and the way in which they have been interpreted in major cases (involving the internet or not), is the best safeguard for any journalist against libel suits.

Key defences

The most common defences used by publishers when sued for defamation are:

- Justification (or 'truth'). If you can prove the substantial truth of what you have written or broadcast, you cannot be found liable.
- Honest comment. This defence was, until recently, known as 'fair comment' but a Supreme Court judge usefully renamed it (*Spiller v Joseph* [2010] UKSC 53 [117]). It helps protect opinion. The defendant must prove the words were an opinion based on true facts and the opinion was honestly held. The issue must be one of public interest.
- Privilege. This defence recognizes the special status of the information being reported and the importance of the journalist's role in reporting it. The proceedings of Parliament and most courts are covered by absolute privilege meaning that people can speak freely there with no fear of a libel writ. Fair and accurate reports of things said there enjoy the privilege defence too. For reporters in most circumstances, however, the key defence is qualified privilege, which rewards diligent reporting. If you have written a fair and accurate report on a matter of public interest, without malice, you may succeed *in this defence*. An important case in 1999 (*Reynolds v. Times Newspapers Ltd and Others* [1999] UKHL 45) established a version of this called the Reynolds Defence which gave courts a series of duty/interest tests by which to measure the reporter's diligence – see box below. This has become known as the 'public interest defence'. These tests are worth memorizing, since they reflect the good habits any diligent reporter should be applying anyway.

Reynolds Defence

In his comments on a libel case between *The Times* and the Irish Prime Minister, Lord Nicholls outlined ten points that a court (and therefore a journalist) should consider when deciding if a report was the product of responsible journalism and, even if it defamed someone, could be defended in law:

1. The seriousness of the allegation. The more serious, the more the public is misinformed, the more the individual harmed, if the claim is untrue.
2. The nature of the information. Is it a matter of public concern?
3. The source of the information. Is the source reliable?
4. The steps taken to verify the information. What checks were done?
5. The status of the information. Has it already been part of a trustworthy investigation?
6. The urgency. Did the news have to be published or broadcast then?
7. Whether comment was sought. Were the claims put to the plaintiff?
8. Whether the article contained the gist of the plaintiff's side, even if comment wasn't sought.
9. The article's tone. Are allegations presented as fact?
10. The circumstance. Was there mischief in the timing?

Nicholls made it clear this was not an exhaustive list. The defence has been codified by the new Defamation Act (see box below).

Reform

The new Defamation Act received the Royal Assent in April 2013 but at the time of writing its provisions had not formally become law. It significantly changes some aspects of libel law. The key ones are outlined in the following box.

All change for the libel laws

In 2013, the UK parliament passed a new Defamation Act. Its most significant proposals for online journalists include:

- a requirement that a statement must have actually caused substantial harm;

- a single publication rule to prevent action being taken repeatedly over, e.g., material in online archives;

- increased protection for websites that host user-generated content, provided they comply with a dispute resolution procedure;

- a clause enshrining the principle that people performing a 'public function' in local authorities could not sue;

- a new statutory defence of 'responsible publication on matters of public interest' (see Reynolds Defence box above) and amendments to the established defences of 'truth' and 'honest opinion';

- action to address libel tourism by ensuring a court will only accept jurisdiction if this is the most appropriate place for a case against a non-European to be heard.

You can read the act in full at www.legislation.gov.uk/ukpga/2013/26/contents/enacted.

The Act aims to end 'libel tourism'. As things stand, if you put something defamatory on your website, you could be sued in any country where it has been downloaded, provided the claimant has a reputation to defend in that country.

In other words, the place of publication is not the journalist's location when he uploads it, nor the company which hosts the site or the server it sits on. Publication happens when someone downloads the article on to their PC, phone or other device.

If you distribute and sell a magazine in a foreign country, you can be sued there too. In that case, courts would look at how many copies had been distributed. In web cases, courts seek data on individual page viewings, although the level of damages does not always correlate with the statistics.

This principle was established in a 2002 case in which a man living in Victoria, Australia, was allowed to sue an American publisher of a website hosted in New Jersey (*Dow Jones & Company, Inc v Gutnick* [2002] HCA 56). In that judgement, Callinan J wrote: 'If a publisher publishes in a multiplicity of jurisdictions it should understand, and must accept, that it runs the risk of liability in those jurisdictions in which the publication is not lawful.'

Two years later, when boxing promoter Don King, a US resident, decided to sue a US-based lawyer who had accused him of being anti-Semitic on websites based in the US, he was given permission to pursue the claim in England (*King v Lewis and Others* [2004] EWCA Civ 1329).

Such cases have fuelled much debate about libel tourism (or 'forum shopping') amid fears that rich claimants will pick countries where they were most likely to succeed. This trend is nothing new but the web makes it easier. Courts in England and Wales have hit back at times. In 2005 a case was judged to be an 'abuse of process' because an allegedly libellous article published on a US subscription-based website had been seen here by only five people, three of whom were linked to the claimant (*Dow Jones and Co Inc v Yousef Abdul Latiff Jameel* [2005] EWCA Civ 75).

The Act also changes the 'multiple publication rule'. Anyone suing for libel must usually do it within a year of when it appeared. With traditional media, there was usually a clear date of publication or broadcast. Today, with online archives of all types of media, material is, says the law as it stands, republished every time someone views an article or item afresh. A key case here was *Loutchansky v Times Newspapers Ltd. & Ors* [2002] EWHC 2726 (QB). The Act establishes a 'single publication rule', preventing a claimant from suing a publisher afresh after the one-year limitation period.

The other publishers

Another challenge for online journalists is how robustly others involved in the publication chain might defend your right to publish. With newspapers, this chain includes the printer and the news agent. Online, it may include a company like WordPress on whose site yours sits, or an ISP hosting your company's servers. Section 1 of the Defamation Act of 1996 offers the defence of innocent dissemination to any such innocent party, who could not have known about the libel.

But ever since a landmark case (*Godfrey v Demon Internet Service* [2001] QB 201), ISPs have been inclined to pre-emptively remove material from their servers once a complaint has been made – just to ensure they are safe. Indeed, swift action is encouraged in a range of media law contexts (see, e.g., the Digital Millennium Copyright Act 1998 in the US and the EU's Electronic Commerce Directive 2000 – see also below).

Wikileaks has famously tried to buck this trend by exploiting the complex technology of the web to disguise who runs and hosts it and where it essentially 'exists', taking on laws internationally in areas even more controversial than defamation, notably national security.

The temptation for hosts and ISPs to tell its users to 'take down' complained-of material without the hassle (and cost) of checking the fairness of the complaint means that there are likely to be many unjustified infringements of free expression happening quietly in the background every day, although sites like www.chillingeffects.org are fighting back on behalf of internet users by monitoring such actions. In the US, the law outlines a procedure which accommodates counter-complaints by the original author of the material after a 'cease and desist' notice is issued (though this happens after the site is disabled or blocked, not before). In Europe, such procedures are not yet explicitly defined but are being reviewed.

User-generated content

In the same way that ISPs play no part in the authorship of journalism on the websites they host, editors cannot anticipate what readers will publish in the 'comment' fields widely available on their web pages. Swift and wide-ranging interaction with readers is one of the fundamental benefits of publishing on the web, fuelling the free flow of information and comment. Yet illegal content of all kinds is an ever-present danger, whether you are a solo blogger who has enabled the comment facility, or a big company hosting interactive features like forums or chatrooms. Long gone are the days when readers' views were only represented on the fixed letters pages of a newspaper, after careful editing by trained journalists. Few have the resources to monitor such live UGC, but all need some kind of moderation process.

An important case in the area of user-generated content (*Karim v Newsquest Media Group* [2009] EWHC 3205 (QB)) established that publishers could rely on Regulation 19 of the E-Commerce Regulations, a piece of European legislation. An article entitled 'Crooked solicitors spent client money on a Rolex, loose women and drink' was published on websites run by Newsquest, a UK regional news publisher. The High Court ruled that the article itself, about a lawyer being struck off, was not defamatory because it was a fair and accurate report of a tribunal and covered by absolute privilege. Newsquest escaped liability for defamatory comments posted beneath the story thanks to the directive. To enjoy this protection, it is vital that the organization controlling a site 'upon obtaining such knowledge or awareness [of serious illegality], acts expeditiously to remove or to disable access to the information'. As we discuss in Chapter 9, most news companies use their readers as moderators of UGC on their sites, providing a clear way for alerts to be sent in, and a procedure for acting on them swiftly if necessary.

Football fans' forums seem to have provided particular challenges in this regard. An independent forum for Sheffield Wednesday fans, owlstalk.co.uk, hit the headlines in 2007 when the club sued the site's owner for allowing some fans to pursue an often libelous 'sustained campaign of vilification' against the club chairman. The suit was later dropped, but the case was also significant for the attempt by the club to gain a so-called 'Norwich Pharmacal' order (see 'Privacy' section below).

Live reporting

In an era when journalists are increasingly using tools like Twitter and liveblogs (which provide a running commentary on an event or breaking story, often with readers' contributions), awareness of defamation dangers is more important than ever. The first Twitter libel case in England – *Cairns v Modi* [2012] EWHC 756 (QB) – saw New Zealand cricketer Chris Cairns win £90,000 in damages and £400,000 in costs over a single tweet by a cricket administrator, who had accused him of match fixing. Although neither party was a journalist, the profile of the tweet was raised greatly when the cricket website Cricinfo ill-advisedly repeated the allegation. More wisely, it admitted its error, paid Cairns £7,000 in damages and published an extensive interview with him about the whole affair – another good example of the benefits of quick action when you know you are wrong.

Since reporters are now allowed to tweet from court (see 'Contempt' section below) without the judge's permission, journalists should acquaint themselves with the demands of the privilege defence which is a complete bar to a libel action. The three requirements are that reports should be fair, accurate and contemporaneous reports of a hearing held in public. Tweets are clearly as contemporaneous as it gets, but fairness and accuracy may be harder to achieve in a series of 140-character updates than in a carefully sub-edited summary of a day's evidence.

COPYRIGHT (Intellectual Property)

Overview

Journalists make money from their professional expertise and the artefacts, written, audio or visual, they create. The laws of intellectual property (IP) protect this material and ensure that journalists (and all kinds of creative people) can be fairly rewarded.

These laws are an essential safeguard, since practically – particularly on the web – it is very easy to steal the products of our labour by, for instance, copying and pasting text or lifting an image. Knowledge of these laws enables you to protect your work and, equally importantly, to avoid using others' work without permission.

However, in the area of IP, the lawless side to the web is really creating some major headaches. A consumer study by Ofcom (Ofcom, 2012) found one in six people believed they had downloaded or accessed online content illegally over a three-month period. This isn't just words and pictures – copyright is brought into play with 'piracy' of movies and music. You may well have read about Napster and Pirate Bay.

But the fact that lots of people routinely take and republish, for example, photographs online and 'get away with it' does not make it right or lawful. For a journalist to do this is self-defeating. If you are careless about other people's IP, why should others respect yours?

The good news is that reporters have special protection when using others' material for journalistic purposes.

The basics

In the UK, the Copyright Designs and Patents Act 1988 protects 'original literary, dramatic, musical or artistic works', 'sound recordings, films or broadcasts' and 'the typographical arrangement of published editions'. Such materials are protected regardless of whether there is an explicit copyright warning or a '©' sign. For journalists, this covers text, images, audio, video and page layouts.

Who owns the copyright varies according to the circumstances. News publishers employing staff journalists generally own the copyright to material produced by them, unless an individual's contract states otherwise. In contrast, a freelance writer or video journalist would be the 'first owner' of his or her work. (A minor complication arises with work created before 1 August 1989 – a photograph by a freelancer belongs to whoever commissioned it.)

Importantly, there is no copyright in facts, news or information. The law is not intended to stifle ideas – merely to protect the way they are expressed when someone has had to put a degree of effort, skill or creativity into doing so. While there is copyright in formally delivered spoken words (like an interview or a speech), recording words in any format to report current events is specifically allowed.

Transferring and protecting copyright

Copyright can be 'assigned' to another user of material or a publisher can be 'licensed' to use the work in a particular way (for instance, in a newspaper but not on an associated website). When a freelancer sells his work, he is effectively doing one or the other, and it is important to get the precise terms of the deal in writing. Likewise, if you need to use another's picture to illustrate an article, you should get written permission from the photographer, whether money changes hands or not. Websites such as freelanceuk.com offer excellent advice on such things.

The 24/7 nature of online journalism means information is circulated rapidly, with rivals monitoring each other to keep up with the news. Because information is not copyright-protected, it is acceptable, for instance, to 'lift' facts from another source, provided you express the information in a new way. Of course, there are other legal and ethical dangers in using facts you have not personally checked. At the very least, it is often appropriate to credit the news source until you have verified information, which is why you often hear, for instance, the BBC saying 'Reuters is reporting ...' when a story is first breaking. Regardless of the law, merely regurgitating news found by others – famously described as 'churnalism' (Davies, 2008) – is not a rewarding use of your time, and may simply mean you are in a chain of gossip or, worse, misinformation.

Cases that come to court often hinge on lawyers arguing over whether the copyright breach is 'substantial'. But the Act provides a specific defence, known as fair dealing, for those reporting current events. This allows journalists to use verbatim material from other sources, or broadcast small parts of others' audio or video work, provided that:

- the material is used 'fairly' – you must only use a reasonable chunk and not take unreasonable commercial advantage;
- you acknowledge the source, by providing a suitable title or description, and naming the author or creator.

Importantly, this defence does *not* cover still photographs. The Act also specifically allows fair dealing for 'criticism or review', important for journalists who review books, TV shows, films, etc.

A separate, and rarely used, public interest defence also enables copying without permission where the purpose is to expose an immoral work or one that incites immoral behaviour.

It is also worth online journalists knowing about the Creative Commons, which has emerged to help people 'take full and legal advantage of the Internet's unprecedented wealth of science, knowledge and culture'. See box below.

Creative Commons

Creative Commons (CC) is a non-profit organization that offers free legal tools and technology to help people share their work online safely. It offers six types of licence. Its outreach manager Fred Benenson suggested in an interview (Townend, 2009a) that journalists could take advantage of this system by:

1 Releasing their work online under a CC licence. Al Jazeera and Wired.com have both released material using CC licences.
2 Using the CC search tool at search.creativecommons.org to find material available. Mr Benenson said: 'Whether this is a photo to accompany an article or a MP3 to put in the background of a video, CC licences lower the transaction costs of acquiring usable material online.'

Figure 13.2   The Creative Commons logo. (Creativecommons.org)

Aggregators

One of the services PR firms offer for clients is to monitor media coverage, either of the client's own business or of news relevant to it. Online, such firms can automate the presentation of such content, using 'spider' technology to generate summaries of or links to many stories. Such processes are known as aggregation or skimming. The Newspaper Licensing Agency, a firm owned by UK newspapers and originally set up to give licences for the use of print cuttings, pursued a test case against media monitor Meltwater News.

The case (*Newspaper Licensing Agency & ors v Meltwater Holding BV & ors* [2011] EWCA Civ 890) established not only that Meltwater should pay for using headlines and extracts from news sites, but that its subscribers needed a separate licence. The Supreme Court in 2013 overturned a ruling which suggested anyone simply browsing a newspaper site was infringing copyright, but referred the case to the European Court of Justice to establish an EU-wide application of these principles. Interestingly, the latter court had earlier ruled that a 'literary work' as short as an 11-word headline could be copyright-protected. In a separate case between Meltwater and Associated Press (a news agency owned by US newspapers), Meltwater was judged to have infringed copyright law there by failing to pay for headlines and excerpts.

Reform

Amid fears that IP laws block economic growth and innovation, a recent review (Hargreaves, 2011) proposed creating the world's first Digital Copyright Exchange, to make the buying and selling of licences more efficient. The government later announced plans to create this.

CONTEMPT

Overview

It is an important principle in democratic societies that the judicial system – which wields huge state power over individuals – is open to scrutiny and held accountable.

Generally, the courts are open to the press and public, and the media play an important role in ensuring trials are scrutinized and in communicating to citizens how justice has been administered.

But it is also an important principle that justice is fair. The media does not merely report on crime and the courts to fulfil its noble function as democratic watchdog. Cases often make cracking stories, with clear goodies and baddies, full of drama and emotion. The process of justice – the systematic and controlled gathering, presentation and evaluation of evidence – is often at odds with the ways of journalism. Major crimes often become the focus of a very competitive 'feeding frenzy' as rival media battle to find new angles. A good example of this was the case of Christopher Jefferies, the landlord of Joanna Yeates who was murdered in Bristol in 2010. He was never charged, but his arrest for questioning fuelled a spate of defamatory articles about him which led to actions both for libel and contempt.

The law of contempt has evolved to stop such 'trial by media', by putting limits on freedom of expression.

Contempt is another area of law where the competitive pressure in the digital age to report swiftly can lead to legal problems. As we shall see, anyone can be found guilty of contempt, including ordinary people commenting on a case, being disruptive in the public gallery of a courtroom or breaking jury rules.

The basics

A priority concern in most contempt cases is to ensure that any case which does or may involve a jury is not seriously 'prejudiced'. This is because juries are ordinary people and not trained lawyers.

Such prejudice might, as in the Jefferies case, involve the publication of unverified gossip. It might also consist of true facts which, for good legal reasons, are not being shared with the jury, such as previous convictions. It might be something as relatively banal as recording a hearing without permission.

The key act in England and Wales, detailed in the box below, is the Contempt of Court Act of 1981.

Contempt of Court Act 1981

- *Substantial risk.* The act says that a publisher is guilty of contempt if it publishes material which 'creates a substantial risk that the course of justice in the proceedings in question will be seriously impeded or prejudiced'.

- *Active proceedings.* The proceedings don't have to be an ongoing trial. Liability covers the period that proceedings are 'active', which might be triggered by an arrest or even a warrant.

- *Strict liability.* Contempt under the act is a crime of strict liability – it is irrelevant whether the publisher intended to interfere with justice or not.

- *Defences.* Journalists can claim a defence if their report is on a matter of public affairs and raises a prejudice which is merely incidental to the proceedings, or if they didn't know proceedings were active and could reasonably not have been expected to know.

Contempt – alive and kicking

In 2008, Richard Danbury argued that contempt was declining. The media were getting away with publishing things that they didn't used to, and technology was likely to accelerate the trend. 'Because the internet is outside the jurisdiction of the court, easily searchable, and historical in nature, the law of contempt risks becoming unenforceable. And because of the way that it is developing, that risk is being magnified' (Danbury, 2008). He realized that archived news online posed a big problem and also understood that people other than trained journalists were increasingly likely to commit contempt.

This proved prophetic. There have been well-publicized instances of contemptuous material being widely disseminated by non-journalists on social networks, primarily Twitter. Some have broken court injunctions intended to protect someone caught up in scandal (see 'Privacy' section below). In 2012, after professional footballer Ched Evans was convicted and jailed for raping a 19-year-old, her identity, which is protected in law, was widely discussed on Twitter.

One high-profile case did involve a non-journalist and a social network, but the guilty woman was a juror not a blogger. Mother-of-three Joanna Fraill was on the jury in a complex drugs trial in 2010. There were eight defendants on numerous charges and two previous trials had already collapsed. Some way into the trial, the 40-year-old used Facebook to exchange messages with one of the defendants and also admitted having done a web search on another defendant. She was jailed in 2011 for eight months.

She was not the first juror to disobey a judge's express command only to assess the case on the facts in court. Joshua Rozenberg wrote that it was not unique to the internet age and recalled the 1993 double murder trial which had to be abandoned after it was discovered that four members of the jury had consulted a ouija board before finding him guilty. 'Since 'ouija' means "yes-yes", Young might well have felt that he did not receive a fair trial,' was Rozenberg's dry postscript (Rozenberg, 2011).

The first line of the Fraill judgement said: 'This is a troublesome case and, we must do our best to ensure, an exceptional case.' The court must have been dismayed, then, when former university lecturer Theodora Dallas was jailed in January 2012 for conducting internet research during an assault trial in Luton, which also later collapsed. There have been similar problems elsewhere, notably Canada and the USA.

So if Danbury was right to see how new media might entangle ordinary people in media laws, he perhaps under-estimated the Contempt of Court Act's staying power. Attorney General Dominic Grieve wrote in 2012 his belief that the act was 'a sound piece of legislation for the modern age' (Grieve, 2012) and it has become clear in recent years that the contempt laws are still very much alive and kicking.

Tweets in court

A new Rubicon was crossed for court reports in 2011 when Lord Judge, Lord Chief Justice, ruled that bona fide reporters could tweet from court without asking for permission. He said laptops and hand-held devices were important parts of open justice, as long as use was silent. Reporters must still take care, however. Shortly afterwards, at the trial of football manager Harry Redknapp on tax-evasion charges in 2012, the judge banned Twitter use after a reporter allegedly tweeted the name of a juror and also reported evidence that had been heard in the jury's absence. The Attorney General apparently decided to take no further action, but such errors are clearly more likely when reporting live online.

It should be emphasized that photography in court or its precincts is still strictly banned. Section 9 of the 1981 act also bans recording devices 'except by leave of the court'. Lord Judge's Twitter ruling, contained in a 'Practice Guidance' published on judiciary.gov.uk (Judge, 2011), points to earlier guidelines which say the key tests for allowing recording are whether there is a 'reasonable need' and the likely impact on proceedings. Such leave still appears very rare.

Lord Judge made clear that members of the public in court still needed to ask the judge's permission to use phones or laptops. This returns us to the thorny problem of the status of ordinary citizens as reporters in court. Journalists who attend court as part of their training will know that, after establishing permission even to take notes, courts can be peculiarly sensitive to what they plan to report and where. Writers such as Heather Brooke (2011) have argued these uncertainties are symptoms of a justice system which is too secretive. Trends in mainstream journalism are not helping, as the number of people dedicated to court reporting declines in newsrooms squeezed for resources. The Justice Gap (thejusticegap.com) is one campaign trying to open up the justice system and encourage citizen journalism. It claims 'it is perfectly possible for a member of the public to report on a court case' and offers explicit advice on how to approach it.

Contempt and archives

Online archives have also been implicated in contempt issues. During the trial in July 2012 of PC Simon Harwood for killing Ian Tomlinson, the judge ordered the *Daily Mail* to remove archive articles on its website which reported previous allegations of misconduct against him. The old articles were considered both 'published' and prejudicial. The judge had, as invariably judges do, guided the jury not to search the web for background information but did not make the ruling because he thought they would disobey him. Rather, he feared a search by a juror for reports of the current trial (which was permitted) was likely to throw up the earlier reports.

Pictures can get you in trouble too. The first online contempt case in England and Wales (*Attorney General v Associated Newspapers Ltd and News Group Newspapers Ltd* [2011] EWHC 418) led to fines for the *Sun* and the *Daily Mail*, who both published on their websites an uncropped image of the defendant in a murder case holding a pistol. Both took the image down within hours and the jury in the murder trial was not discharged, but the contempt ruling still went against them.

Reform

The Law Commission published a consultation paper in 2012 proposing reform of the contempt laws in the light of digital challenges. Its proposals include putting into statute the right for courts to order news organizations to take down prejudicial archive material and introducing a new crime for jurors doing background research.

PRIVACY

Overview

The explosion in communications technology has made privacy a hot topic. Facebook's one billion users happily share all sorts of private information online, usually to a circle well beyond their nearest and dearest. We can take a picture on our phone and publish it instantly. Material we used to share with one or two people is now shared among many more.

Yet however cavalier the digital generation seems about such 'self-publishing', resentment of media intrusion into the private space seems higher than ever.

It was serious and sustained breaches of privacy, in the form of mobile-phone hacking, which led to the closure of the *News of the World* newspaper in 2011, multiple court actions against journalists and others, and to the Leveson Inquiry into press standards. Leveson's final report recommended another overhaul of media regulation in the UK, and at the time of writing politicians and editors are haggling over what it should entail.

That case has been by far the most high-profile 'privacy' story in recent years, and yet its relevance for online journalists is still unclear. True, it involved (newspaper) journalists making use of modern technology (mobile phones) but they were breaking distinct laws governing such technology. The material was also published online but in his 2000-page report of the inquiry, only a very few pages cover the internet. He has been quoted since as suggesting new laws are needed to prevent 'mob rule' online and what he termed 'trial by Twitter' (BBC, 2012).

The hacking scandal fuelled a general public intolerance of privacy breaches. Highlighting significant moves by press regulators 'on developing privacy rights around identity, health and children' in an article written before the *News of the World* scandal exploded, Chris Frost wrote: 'Developments in privacy seem to be led by a clear expectation from the public of greater privacy rights and a freedom from media intrusion, paradoxical at a time when intrusion into privacy by the state has never been greater' (Frost, 2010b).

The scandal and uncertainty surrounding the post-Leveson press regulatory regime seem to have reined in the tabloids too – none published topless photos of the Duchess of Cambridge after they were printed in a French magazine in 2012.

The basics

Many laws affecting journalists might be said to touch on privacy issues, such as those of trespass, data protection (see below) or court restrictions on identifying children or sex crime victims. But in the current context, we mean the general right to a private life. In the UK, this right is now guaranteed in the 1998 Human Rights Act (see box below).

Rights to privacy

Article 8 of the ECHR was enshrined in UK law in the Human Rights Act. Judges must take account of the Act in relevant cases, and this article (with Article 10 guaranteeing Freedom of Expression) has been repeatedly cited in media law cases, even though the convention was originally devised to protect citizens from abuses of state power, not nosy journalists.

Article 8 says:

Right to respect for private and family life

Everyone has the right to respect for his private and family life, his home and his correspondence. There shall be no interference by a public authority with the exercise of this right except such as is in accordance with the law and is necessary in a democratic society in the interests of national security, public safety or the economic well-being of the country, for the prevention of disorder or crime, for the protection of health or morals, or for the protection of the rights and freedoms of others.

UK journalists are expected to abide by the PCC Editors' Code of Practice. While imminent press regulation reform may amend this, any new code is likely to include a similar – if not much tougher – set of principles. Clause 3 states:

Everyone is entitled to respect for his or her private and family life, home, health and correspondence, including digital communications.

Editors will be expected to justify intrusions into any individual's private life without consent. Account will be taken of the complainant's own public disclosures of information.

It is unacceptable to photograph individuals in private places without their consent.

Note – Private places are public or private property where there is a reasonable expectation of privacy.

Before the Human Rights Act, there was no similar explicit right to privacy. Such rights as the courts had established in England and Wales had evolved from the laws on Breach of Confidence. Many people still believe that this country needs an explicit Privacy Act, passed by Parliament. Victims of intrusion like Max Mosley, who won record damages for breach of privacy after the *News of the World* plastered his sado-masochistic sex life over its paper and website, believe editors should be legally obliged to tell subjects of intrusive stories before they publish. This would give the subject time to apply for an injunction to prevent publication. Mosley's attempt to establish this failed in the European Court of Human Rights in 2011.

Victims of media intrusion suing for breach of privacy, or those seeking an injunction to stop publication, must undergo a two-stage test. The test was explained by Mr Justice Eady in the Night Jack case (detailed below) in 2009:

> One must ask, first, whether the claimant had a reasonable expectation of privacy in relation to the particular information in question and, if so, then move to the second stage of enquiring whether there is some countervailing public interest such as to justify overriding that *prima facie* right. (*Author of a Blog v Times Newspapers* [2009] EWHC 1358 (QB))

Stephen Sedley, a former judge, characterized this as the 'balance between the entitlement of the public to know about things that matter and the right of individuals (including famous ones – why else would anyone care?) to some space of their own' (Sedley, 2012).

The outcome of the Mosley case surprised many journalists. The story featured a married man who was a high-profile figure in Formula One caught on video in an orgy, so the paper thought it was on solid ground. But Judge Eady disagreed, saying: 'It is not for the state or for the media to expose sexual conduct which does not involve any significant breach of the criminal law … It is not for journalists to undermine human rights … merely on grounds of taste or moral disapproval' (*Mosley v News Group Newspapers Ltd* [2008] EWHC 1777 (QB) (24 July 2008)).

Twitter

The media's hackles were raised in 2011 after a spate of injunctions, colloquially known as 'gagging orders'. Injunctions can be made by judges in all kinds of contexts. Breaking such orders will land you in court for contempt but they are dealt with here because courts have been increasingly using them to protect individuals' privacy. It is an added vexation for journalists that while they have had to obey such orders, non-journalists have frequently – and in huge numbers – been able to flout them via social media.

Before the phone-hacking scandal, the biggest row concerned a married footballer's affair with a model. She gave her account of the alleged relationship to the *Sun*, but the paper did not name him. A temporary injunction banned any further press publication but his identity was widely spread on social media. The footballer launched a legal action against Twitter itself, sparking even more users to tweet and re-tweet his identity. The *Sun* applied to have the ban lifted but Mr Justice Eady judged it should stay (*CTB v News Group Newspapers Ltd & Anor* (No 2). [2011] EWHC 1326 (QB)), a ruling described by one legal commentator as 'a trenchant endorsement of the continued utility in the internet age of anonymized privacy injunctions to protect private and family life, in spite of the matter becoming an "open secret"' (5RB, 2011).

It was such an open secret that a Scottish paper, not covered by the injunction, had identified the player, as had the *Times of India*. Later on the day of Eady's judgement, Liberal Democrat MP John Hemmings controversially used parliamentary privilege to defy the ban and name the player in the House of Commons as Ryan Giggs, which effectively killed the injunction. However, it was not until months later that Giggs formally gave up his anonymity in the High Court.

A report by a parliamentary committee in 2012 urged the Attorney General to be more willing to bring actions for contempt for online breaches, and urged courts making injunctions to ensure the claimant serves notice on sites such as Facebook and Twitter, as well as traditional news outlets.

Anonymous journalism

Journalists are generally expected to put a name to their work, but the growth of blogging has seen many writers (rarely trained journalists) choose to hide behind a pen name. A detective constable with the Lancashire constabulary gave his forthright views of the police in an anonymous blog called Night Jack. A journalist on *The Times* discovered his identity. The blogger secured an interim injunction to stop his exposure but this was overturned by Mr Justice Eady. The judge said the officer did not have a 'reasonable expectation of privacy' because his blogging was 'essentially a public rather than a private activity', analogous to journalism because he was making serious criticisms of the police. *The Times* could name him.

The decision was hailed as a victory for freedom of expression and the public interest by *The Times* and as a sad day for democracy by others, who feared the valuable 'front line' information provided by bloggers writing anonymously would be lost. No blogger, it now appears, can rely on hiding behind a false name. His exposure meant the end of a unique source of 'inside info' on the police, but it also meant that his bosses could plug a potentially compromising 'leak' in their ranks.

An archive of Night Jack's blog has been published by a fan at nightjackarchive.blogspot.co.uk. And the saga went on – the officer, Richard Horton, filed a claim for breach of confidence, misuse of private information and deceit against *The Times* after it emerged that one of its reporters hacked into his email account. The paper settled for a reported £42,500 plus costs.

The value of such anonymity is an ethical as well as legal question. Paul Staines has long been outed as the man behind the forthright political blog Guido Fawkes (order-order.com), but that doesn't seem to have been a bar to his success or influence (see box below).

Dr Brooke Magnanti gained notoriety by blogging details of her life as a call girl under the pseudonym Belle de Jour, and now happily blogs about 'sex, policy and related issues' but has offered a much re-blogged article entitled 'How to Blog Anonymously' (Magnanti, 2012).

Anonymity – and when you lose it

Inspired by the uncompromising journalism of Kelvin MacKenzie's *Sun* newspaper in the 1980s and the US blog The Drudge Report, Paul Staines set up his award-winning Guido Fawkes blog in 2004. 'The primary motivation for the creation of the blog was purely to make mischief at the expense of politicians and for the author's own self-gratification,' he reports on his website. He was 'unmasked' by the *Guardian* online in 2005, but lost his anonymity once and for all after a BBC Radio 4 *Profile* programme in 2007. His blog has gone from strength to strength and still employs the third person 'Guido' voice, but he says losing his anonymity had drawbacks. 'Confirming I was the author brought the baggage of my political history to attention and allowed people to frame me in terms of background. The blog was more careful to fire at all parties and was less clearly anti-Labour in the early years.' It also made

Figure 13.3   Paul Staines runs the right-wing Guido Fawkes political blog. (Source: Alex Folkes/Fishnik Photography)

it harder for him to slip into events unnoticed and 'put people more on their guard with me'. Although a trenchant critic of established journalists – notably Parliamentary lobby correspondents – he believes the right to report anonymously is important: 'Anonymous journalism is essential when people are in hostile environments – be they occupational or by the nature of the regime they live under – China, Iran, Cuba etc. The former get fired, the latter get jailed.'

The traditional ethical view is that journalists should avoid anonymity if at all possible, be up front with people they interview and put their name to their work. Only certain investigative projects (discussed elsewhere in Chapter 7) might justify acting anonymously.

Closed justice

Iris Robinson, a former politician and wife of Northern Ireland's First Minister, suffered serious depression after her affair with a 19-year-old man was revealed. During her attempt (*Robinson v Sunday*

Newspapers [2011] NICA 13) to maintain a privacy injunction preventing papers from republishing pictures of her during her rehabilitation, the Court of Appeal decided such an injunction hearing should be held in private. While acknowledging that any reporting restrictions to prevent the publishing of intimate medical evidence were likely to be honoured by official news organizations, the court explicitly pointed to the risk of others disseminating the information on social networks. This has led to speculation that this may set a precedent for holding other such hearings in private – contravening the important principle of open justice.

Data protection

The growth of data journalism is enabling a new generation of online journalists to exploit an unprecedentedly rich source of statistics, reports and databases. But there are legal dangers associated with such work.

Long gone are the days when the government and private companies held our information on paper in locked filing cabinets. Data about us is held in digital files by everyone from our doctor to our bank, Amazon to Facebook. Data is at the heart of our schizophrenic relationship with technology, meaning we crave the innovations which make our lives easier but balk at the implications of all this data for some of our most cherished freedoms. Recurring debates about, for instance, CCTV cameras in town centres and the Communications Data Bill in the UK illustrate these tensions.

Disgruntled subjects of stories they don't want told often tell journalists they can't write anything because of 'data protection'. This is almost always nonsense. The main law governing stored information is the Data Protection Act of 1998, although proposals for new DP regulations currently being considered by the European Union are likely to have an impact too.

Online journalists need to know five key things about the Act:

- News outlets and freelance journalists are likely both to 'process' data (i.e. store and use structured private information about people, such as their phone number) and to seek to persuade others to disclose data.
- Those who hold such data, in any format, must register as 'data controllers' and ensure it is handled and stored securely, for limited purposes and in accordance with the person's lawful rights.
- The National Union of Journalists has advised freelance journalists to register as data controllers to avoid breaking the law.
- While this imposes obligations on journalists, Section 32 of the Act explicitly exempts them from having to disclose 'journalistic material' when asked to. This means, among other things, that your contacts book is protected.
- The Act contains specific criminal offences of unlawfully obtaining, disclosing or procuring of personal data. If a journalist can prove he/she offended in order to prevent or detect crime, or that the breach was otherwise 'in the public interest', a conviction may be avoided.

Full details of the Act can be found on the Information Commissioner's website (www.information commissioner.gov.uk) and specific advice for journalists at www.pcc.org.uk.

The area of reader comments (or user generated comment) is also relevant here. In the Sheffield Wednesday case mentioned above, the plaintiffs asked the High Court for a so-called Norwich Pharmacal order. Such orders relate to a 1974 case that long predates the web, and oblige those who run or host sites to disclose the identities of anonymous contributors who someone wants to sue, even if the owner had nothing to do with the offensive material. The High Court in the Wednesday case ruled that the DPA provided no protection in those circumstances – fans making defamatory comments about the club chairman – and ordered the identities of five contributors (out of 14 sought) to be revealed, stating that the members' rights to anonymity and freedom of expression were outweighed by the claimants' right to reputation. The case was later dropped.

Stay informed

Media law online is fast evolving and the working journalist must take responsibility for keeping him/herself up-to-date. There are excellent law updates provided at www.holdthefrontpage.co.uk/category/news/law/ and on the websites of media law firms such as www.5rb.com. Transcripts of many key cases in Britain, Ireland and Europe can be found at www/bailii.org.

>>Summary<<

1 Judicial and regulatory systems around the world are struggling to accommodate new challenges posed by the internet to rules made to cope with traditional print and broadcast media. Not least among those challenges is that ordinary people, with no journalism training or tie to traditional media outlets, are now effectively acting as journalists. Their status in law, and the consequences for professional journalists of their media misdemeanours, remain uncertain.

2 The best journalism is what one might call 'oppositional' (Jones and Salter, 2012) – it challenges powerful interests like governments and big business, who control the very laws and regulations by which we must abide. In many areas, restrictions are widening as the implications of technology sink in, but journalists in democracies should take courage from the many parts of law which attempt to defend free speech, and from the many forces online challenging censorship.

3 Media law has been fast-changing for at least a generation, but the web has rapidly accelerated the pace of change. More than ever, diligent journalists need to keep up with developments.

4 The big cases make the headlines and affect case law, but in the West at least, journalists are still rarely in the dock. Perhaps the biggest danger for young journalists is self-censorship – allowing the law to cow you into tepid reporting. There is no need and no excuse for that, not least because you are part of a vigilant international community of people dedicated to free speech. That privilege is something to enjoy and defend.

5 Journalists are trained to ask questions, and this shouldn't stop when the final interview is complete. Is this defamatory? Am I covered if it is? Do I have permission to use this extract/picture/video? And in this, as in every aspect of your work, don't be afraid to admit your doubts. If you don't know, ask someone who does.

EXERCISES

1 Look at the interactive parts of some major news websites and compare how they moderate user-generated content. How clear are the guidelines and is there any evidence of posts being removed to avoid legal action?
2 Dip into the judgements of some of the cases mentioned in this chapter available at bailli.org and write a media law blog summarizing the ruling for a general readership.
3 Draw up a series of template contracts to prepare for when you try to sell your freelance work.

FURTHER READING

Brooke, Heather. 2011. *The Silent State*. London: Windmill Books.
   Familiar through her early career with American journalism, Brooke casts a semi-outsider's light on some fusty corners of the British government and judiciary.
Frost, Chris. 2011. *Journalism Ethics and Regulation*. 3rd edn. Harlow: Longman.
   Frost provides the context for the current regulatory climate in British journalism and is not afraid to champion morals in the newsroom.
Guardian Media Law: www.guardian.co.uk/media/medialaw/
Hold the Front Page: www.holdthefrontpage.co.uk/category/news/law/
   Keep up-to-date with legal and regulatory developments and debates on these sites, giving an international, national and regional perspective.
Hanna, Mark and Dodd, Mark. 2012. *McNae's Essential Law for Journalists*. 21st edn. Oxford: Oxford University Press.
   The chunky bible for news desks and students alike, also recommended for those studying for NCTJ exams.
Jones, Janet and Salter, Lee. 2012. *Digital Journalism*. London: Sage.
   Chapter 9 offers an erudite and detailed international perspective on the legal pressures on journalists, and is a repository of eye-catching cases from around the world.

CHAPTER 14

How the Internet Transformed Journalism

INTRODUCTION

What is most remarkable is how quick it has been. A little over 25 years ago, newspaper reporters were still writing stories on typewriters. If you were born in the 1990s, you are part of the generation of digital natives that grew up using the World Wide Web. While older generations (digital immigrants) may marvel how we can send an email to New York at the blink of an eye, when a letter sent in the post would take days or even weeks to arrive, younger people (the digital natives) take it for granted. Computers have become truly pervasive in the home and workplace. The internet is now a utility, just like water and electricity and it is something we rely on day-to-day.

This concluding chapter provides an important opportunity to consider how we got to where we are today and understand how the internet and associated digital technologies have revolutionized the way we work as journalists.

It is worth reflecting on how we have moved from information scarcity to information over-supply. We no longer have to wait for a newspaper to be published or for the ten o'clock news on TV – news is ubiquitous. News is on-demand and on our desktop computers, tablets, e-readers and smartphones 24 hours a day. Yet a question remains about how much of what is going on in the world we understand and it is common to hear people complain about suffering from information overload and poor quality journalism.

Ian Hargreaves (2003) describes how news is now all around us, a phenomenon he terms 'ambient news'.

> News, which was once difficult and expensive to obtain, today surrounds us like the air we breathe. Much of it literally ambient: displayed on computers, public billboards, trains, aircraft, and mobile phones. Where once news had to be sought out in expensive and scarce news sheets, today it is ubiquitous and very largely free at the point of consumption.

Technology is central to the development of the media industry and it's important we understand where we are going and where we've been. We are not suggesting that you quit journalism to become computer scientists, but it's worth noting that these once distinct professional fields are moving closer together.

Academic David Domingo (cited in Steensen, 2011) argues that research about online journalism in the first decade of its existence was partly paralysed by what he labels 'utopias of online journalism'. These utopias were especially related to how hypertext, multimedia and interactivity would foster innovative approaches that would revolutionize journalism.

There is a long history of techo-optimism which suggests that technological developments are mostly beneficial to society and underplays the negatives such as potential loss of privacy. In the area of journalism, the development of blogging tools allowed more people to publish content and take part in the political debate than was possible through mainstream, mass media. However, as we will see later on in this chapter, *Guardian* journalist Nick Davies (2008) highlights how the rise of the internet has, in some respects, reduced the quality of journalism and led to weaker public discourse. Hargreaves (2003) warns that there are downsides to the 'new news culture'. The biggest problem with online news is that 'Because there is so much of it, we find it difficult to sort the good from the bad'. Indeed, as journalists we now no longer just go out and find stories, but a new role exists of helping our users judge the reliability and quality of existing online sources of information.

It's obvious that technology will continue to change. It will constantly act to shape how the media operates and our role as journalists. It's important that we consider the opportunities and threats that any new piece of technology presents journalists. In short, the battle moving forward is how we cope with constant change while ensuring we keep to our ethical beliefs and not lose sight of the purpose of journalism.

>>OBJECTIVES<<

In this chapter, you will learn:

1 the important difference between the internet and the World Wide Web;
2 how the web developed with liberal principles based on open source and free sharing of content;
3 how the early principles of the web clashed with economics of newspaper publishing;
4 the strengths and limitations of print, broadcast and internet publishing;
5 the importance of mobile devices, access to bandwidth and fast download speeds for the development of journalism.

MILESTONES IN TECHNOLOGY

1969: CompuServe – content and distribution

This was a major ISP (Internet Service Provider) that gave access to online text-based services and to the World Wide Web in the 1990s.

1974: Ceefax – Content

Ceefax (pronounced 'See Facts') is the BBC's electronic teletext information service transmitted via the analogue TV signal.

1981: BBC Micro – Hardware

The BBC Microcomputer System, a home computer, was launched by Acorn Computers as part of the BBC's computer literacy project to teach computing in schools. It introduced a generation of children to the basic computer language.

1982: ZX Spectrum – Hardware

Costing under £100, 'the Specy', as it was known, became the first mass market home computer. Developed by British maverick inventor Sir Clive Sinclair.

1994: Netscape Navigator – software

Early browser software for surfing the web. It lost market share to Microsoft's rival browser Internet Explorer which, controversially, was bundled with Windows 95 operating system (OS) giving the company a massive advantage.

1994: *Daily Telegraph* – content

The first UK national daily newspaper on the web was initially known as Electronic Telegraph.

1995: GeoCities – content distribution

Popular free web hosting allowed anyone to publish a personal website. A precursor to participatory tools such as Blogger.com.

1997: BBC Online – content

BBC Online, which includes BBC News and BBC Sport, is funded by the licence fee. The site redirects to the advertizer-funded BBC.com when accessed outside the UK.

1998: Google – search and applications

Google launches its search site. Google has since launched numerous other services which are important to journalists including: AdWords (online advertising network), Google Drive (cloud computing and online applications), Google News (news aggregator) and Google Scholar (search engine of academic literature).

1999: BlackBerry from Research in Motion (RIM) – hardware

A line of smartphones aimed initially at business users, but later became popular with young people. Known for it's easy to use keyboard and 'push' email system, the BlackBerry was used as a communication tool during the Arab spring and London riots of 2011.

1999: Blogger – content distribution

Launched by Pira Labs and eventually bought by Google, Blogger led to a boom in blogging, particularly after the terrorist attacks on 11 September 2001 in the USA.

2004: Facebook – content distribution and applications

Profile-based social media site founded by Mark Zuckerberg. Includes numerous social applications such as email, message boards and real-time chat.

2005: YouTube – content distribution

Video sharing site designed to make sharing content easy among friends. Now a major tool for the publication of user generated video content as well as video from mainstream media.

2006: Twitter – content distribution and applications

A form of micro-blogging it enables its users to send and read text-based messages of up to 140 characters, known as 'tweets'.

2007: Apple iPhone

One of the most popular touch-screen smartphones on the market. The latest version allows users to shoot digital still images, record audio and video, download apps, browse the web and carry out basic editing. A great example of a convergent technology.

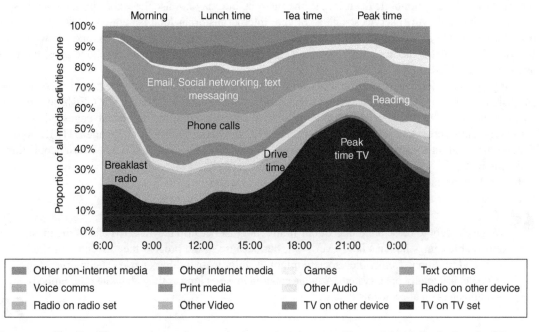

Figure 14.1   The chart illustrates take-up of communication services since 2000. The graph highlights the rise of mobile phones and digital TVs, where over nine out of ten households have access to these services. (Source: Ofcom)

THE WEB IS NOT THE INTERNET

How do you imagine the internet to look? You may view it as being content – words, pictures, audio and video that appear on a computer screen. But what you are describing here is the World Wide Web and not the internet.

The internet is usually described as a global 'network of networks'. To put it simply, it's a global network of computer servers interlinked by telephone lines and high speed data lines. The main core of the internet uses fast fibre optic cables where data is passed at the speed of light (so that's really fast!). But data also flows over old-fashioned copper lines which can slow up the data flow; this particularly applies to the 'last mile' connection – the telephone lines that connect your local telephone exchange with your home.

Before the invention of the web, email and Usenet newsgroups (virtual message boards) were some early uses of the internet. These technologies were purely text based. This is important to highlight for two reasons: First, the internet and the web were never 'just' technologies. A social and human interactive element existed right from the start. In the early days, people referred to the 'social web' where people would communicate in real-time in virtual chatrooms. Within this context, it would seem natural that a social media site like Facebook would build upon popular early internet social tools such as Usenet Newsgroups, Internet Relay Chat (IRC) – text-based real-time chat and instant messaging software. What is unique about Facebook is how successful it has been in harvesting personal data and the information we give out about ourselves in online conversations for advertizing purposes.

HOW DO MOBILE APPS USE THE INTERNET?

The distinction between the internet and the web can be confusing. Smartphone and tablet apps (computer programs which run on mobile devices) use the internet, but may not use the web. The same applies to voice over internet (VoIP) services such as Skype. Internet historian John Naughton (2000) provides a useful analogy. He says the best way to explain the difference between the internet and the web is to imagine the internet is the tracks of a railway network. Things like Skype, mobile phone apps, the web and email are different types of 'train' that run over the railway network.

Using concepts from earlier hypertext systems, the World Wide Web was begun in 1992 by the Englishman Sir Tim Berners-Lee and Robert Cailliau from Belgium, working for CERN in Geneva, Switzerland. In 1990, they proposed building a 'web of nodes' storing 'hypertext pages' viewed by 'browsers' on a network, and released the web in 1992. Hypertext Markup Language (HTML) allows text, pictures and other elements to intermingle on the computer screen and this is what most people think is the internet.

John Naughton in *A Brief History of the Future* (2000) writes:

> **"** We owe a debt to these architects of our future, not just because they created one of the most remarkable things humans have ever built, but because in the process they invented institutions and traditions from which society might usefully learn a thing or two. The internet, for example, is a totally open system. Anyone can join in, so as long as they obey the rules embedded in its technical protocols. **"**

Unlike so much of the proprietary software we use, like Microsoft Word or Adobe InDesign, the internet and the web were based on open standards and distributed for free. We can only speculate how successful the web would have been if it had been patented. Naughton writes:

> Not a single line of the computer code which underpins the net is proprietary; nobody who contributed to its development has ever made a cent from intellectual property rights in it. In the age of the bottom line, where the default assumption is that people are motivated by money, rather than altruism, and where software is the hottest intellectual property there is, this is surely extraordinary.

Along with the social web, we can see that a culture of free exchange of knowledge existed on the web from the very start. There is now an assumption that content on the web will be free among most web users; after all, that's how it was set up. As a journalist you may have identified a problem here. The free nature of the web clearly presents problems to those media organizations that rely on the sale of digital content to generate revenue. The problem of how media publishers generate revenue from content which is distributed in digital format, and therefore easily copyable, presents a challenge to the future success of online journalism. It's worth considering what types of content you are willing to pay for on the internet. If you use Facebook, would you be willing to pay for it? If so, how much would you pay a month?

THE WEB GETS POLITICAL

A strong liberal and entrepreneurial ethos existed among early adopters of the web in 1994 and 1995. Early internet freedom groups were anti-censorship and pro-free speech. These ideals clashed with growing concern in mainstream media that children could access inappropriate material and the rise of cyber-terrorism. Many people remain concerned about how much data companies and governments are collecting about our online activities. Today cyber-liberty groups such as the UK's Open Rights (www.openrights group.org) continue to campaign for internet freedom.

On the political front, in an era where 'anyone can publish' a much wider selection of views appeared online than was previously supported by mainstream media. This led to an expansion of online political debate and this has been a cause of concern for authoritarian regimes in many parts of the world including China and those across the Middle East.

OPEN SOURCE MOVEMENT

Early internet users were liberal-minded when it came to copyright control. The open source movement, where the source code for software programs is made available for free, highlights the open and sharing nature of internet communication. Hundreds of software developers throughout the world, usually working for free, have created some fantastic open source software including operating systems, such as Linux, a rival to Microsoft Windows as well as many CMS. Internet theorist Yochai Benkler (2006), who writes extensively on the new economics of the internet, describes the collaborative and social nature of the internet which is based on 'non-monetary motivations' which are having a transformative impact on the 'dynamics of markets and the possibilities of freedom'.

Others have described this as an online 'gift economy' where internet users create work, whether it be software or YouTube videos for free, and don't seek payment for their efforts. Unfortunately, journalists have to make a living and will want to be paid for their work.

THE LAUNCH OF NEWSPAPER WEBSITES

In 1994, traditional media organizations made their first tentative steps onto the internet. In November 1994 the Electronic Telegraph, from the *Telegraph* newspaper group, was launched as the UK's first newspaper website. Its first editor Derek Bishton (2001) says:

> **66** Our brief was simple: explore this new medium; evaluate the usefulness of establishing the Telegraph as an online brand; learn about the technology and the commercial possibilities. The last point, although the most alien for journalists, was clearly uppermost in the thoughts of the proprietor at the time. **99**

Entrepreneurism has been embedded in online journalism since an early stage in a way that has not happened in the traditional media. A major step on the path came in 1998 when the news aggregate and gossip site called the Drudge Report broke the Monica Lewinsky story. Lewinsky was an intern that had an affair with President Bill Clinton. The story was enormous and carried on for months. It demonstrated how an online operation run by just a few adaptable people could be more relevant than the mainstream media.

In December 1997 BBC Online started. It is funded by the licence fee and does not seek to make a profit. While most people are staunch supporters of the quality of BBC journalism (commonly regarded as some of the finest in the world), commercial rivals complain they cannot compete with a well-funded BBC. The majority of news sites are profit-making enterprises and are forced to rely heavily on limited revenue from online advertizing and other sources.

GENERATING REVENUE

Paywalls around sites, where users have to pay to access news content, have been mooted over the years. It had been generally agreed that it only worked when you had a high value audience who would pay for top notch information. The *Financial Times* and *The Economist* paywall is an example of this and they are commonplace in many areas of B2B (business-to-business) online publishing. However, both the *FT* and *The Economist*'s paywalls are porous (or metered), that's to say that specific numbers (often between 10 to 20 stories a month) can be accessed for free before a charge is applied. This has been criticized by some media observers as it rewards those fickle users who get news from a wide range of websites and discourages loyalty to a single news brand.

In July 2010, News Corporation put all the content of *The Times* as well as the *Sunday Times* behind a non-penetrable paywall which gave no content away for free. This was viewed as a risky strategy that saw *The Times* lose a huge number of users overnight who had previously enjoyed unlimited free access.

Trying to determine whether paywalls work in the UK – whether porous or non-penetrable – has so far been impossible. Newspapers that have them rarely give answers to the following key questions:

1 How many unique visitors did you lose when you started charging for content?
2 What impact did the loss of users have on revenue from banner advertizing?
3 How much money do you make through subscriptions/membership fees?
4 How many digital-only subscribers do you have? How does this compare with the numbers who subscribe to the newspaper print edition (and get digital access as a free added bonus)? Newspapers can be reluctant to unbundle this data.

As revenue from the sale of newspapers in printed format continues to fall, it is likely that newspapers will launch more innovative ways to bring in much-needed revenue. Journalists feel that giving away content for free on the web is simply not sustainable over the long term. Users need to accept that journalism needs to be paid for in digital format as they have traditionally paid for it in print.

There are certainly interesting models to explore. In 2012 the majority of the newspaper brands in Slovenia took part in a national paywall, modelling a similar experiment in Slovakia the previous year. In both countries, each of the main publishers puts an amount of premium content behind the paywall. Readers pay one fee to gain access to the premium content from all the participating newspaper publishers.

NEWS AS A COMMODITY

In the online world, mainstream news organizations like the BBC and the *Guardian* compete with a bewildering array of commercial and non-journalistic websites which aggregate news content. 'Every organization is now a media entity, engaged in creating and disseminating messages among its staff, customers, and partners to achieve business objectives,' states the Future Exploration Network Report (Future of Media, 2008).

Search engines and ISPs, such as Yahoo!, AOL, MSN and Virgin Media, pay for pre-packaged content from wire agencies such as Reuters and Press Association (better known as PA). This kind of content is easy to spot as you see the same articles appearing on many different sites with perhaps only a headline or intro paragraph changed, an editing process crudely known as top 'n' tailing a news story.

Corporations realize that news content is popular with audiences; but the model can only work if news is obtained as cheaply as possible. These sites rarely employ reporters to write original stories, just content editors who spend their working days chained to their desks re-packaging existing content.

IMPACT OF THE NET ON WORKING PRACTICES

Nick Davies in his book *Flat Earth News* (2008) captured the daily experience of many reporters in an example of a young provincial newspaper reporter who kept a work journal for him. In this reporter's working week, he turned out 48 stories – and yet he spent a total of only three hours out of the office and spoke face to face to only four people. That is what Davies defined as 'churnalism'. Davies says:

No reporter who is producing nearly 10 stories every shift can possibly be doing their job properly. No reporter who spends nearly 95 per cent of the time crouched over a desk can possibly develop enough good leads or build enough good contacts. No reporter who speaks to so few people in researching 48 stories can possibly be checking their truth.

All local and regional media outlets in Britain – print and broadcast – have been swamped by a tide of churnalism. The scale and quality of coverage has been swept away. But the tide has not stopped in the provinces. The big national outlets can still support some real journalism, but here too, churnalism has swept through newsrooms.

"

ONLINE NEWS TODAY

Today media is demand-led rather than supply-led. We use technologies that allow us to personalize and control our media interactions. It is worth reflecting on the devices that you use to consume text, audio, video and images. Most people choose devices based on what is most convenient to them when they are at home, travelling or at work and based on the type of content they are viewing.

The following list highlights some of the strengths and weaknesses of different media, but you may wish to add to the list:

a) Print: News in paper newspapers and magazines:

- o Portable: A paper newspaper or magazine can be taken wherever the user likes. It doesn't matter if they lose it, and a printed magazine or newspaper requires no batteries.
- o Tangible: It's something you can hold. People like the look, feel, and smell of newspapers.
- o Archive: Paper is a permanent record. It can be archived in libraries, although paper is difficult to search compared to text stored in digital format.
- o Branding: People read their favourite newspapers and magazines because it says something about them. There is a stereotype of a *Guardian* newspaper reader that is different to someone who reads a tabloid such as the *Daily Star*. Hairdressers and advertizing agencies have glossy magazines, like *Vogue* and *GQ*, hanging around their premises to create a particular impression to their customers.

b) Broadcast: Radio and TV news:

- o Live and emotional: News can be brought live to the viewer or listener. TV and radio is best for news where there is emotion and drama.
- o Always-on: 24-hour cable TV channels are always on – broadcasting 24 hours day.
- o On-demand: Sites such as BBC iPlayer form a searchable online archive of previous shows. Audiences use PVRs (personal video recorders) such as Sky Plus and TiVo to record, pause and rewind live TV. However, while it's possible to search via programme title, it's far harder to search content within a broadcast.
- o Interactivity: TV and radio content is mostly designed to be passively consumed from a comfortable sofa. Many TV formats are experimenting with a greater depth of interactivity and there is likely to be more growth here as more people access streaming video broadcasts on their living TV set using smartTVs, games consoles and set top boxes such as Apple TV.

c) Online news:

- o Archive: The web is a global archive of digital content. It has the facility to store large amounts of content, and digital content in text format is easily searchable.
- o Portable: Some devices are portable, others are fixed.
- o Interaction: Online news is often highly interactive and user's can contribute content.

o Multimedia: Can deliver a range of text, audio and video content and very cheap to distribute content. News can be updated easily throughout the day.

o Reading text from a computer screen can cause eyestrain. However, e-readers and tablet computers make the experience a pleasure.

Consider the strengths and weaknesses of different media above as a way to:

1 Consume news and entertainment content.
2 Interact or contribute your own views – how involved can you get with the media?
3 Personalize the experience so you only see news you are interested in.
4 Generate revenue for the producers of content – is the media device a good advertizing tool?
5 Distribute content – who pays the costs of distribution: publishers, the consumer or mixture of both?

THE NETWORK AND DEVICES

Increased demand for bandwidth

Bandwidth refers to the amount of data that can be passed through a channel. Imagine a pipe of liquid – the larger the dimensions of the pipe, the more liquid can flow through it. The pressure on internet infrastructure is greater than it has ever been as we are downloading increasingly more data thanks to the popularity of video sites such as BBC iPlayer, YouTube and Apple iTunes.

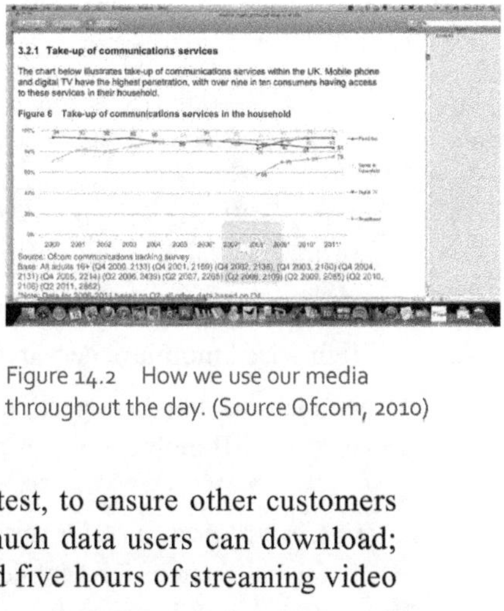

Figure 14.2   How we use our media throughout the day. (Source Ofcom, 2010)

A report by UK media regulator Ofcom (2011) states: 'Residential fixed broadband customers are using on average 17 Gigabytes (GB) of data per month, the equivalent to streaming 12 hours of BBC iPlayer HD video. It was found that data use has increased sevenfold over the past five years [up to November 2011].'

Many internet service providers (ISPs) routinely slow the speed, a tactic known as 'bandwidth throttling' or 'traffic shaping', of high bandwidth users at peak, evening times when demand is greatest, to ensure other customers do not suffer slow speeds. Cheaper internet packages limit how much data users can download; some cap data to as little as 10GB a month, the equivalent of around five hours of streaming video a month.

Lack of bandwidth on fixed line and mobile broadband is a serious problem for the media industry and is likely to get worse in the future as we become more reliant on the internet for the delivery of streaming HD and even 3D video content.

How mobile phones changed journalism

Over the last 20 years mobile phones have taken over our lives and become symbols of both fashion and status. Shane Richmond (2010) technology journalist for the *Daily Telegraph* newspaper says: 'Every year since 2007, mobile phone users in the US have been making fewer and fewer calls. Americans use their phones to

Figure 14.3　Broadband speeds: areas of North Scotland, Wales and North-West of England (the darkest areas) have the slowest broadband speeds. The South of England (the lightest areas) have some of the fastest speeds. (Source: Ofcom, 2011/Google Maps)

text, to email, to surf the web, to take photos, to play games, to listen to music – but to talk to each other? It's almost an afterthought.' Mobile phones have turned into smartphones or what Richmond says is 'effectively, a mobile computer that happens to make phone calls'.

The types of things we use our mobile phones for include:

1　To remain connected wherever we are.
2　To consume news and entertainment – they have moved from being the third screen to being the first screen, i.e. the primary way that some people, particularly the young, access content.
3　To create multimedia in text, images, video and audio formats – smartphones are the ultimate convergence technology when it comes to this.
4　To carry out basic image, audio and video editing before we send the content to a newsroom using an internet connection – mobile phones, and apps for smartphones, act as mini-editing studios.

As we write this, the main battle in mobile technology is between Apple devices and those that run the Android operating system such as those manufactured by the Korean electronics giant Samsung. Apple place great emphasis on modern design and generate an awe that is truly extraordinary and alarming. Academics Heidi Campbell and Antonio La Pastina (2010) write: 'A key example is the rhetoric of the "cult of Macintosh", in which Apple has become a cult brand whose status is supported by religious like stories and images.' Thus, iPhones are promoted as a 'redeeming technology' which will improve the lives of their users.

High-speed mobile access in the UK remains patchy and is largely focused on metropolitan areas.

Mobile broadband connections are usually accessed using a SIM card placed in smartphones, tablet devices or USB mobile dongles plugged into laptops.

- *General packet radio service (GPRS)*: One of the slowest connection speeds available over the Global System for Mobile Communications (GSM) mobile networks, the most commonly used digital mobile network.
- *Enhanced Data Rates for GSM Evolution (EDGE)*: In the days before third generation (3G) phones, EDGE was sometimes known as 2.5G. It's still common to see the big 'E' symbol appear on your phone and it provides speeds four times faster than GPRS. At maximum speeds of between 75 and 135 Kbps, it's good for checking emails and downloading mobile optimized websites. However, it will take many minutes to download a full website.
- *High Speed Packet Access (HSPA)*: This system works on 3G phones. It has the potential to allow broadband speed and is one of the fastest speeds available. It works over 3G with location-based maps based on transmitter positions and GPS.
- *Fourth generation (4G)*: The fastest mobile broadband available, launched in the UK in 2012. It should be fast enough to allow the download of video in HD and for viewing of video in 3D.

As mobile devices become cheaper and mobile broadband increases in speed, as journalists we need to ensure our content is available on all the devices that are likely to be popular in the future with our users.

THE RISE OF TABLET DEVICES

There is a debate over whether tablet devices, such as the Apple iPad and Amazon Kindle and Samsung Galaxy ranges, will reinvigorate journalism.

There is a lot to recommend them. They make reading long-form journalism, longer news articles and features, much easier on the eye than reading from a bright computer monitor. They have the portability of smartphones, but with much bigger screens – 9.7 inches in the case of the iPad. It is likely that tablet computers will get much thinner, lighter and cheaper in the future.

Tablet apps (software applications) allow for the reproduction of newspaper and magazine pages, including a neat ability to give the impression of turning newspaper pages. It also allows users to view video clips directly off the page. Yet some believe this is a step backwards in delivery of content. Paper-based newspapers and magazines traditionally promote a linear form of consumption where people read them from the front to the back. On the web, we are used to navigating using hyperlinks in a non-linear way that some say is more efficient.

However, media publishers are particularly interested in tablet computers as they provide a rare opportunity to generate revenue from digital content. In contrast to the web, where a 'culture of free' content exists, tablet owners are used to paying to download content using app stores.

PREDICTING THE FUTURE (BASED ON THE PAST)

John Naughton (2010) observed that living through today's media revolution is

> like being a resident of St Petersburg in 1917, in the months before Lenin and the Bolsheviks finally seized power. It's clear that momentous events are afoot; there are all kinds of conflicting rumours and theories, but nobody knows how things will pan out. Only with the benefit of hindsight will we get a clear idea of what was going on.

So in short, the future is up to you to discover. One of the best ways to approach this task is to talk to people. It is well worth discussing your ideas for new journalism websites and apps with friends who have a knowledge of computing. Take an experimental and entrepreneurial approach.

Futurist Ross Dawson Future of Media Report, 2008 says: 'In uncertain times, don't try to predict the future. Systematically explore possible futures.' So instead of waiting for the big idea to come to you, launch new sites in beta format to test the market. You'll get feedback from your users, you'll then make improvements and then you'll launch something better.

Questions to help you think about the future

We can assume that prices in computing will come down over time as products gain mass appeal and manufacturing costs fall. The famous Moore's Law predicts that computing power doubles every 18 months to two years. In short, computers get faster and cheaper very quickly. Battery power has often been a problem for mobile devices. But the development of power efficient, high-performance chips, hopes to solve this problem.

Devices no longer need large hard drives as cloud-based storage systems such as Dropbox, Google Drive and Apple's iCloud become popular.

Accessing content on small-screen mobile devices can be a frustrating experience. So can you think about how the experience could be improved? Many manufacturers are experimenting with voice control and allowing users to browse the web using blinks of the eye. Motion control is used on games consoles such as Microsoft's Xbox – how could this be used on other devices?

There is likely to be far more growth in on-demand streaming TV services. As we write this, by far the most popular tools are online video sites YouTube, NetFlix, BBC iPlayer and Hulu (in the USA). Accessing the internet on a TV from the sofa is still a frustrating experience though.

Wearable technology is likely to be important in the future. Manufacturers are working on watches and even glasses that allow us to make calls and interact with the online services.

Driving forces that *may* shape the future of media

Increased media consumption

It is now commonplace for multiple media streams to be consumed simultaneously. Younger users in particular are becoming adept at dividing their attention. During TV adverts breaks they read emails, send texts and tweets. The impact of advertizing is likely to decrease as broadcasters will never have our full attention.

Audiences are fragmented

People consume content through a range of fragmented channels. While the number of new media outlets has expanded offering users more choice, the pot of money from advertizing has not vastly increased. This means that content creators will need to create content with limited funds.

Participation and social

As we have seen, the web is not just a technology. Its social roots can be traced back to when the web was invented and it is likely that we will see many more social applications emerge. Users will continue to participate in media and generate content – some of it will be useful for journalists and some of it will be terrible. It is likely we will see more amateur stars emerge on the internet.

More user control

Most people hate seeing or listening to adverts and do everything they can to avoid them. There is also a lot of wastage in advertizing – baby food ads are watched by people without children and car adverts are seen by people who don't drive. So on-demand TV streaming sites in the USA are allowing users to choose, from a limited option of adverts, which ones they want to be shown. Short of being able to fast forward through the adverts completely, this is surely an improvement on things.

The internet is everywhere!

The internet is likely to appear on yet more devices. As we write this, the latest buzz is to do with wearable technology such as internet-enabled watches and glasses. Devices are likely to be controlled in new ways using speech, hand gestures or even blinks of the eye.

Limitations

There are always factors that limit the roll out of new technologies.

New revenue models

Apple's iTunes and their App Store is one of the most successful examples of charging for online content. Finding new ways to 'monetize' digital content (generate revenue from journalism) is seen as crucial for most newspapers.

Will internet connectivity improve?

Access to highest broadband speeds, delivered via fixed line, is often limited to those who live in metropolitan areas. Those who live in rural areas are often forced to put up with appallingly slow speeds. While networks are rolling out high speed 4G mobile broadband services, surfing the net on a smartphone remains a slow and frustrating experience when in a poor mobile area. The rate of change means there is massive pressure on the network as content creators deliver high bandwidth services, such as HD and even 3D video.

Privacy

The extent that services can be personalized is often limited by privacy concerns of users. Rightly in our view, many people are concerned that companies and governments can track their movements via their mobile devices.

Cyber-threats

Cyber-crime is divided into two broad categories – attacks on the individual and attacks on governments/ corporations. Phishing, the act of attempting to acquire private information fraudulently, such as usernames and passwords, is a growing problem. The websites and social media accounts of news organizations are often targets for hackers and various political groups around the world.

Rights management

Television and media organizations pay vast sums of money for the exclusive right to broadcast sporting events, movies and the latest American sitcoms first. Licences are usually sold by content producers based on territory, i.e. a single broadcaster will pay for the exclusive rights to broadcast an event or a show first within their own country. Rights are sometimes treated separately, so for some sports events different companies will be able to broadcast it live on TV, internet and radio. A separate deal may be arranged with those media companies looking to broadcast highlights packages (i.e. non-live).

>>Summary<<

1 The words 'internet' and the 'World Wide Web' are frequently used interchangeably, but they have different meanings. The internet is a global network of computers that form the 'railway tracks' which 'carry' the web. Other applications like Skype and mobile apps run over the internet, but are not 'the web'.

2 We are living through an era of 'informed bewilderment' (Castells) and 'ambient news' (Hargreaves) where we are surrounded by information, yet are confused. As well as reporters of news, journalists are also interpreters of the mass of online content and data created by others.

3 A liberal and open source ethos characterized the early web which promoted the sharing of knowledge for free. This has presented key challenges to media organizations who seek to generate revenue from their online content.

4 Early academic study of the internet was often characterized by techno-optimism. This highlighted the social good of technology, rather than focusing on the negatives. In contrast, early tabloid reporting promoted fears to do with pornography, copyright abuse (music and software piracy) and cyber-crime.

5 Smartphones provide new ways to deliver content to users on the go, but the UK is crippled by slow broadband speeds compared to many countries.

EXERCISES

1 Ian Hargreaves (2003) describes how news is now 'all around us', a phenomenon he terms ambient news. From 6 a.m. to midnight make notes of when, how and on what device you consumed news. How does news come to you? Did you actively seek it (like buying a newspaper) or did it come to you (e.g. via a link on social media, a TV on in the pub or via electronic signs while waiting for public transport)?

2 'In uncertain times, don't try to predict the future. Systematically explore possible futures,' says futurist Ross Dawson. There are a few trends that are emerging:

   o Internet connections will continue to get faster (both fixed line and mobile).
   o The price of home computers will continue to fall.
   o More people around the world will access the internet on mobile devices rather than desktop computers.
   o More types of content and services will be delivered in digital format, rather than in hard copy.
   o Wearable technology, like internet-enabled watches and glasses, are growing in importance.

   How do you think these trends will alter the media landscape? Without thinking about cost, think of ideas for new websites, mobile apps or devices that will exploit these trends.

3 Dan Gillmor describes a 'Multiple directional flow of news and information on which the audience plays a vital role'. Draw up a list of ways that a favourite news website interacts with its visitors. Do you think it provides a mostly passive or interactive experience?

FURTHER READING

Future of Media. 2008. Future Exploration Network [viewed 30/8/2012]. Available: www.futureexploration. net/future-of-media/

A fascinating report into the future of media covering trends, strategies and frameworks.

Hargreaves, Ian. 2003. *Journalism: Truth or Dare?* Oxford: Oxford University Press.

In this classic text, Hargreaves outlines the rise of ambient news.

Naughton, John. 2012. *From Gutenberg to Zuckerberg: What You Really Need to Know about the Internet*. London: Quercus.

The *Observer* newspaper technology columnist and internet historian documents the historical and technological roots of the internet.

Steensen, Steen. 2011. Online Journalism and the Promises of New Technology, *Journalism Studies*, 12(3): 311–27.

The 'success' of online journalism is often measured by the extent it utilizes technology.

REFERENCES

5RB, 2011. Case report on *CTB v News Group Newspapers Ltd & Anor* (No. 2) [viewed 14/4/2013]. Available: www.5rb.com/case/CTB-v-News-Group-Newspapers-Ltd--Anor-%28No-2%29

Akdeniz, E., Walker, C. and Wall, D. (eds). 2000. *The Internet, Law and Society*. London: Longman.

Allan, S. (ed.). 2005. *Journalism: Critical Issues*. Maidenhead: Open University Press.

Alps, T. 2010. Hey, Clay Shirky – TV is Just as Valuable as the Net, *Guardian* 1/7/2010 [viewed 29/8/2011]. Available: www.guardian.co.uk/media/organgrinder/2010/jul/01/clay-shirky-television-vs-internet

Anderson, C. 2006. *The Long Tail: How Endless Choice is Creating Unlimited Demand*. London: Business Books

Andrews, R. 2011. The *Guardian* Still Mulling Its iPad Options. 24/1/2011 [viewed 23/8/2012]. Available: http://paidcontent.org/2011/01/24/419-the-guardian-still-mulling-its-ipad-options/

Anon., 2003. *The Times Style and Usage Guide*. New edn. London: Times Books.

Associated Press. 2002. *Stylebook and Briefing on Media Law: With Internet Guide and Glossary*. Rev. and updated edn. Cambridge, MA: Oxford: Perseus.

Baines, D. and Kennedy, C. 2010. An Education for Independence: Should Entrepreneurial Skills Be an Essential Part of the Journalist's Toolbox?, *Journalism Practice*, 4(1): 97–113.

Barker, M. and Petley, J. (eds). 2001. *Ill Effects: The Media Violence Debate (Communication and Society)*. London: Routledge.

Barnett, S. and Brevini, B. 2012. The Media-Industrial Complex: Comparing the Influence of Murdoch and Berlusconi? Reuters Institute for the Study of Journalism, 25/6/2012 [viewed 12/3/2013]. Available: http://podcasts.ox.ac.uk/media-industrial-complex-comparing-influence-murdoch-and-berlusconi-audio

Barry. A.M.S. 1997. *Visual Intelligence: Perception, Image and Manipulation in Visual Communication*. New York: State University of New York Press.

Barthes, R. 1983. 'The Photographic Message' in S. Sontag (ed.), *Barthes: Selected Writings*. Oxford: Oxford University Press.

Bartlett, R. 2011. Jay Rosen on a 'golden age' of press freedom, 13/3/2011 [viewed 16/8/2013]. Available: www.journalism.co.uk/news/-media140-jay-rosen-on-a-golden-age-of-press-freedom/s2/a543689/

BBC (n.d.) Editorial Guidelines – Guidance – Moderation, Hosting, Escalation and User Management – Part 1: Hosting, Moderation and Escalation [viewed 29/8/2012]. Available: www.bbc.co.uk/editorialguidelines/page/guidance-moderation-hosting#scope-and-level-of-moderation

BBC. 2011. Leveson Inquiry: 'Newsroom Pressure' on Ethics, 8/12/2011 [viewed 14/4/2013]. Available www.bbc.co.uk/news/uk-16097382

BBC. 2012. Leveson: Internet Needs New Privacy Laws, 7/12/2012 [viewed 14/4/2013]. Available: www.bbc.co.uk/news/uk-20636697

Beck, J.N. 2012. *WordPress*. 2nd edn. Berkeley, CA: Peachpit.

Beckett, C. 2008. *SuperMedia: Saving Journalism So It Can Save the World*. Malden, MA: Wiley.

Belam, M. 2007. Remembering myBBC, BBC Blogs, 15/12/2007 [viewed 29/8/2011]. Available: www.bbc.co.uk/blogs/bbcinternet/2007/12/remembering_mybbc.html

Bell, S. 2010. *If ... Bursts Out*. London: Jonathan Cape.

Benkler, Y., 2006. *The Wealth of Networks: How Social Production Transforms Markets and Freedom*. New Haven, Conn.; London: Yale University Press.

Berger, J. 1972. *Ways of Seeing*. Harmondsworth: Penguin/London: BBC.

Bishton, D. 2001. From ET to TD. *Telegraph*, 1/1/2001 [viewed 30/8/2012]. Available: www.telegraph.co.uk/news/1471964/From-ET-to-TD.html

Blackhurst, R. 2005. The Freeloading Generation, *British Journalism Review*, 16(3): 53.

Block, M. 1997. *Writing Broadcast News*. Chicago: Bonus Books Inc.

Boutin, P. 2008. Twitter, Flickr, Facebook Make Blogs Look So 2004, Wired, 20/10/2008 [viewed 30/8/2012]. Available: www.wired.com/entertainment/theweb/magazine/16-11/st_essay

Boyd. A. 2005. *Broadcast Journalism*. 5th edition. Oxford: Focal Press.

Boyd, A., Stewart, P.S. and Alexander, R. 2008. *Broadcast Journalism, Techniques of Radio and Television News*. 6th edition. London: Focal Press.

Bradshaw, P. 2011. Has Investigative Journalism Found Its Feet Online? (Part 1), 23/8/2011 [viewed 13/4/2013]. Available: http://onlinejournalismblog.com/2011/08/23/has-investigative-journalism-found-its-feet-online-part-1/

Bradshaw, P. 2011. *The Online Journalism Handbook: Skills to Survive and Thrive in the Digital Age*. Harlow: Longman.

Bradshaw, P, 2012. Torchbearer data is a journalist's dream, *Daily Telegraph*, 21/6/2012 [viewed 14/4/2013]. Available: http://www.telegraph.co.uk/sport/olympics/olympic_infographics_and_data/9347011/Paul-Bradshaw-torchbearer-data-is-a-journalists-dream.html

Bradshaw, P. 2011. Objectivity Has Changed, Why Hasn't Journalism? Online Journalism Blog, 3/3/2011 [viewed 14/4/2013]. Available: http://onlinejournalismblog.com/2011/03/03/objectivity-has-changed-why-hasnt-journalism/

Briggs, M. 2007. *Journalism 2.0: How to Survive and Thrive*. University of Maryland Philip Merrill College of Journalism and the Knight Citizen News Network. [viewed 14/4/2013] Available: http://www.j-lab.org/Journalism_20.pdf

Briggs, M., 2012. *Journalism Next*. Washington: CQ Press.

Briggs, M. 2013. *Entrepreneurial Journalism*. London: Sage/CQ Press.

Brooke, H. 2011. The Press Will Die if It Fails in Its Duty to Serve the Public Interest. *The Times*, 27/9/2011 [viewed 19/8/2013] Available: http://heatherbrooke.org/2011/article-journalisms-unique-selling-point-is-the-public-interest/

Brooke, H. 2011. *The Silent State*. London: Windmill Books.

Brooke, H. 2012. The Future of Investigtaive Journalism. *The House Magazine*. 1/4/2012

Brooker, C. 2008. Online POKER Marketing could Spell the NAKED End of VIAGRA Journalism as We LOHAN Know It. *Guardian*, 21/7/2008 [viewed 9/9/2012]. Available: www.guardian.co.uk/commentisfree/2008/jul/21/charliebrooker.pressandpublishing

Bruns, A. 2003. Gatewatching, Not Gatekeeping: Collaborative Online News, *Media International, Australia Incorporating Culture and Policy: Quarterly Journal of Media Research and Resources*, 107: 31–44.

Bruns, A. 2010. Coverage of Breaking News by UK News Sites, Snurblog, 14/10/2010 [viewed 9/8/2012]. Available: http://snurb.info/node/1405

Bull, A. 2010. *Multimedia Journalism: A Practical Guide*. London: Routledge.

Bunker Radio, 30/6/2012 [viewed 2/6/2012]. Available: www.kentbusinessradio.co.uk/one-third-of-uk-now-listen-to-internet-radio

Butterworth, S. and Johannes, J., 2009. 'Regulating Journalism and Newsgathering', in D. Goldberg, G. Sutter and I. Walden (eds), *Media Law and Practice*. Oxford: Oxford University Press.

Cadman, S,. (2008) Interviewed by Paul Lashmar.

Campbell, H.A. and La Pastina, A.C. 2010. How the iPhone Became Divine: New Media, Religion and the Intertextual Circulation of Meaning, *New Media & Society*, 12(7): 1191–207.

Carlson, N. 2011 Leaked: AOL's Master Plan, 1/2/2011 [viewed 4/4/2013]. Available: www.businessinsider.com/the-aol-way

Carlyle, T. 1841. *On Heroes, Hero-Worship, and the Heroic in History*. London: Chapman & Hall.

Carr, F. 2002. Common Convergence Questions, 14/11/2002 [viewed 9/2/2011]. Available: www.poynter.org/uncategorized/3354/common-convergence-questions/

Carroll, B. 2010. *Writing for Digital Media*. London: Routledge.

Castells, M. 2001. *The Internet Galaxy: Reflections on Internet, Business, and Society*. Oxford: Oxford University Press.

Caton, J. 2010. A Look Back at the Last 5 Years in Blogging, Mashable, 3/8/2010 [viewed 9/2/2011]. Available: http://mashable.com/2010/08/03/last-5-years-blogging/

Cenite, M. et al. 2009. Doing the Right Thing Online: A Survey of Bloggers' Ethical Beliefs and Practices, *New Media & Society*, 11(4): 575–97.

Clifton, B. 2010. *Advanced Web Metrics with Google Analytics*. 2nd edn. Hoboken, NJ: Wiley.

Cohen. S. 1972. *Folk Devils and Moral Panics*. St Albans: Paladin.

Colgan, J. 2011. How Online Audio Tools Can Help Journalists, Poynter.org, 29/12/2011 [viewed 14/4/2013]. Available: www.poynter.org/how-tos/digital-strategies/157307/how-online-audio-tools-can-help-journalists-and-journalism/#.TvyMzOO6Nbc.twitter

Commission for Rural Communities. 2011. Mind the Gap: Digital England – a Rural Perspective [viewed 29/8/2011]. Available: http://crc.staging.headshift.com/2009/06/17/crc-104-mind-the-gap-digital-england-a-rural-perspective/

comScore (n.d.) Methodology [viewed 29/8/2011]. Available: www.comscore.com/About_comScore/Methodology

Copeland, D. 2012. Best Practice for Writing for Online Readers, ReadWrite.com [viewed 6/3/2013]. Available: http://readwrite.com/2012/03/16/best_practices_for_writing_for_online_readers

Crisell, A. and Starkey, G. 2009. *Radio Journalism*. London: Sage.

Crook, T. 1998. *International Radio Journalism*. Oxford: Routledge.

Curran, J, and Seaton, J. 2009. *Power without Responsibility: The Press and Broadcasting in Britain*. 3rd edn. London: Routledge.

Cushing, T. 2012. The Rise of the 'Professional Amateur' and the Fall of Gated, Exclusionary 'Clubs', TechDirt, 8/2/2012 [viewed 3/6/2013]. Available: www.techdirt.com/articles/20120201/09311617622/rise-professional-amateur-fall-gated-exclusionary-clubs.shtml

Danbury, R. 2008. Can I Really Report That? The Decline of Contempt. Reuters Fellowship Paper, Oxford University.

Davies, N. 2008. *Flat Earth News: An Award-Winning Reporter Exposes Falsehood, Distortion and Propaganda in the Global Media*. London: Chatto & Windus

Dawson, T. (2013) Help Yourself: New Ways to Make Copyright Pay, NUJ [viewed 2/3/2013]. Available:www.nujtrainingwales.org/news/make-copyright-pay-free-new-download

de Burgh, H. (ed.). 2008. *Investigative Journalism: Context and Practice*. Oxford: Routledge.

Dean, J. 2010. *Blog Theory: Feedback and Capture in the Circuits of Drive*. Cambridge: Polity.

Doctor, K. 2010. *Newsonomics: Twelve New Trends that Will Shape the News You Get*. New York: St. Martin's Press.

Doctor, K. 2011. The Newsonomics of Oblivion. Nieman Journalism Lab [viewed 4/4/2013]. Available: www.niemanlab.org/2011/03/the-newsonomics-of-oblivion/

Dodd, M. 2011. Online Libel Cases Double. *Independent*, 26/8/2011 [viewed 14/4/2013]. Available: www.independent.co.uk/news/uk/crime/online-libel-cases-double-2344452.html

Dube, J. 2003. Writing News Online, Poynter, 14/7/2003 [viewed 9/11/2011]. Available: www.poynter.org/how-tos/digital-strategies/web-tips/13605/writing-news-online/

Dubner, S. 2012. 'Homicide Victims Rarely Talk to Police' and Other Horrible Headlines, Freakonomics [viewed 3/6/2013]. Available: www.freakonomics.com/2012/12/05/homicide-victims-rarely-talk-to-police-and-other-horrible-headlines/

Durrani, A. 2012. PPA Conference: Tim Brooks on *The Times* 'Paywall Failure' and Mail's 'World Success'. *Media Week*, 9/5/2012 [viewed 30/8/2012]. Available: www.mediaweek.co.uk/news/1131096/PPA-Conference-Tim-Brooks-Times-paywall-failure-Mails-world-success/

Economist, The. 2001. High-speed Internet Access: Broadband Blues, 21/06/2001 [viewed 29/8/2011]. Available: www.economist.com/node/666610

Economist, The. 2006. The Newspaper Industry: More Media, Less News, 24/08/2006 [viewed 29/8/2011]. Available: www.economist.com/node/7827135

Economist, The. 2011. Julian Assange and the New Wave [A special report on the news industry], 7/7/2011 [viewed 20/12/12]. Available: www.economist.com/node/18904166

Economist, The. 2011. Impartiality: The Foxification of News, 7/7/2011 [viewed 20/12/12]. Available: www.economist.com/node/18904112

Economist, The. 2011. Social Media: The People Formerly Known as the Audience, 7/7/11 [viewed 21/8/2012]. Available: www.economist.com/node/18904124

Economist, The. 2011. Brain Scan: Disrupting the Disrupters, 3/9/2011 [viewed 10/10/2011]. Available: www.economist.com/node/21527020

Economist Group. 2011. Media Information: Audience [viewed 29/8/2011]. Available: www.economistgroupmedia.com/products/economist-online/audience/

Egawhary, E. 2010. Your Next Scoop is Hiding in a Spreadsheet, *Television*, May, 47(5): 26–7.

Elliot, C. 2012. Headlines Are More Easily Misunderstood Online, *Guardian*, 16/9/2012 [viewed 6/3/2013]. Available: www.guardian.co.uk/commentisfree/2012/sep/16/headlines-more-easily-misunderstood-online

Etling, B., Kelly, J., Faris, R. and Palfrey, J. 2010. Mapping the Arabic Blogosphere: Politics and Dissent Online, *New Media & Society*, 12(8): 1225–43.

Evans, H. 1997. *Pictures on a Page: Photojournalism, Graphics and Picture Editing*. London: Paladin.

Evans, H. 2000. *Essential English: For Journalists, Editors and Writers*. Rev. edn. London: Pimlico.

Evans, J. and Hall, S. 1999. *Visual Culture: A Reader*. London: Sage.

Fenton, N. 2009. *New Media, Old News: Journalism and Democracy in the Digital Age*. London: Sage.

Frost, C. 2007. *Journalism Ethics and Regulation*. London: Pearson.

Frost, C. 2010a. Current Issues on Journalism Ethics, in P. Lashmar (ed.), *Journalism: Cutting Edge Commentaries on the Critical Issues Facing Journalism at the Practical, Theoretical and Media Industry Level*. The Marketing & Management Collection, London: Henry Stewart Talks Ltd.

Frost, C. 2010b. The Development of Privacy Adjudications by the UK Press Complaints Commission and Their Effects on the Future of Journalism, *Journalism Practice*, 4(3): 383–93.

Frost, C. 2011. *Journalism Ethics and Regulation*. 3rd edn. Harlow: Longman.

Future of Media. 2008. Future Exploration Network [viewed 30/8/2012]. Available: www.futureexploration.net/future-of-media/

Gaber, I. 2009. Three cheers for Subjectivity: or the crumbling of the seven pillars of journalistic wisdom. *International Journal of Communications Law and Ethics*, 14(5).

Gardner, S. 2010. *Blogging for Dummies*. 3rd edn. Hoboken, NJ: Wiley.

Geere, D. 2012. One Third of UK Now Listen to Internet Radio, Business Radio Bunker, 30/6/2012. [viewed 16/8/2013] Available: www.kentbusinessradio.co.uk/one-third-of-uk-now-listen-to-internet-radio

Gilligan, A. 2011. Phone Hacking: My Big Fear Is This Scandal Could Damage Investigative Journalism, *Telegraph*, 10/7/2011 [viewed 13/7/2012]. Available: www.telegraph.co.uk/news/uknews/phone-hacking/8628148/Phone-hacking-My-big-fear-is-this-scandal-could-damage-investigative-journalism.html

Gillmor, D. 2004. *We the Media: Grassroots Journalism by the People, for the People*. Farnham: O'Reilly.

Glasgow, F. (ed.). 2008. *Small Business Finance All-in-one for Dummies*. London: J. Wiley & Sons.

Goldsmith, J. and Wu, T. 2008. *Who Controls the Internet?* Oxford: Oxford University Press.

Gomez-Mejia, L. et al. 2007. 'Developing an Effective Whistleblowing Policy', in *Managing Human Resources*, 5th edn. Upper Saddle River, NJ: Pearson Prentice Hall.

Gray, J., Bounegru, L. and Chambers, L. 2012. *The Data Journalism Handbook*. Cambridge: Open Knowledge Foundation.

Greenslade, R. 2003a. Their Master's Voice, *Guardian*, 17/2/2003 [viewed 13/7/2012]. Available: www.guardian.co.uk/media/2003/feb/17/mondaymediasection.iraq

Greenslade, R. 2003b. *Press Gang: How Newspapers Make Profits From Propaganda*. London: Pan.

Greenslade, R. 2010a. Is iPad Really Digital Savior of Newspapers? Don't Bet on It, *Evening Standard*, 2/6/2010 [viewed 23/10/2012]. Available: www.standard.co.uk/business/markets/is-ipad-really-digital-saviour-of-newspapers-dont-bet-on-it-6475879.html

Greenslade, R. 2010a. Journalistic Blogging Is Fair, Balanced and Ethical, *Guardian*, 29/8/2010 [viewed 8/29/2012]. Available: www.guardian.co.uk/media/greenslade/2010/jul/29/blogging-trinity-mirror

Greenslade, R. 2010. Journalists as Entrepreneurs? That's Fine, But Not if They Have to Sell Advertising, *Guardian*, 8/9/2010 [viewed 13/4/2013]. Available: www.guardian.co.uk/media/greenslade/2010/oct/08/entrepreneurs-digital-media

Greenslade, R. 2012. Mail Online Goes Top of the World, *Guardian*, 25/1/2012. [viewed 30/8/2012]. Available: www.guardian.co.uk/media/greenslade/2012/jan/25/dailymail-internet?INTCMP=SRCH

Greenslade, R. 2012. Research Reveals Popularity of Live Blogging, *Guardian*, 20/11/12 [viewed 4/3/2013]. Available: www.guardian.co.uk/media/greenslade/2012/nov/20/blogging-cityuniversity

Greenwald, G. 2012. Conservatives, Democrats and the Convenience of Denouncing Free Speech, *Guardian*, 19/9/2012 [viewed 13/7/2012]. Available: www.guardian.co.uk/commentisfree/2012/sep/16/conservatives-democrats-free-speech-muslims

Grey, S. 2006. *Ghost Plane: The Inside Story of the CIA's Secret Rendition Programme*. London: Hurst & Company.

Grieve, D. 2012. Contempt Laws Are Still Valid in the Internet Age, *Guardian*, 8/2/2008 [viewed 14/4/2013]. Available: www.guardian.co.uk/commentisfree/2012/feb/08/contempt-of-court-act-internet

Guardian. 2010. Afghanistan War Logs: The Unvarnished Picture, editorial, 25/7/2010 [viewed 12/4/2013]. Available: www.guardian.co.uk/commentisfree/2010/jul/25/afghanistan-war-logs-guardian-editorial

Hall, A. 2003. Cannibal on Trial for Murder, *Evening Standard*, 20/12/2003.

Hall, S. 1977. Culture, the Media and the Ideological Effect, in J. Curran, M. Gurevitch and J. Woollacott (eds), *Mass Communication and Society*. London: Edward Arnold.

Hall, S. 1980. Encoding/Decoding, in Centre for Contemporary Cultural Studies (ed.). Culture, Media, Language: Working Papers in Cultural Studies, 1972–79. London: Hutchinson.

Hall, S. 1981. The Determinations of News Photographs, in S. Cohen and J. Young (eds), *The Manufacture of News: Social Problems, Deviance and the Mass Media*. London: Constable.

Halliday, J. 2010. Times Loses Almost 90% of Online Readership, *Guardian*, 20/7/2010 [viewed 30/8/2012]. Available: www.guardian.co.uk/media/2010/jul/20/times-paywall-readership

Hammersley, B. (2004) Audible Revolution: Online Radio is Booming Thanks to iPods, Cheap Audio Software and Weblogs, *Guardian*, 12/2/2004 [viewed 2/6/2012]. www.guardian.co.uk/media/2004/feb/12/broadcasting.digitalmedia

Hanna, M. and Dodd, M. 2012. *McNae's Essential Law for Journalists*. 21st edn. Oxford: Oxford University Press.

Hargreaves, I. 2003. *Journalism: Truth or Dare?* Oxford: Oxford University Press.

Hargreaves, I. 2011. Digital Opportunity – A Review of Intellectual Property and Growth. IPO May 2011 [viewed 14/4/2013]. Available: www.ipo.gov.uk/ipreview-finalreport.pdf

Heathfield, D., Punter, S. and Thayer, K. 2011. Journalists Talk Video Journalism, 31/1/2011 [viewed 12/4/2013]. www.youtube.com/watch?v=5p9akcmSxl8

Heilmann, C. 2012. Web Enabled Video at News: Rewired, 2/2/2012 [viewed 12/4/2013]. Available: http://christianheilmann.com/2012/02/02/web-enabled-video-at-newsrewired

Helsper, E. 2008. *Digital Inclusion: An Analysis of Social Disadvantage and the Information Society*. London: Department for Communities and Local Government.

Herbert, J, and Thurman, N. 2007. Paid Content Strategies for News Websites, in *Journalism Practice*, 1(2): 208–26.

Hicks, W. 2008. *Writing for Journalists*. 2nd edn. London; New York: Routledge

Hill, S. 2002. Lastminute Lines Up 100 More Sackings, *Sunday Express*, 22/9/2002.

Hitwise (n.d.) Internet Usage, Internet Statistics – How We Do It [viewed 29/08/2011]. Available: www.hitwise.com/uk/about-us/how-we-do-it

Hobsbawm, J. 2011. Time to Stop Anonymous Commenting, Dale & Co. [viewed 28/8/2012]. Available: www.iaindale.com/posts/time-to-stop-anonymous-commenting

Holzner, S. 2011. *Joomla! for Dummies*. 2nd edn. Hoboken, NJ: Wiley.

Huang, E. et al. 2006. Facing the Challenges of Convergence, *Convergence: The International Journal of Research into New Media Technologies*, 12(1): 83.

Hudson, G. and Rowlands, S. 2007. *The Broadcast Journalism Handbook*. London: Longmans.

Hughes, J., Petley, J. and Rohloff, A. (eds). 2013. *Moral Panics in the Modern World*. London: Bloomsbury.

Hunter, M. et al. 2011. Story Based Inquiry: A Manual for Investigative Journalists, UNESCO [viewed 12/4/2013]. http://unesdoc.unesco.org/images/0019/001930/193078e.pdf

Independent. 2009. Leading Article: Search-engine Showdown, 10/10/2009 [viewed 30/8/2011]. Available: www.independent.co.uk/opinion/leading-articles/leading-article-searchengine-showdown-1800591.html

IPC. 2011. NME Media Pack [viewed 29/08/2011]. Available: www.nme.com/mediapack/

Jarvis, J. 2009. The Future of News Is Entrepreneurial, Buzz Machine, 1/11/2009 [viewed 13/4/2013]. Available: http://buzzmachine.com/2009/11/01/the-future-of-journalism-is-entrepreneurial/

Jarvis, J. 2009. *What Would Google Do?* London: Collins.

Jarvis, J. 2012. Big Media Companies Need to Reinvent Online Video [viewed 12/4/2013]. Available: www.beet.tv/2008/10/jeff-jarvis-big.html

Java, A., Song, X., Finin, T. and Tseng, B. 2007. Why We Twitter: Understanding Microblogging Usage and Communities, in Proceedings of the 9th WebKDD and 1st SNA-KDD 2007 Workshop on Web Mining and Social Network Analysis, ACM.

Jenkins, H. 2008. *Convergence Culture: Where Old and New Media Collide*. New York; London: New York University Press.

Jenkins, S (2010). Interview on BBC Radio 4 Today programme. Date unknown.

Johnson, D. and Post, D. 1996. Law and Borders: The Rise of Law in Cyberspace, *Stanford Law Review*, 48: 1367.

Jones, J. and Salter, L. 2012. *Digital Journalism*. London: Sage.

Kaplan, A.M. and Haenlein, M. 2010. Users of the World, Unite! The Challenges and Opportunities of Social Media, *Business Horizons*, 53(1): 59–68.

Keeble, R. 2008. *Ethics for Journalists*. London: Routledge.

Keen, A. 2008. *The Cult of the Amateur: How Blogs, Myspace, Youtube and the Rest of Today's User-Generated Media Are Destroying Our Economy, Our Culture, and Our Values*. Rev. edn. London: Nicholas Brealey.

Keiran, M. (ed.). 1998. *Media Ethics*. Oxford: Routledge.

Kieran, M. 2000. The Regulatory and Ethical Framework for Investigative Journalism, in H. de Burgh (ed.), *Investigative Journalism: Context and Practice*. London: Routledge.

Kirkpatrick, D. 2011. *The Facebook Effect: The Real Inside Story of Mark Zuckerberg and the World's Fastest-Growing Company*. Updated edn. London: Virgin.

Kiss, J. 2006. How to Get Started as a Freelance Journalist, Journalism.co.uk, 3/4/2006 [viewed 13/4/2013]. Available: www.journalism.co.uk/news-freelance/how-to-get-started-as-a-freelance-journalist/s12/a51787/

Knight, A.D. (2008) Who Is a Journalist?, *Journalism Studies*, 9(1): 117–31.

Koblin, J. 2009. Twitter Culture Wars at *The Times*: 'We Need a Zone of Trust,' Bill Keller Tells Staff, *New York Observer*, 14/5/09 [viewed 5/4/2013]. Available: http://observer.com/2009/05/twitter-culture-wars-at-ithe-timesi-we-need-a-zone-of-trust-bill-keller-tells-staff/

Kolodzy, J. 2006. *Convergence Journalism: Writing and Reporting Across the News Media*. Oxford: Rowman & Littlefield.

Kovach, B. and Rosenstiel, T. 2003. *The Elements of Journalism*. London: Atlantic Books.

Krotoski, A. 2010. Cognitive Surplus, the Soma of Television and Being on *Newsnight* with Clay Shirky, 30/06/2010 [viewed 29/8/2011 2011]. Available: http://alekskrotoski.com/post/media-cognitive-surplus-the-soma-of-television-and-being-on-news

Kuhn, M. 2007. Interactivity and Prioritizing the Human: A Code of Blogging Ethics, *Journal of Mass Media Ethics*, 22(1): 18–36.

Lashmar, P. 2000. The Importance of Investigative Journalism. Media Section, *Independent*, 17/10/2000.

Lashmar, P. 2008a. Sub-prime – the Death of Financial Reporting or a Failure of Investigative Journalism? Paper for the Future of Journalism Conference at the University of Bedfordshire, October.

Lashmar, P. 2008b. Minimising Evidence and Protecting Your Source, *Press Gazette*, 2/2/2008 [viewed 12/4/2013]. Available: www.pressgazette.co.uk/story.asp?storycode=40269

Lashmar, P. (ed.). 2010. *Journalism: Cutting Edge Commentaries on the Critical Issues Facing Journalism at the Practical, Theoretical and Media Industry Level*, The Marketing & Management Collection, London: Henry Stewart Talks Ltd.

Lashmar, P. 2013. 'Journalist, Folk Devil?' in *Moral Panics in the Contemporary World*, by Amanda Rohloff, Chas Critcher, Jason Hughes and Julian Petley (eds). Bloomsbury Academic.

Lasica, J.D. 2002. The Promise of the Daily Me, Online Journalism Review [viewed 29/8/2011]. Available: www.ojr.org/ojr/lasica/1017779142.php

Lavrusik, V. 2010. The Future of Social Media in Journalism, Mashable, 13/9/2010 [viewed 9/8/2012]. Available: http://mashable.com/2010/09/13/future-social-media-journalism/

Leigh, D. 2007. Inaugural Lecture as Anthony Sampson Professor of Reporting, at City University London, 1 November.

Leigh, D. 2010. Iraq War Logs: An Introduction, *Guardian*, 22/10/2010 [viewed 13/4/2013]. Available www.guardian.co.uk/world/2010/oct/22/iraq-war-logs-introduction

Leigh, D. 2011. Leveson Inquiry: *Guardian* Journalist Justifies Hacking if in the Public Interest, *Guardian*, 6/12/2011 [viewed 13/7/2012]. Available: www.guardian.co.uk/media/2011/dec/06/leveson-inquiry-guardian-phone-hacking

Leveson, L.J. Brian. 2012. *An Inquiry into the Culture, Practices and Ethics of the Press*. London: TSO (The Stationery Office).

Lewis, C. 2004. The Journalist and the Whistle Blower: A Symbiotic Relationship, in R. Callan and G. Dehn (eds), *Whistleblowing Around the world: Law, Culture and Practice*. London: ODAC & PCAW.

Lewis, P. 2012. Talk at the Media Education Conference at Bournemouth University, 12 September.

Lewis-Hasteley, H. 2011 'You should have your tongue ripped out': the Reality of Sexist Abuse Online, *New Statesman*, 3/11/2011 [viewed 28/8/2012]. Available: www.newstatesman.com/blogs/helen-lewis-hasteley/2011/11/comments-rape-abuse-women

Locke, L. 2012. Flipboard Starts Integrating Audio into Its App, BBC News, 16/5/2012 [viewed 14/4/2013]. Available: www.bbc.co.uk/news/technology-18080023

Lord Chief Justice. 2011. Practice Guidance: The Use of Live, Text-Based Forms of Communication Including Twitter from Court for the Purposes of Fair and Accurate Reporting [viewed 14/4/2013]. Available: www.judiciary.gov.uk/JCO%2fDocuments%2fGuidance%2fltbc-guidance-dec-2011.pdf

Lynch, L. 2010. We're Going to Crack the World Open, *Journalism Practice*, 4(3): 309–18.

Machin, D. and Niblock, S. 2006. *News Production: Theory and Practice*. Oxford: Routledge.

Magnanti, B. 2012. How To Blog Anonymously (and How Not To), blog on The Sex Myth, 10/5/2012 [viewed 14/4/2013]. Available: http://sexonomics-uk.blogspot.co.uk/2012/05/how-to-blog-anonymously-and-how-not-to.html

Mair, J. 2011. Is Investigative Journalism Dead or Alive? *Huffington Post*, 26/8/2011 [viewed 13/4/2013]. Available: www.huffingtonpost.co.uk/john-mair/is-investigative-journali_b_937968.html

Mair, J. and Keeble, R. (eds). 2011. *Investigative Journalism: Dead or Alive?* Bury St Edmunds: Arima Publishing.

Marr A. 2004. *My Trade: A Short History of British Journalism*. London: Macmillan.

Marr, A. 2006. Brave New World, *British Journalism Review*, 17(1): 29.

Marsh, D. 2007. *Guardian Style*. London: Guardian Books.

Marshall, S. 2012. Five Examples of iPhone Journalism from BBC 5 Live's Nick Garnett, Journalism.co.uk, 13/12/2012 [viewed 31/8/2011]. Available: www.journalism.co.uk/news/five-examples-of-iphone-journalism-from-bbc-5-live-s-nick-garnett/s2/a551533/

McAdams, M. 2005. *Flash Journalism: How to Create Multimedia News Packages*. Oxford: Focal Press.

McAdams, M. 2011 Reporter's Guide to Multimedia Proficiency [viewed 8/29/2011]. Available: www.jou.ufl.edu/faculty/mmcadams/PDFs/RGMPbook.pdf

Mckane, A., 2006. *News Writing*. London: Sage.

McLuhan, M. 1964. *Understanding Media: The Extensions of Man*. New York: McGraw Hill.

McMorrow, C. 2012. Ernst & Young Insight: Getting to the Core of Successful Entrepreneurs: Eight Things Top Entrepreneurs Do Differently, [viewed 16/8/2013]. Available: http://business.financialpost.com/2012/06/05/ernst-young-insight-getting-to-the-core-of-successful-entrepreneurs-eight-things-top-entrepreneurs-do-differently/

Messner, M. and DiStaso, M.W. 2008. The Source Cycle, *Journalism Studies*, 9(3): 447–63.

Meyer, P. 2004. *The Vanishing Newspaper: Saving Journalism in the Information Age*. London: University of Missouri Press.

Montague, B. and Amin, L. 2012. *FOIA Without the Lawyer – a Logan Handbook*. London: Centre for Investigative Journalism.

Murdoch, R. 2005. Speech by Rupert Murdoch to the American Society of Newspaper Editors, 13/4/2005 [viewed 30/8/2012]. Available: www.newscorp.com/news/news_247.html

Nass, C. 2010. Thinking About Multitasking: It's What Journalists Need to Do, Nieman Reports [viewed 9/8/2012 2012]. Available: www.nieman.harvard.edu/reportsitem.aspx?id=102398

Naughton, J. 2000. *A Brief History of the Future: The Origins of the Internet*. London: Phoenix.

Naughton, J. 2010. Everything You Need to Know about the Internet, *Observer*, 20/6/2010 [viewed 30/8/2012]. Available: www.guardian.co.uk/technology/2010/jun/20/internet-everything-need-to-know

Naughton, J. 2011. All the news fit to print, but only if it ups the online hits, *Observer*, 17/4/2011 [viewed 19/8/2012]. Available: http://www.theguardian.com/technology/2011/apr/17/news-websites-driven-by-ratings

Naughton, J. 2012. *From Gutenberg To Zuckerberg: What You Really Need to Know about the Internet*. London: Quercus.

Naughton, J. 2012. 'Graphic designers are ruining the web'. The Observer, 19/2/2012 [viewed 8/29/2011]. Available: www.guardian.co.uk/technology/2012/feb/19/john-naughton-webpage-obesity

Negroponte, N. 1995. *Being Digital*. London: Coronet.

Nel, F. 2010. Laid Off: What Do Journalists Do Next? Published by the Journalism Leaders Programme at the School of Journalism, Media &Communication at the University of Central Lancashire (UCLAN).

Netimperative. 2009. Top 10 Sites 'account for nearly half UK total web browsing', [viewed 29/08/2011]. Available: www.netimperative.com/news/2009/may/top-10-sites-2018account-for-nearly-half-uk-total

Newman, N. 2009. *The Rise of Social Media and Its Impact on Mainstream Journalism*. Oxford: Reuters Institute for the Study of Journalism.

Newman, N. 2011. *Mainstream Media and the Distribution of News in the Age of Social Discovery*. Oxford: Reuters Institute for the Study of Journalism.

Niblock, S. 2011. *Journalism: A Beginner's Guide*. London: OneWorld.

Niblock, S. 2012. *The Fifth Estate: Media Training and Professionalism*. London: Palgrave Macmillan.

Nielsen (n.d.) Online Measurement [viewed 29/8/2011]. Available: www.nielsen.com/us/en/measurement/online-measurement.html

Nielsen, J. 2003. Information Foraging: Why Google Makes People Leave Your Site Faster, 30/6/2003 [viewed 5/4/2013]. Available: www.nngroup.com/articles/information-scent/

Nielsen, J. 2010. *Eye Tracking Web Usability*. Berkeley, CA: New Riders.

Ofcom (n.d.), Digital Communications Mapped Out across UK [viewed 30/8/2012]. Available: consumers. ofcom.org.uk/2011/11/digital-communications-mapped-out-across/?lang=cy

Ofcom. 2011. The State of the Communications Nation, 1/11/2011 [viewed 5/4/2013]. Available: media.ofcom. org.uk/2011/11/01/the-state-of-the-communications-nation-2/

Ofcom. 2012. Online Copyright Infringement Tracker Benchmark Study Q3 2012 [viewed 14/4/2013]. Available: http://stakeholders.ofcom.org.uk/market-data-research/other/telecoms-research/copyright-infringement-tracker/

Osbourne, H. 2012. 'MoneySavingExpert.com Turns £87m in Profit – and Vows to Fight On', *Guardian*, 1/6/2012. [viewed 16/8/2013] Available: www.theguardian.com/money/2012/jun/01/moneysaving-expert-87m-profit

Pape, S. 2006. *Feature Writing: A Practical Introduction*. London: Sage.

Park, H.W. 2003. Hyperlink Network Analysis: A New Method for the Study of Social Structure on the Web. *Connections*, 25(1): 49–61.

Peer, L. and Ksiazek, T. 2011. Youtube and the Challenge to Journalism, *Journalism Studies*, 12(1): 45–63.

Penny, L. 2010. How Twitter Changed the Face of Dissent, *New Statesman*, 20/12/2010 [viewed 9/8/2012]. Available: www.newstatesman.com/blogs/laurie-penny/2010/12/information-solidarity

Peston, R. 2009. Peston's Picks: What Future for Media and Journalism?, BBC, 29/8/2009 [viewed 31/8/2001]. Available: www.bbc.co.uk/blogs/thereporters/robertpeston/2009/08/what_future_for_media_and_jour. html

Peston, R. 2009. What Future for Media and Journalism? BBC, 29/8/2009 [viewed 31/8/2011]. Available: www. bbc.co.uk/blogs/thereporters/robertpeston/2009/08/what_future_for_media_and_jour.html

Peters, M. 2011. 6 Game-Changing Digital Journalism Events of 2011, Mashable, 28/12/2011 [viewed 9/10/2012]. Available: http://mashable.com/2011/12/28/digital-journalism-2011/

Petley, J. 2011. *Film and Video Censorship in Modern Britain*. Edinburgh: Edinburgh University Press.

Pew Project for Excellence in Journalism. 2010. How Blogs and Social Media Agendas Relate and Differ from the Traditional Press [viewed 8/30/2012]. Available: www.journalism.org/analysis_report/new_media_old_media

Pew Project for Excellence in Journalism. 2012. The Demographics of Mobile News, 11/12/2012 [viewed 4/3/2013]. Available: www.journalism.org/node/31859

Phillips, R. 2013. Talk to Brunel University Journalism Students, 12 March.

Pilger, J. (ed.). 2005. *Tell Me No Lies: Investigative Journalism that Changed the World*. London: Pan.

Ponsford, D. 2012. *Times* and *Sunday Times* Digital Sales Power Ahead, Press Gazette, 15/2/2012 [viewed 30/8/2012]. Available: www.pressgazette.co.uk/story.asp?sectioncode=1&storycode= 48755&c=1

Press Gazette. 2012. Ex-Loaded Editor Daubney's Six of the Best: 'Best editor? Hands down, Andy Coulson', 5/9/2012 [viewed 6/9/2012]. Available: http://blogs.pressgazette.co.uk/wire

Preston, P. 2010. Rupert Murdoch's Daily iPad Venture Looks Thin in the Profits Column, *Observer*, 28/11/2010 [viewed 23/8/2012]. Available: www.guardian.co.uk/media/2010/nov/28/rupert-murdoch-steve-jobs-ipad-the-daily

Prior, M. 2005. News vs. Entertainment: How Increasing Media Choice Widens Gaps in Political Knowledge and Turnout, *American Journal of Political Science*, 49(3): 577–92.

Quinn, S. 2004. An Intersection of Ideals: Journalism, Profits, Technology and Convergence, *Convergence: the International Journal of Research into New Media Technologies*, 10(4): 109.

Quinn, S. and Filak, V, 2005. *Convergent Journalism: an Introduction: Writing and Producing Across Media*. Oxford: Focal.

Race Online. 2011. Manifesto – We're All Better Off When Everyone's Online [viewed 8/29/2011]. Available: http://raceonline2012.org/manifesto

Randall, D. 2000. *The Universal Journalist*. 2nd edn. London: Pluto Press.

Ray, V. 2003. *The Television News Handbook*. London: Macmillan.

Reade, B. 2011. Let's Look After Our Victims More than Our Criminals, *Mirror*, 27/1/2011 [viewed 9/8/2012]. Available: www.mirror.co.uk/news/uk-news/lets-look-after-our-victims-more-106890

Reuters Institute for the Study of Journalism. (2012) The Reuters Institute Digital Report 2012 [viewed 15/8/2012]. Available: reutersinstitute.politics.ox.ac.uk/index.html

Richmond, S. 2008. How SEO is Changing Journalism, *British Journalism Review*, 19(4): 51–5.

Richmond, S. 2010. Making a Call on a Mobile? Surely Not. *Telegraph*, 12/8/2010 [viewed 30/8/2012]. Available: www.telegraph.co.uk/technology/mobile-phones/7941655/Making-a-call-on-a-mobile-Surely-not.html

Robertson, G. 1983. *People Against the Press*. London: Quartet Books.

Rogers, S. 2013. *Facts Are Sacred: The Power of Data*. London: Faber & Faber.

Rosen, J. 1999. *What Are Journalists For?* New Haven, Conn.: Yale University Press.

Rosen, J. 2006. The People Formally Known as the Audience, PressThink, 27/6/2006 [viewed 4/4/2013]. Available: http://archive.pressthink.org/2006/06/27/ppl_frmr.html

Rozenberg, J. 2011. Facebook Juror Trial Shows Contempt in Other Ways, *Guardian*, 15/6/2011 [viewed 14/4/2013]. Available: www.guardian.co.uk/commentisfree/libertycentral/2011/jun/15/facebook-trial-jury-joanne-fraill

Rusbridger, A. 2010. The Hugh Cudlipp Lecture: Does Journalism Exist? *Guardian*, [viewed 29/8/2011 2011]. Available: www.guardian.co.uk/media/2010/jan/25/cudlipp-lecture-alan-rusbridger

Rusbridger, A. 2011. Hacking Away at the Truth [viewed 19/8/2012] Available: http://theorwellprize.co.uk/events/past-events/alan-rusbridger-hacking-away-at-the-truth/

Sabbagh, D. 2011. Welcome to the Toilet-talking, Midnight Phone-junkie Generation, *Guardian*, 4/8/2011 [viewed 29/8/2011]. Available: www.guardian.co.uk/technology/2011/aug/04/welcome-toilet-midnight-phone-junkies

Salmon, F. 2011. The State of the Blog, *Columbia Journalism Review* [viewed 29/8/2012]. Available: www.cjr.org/the_audit/the_state_of_the_blog.php

Schneider, M. 2009. How to: Launch Your Own Indie Journalism Site, Mashable, 24/9/2009 [viewed 9/9/2012]. Available: http://mashable.com/2009/09/24/indie-journalism-guide/

Schudson, M. 2003. *The Sociology of News*. New York: W.W. Norton & Co.

Sedley, S. 2012. The Goodwin and Giggs Show, *London Review of Books*, 33(12): 3.

Shiels, M. 2009. Twitter Responds on Iranian Role. BBC, 17/6/2009 [viewed 9/10/2012]. Available: http://news.bbc.co.uk/1/hi/technology/8104318.stm

Shirky, C. 2008. *Here Comes Everybody: The Power of Organizing Without Organizations*. New York: Penguin.

Shirky, C. 2010. *Cognitive Surplus: Creativity and Generosity in a Connected Age*. New York/London: Penguin.

Shirley, S. 2012. On the *Today* programme, 14/9/2012. Available: http://news.bbc.co.uk/today/hi/today/newsid_9751000/9751826.stm

Shukmann, D. n.d. Pieces to Camera, BBC College of Journalism Video [viewed 12/3/2013]. www.bbc.co.uk/academy/collegeofjournalism/how-to/how-to-report?page=2

Singer, J. et al. 2011. *Participatory Journalism: Guarding Open Gates at Online Newspapers.* Oxford: Wiley-Blackwell.

Sky News. n.d. Sky News Blogs – House Rules [viewed 8/29/2012]. Available: http://blogs.news.sky.com/about/house_rules.html.

Smith, J. and National Council for the Training of Journalists. 2007. *Essential Reporting: the NCTJ Guide for Trainee Journalists.* London: Sage.

Smith, P. 2010. Link to the Past: Why Do Some News Sites STILL Not Link Out in 2010? [viewed 29/8/2012]. Available: http://psmithjournalist.com/2010/08/link-to-the-past-why-do-journalists-still-not-link-to-each-other/.

Snoddy. R. 1993. *The Good, The Bad and The Unacceptable.* London: Faber & Faber.

SnurBlog. 2010. Coverage of Breaking News by UK News Sites, 14/10/2010 [viewed 5/4/2013]. Available: http://snurb.info/node/1405

Sontag, S. 1979. *On Photography.* Harmondsworth: Penguin.

Sparrow, A. 2012. Fuel Panic: Petrol Prices Rise Demand Rockets, *Guardian*, 30/4/2012 [viewed 9/8/2012 2012]. Available: www.guardian.co.uk/politics/blog/2012/mar/30/fuel-panic-petrol-live

Starkman, D. 2011, Confidence Game: The Limited Vision of News Gurus, *Columbia Journalism Review*, 8/11 [viewed 13/4/2013] Available: www.cjr.org/essay/confidence_game.php

Steensen, S., 2009. Online feature journalism, *Journalism Practice*, 3(1), 13–29

Steensen, S., 2011. Online Journalism and The Promises of New Technology, *Journalism Studies*, 12(3): 311–327.

Sternberg, J. 2011. Why Curation Is Important to the Future of Journalism, Mashable, 10/3/2011 [viewed 8/28/2012]. Available: http://mashable.com/2011/03/10/curation-journalism/

Stevens, C., 2011. *Designing for the iPad: Building Applications that Sell.* Hoboken, N.J.: Wiley.

Stoddard, K. 2010. news:rewired #1: George Brock intro, Kevin Marsh keynote. Librarian of tomorrow. [viewed 9/2/2011 2011]. Available: http://librarianoftomorrow.wordpress.com/2010/01/19/newsrewired-1-george-brock-kevin-marsh/

Stray, J. 2010. Why link out? Four journalistic purposes of the noble hyperlink, Nieman Journalism [viewed 29/8/2012]. Available: www.niemanlab.org/2010/06/why-link-out-four-journalistic-purposes-of-the-noble-hyperlink/

Surowiecki, J,. 2004. *The Wisdom of Crowds: Why the Many Are Smarter Than the Few and How Collective Wisdom Shapes Business, Economies, Societies and Nations,* New York: Anchor Books.

Tavakoli-Far, N. 2011. What makes a great entrepreneur? BBC World Service, 14/7/2011 [viewed 13/4/2013] Available www.bbc.co.uk/news/business-14032584

Technorati, 2011 State of the Blogosphere 2011: Introduction and Methodology. [viewed 30/8/2012] Available: http://technorati.com/social-media/article/state-of-the-blogosphere-2011-introduction/.

Techradar, 2009. Reviews guarantee [viewed 9/8/2012]. Available: www.techradar.com/news/world-of-tech/techradars-reviews-guarantee-622749

Thompson, K. 1998. *Moral Panics.* London: Routledge.

Thompson, R. 2007. *Writing For Broadcast Journalists.* Abingdon, Oxford: Routledge.

Thornburg, R. M. 2011. *Producing Online News.* Washington, DC: CQ Press.

Thurman, N.J. and J. Herbert, 2007. Paid content strategies for news websites: An empirical study of British newspapers' online business models, in *Journalism Practice*, 1(2), 208–226.

Thurman, N.J. and B. Lupton, 2008. Convergence calls: Multimedia storytelling at British news websites *Convergence: The international journal of research into new media technologies*, 14(4), 439–455

Total Politics, 2011 Top 100 UK political blogs 2011 [viewed 28/8/2012] Available: www.totalpolitics.com/blog/259027/top-100-uk-political-blogs-2011.thtml

Townend, J. 2009a. Creative Commons Q&A: How can journalists get the most out of it? 6/1/2009 [viewed 14/4/2013]. Available: www.journalism.co.uk/news-features/creative-commons-q-amp-a-how-can-journalists-get-the-most-out-of-it-/s5/a533141/

Townend, J. 2009b. Journalism in Crisis 09: 'Recognising one's subjectivity allows one to be fair' Ivor Gaber tells conference, Journalism.co.uk, 19/5/2009 [viewed 13/7/2012]. Available: www.journalism.co.uk/news-events-awards/journalism-in-crisis-09--recognising-one-s-subjectivity-allows-one-to-be-fair-ivor-gaber-tells-conference-/s14/a534489/

Townend. J. 2009. Student Journalists as entrepreneurs, Journalism.co.uk, 30/11/2009 [viewed 13/4/2013] Available: http://blogs.journalism.co.uk/2009/11/30/journalism-students-as-entrepreneurs/

Tynan, D. 2009. My Job and Welcome to It, 10/5/2010 [viewed 5/4/2013]. Available: http://tynanwood.com/blog/?p=56

van Dijck, J., 2009. 'Users like you? Theorizing agency in user-generated content', *Media, culture, and society*, 31(1).

W3Techs.Com 2012. Usage of Content Management Systems for Websites, August 2012, W3Techs Monthly Survey.

Waisbord, S. 2001. Why Democracy Needs Investigative Journalism, *Electronic Journal of the US Department of State*. [online] 6(1) 14–17.

Waldman, S., 2010. Creative disruption: why you need to shake up your business in a digital world. Harlow: Financial Times Prentice Hall

Wallsten, K., 2005. Political blogs and the bloggers who blog them: Is the political blogosphere and echo chamber, American Political Science Association's Annual Meeting. Washington, DC, September 2005, pp. 1–4.

Wardle, C., 2007 User generated content and public service broadcasting, Networked Knowledge blog 19/5/2010 [viewed 4/4/2013]. Available:http://clairewardle.com/2010/05/19/user-generated-content-and-public-service-broadcasting/

Wardle, C., 2010 How social networkers use news, BBC Academy, 19/07/2010 [Viewed 5/4/2013] Available: http://bbcjournalism.oup.com/blog/posts/how_social_networkers_use_news_1

Wayne, J. 2009. Sue Cross on the news industry's bleak state, bright future, Online Journalism Review [viewed 29/8/2011] Available: www.ojr.org/sue-cross-on-the-news-industrys-bleak-state-bright-future/

Webster, F. 2012. Interview with Paul Lashmar, 20 September 2012.

Weitzman, M, 2010 The Economist.com data migration to Drupal, 1/10/2010 [viewed 9/9/2012]. Available http://drupal.org/node/915102

Wells, L. (ed.) 1997. *Photography: A Critical Introduction*. Oxford: Routledge

White, A. 2011. Using online tools and techniques to get a job in journalism: advice from the experts. *Guardian* 11/8/2011. [viewed 13/4/2013] Available: http://careers.guardian.co.uk/journalism-job-tips.

White D. M. 1950. 'The gate keeper: A case study in the selection of news', *Journalism Quarterly*, 27: 383–391.

White, T. and Barnas, F. 2002. *Broadcast News Writing, Reporting, and Producing*. London: Focal Press.

White, T. and Barnas, F. 2010. *Broadcast News Writing, Reporting and Producing*. 5th edn. Oxford: Focal Press.

Williams, A and Franklin, B. 2007. *Turning Around the Tanker: Implementing Trinity Mirror's Online Strategy*. Cardiff University.

Wilson, R. 2012. Hislop: Eye Success Down to Investment in Investigative Journalism, Press Gazette, 28/8/2012 [viewed 12/4/2013]. www.pressgazette.co.uk/story.asp?sectioncode=1&storycode=49912&c=1

Wolber, D. et al. 2011. App Inventor: Create Your Own Android Apps. Beijing: O'Reilly Media.

Woodward, B. 2006. *The Secret Man: The Story of Watergate's Deep Throat*. New York: Simon & Schuster.

Wren, A . 2011. How to Build and Monetise a Blog, *Guardian*, 2/9/2011 [viewed 13/4/2013]. Available: www.guardian.co.uk/money/2011/sep/02/how-to-build-and-monetise-a-blog?INTCMP=SRCH

Yahoo! 2010. *The Yahoo! Style Guide: The Ultimate Sourcebook for Writing, Editing, and Creating Content for the Digital World*. London: Macmillan.

Zak, E. 2012. 4 Questions with Anjali Mullany, Social Media Editor at Fast Company, 10,000 Words, 21/5/2012 [viewed 8/29/2012]. Available: www.mediabistro.com/10000words/4-questions-with-anjali-mullany-social-media-editor-at-fast-company_b13272#more-13272

Index

A

Adobe 16, 117, 207
advertisers 9, 62–3, 88, 187
advertising 17, 28–9, 34, 186–8, 196, 268
  banner 34, 36
  CPM (page impression cost) 34, 41, 187
  Google 187
  mixing with editorial 173, 187, 193
  nme.com 39
  or paywall 263
  PPC (pay per click) 186
  revenue 1, 26, 30, 43, 173, 262
  takeover 187
advertorials 186–7
affiliate marketing 178, 186–7
Afghanistan (war) 19, 74, 125, 162, 174
aggregation 30–2
  content 161–2
aggregators 30–1, 174, 245
amateur journalists 144, 163, 165
analytics software 26, 34, 37
Anderson, Chris 28, 164, 272
Android 15, 210–12, 266
  emulator 211
anonymity 156, 251–2, 254
anonymous journalism 251–2
AOL 41, 161, 173
APIs (application programming
  interfaces) 23
Apple 15, 28, 88, 211–12, 266
  app store 269
  iMovie 16, 76, 114, 117
  iOS 15, 212
  iPod 83, 88, 112
  iPod Touch 15
  iTunes 83, 88, 93, 100, 211
apps 13, 15, 75, 213, 266–7
  audio 93
  creating 15, 210, 212
  iOS 210–11
  for journalists 15
  selling 212
Arab Spring 141

Assange, Julian 125–6
Audacity (software) 76, 95–6
audience 18–19, 25, 27, 147, 165,
    182, 215
  ABC1 36, 39
  for audio 83, 90
  blogs 164
  breaking news 52
  forming at article level 33
  fragmented 28, 268
  newspaper 8
  niche 28
  nme.com 39
  passive 26, 145, 176
  people formally known as 18, 27, 226
  platform-neutral 11
  print decline 8
  as producers 18
  profile 39
  pseudo-empowerment 19
  trust 223, 227–8
  or user? 26
  for video 104
  for websites 26
audio 83–5, 88–9, 98
  convergence 84
  history 85
  packages 89
  part of digital workflow 198
  recording on smartphone 13
  slideshows 76–7
  writing for 89–90
audio files 99
AudioBoo 16, 93–4, 201
Audition (Adobe software) 95

B

Baghdad Blogger (Salam Pax) 162
Ball, James 127
Bambuser (broadcast software) 16
bandwidth 257, 265
Barling, Kurt 108
Barnett, Steve 129, 226, 228

BBC 11, 262
  audio 88, 98
  commercial rivals 226
  data journalism 21-2, 80
  editorial guidelines 157
  iPlayer 104, 264–5, 268
  licence fee 226, 258, 262
  online 29, 58
  radio 85–6
  social media 157–8
  student finance calculator 21
  twitter usage 175
  user participation 19, 154
  video 104
BBC Breakfast 153
BBC College of Journalism 111, 119
BBC London 108–9
BBC Micro (computer) 258
BBC MyBBC 29
BBC News 38, 52
BBC Online 208, 258, 262
BBC Surrey 58
Beanland, Kristina 97
Bell, Steve 80–1
Benkler, Yochai 261
Berners-Lee, Tim 205, 260
Bernstein, Carl 123
BlackBerry 258
Blackhurst, Chris 232
Blogger.com 15, 161, 166, 200,
    258–9
bloggers 160, 162–4, 174, 223
  aggregators 31
  business 172
  citizen journalists 173
  female 172
  as gatekeepers 170
  as journalists 238
  legal issues 242, 247, 251
  newspapers 175
  use by newspapers 174
blogging 160–1, 173, 186, 230, 251,
    259, 274–5
  death of? 175

blogging *cont.*
  as journalism 173–4
  live 14, 51–3, 64
blogging communities 162, 164
blogging tools 257
blogosphere 163, 174, 176
  political 164–5
blogs 18, 59, 151, 160–77, 186, 188, 197,
    200, 252
  code of conduct 230
  defined 161
  fake (flogs) 176
  political 164–5, 172, 174
  post 161, 166, 169–71, 200
  self-expression 176
  successful 161, 173, 186
  war 162
bounce rate 36
Bradshaw, Paul 22, 127, 134–6, 181, 223
Briggs, Mark 179, 182
broadband, speeds 269
broadcast journalists 4, 236
broadcast media 27, 48, 85, 89–90, 96,
    146, 197–8, 254, 264, 269
Brooke, Heather 131, 233
Brooker, Charlie 210
Bruns, Axel 225
BSkyB 13, 107
Burgh, Hugo de 122–3, 128, 130
business angels 181, 184
business plans 188
Butcher, Mike 184
BuzzTouch (app design) 211

C

Cadman, Simon 89
Caerphilly Observer 185
camera 15, 68–9, 112, 114
  digital 66, 68, 74, 156
  flash 68, 70, 152
  piece to 108
  smartphone 68, 102, 112
cannibalization 214–16
Canon, EOS 69, 112
captions 50, 71, 73, 77, 198, 208
  video 115
  writing 71–2, 78
CAR (computer-assisted reporting)
    19, 134
cartoons 81
Carvin, Andy 141
Castells, Manuel 270
CCTV footage 105–6, 238
celebrity 23, 26, 222
celebrity news 29, 38, 40, 56–7, 66
censorship 221, 254

Centre for Investigative Journalism
    129, 137
churnalism 122, 244, 263–4
citizen journalism 144–5, 158, 162, 164,
    173–4, 185, 248
Clegg, Nick 74, 76
clichés 57, 67, 90
cloud computing 15, 75, 199, 258, 268
CMS 35, 50–1, 160, 166, 198, 200
  categories 166, 170, 176, 196, 201,
    203, 205, 209
  commercial 199–200
  most popular 166, 200
  sections 201, 203, 205, 209
  software 167, 172
  tags 170–1, 209–10
  text editors 51, 169, 203
CNN 15, 29, 141, 175
Codes of conduct 229
collaborative journalism 7, 18, 143, 158
collective intelligence 18, 33
commentary (audio) 77–8, 96, 107, 110,
    116, 164
comments 171–2, 239, 242, 253
commercial pressures 9, 225, 228
commissioning editors 17, 189–92
communities 19, 109, 142–3, 145, 147
composition 70–1, 73–5
comScore 38, 40
contacts 41, 56, 150–2, 189–91
contempt 246–8, 251
  guilty of 246–7
  laws 248–9, 276
contempt of court Act 246–7
content
  communities 143, 158
  sharing 154, 259
  snacking 49
content management systems, *see* CMS
context articles 51
convergence 10–13, 84, 105, 174
convergent technology 259
conversation 18, 56, 145, 150, 220
copy (text of a story) 13–14, 48–9, 51,
    54–5, 198, 201, 231, 237
copyright 79, 243–4, 246, 261
corrections 228
courts 64, 234, 238–41, 244,
    246–50
  twitter 243, 248, 251
CoverItLive (live blogging tool) 52, 64
creative commons 80, 245
creative disruption 8
criminal law 234, 251
Crook, Tim 221
Cross, Sue 29
crowdsourcing 121, 134–5

CSS (Cascading Style Sheets) 161,
    202, 205
curation 19, 72, 162, 165, 174, 176
Curran, James 219
cyber-crime 269–70
cyber-terrorism 261

D

Daily Express 190
Daily Mail 40, 66, 190–1, 215, 239, 248
daily me (theory of personalization)
    29, 142
Daily Mirror 54, 57, 200
Daily Star 219, 231, 264
Daily Telegraph 25, 72, 126, 197, 200,
    215, 258, 262
Danbury, Richard 247
DAR (Digital Audio Recorders) 85, 94–5
data, visualizing 20, 22
data journalism 7, 19–22, 134, 207, 253
data protection 134, 249, 253
Davies, Nick 10, 122, 124, 231, 244,
    257, 263
Dawson, Ross 267
deadlines 198–9, 225
Dean, Jodi 175
declarative lifestyles 156–7
defamation 221, 239–40, 242–3
defamatory 172, 239, 241, 243, 254
democratic society 20, 129, 228, 246, 250
Denton, Nick (Gawker.com) 173
Digg (news site) 33, 147
digital assets 166, 198
Digital Audio Recorders, *see* DAR
digital divide 41
digital natives 256
digital newsroom 197, 200, 214
digital technology 10, 27, 41, 225
digital workflow 198–9
displacement 214–15
Doctor, Ken 8
Douglas, Paul 63
Dreamweaver (Adobe) 202
Drudge Report 252, 262
Drupal 167, 200, 202
Duggan, Mark (shooting) 109

E

e-readers 49, 61–2, 265
early internet users 156, 261
echo chamber (theory) 164
Economist, the 4, 58, 202, 207, 262
editing 224, 242
  audio 91, 95, 97, 231
  photos 75
  video 105, 112–14

editorial team 8, 74, 158, 197–8, 203
entertainment news 40, 222
entrepreneurial journalism 179–81
entrepreneurs 179–81, 183–4, 192
ethics 9, 220, 225, 227–8, 230, 232,
    234, 257
    codes of 174, 226, 230, 234
European Court of Human Rights 124, 250
Evans, Harry 67, 72, 76
EXIF (data) 152
extensions (CMS) 201, 203, 210, 212
eyeball chart 25, 38
eyewitness accounts 56, 83, 120, 147
eyewitnesses 51, 54, 56, 91, 108–9,
    121, 147

F

Facebook 28, 41, 143, 147, 151, 155,
    259–61
    chat 159
    comparison with blogs 160
    friends 151, 156
    groups 153, 158
    history 143
    legal 247, 249, 251, 253
    pages 151–3
    photos 157
    profiles 151, 155
    search 151
    social news 31, 142, 153–4
    users 144, 153
fairness 90, 223–4, 227, 242–3
feature articles 8, 32, 61, 191
filming 110, 114, 116, 118
Final Cut Pro (software) 114,
    117, 200
Flat Earth News 10, 122, 231, 263
Flickr 18, 80, 121, 143, 147
Flipboard (app) 32
fourth estate 128, 220
François Nel 9
free speech 172, 221, 236, 239, 254
freedom of expression 220–1, 227, 229,
    239, 246, 251, 254
freedom of information (FOI) 126, 131–2,
    134
freedom of press 228
freelance journalist 9, 16–18, 180–2,
    189–93, 253
Frost, Chris 228–9, 249
ftp (file transfer protocol) 99
Fyrne, James 199

G

Gaber, Ivor 222–3
games consoles 104, 264, 268

Garnett, Nick 14
gatekeeping 31, 145, 170, 225
gatewatching 225
Gawker.com 173
Gibson, Janine 213
gif (file format) 70
gift economy 9, 262
Giggs, Ryan 251
Gilligan, Andrew 233
Gillmor, Dan 18, 145, 162, 270
Gilmour, Kim 17
Google 9, 28, 35, 38, 81, 170, 258
    advertising 187–8
    alerts 151
    analytics 34–6
    calendar 199
    fusion tables 22, 81
    images 79
    maps 22
    news 23, 30, 81, 258
    scholar 258
    search 17, 209
    seo issues 50, 199, 208–9
    site map 209
    spreadsheet 199
    trends 38
Google AdSense 187–8
Google AdWords 188, 258
Google Drive 258, 268
Google Play (app store) 15, 211–12
graphics 66, 80–1, 116
Greenslade, Roy 53, 193, 213, 226
Guardian 7, 12, 20, 38, 58–9, 79, 81, 88,
    94, 105, 118,
    124, 145, 215, 264
    app 213
    data journalism 7, 21
    eyeball chart 38
    live blogging 53
    newsroom 197
    phone hacking 124
Guido Fawkes (blog) 161, 164, 252

H

Hall, Stuart 78
Hammersley, Ben 88
Hargreaves, Ian 256–7
Hari, Johann 232
headlines 49–50, 57–8, 101, 168–9, 198,
    200, 209
    tabloid 57
    writing 50, 57, 64
HelpMeInvestigate.com 135
High Court 131, 136, 243, 251, 253
High Speed Packet Access (HSPA) 266
Hislop, Ian 123

hoaxes 150–1
Hobsbawm, Julia 172
Hootsuite (social media) 16, 51
Horton, Richard 252
hosting 166–7, 172–3, 272
HTML (Hypertext Markup Language)
    205, 260
HTML 5 117, 205
Huffington Post 8, 161, 173–4
human rights 124, 250–1
hyperlinks 169, 198, 208, 267
hyperlocal 163, 185

I

IDEs (integrated development
    environment) 211
Independent Radio News (IRN) 89, 91
InDesign (design software) 214, 261
infographics 80–2
information gatekeepers 31, 145, 158
information overload 19, 33, 48, 256
information scarcity 9, 19, 256
injunctions 250–1
integrated development environment,
    see IDEs
intellectual property (IP) 243–4, 261
interaction 37, 264
interactivity 207, 238, 257, 264
internet 10, 27–8, 40–1, 146, 215, 256–7,
    260–1, 265, 268–70
    radio 88
    service providers, see ISPs
    streaming 88
    threat to journalism? 1
Internet Relay Chat, see IRC
interviews 55–6, 77–8, 90–3, 95–8, 104,
    108, 110–15, 151,
    192, 231–2, 252
intros 49, 55, 60–1, 91, 101, 111, 209, 263
intrusions into privacy 76, 249–50
investigations 122–4, 134–6
investigative journalism 122
    CAR 135
    death of? 126
    defined 122
    fourth estate 128
    history 123
    new models 136
    phone-hacking 124
    WikiLeaks 126
investigative journalists 121–2, 129–30,
    134
IP, see intellectual property
iPad 11, 15, 213–14, 267
    audio 83
    camera 112

iPad *cont.*
   creating content 213–14
   magazine 214
   screen 213
iPhone 93–4, 193, 259, 266, 274
   apps 181, 210, 212
   camera 69
   operating system 15
   record calls 93
   video 102, 112, 117
Iran 125–6, 142, 156, 252
Iraq (war) 125, 162, 174
IRC (Internet Relay Chat) 143, 260
IRN (Independent Radio News) 89, 91
ISPs (internet service providers) 38, 242, 263, 265
ITV 28, 127, 146

J

Jarvis, Jeff 9, 103, 178–9, 183
Java 207, 211
JavaScript 205, 207
Jenkins, Henry 27, 178
Jenkins, Simon 86
Johann Hari 232
Joomla 200–3
   articles 203
   extensions 201, 203, 210
   layout 202
   text editor 203
   user manager 203
journalism
   as conversation 18–19, 150, 158, 161, 176
   fourth estate 128
   long-form 61, 267
   new model of 18
   role 2, 7, 9, 18, 41, 126, 174, 228
   social 18–19
   students 36, 230
journalist
   skills 2, 9, 11, 122
   use of social media 147
journalists
   mobile 13–14
   social 18–19, 24
journalist's role 198, 240
jpeg (file format) 70
jurisdictions 236, 241, 247
jury 246–8

K

Keeble, Richard 126
Keen, Andrew 163
Kieran, Matthew 222
Kiss, Jemima 189
Kleinman, Zoe 149

Knight, Alan 160
Kolodzy, Janet 11
Kovach, Bill 7, 10
Krotoski, Aleks 146, 165

L

laptops 11, 248, 266
LBC (London Broadcasting Company) 86
Ledgard, Chris 83, 98–9
Leigh, David 234
Leveson (Lord) 236, 249
Leveson, Inquiry 124, 219, 226, 228, 231–2, 234, 249
Lewis, Martin 178
Lewis, Paul 118, 120–1, 127, 132–3, 178–9
Lewis-Hasteley, Helen 172
libel 240–2, 246
   tourism 241–2
link bait 59
link economy 19
LinkedIn 151, 154
linking 57, 147, 159, 169–71, 187, 223
Linux 261
Little White Lies 182
live TV 145, 264
long-form journalism 213, 215
long tail theory 28, 164
loyalty (user loyalty to media brand) 29, 32, 34, 37, 142, 154, 262
Luci Live (broadcast tool) 14, 16
Luckhurst, Tim 132
Lynch, Lisa 126

M

magazine articles 48
magazine readers 26
magazines 67, 190–1, 215, 264, 267
   iPad 213
   print 8, 13
   on tablet 213
Magnanti, Brooke (Belle de Jour) 252
MagPlus (iPad design) 214
mainstream media 145, 162–5, 173–5, 227, 261–2
Mair, John 126
Manning, Bradley 126, 132
market
   online news 26, 37, 59
   size of 188
   smartphone 259
   study of 199
   testing 267
Marr, Andrew 47
Mashable.com 274, 278, 280–2
Mason, Paul 161, 177

mass media 27–9, 146, 257
McLuhan, Marshall 86
media
   business of 9, 16, 173
   horizontal 144–5
   hot 86
   publishers 9, 31, 153, 210, 261, 267
   traditional 27, 104, 144–5, 174, 189, 220, 242
microphone 85, 89, 94–5, 101, 112, 115
mobile 11, 14–15, 184, 210, 270
   broadband 14, 265–7, 269
   devices 14–15, 37, 88, 117, 260, 267, 269
   users 50, 198
mobile phones 11, 14, 154, 265–6
   audio 85, 88
   camera 66, 69, 152, 229
   hacking 249
   recording calls 93, 233
   smartphones 14, 93, 111
   UGC 105, 225
   use in protests 156
MoneySavingExpert 178
moral panics 224
Mosley, Max 250–1
mp3 (file format) 94–6, 245
MPs' expenses 131–2, 134
multi-tasking 33
multimedia mindset 8–9
Murdoch, Rupert 126, 226
MySQL 202, 206

N

Nass, Clifford 33
National Council for the Training of Journalists, *see* NCTJ
National Union of Journalists, *see* NUJ
Naughton, John 40, 260–1, 267
NCTJ (National Council for the Training of Journalists) 4, 55, 105
Negroponte, Nicholas 29, 142
NetFlix 268
New Statesman 61, 232
New York Times 19, 147, 175
Newman, Nic 154, 156, 174
news
   agenda 40, 129, 145, 187, 222, 224, 226
   aggregators 30–1, 258
   breaking 143, 150
   bulletin 89, 101
   distribution 31, 142
   scraper sites 30
News Corp 107, 262
news-u-like 40

news websites
  headlines 57
  images 66, 76
  independent 8, 27, 165, 196
  linking policy 170
  major 82, 255
  market-driven 26, 43
  revenue 186
  RSS 31
newspaper reporters 105, 256
newspaper websites 31, 262
  local 37, 107, 176
newspapers 8, 26–31, 33, 215, 226, 234,
    238, 242, 249, 253, 256, 263–4
  agenda 38
  apps 213
  decline in print sales 215
  ethics 234
  giving away content for free 215
  local 106, 136, 163, 185
  national 8, 219, 226
  news list 145
  paywall 262
  photography 73–4, 76
  print 28, 264
  printed 40, 213–15
  regulation 227
  revenue 263
  roles on 145
  shift work 191
  use of blogs 174
  use of social media 175
  use of tablets 267
  use of video 105
newsprint 8, 31, 47
newsrooms 10, 25, 84, 197–8,
    225, 264
Niblock, Sarah 79, 84, 224–5
niche interests 18, 28–9
niche sites 28, 164, 185, 199
Nielsen, Jakob 49, 203
nme.com 39, 203–4
NUJ (National Union of Journalists) 10,
    194, 229, 231
NUJ Code of Conduct 229

O

objectivity 222–3
Observer, the 28, 134, 197
Ofcom 227, 244
online
  archives 238, 241–2, 248
  communities 19, 146, 159, 200
  identity 156
  markets 160, 163, 179, 181, 194, 199
  users 26, 49, 161

open source 9, 95, 166, 200, 261, 270
  CMS 200, 202, 206
operating system (OS) 15, 210, 258,
    261, 266
opinion (style of writing) 58–9, 162, 229
opinion
  blogging 59
  honest 241
  legal (based on true fact) 240
opt-in 187
OS, see operating system

P

Pape, Susan 61
participation 143, 155, 268
  active 155
  political 40
passive receivers 27, 145, 155
paywall 262–3
PCC Editors' Code of Practice 250
PeerIndex 152
Penny, Laurie 61, 161
Peppiatt, Richard 220, 231
permalinks 168, 176
personal recommendation 31, 142, 189
personalization 29, 31–2
personalized news 28, 32
Peston, Robert 11
Petley, Julian 224
Phillips, Ronke 127
phone-hacking 2, 124, 129, 226–7,
    249, 251
photo galleries 62, 76, 203
photographer 14, 66, 74–5, 78, 80, 244
photographs 66–7, 69, 147, 230, 245
  cameras 69
  captions 71, 73
  composition 70, 74
  editing 75
  slideshow 76
photography 66, 69, 72–4, 88, 162, 248
Photoshop 75, 168, 194, 230
Photoshop Elements 69, 208
PHP 202, 206
picture editors 71, 73–4, 76
piracy 244, 270
PlayStation (Sony) 143
plugins 117, 171, 205
  CMS 167, 170, 176, 210
  free media player 99
  WordPress 171, 201
pluralism (number of media outlets) 13,
    163–4
podcasts 83, 88, 100, 185
  Guardian 88
  most popular 88

prejudices 222, 246–7
press releases 17, 55–6, 122, 231
Prior, Markus 40
privacy 37, 76, 129, 156–7, 221–2, 227, 234,
    238, 249–51, 253, 269
Private Eye 123–4
pro-am 144
product reviews 62–3
production process 19, 198–9, 201
programming languages 161, 203, 207,
    211
protests 121, 141–2, 156, 161, 258
public interest 128–30, 157–8, 222, 225–6,
    229, 233–4,
    240–1, 250–1
public interest journalism 26, 29
puns 57, 227
python (programming language) 207

Q

Quinn, Stephen 12, 113

R

radio 14, 27, 83, 85–6, 90, 98, 146, 264
Randall, David 58
Ray, Vin 115
Reade, Brian 60
recording audio 84, 93, 102, 115, 259
Reeves, Marc 193
revenue 10, 178, 261
  generating 186, 262
  from journalism 9, 39, 41, 62, 178,
    186–7, 213, 263, 265, 267, 270
Reynolds Defence 240–1
Richmond, Shane 33, 266
riots 7, 14, 102, 109, 118, 230
Rosen, Jay 18, 27, 144, 178, 223
Rosenstiel, Tom 7, 10
Rozenberg, Joshua 247
RSS (syndication) 31–2, 57, 59, 83, 88, 100
RSS readers 31
Rusbridger, Alan 129

S

Salmon, Felix 174
Saltzis, Kostas 52
Scott, CP 193
script 90, 96–7, 104–5, 107–8, 111, 116,
    118, 231
search
  keywords 58, 208
  social media 51, 148, 151–2, 176
Search Engine Optimization, see SEO
search engines 17, 30–1, 33–4, 36, 43, 50,
    57–8, 63–4, 117,
    170, 173, 208–10, 258

search keywords 208
self-censorship 254
SEO 50, 57, 63, 194, 199, 208, 210
    data 198
    importance of 208
    keywords 209
    tips 209
Sharma, Sutish 91–2, 97
Shirky, Clay 18, 27, 146, 178–9
shots 77, 105, 108, 110–11, 113–15, 118
Shukmann, David 111
Silicon Valley 180, 183
Sky News 102, 174
Sky Plus (PVR) 264
Skype 14, 16, 184, 260, 270
slideshow 76–7
smart TVs 1, 48, 104
smartphone, apps 146
smartphones 11, 13, 24, 213, 258, 266, 269
    app creation 210–11
    apps 15, 260
    audio 94
    images 70, 75
    operating system 15
    reading text 49
    second screen 145
    use by eyewitnesses 51
    use by reporters 13–16, 24
    video 111–12
sms (text message) 12, 143
social bookmarking sites 33
social media 7, 16, 18, 31, 51, 132, 142–5,
        147, 151, 156–7,
        175, 186, 190, 251
    accounts 147, 150–1, 269
    authenticity 155
    compared with mass media 146
    criticism 146–7
    embedded in news production 147
    finding stories on 150
    hoaxes 151
    improving use of 150
    monitoring of 147
    most shared stories 154
    page 142, 158
    publishing pictures from 157
    as second screen 145
    sharing content on 210
    tools 66, 166
    use by eyewitnesses 147
    use by journalists 147
    use in protests 156
    use to build audience 147
    user engagement with 154
social media sites 2, 18, 23, 34, 43, 141–3,
        146–7, 154–5,
        157–8, 175–6, 260

social networking 18, 60, 259
social news 18, 31
social web 31, 260–1
SoGlos (hyperlocal site) 199
sound effects 98, 116
SoundCloud 16, 88, 93
SoundSlides 76
sources 126, 132–5, 145, 174–5, 177, 226,
        240, 245
    anonymous 132
    blogs 174
    CAR 134
    confidential 132–3
    news 30, 49–50, 244
    protecting 133, 229
    social media 132, 145, 151–2, 158
Southern Daily Echo 105
sport 40, 57, 154, 164, 170, 185
Spotify 83
spreadsheets 19–20, 22, 130, 199
staff journalists 105, 189, 244
Staines, Paul (blogger) 161, 252
start-ups 184
statistics 9, 19, 50, 122, 207, 253
Steensen, Steen 61, 257
Steward, Sue 72–3, 76
Stone, Mark 102, 111
stories
    breaking 127, 154, 243
    developing 51–2
    funny 154, 159
    investigative 127, 130
    summary 51–2
Storify 18, 176
storytelling 12, 61, 98, 104
streaming video 83, 214, 265
style guide
    design 197, 207–8
    editorial 207–8, 216
sub-editors 71, 197–8
Sun, the (newspaper) 40, 57, 225–7, 248,
        251
Sunday Express 54
Sunday Times 28, 124, 190, 212, 227, 262
Survey Monkey 38

T

tablets 8, 11–14, 61, 117, 212–14, 265, 267
    apps 62, 146, 213, 215, 260, 267
    creating content 213–14
    operating systems 15
    reading text 49
    second screen 146
tabloids 54, 58, 124, 234, 249, 264
TechCrunch 173, 184
techno-optimism 10

TechRadar 63
themes, CMS 166–8, 176, 200, 208
Thurman, Neil 53
Times, the 226, 240, 242, 250
TiVo 264
Tomlinson, Ian (newspaper vendor) 120–1,
        127, 248
tools
    data journalism 22
    reporting 13
    social media crowdsourcing 159
traditional Journalism 9
traditional journalistic news values
        41, 147
traffic 34, 36, 41, 178, 196, 210
trolling 171–2
Tumblr 15, 160, 166
tv
    channels 28
    journalism (versus online video) 103
    news 103–4, 107, 147, 264
    watching 26, 214
TweetDeck (software) 51, 150, 154
tweets
    celebrity 151, 251
    in court 243, 248
    curation 53
    eyewitness 51, 141
    hoaxes 150–1
    legal issues 236, 243
    mobile journalists 14
    police incidents 80
    use in protests 60, 141, 156
Twitter 32, 142, 145, 147, 153, 259
    accounts 32, 150, 152
    distribution of news 31
    eyewitness material 148
    followers 51, 143, 147–8, 152–3, 159
    freelance use 190
    legal 238, 247, 251
    protests 156
    searching 151–2
    sharing news 154
    trending 32
    use in protests 60, 121, 141
Twitter and Facebook users 147

U

UGC 18, 27, 75, 105, 143,
        146–7, 158
    legal issues 241–3
    video content 105
undercover reporting 130–1, 233
uploading media to web 99, 116, 166
usability 49, 203
usenet (newsgroups) 143, 260
user-generated content, *see* UGC

users
  analytics 33, 36
  fickle 262
  heavy news 19
  passive 27

V

video
  apps 16
  CCTV 106
  embedding on website 117
  Flash 117, 205, 207
  iPad 117, 207
  legal issues 231
  low standards online 105
  newspaper usage 105
  over broadband 269
  shooting 115
  streaming 16, 42
  use in protests 141, 156
  use on tablets 214
  Wordpress 171
  working with 103
  writing for 106–7
video camera 18, 49, 111
video content 106, 198, 265
video journalist (VJ) 103–4, 112, 244
video sites 143, 207, 265

Vimeo (video site) 104, 114, 117, 171, 214
viral marketing 31
visitors
  unique 34, 36, 263
  to websites 25–6, 30, 34, 36–7, 43, 186, 188
VJ, see video journalist
voice 83, 88, 97–8, 101

W

Waldman, Simon 8
Wardle, Clare 19
Washington Post 123, 175, 223, 228
wav (file format) 94, 96
wearable technology 268–70
web host 166–7
weblogs 160, 174
website hosting 166–7, 171, 202
  legal 242
Webster, Fiona 190
whistleblowers 132–3
whistleblowing 132
wi-fi 13, 17, 24
wiki 143
WikiLeaks 19, 124–7, 132, 223, 242
Wikipedia 151, 232
Woodward, Bob 123

Wordle 80
WordPress 15, 99, 166–71, 176, 200–1, 209, 242
  dashboard 167
  installing 167
  mobile 210
  plugins 171
  text editor 169
  theme 168, 170
  wordpress.com (hosted) 161, 166–7, 171
World Wide Web 10, 256–7, 260, 270

X

Xbox (Microsoft) 268
Xcode (app developer software) 211

Y

Yahoo!
  personalization 29
  pipes 23
  style guide 50, 58
YouTube 104, 117, 156, 259, 265, 268
  videos 31, 33, 262

Z

Zeebox (social media app) 146
Zoom H4N 94
Zuckerberg, Mark 259